Pindar's Victory Songs

TRANSLATION

INTRODUCTION

PREFACES

Frank J. Nisetich

THE JOHNS HOPKINS UNIVERSITY PRESS

BALTIMORE AND LONDON

PINDAR'S VICTORY SONGS

This book has been brought to publication with the generous assistance of the David M. Robinson Publication Fund.

The Johns Hopkins University Press, Baltimore, Maryland 21218
The Johns Hopkins Press Ltd., London

Library of Congress Cataloging in Publication Data

Pindarus.
Pindar's Victory songs.

Bibliography: pp. 359–60.
Includes index.
I. Nisetich, Frank J. II. Title.
PA4275.E5N57 884'.01 79-3739
ISBN 0-8018-2350-1 ISBN 0-8018-2356-0 pbk.

Title page illustration: Inside of red-figured cup showing a running warrior in bronze. Musée du Louvre, Paris. Photo by Chuzeville.

CONTENTS

FOREWORD

Most of those who can read Pindar in the original would agree that he is one of the greatest poets of Greece, and indeed of Europe. Since the sixteenth century a succession of modern poets has felt his influence; Ronsard and Cowley, Gray and Hölderlin come to mind. But not all those who acknowledge his greatness do so wholeheartedly; and though there are several good modern translations, he is less read and understood by people who do not read Greek than any other of the great Greek poets. How can we account for this?

Firstly, he is commonly thought to be a difficult poet. True, his language is not easy; but the reader who perseveres a little will become used to his style, syntax, and vocabulary, and will soon find him nowhere near so difficult as he seems at first. His text is a good deal better preserved than that of Aeschylus or Sophocles; so far as language is concerned, he is the easiest of the three. Some of his poems, it is true, are in a complicated metre; but about half are in dactylo-epitrite, whose main features can be explained in half a page.

Much of the difficulty of understanding him lies in the seemingly abrupt and arbitrary transitions from one topic to another. There has been endless debate as to whether a Pindaric ode has unity, and if so in what that unity consists. Until lately most scholars held that it had none. The only surviving complete poems by Pindar are the four books of choral odes celebrating victors in the great Panhellenic games. It is easy to see that certain elements occur regularly in these odes, though in an order that varies a good deal. An ode will name the victor, list his victories, and praise him for his skill and valour; it will praise his city and his family, and will sometimes praise other members of it and enumerate their victories. The victory is seen against the background of a distinctive world outlook, very different from our own; until lately scholars, viewing Pindar as a lyric poet like modern romantic lyric poets, took this to be a peculiar compound of his own invention. In fact it is the ordinary world outlook of the archaic Greek religion, and has a great deal more in common with that of the Athenian tragedians than has usually been supposed. Pindar has been less esteemed than they because he has been held to take a narrow and restricted view of life, typical of the declining aristocracy to which he and his patrons belonged. But in reality the attitude which he expresses differs little from that of the tragedians, who were less concerned with the revolutionary thought of their contemporaries than is commonly imagined.

For a believer in the religion of archaic Greece, to praise a mortal man is an uncertain and hazardous enterprise. The universe is governed by the gods in their own interest, and not in that of men; man's life is short, his strength feeble, his hopes doomed to disappointment, his prosperity precarious. Yet the gods allow moments of felicity to certain men, usually to men descended from themselves. At such moments, men approach a divine happiness; yet what is their value, if they are doomed to be forgotten? Only one means of perpetuating them is at hand, that of having them made immortal by the art of a poet inspired by Apollo and the Muses. The poet will protect his client against the oblivion which overwhelms most human actions; he will also protect him against the envy which attends all human triumphs. Both the poet and the victor fight, aided by the gods, against envy and oblivion.

In setting the victor and his triumph against the backcloth furnished by this religion, the poet often enunciates the simple and eternal truths which a believer in it must accept. Taken alone, they would seem, in the usual and pejorative sense, commonplaces; taken in the context of the poem, they derive potency from their application to a concrete situation. The poet often illustrates these truths by narrating, or by mentioning more briefly, a myth about the deeds of gods and heroes; such a myth is another of the constantly recurring elements of the victory ode. The myth commonly celebrates the power and splendour of the gods, on which all human success depends.

A new critical approach, adopted only during the last twenty years, has greatly reduced the difficulty of understanding this world outlook and the artistic conventions it gave rise to. Rejecting the assumption, inspired by romanticism, that Pindar gave expression to his personal beliefs and sentiments, Elroy L. Bundy drew attention to the importance of poetic convention in his work, a convention created by the need to praise the victor against a background furnished by the standard world outlook of archaic Greece. In two detailed studies of Pindaric odes, he showed how regularly certain commonplaces of encomium recur in Pindar's work. He found the clue to the solution of the problem of the unity of the victory ode in the requirement of the genre that the poet praise the victor.

Bundy died in December, 1975, aged fifty-one, without publishing the new work on Pindar which he was preparing. I know from talks with him in 1969 that he regretted the forbidding dryness of his earlier publications and the somewhat formidable technical terminology which he invented to describe the recurring features of the odes and the various modes of transition between them which the poet used. We must hope that at least part of his later work will eventually be published, and in a form which he would have approved.

Since then several other scholars have worked along his lines, in Europe as well as in America. Some of them have used the new approach mechanically, and so weakened its effect; some have pushed it to the extreme of denying to Pindar all but a very few personal or historical allusions. This is a mistake; Pindar was a human being, writing for other human beings in a particular and individual social and historical environment. In each victory ode he sets the concrete fact of the individual victor's triumph against the permanent backcloth of the archaic Greek religious outlook. But in general the work of Bundy and the other American scholars who have pioneered the new approach has had an exhilarating effect upon Pindaric scholarship. That will be clear to the readers of the first translation of Pindar by a scholar thoroughly sympathetic to the new movement and its attitudes.

Frank Nisetich could not have made his translation without having a genuine gift for translation into verse. But his version could not have been so good if he had not been aided by the increased understanding of Pindar's aims and methods which his familiarity with the latest Pindaric scholarship has given him. He is the first translator to present Pindar as he is seen by the adherents of a new and growing movement in criticism, and he has the literary skill to take full advantage of this opportunity. I believe that his translation will have a notable success.

Hugh Lloyd-Jones
Regius Professor of Greek
Oxford University

PREFACE

This is a translation of Pindar's odes, the epinician odes or songs written to celebrate victories gained in the athletic games of ancient Greece. My main concern in translating them was to make them accessible to a contemporary audience. But while I have striven for clarity, I have kept also in mind Pindar's terseness and density of expression. It would have been too easy and too much of a betrayal to load Pindar's poetry down with glosses or to spell out all that he left implicit. Where he was reserved or suggestive and I felt he had a reason for being so, I tried to follow him, remembering, as well as I could, the difference between a hint and a mere blur in expression, a veiled meaning and no meaning at all.

Often in reading Pindar the ability to see such differences is simply a matter of being properly informed. Appreciation depends to some extent on familiarity with the kind of poetry Pindar composed. Here the description of Pindar's genre in the Introduction should be of assistance. I have also written a preface to each of the odes. Without unnecessary summary or paraphrase, I tried to give readers the information they would need. To avoid repetition, I often refer in the prefaces to relevant parts of the Introduction. The precise location of these may be found in the Index, under the topic or the ode concerned. Proper names not explained in the prefaces will be found in the annotated Glossary, which is complete, and which I have tried to make detailed enough to substitute for footnotes. Comprehensive entries for *Aigina*, *Argos*, and *Thebes*, for example, contain information relevant to a large number of odes. Geographical names in the Glossary can be located on the maps.

It is a truism that poetry cannot be translated except into other poetry. This is a poetic translation of Pindar, and its poetic qualities, whatever they may be, are necessarily *other* than those to be enjoyed from reading Pindar in Greek. I have found, however, that my best guide to effective poetry has been faithfulness to Pindar's text—to its sense always, to its words and syntactical structures whenever possible within the bounds of English. Readers who find my stanza patterns strange may be interested to know why I devised them. Pindar's own metrical art is described in the section on meter in the Introduction. This is not meant to initiate students of Greek—or anyone else—into the mysteries of metrics, but to give the general reader an idea of the experience of Pindar in the original, the *effect* of his metrical skill on our minds and our feelings. What I chose to do about the meters in English is discussed in the section on translation, under *Melopoeia*. The numbers in parenthesis after each stanza are the line numbers according to Bruno Snell's Teubner text. I owe the terms *turn*, *counterturn*, and *stand* (Pindar's *strophe*, *antistrophe*, and *epode*) to Ben Jonson, and the idea of using them to a suggestion made at the Hellric Poetry Workshop.

I have generally transliterated proper names from Greek into English without passing through Latin first. This usually results in the preservation of dialectal differences: *Kronidas* (Dorian), for example, as opposed to the more familiar *Kronides*. Such direct transliteration seems to be common practice now. I have not, however, adhered to it rigidly. Pindar's *Moisa* (Aiolic) is "Muse," his *Medoisa* is "Medusa," in my rendering. I have kept Persephone, whom readers will recognize, rather than send them to the Glossary in search of Pindar's *Phersephona*. I have also avoided unfamiliar Dorian forms such as *Damater*, *Orestas*, and *Pagasos*, in favor of Demeter, Orestes, and Pegasos. Pindar was capable of using different dialectal forms from poem to poem, even within the same poem. The possible poetic effects of this are briefly discussed in the section on dialect in the Introduction. Such dialectal variation is peculiar to Greek poetry, and I have not striven to preserve it. Only confusion would result in English if *Asklepios* here became *Asklapios* there. In the case of Greek proper names that Pindar did not use, but which do appear in my Introduction and prefaces, I have chosen to preserve traditional spellings. I write Aeschylus instead of Aischylos, Thucydides instead of Thoukydides. There are, however, a few personal names in Pindar that later came to belong to more famous people. The Theban athlete Herodotos is not to be confused with the famous historian Herodotus, whose name I have left in its familiar Latinized form; the same is true of the poets Alcman and Callimachus. Pindar's Alkman and Kallimachos are different people. In sum, I have as a rule transliterated the names Pindar uses directly into English; the others I have spelled in the traditional manner.

The Bibliography at the end is not so much intended to guide readers to a fuller study of Pindar as it is meant to record my indebtedness. My labors would have been more burdensome and less rewarding without W. J. Slater's *Lexicon to Pindar*. My preface to *Olympian 9* relies heavily on George Huxley's treatment of that ode in his book, cited in the Bibliography. W. J. Verdenius's excellent commentary on *Olympian 7* was very useful. Hugh Lloyd-Jones in his article on modern Pindaric interpretation and Mary R. Lefkowitz in her book *The Victory Ode* have, I believe, lifted the veil of obscurity from *Pythian 2*; my preface owes much to their discussions of that ode, cited in the Bibliography, and my rendering would hardly be what it is if I had had to solve the mysteries on my own. The same is true of *Nemean 7*, whose preface and rendering would surely be different had I not read Professor Lloyd-Jones's article. Readers of my Introduction will see how much I owe to David C. Young's interpretation of *Pythian 11*.

This translation received an award from The Translation Center at Columbia University, an award made possible by a grant from The National Endowment for the Arts. I wish to express my gratitude to the Center, and to its executive director, Dallas C. Galvin, for material and moral support. I am also grateful to the University of Massachusetts at Boston for awarding me a Faculty Growth Grant in 1977 and for making available to me the services of two unusually diligent and gifted research assistants: D. A. Chitwood, who selected and obtained the illustrations and did the initial work on the Index and Glossary; and Christine Toll, who helped bring the Index and Glossary to their final state, reading the entire work several times and making many observations. With customary generosity, and no less customary acumen, A. Thomas Cole of Yale University read my translation of the Olympian odes in its penultimate draft and sent me a copious line-by-line critique of what I had done. My rendering of the Olympian odes also owes some improvements to Deirdre Larkin's annotations. Finally, Steven Helmling of the English Department at Rutgers University read and criticized all the odes—the Olympians and some of the Pythians in two different drafts. In the beginning, when the errors were egregious, and in the end, when they were more subtle and difficult to deal with, Mr. Helmling's help was, in all good senses of the word, critical.

I must also thank Robert Fitzgerald for his encouragement at the beginning of this undertaking. Diskin Clay's initial review for The Johns Hopkins University Press became a critical guide for me in bringing the work to completion. To Professor Lloyd-Jones's interest and support, I owe more than I can say. The same is true of my debt to Pamela Starr Nisetich, who worked with me through all phases of this project, discussing everything from the choice of individual words to the length of lines and the shape of the stanzas. She knows better than anyone else what went into this book, from the moment it was conceived until now.

Pindar's Victory Songs

INTRODUCTION

History repeats itself, but the special call of an art
which has passed away is never reproduced. It is as utterly
gone out of the world as the song of a destroyed wild bird.
—Joseph Conrad

I. Historical Background

Pindar's odes, in their original form and purpose, are different from anything modern readers have encountered as poetry before. They are not private, personal, or spontaneous. Pindar received money to compose his poems; he wrote them to be performed by a singing and dancing chorus; and he was required to mention various matters that he might not have mentioned if he were entirely free to follow his inspiration. He certainly had no notion of the kind of book now in the reader's hands, and yet he speaks often with confidence of the distant future. He implies that the family for which he wrote would keep and prize his work from generation to generation. But within a few centuries of his death his musical notations and choreographical directions vanished from the preserved texts. As choral poetry ceased to be composed and was performed less and less, its peculiar poetic conventions lost their meaning. By the time Alexandrian scholars turned to the study of Pindar, his odes had become what they are to us now—mysterious relics of a distant past.

This, however, is only the beginning. The loss of an audience used to the performance of poetry did not have disastrous consequences for the appreciation of Homer or the Greek dramatists, nor is it the sole cause of modern difficulty with Pindar. The audience of a Homeric recitation had the narrative to rely on. The basic plots of the *Iliad* and the *Odyssey* are still there to guide a modern reader. Indeed, the story is seldom absent from the immediate foreground, and when it retires into the background, it is never absent for long. There is nothing so constant to give readers of Pindar their bearings. The victory celebrated in a Pindaric ode may be the starting or the finishing point, but everything in between varies from one ode to the next. Sometimes the connection between the different parts of an ode and the victory commemorated in it is apparent, at other times it is not. At any rate, the victory does not provide the kind of background that the narrative in Homer provides. It does not fasten the poem down in the same way, if at all. In Homeric recitation, moreover, the poetry itself was unaffected by the circumstances of performance. The poet's personality receded into the background. There was no need for him to interrupt the story with interpretation: his characters would express his insights at dramatic moments, and the narrative itself called for an easy-going, straightforward style. The poet might have an evening, perhaps a succession of evenings, to tell his tale; he would not need to resort to compression in order to accomplish his task.

Comparison of Pindar's odes with the odes of Greek drama is perhaps more to the point. Both were meant to be sung and danced by a chorus. Both are characterized by intense compression of style and by a striving on the poet's part to interpret the meaning of things for the audience. Yet even in an ode by Aeschylus, who is in many ways similar to Pindar, audience and reader always have the dramatic context to help follow the thought. In the *Agamemnon*, for example, the Watchman's opening speech puts us at a specific time and place within a larger narrative. We know that the Trojan War has ended, that Agamemnon will soon come home. No matter how complex the reflections of the chorus after the Watchman has left the stage, his prologue, our own acquaintance with the legend, and the dramatic situation never leave our minds. We may be puzzled by words and phrases whose full meaning will emerge later, but we are never adrift as we are at the opening of a Pindaric ode.

In Pindar there is no single story to give the poem its coherence, as in Homer; there is no dramatic background against which to assess the poet's reflections, as in tragedy. Instead of a dramatic stage where actors and chorus portray a single incident from a recognizable mythic tradition, the scene of a Pindaric performance is a temple or a street or a doorstep or a banquet hall somewhere in archaic Greece. Usually, we cannot even be certain what the scene of performance is, so any impact it may have on the poetry itself may escape us. And what the poet tells us from moment to moment cannot be referred to anything with which we are already familiar, so we must take it as it comes, absorbing it and keeping it in mind as well as we can, if we are to have a background at all.

And we will need a background, for we find as we read that almost anything may happen. We may begin with a solemn invocation, but often it is not directed to a recognizable deity but to an abstraction like "Peace" or "Divineness," or to a city or the song itself or a musical instrument. Ostensibly, the poem was written to celebrate a victory at the athletic games of Greece, but the victor himself does not seem to be the center of attention, at least not as we would expect him to be. The poet, for example, is at pains to display the victor's ancestry. He may go back a hundred years to mention an athletic forebear. He may mention living relatives who also happen to be athletes. In this way, more time may go to the victor's family than to the victor himself. His city may also displace him from the limelight. Yet even more peculiar is the poet's manner of praising the victor, when he gets around to it. To us it seems anything but straightforward. He is inclined, for example, to attack people who do not have the victor's virtues, rather than to praise the victor for having them. Sometimes, when no explicit reference is made to the victor, we are unprepared for such attacks. Thus they give the impression of willful cantankerousness. It is only a step from here to the traditional image of Pindar as a poet who habitually disregards the demands of propriety and relevance.

And then there is the mythic portion of the ode. Here we have narrative, but we are quickly disappointed if we expect anything like the narrative in Homer. The poet moves backward, or backward and forward at once. He may interrupt a myth, dismiss it and start another, totally unrelated to the first, at least as far as we can tell immediately. Careful study of the ode may reveal a connection between the two, but the connection may be in the difference between them, not in their similarity. The proverbial statements that occur in the ode, the poet's moralistic pronouncements or observations, may give us the clue to the way in which we should view the myth or myths in it. In any event, we are forced to read the ode with partial understanding from moment to moment. The poet has created a complex structure where words take on special significance. They derive their full meaning, their full effect, from the total impression made by the ode. Only a second, third, and fourth reading will bring out these extra resonances.

A poet whose style is so compressed, whose manner of proceeding is, at first sight, so unpredictable, might well seem incoherent. Pindar's reputation as the supreme lyric poet of Greece keeps interest in him alive, but many who go to his poems to find the reason for his reputation come away disappointed. Those who read him in translation find him too difficult to understand; those who read him in Greek find that his language impresses even before it communicates, and the odes dissolve into a series of purple passages. Pindar's power and his difficulty combine with the loss of appreciation for the genre in which he worked to create the traditional image of him as a poet beholden to nothing but the laws of his own genius. In times when poetry is in a heroic or tragic mode, Pindar's sublimity is admired and emulated, usually at the expense of poetic coherence; in times when poetry has a quieter voice, preferring irony to celebration, Pindar simply goes out of favor.

He seems to be out of favor now, but the present moment may also be propitious for him. Recent progress in scholarship has begun to revise the traditional image of Pindar as a sublime but incomprehensible poet. Having begun to understand him, we have no need to admire him blindly. But he is not easy to understand. He requires preparation. To begin to appreciate him, we need to know something about the kind of poetry he wrote and the times in which he lived.

Pindar, the Victor, and Poetry of Occasion

Every Pindaric ode begins with its occasion, someone's victory in one of the Greek athletic festivals. The most prestigious of these were the four after which the four books of Pindar's odes have been named: the Olympian, Pythian, Nemean, and Isthmian games, often called the "great" or pan-Hellenic games, to distinguish them from the innumerable minor athletic festivals held throughout the Greek world. Any Greek could compete at the great games, but in practice participation was limited to those who could afford it, and these, in Pindar's day, were the members of aristocratic families.

No money prizes were given officially at the great games themselves, but victors on their return home found ample rewards for their efforts. To judge from the number of statues of athletic victors, the number of inscriptions recording their triumphs, and the number of poems written to commemorate them, they did not consider the fleeting moment of glory sufficient: they looked to the future and wanted a place in it. If they competed during Pindar's lifetime and were wise enough to hire him, they were among the thirty-five individuals whose names, with one or two exceptions, we know today only because Pindar celebrated their victories.

Not very much is known in detail about the events surrounding the production of a Pindaric ode. We can only imagine, in a general way, what these events must have been. First was the moment of victory itself. At the four great games the official prize was a crown or garland—of olive at Olympia, laurel at Pytho (Delphi), green parsley at Nemea, and dry parsley at the Isthmos. As the victor advanced to the altar to be crowned by the judges, the criers would announce his name, his father's name, and the name of his city.

After the moment of triumph, the victor might approach the poet and ask him to compose a song virtually impromptu, to be sung by his friends at the site of the games, whether in a procession or at a banquet. But usually, he would ask for a song to be performed on his return home. If this were the case, the poet would have time to compose a more elaborate ode. He would consider the history of the victor's family and city, finding in it something to deepen the significance of the present moment. He might travel with the victor from the site of the games to his native city, composing the ode on the way. On arrival, a chorus of boys or men would be assembled. The poet would instruct them in the movements he wanted them to execute as they sang the ode, explaining, when necessary, the meaning of its more difficult passages. He also wrote the music, usually for harp and flute.

How much time elapsed between the moment the victor was crowned at the games and the moment he witnessed his success being celebrated in song and dance must have varied a great deal. The whole process reached its culmination in performance. When the poet finally left the

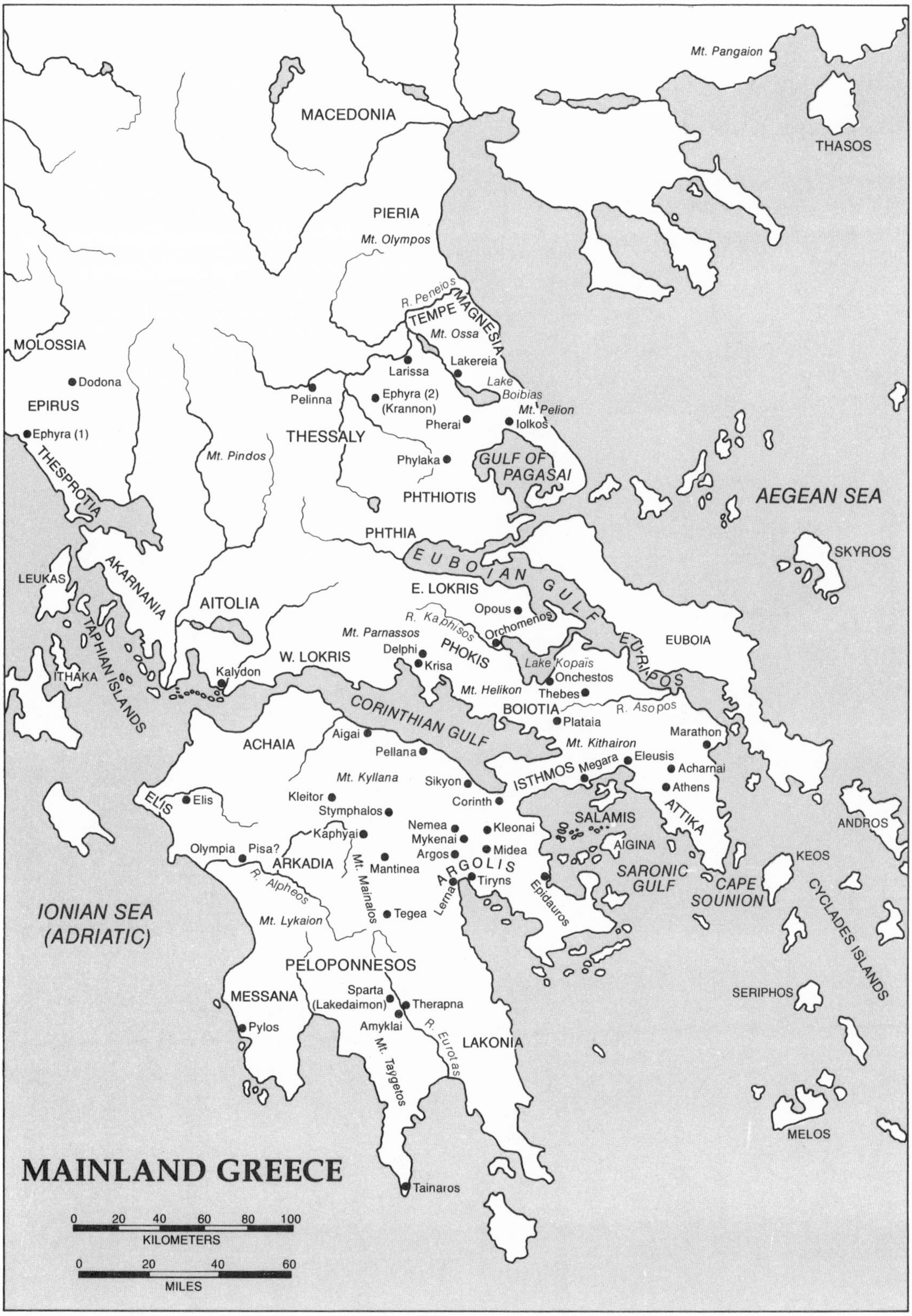
MAINLAND GREECE
Mt. Pangaion
THASOS
MACEDONIA
PIERIA
Mt. Olympos
R. Peneios
TEMPE
MAGNESIA
Mt. Ossa
MOLOSSIA
Dodona
EPIRUS
Ephyra (1)
THESPROTIA
Larissa
Lakereia
Lake Boibias
Pelinna
Ephyra (2)
(Krannon)
Mt. Pelion
Pherai
Iolkos
THESSALY
Mt. Pindos
Phylaka
GULF OF PAGASAI
PHTHIOTIS
AEGEAN SEA
PHTHIA
EUBOIAN GULF
SKYROS
LEUKAS
AKARNANIA
E. LOKRIS
AITOLIA
Opous
TAPHIAN ISLANDS
R. Kaphisos
Orchomenos
Mt. Parnassos
EUBOIA
Delphi
PHOKIS
W. LOKRIS
Krisa
Lake Kopaïs
EURIPOS
ITHAKA
Kalydon
Onchestos
Mt. Helikon
Thebes
BOIOTIA
R. Asopos
CORINTHIAN GULF
Plataia
Aigai
Marathon
ACHAIA
Pellana
Mt. Kithairon
Eleusis
ISTHMOS
Megara
Acharnai
Mt. Kyllana
Sikyon
Athens
Kleitor
ELIS
Elis
Corinth
Stymphalos
SALAMIS
ATTIKA
ANDROS
Nemea
Kleonai
Kaphyai
Mykenai
AIGINA
Olympia
Pisa?
Midea
KEOS
ARKADIA
Argos
ARGOLIS
SARONIC GULF
Mt. Mainalos
Mantinea
Tiryns
CAPE SOUNION
R. Alpheos
Lerna
Epidauros
CYCLADES ISLANDS
IONIAN SEA
(ADRIATIC)
Tegea
Mt. Lykaion
PELOPONNESOS
Sparta
(Lakedaimon)
Therapna
SERIPHOS
MESSANA
Amyklai
R. Eurotas
Pylos
LAKONIA
Mt. Taygetos
MELOS
Tainaros
0 20 40 60 80 100
KILOMETERS
0 20 40 60
MILES

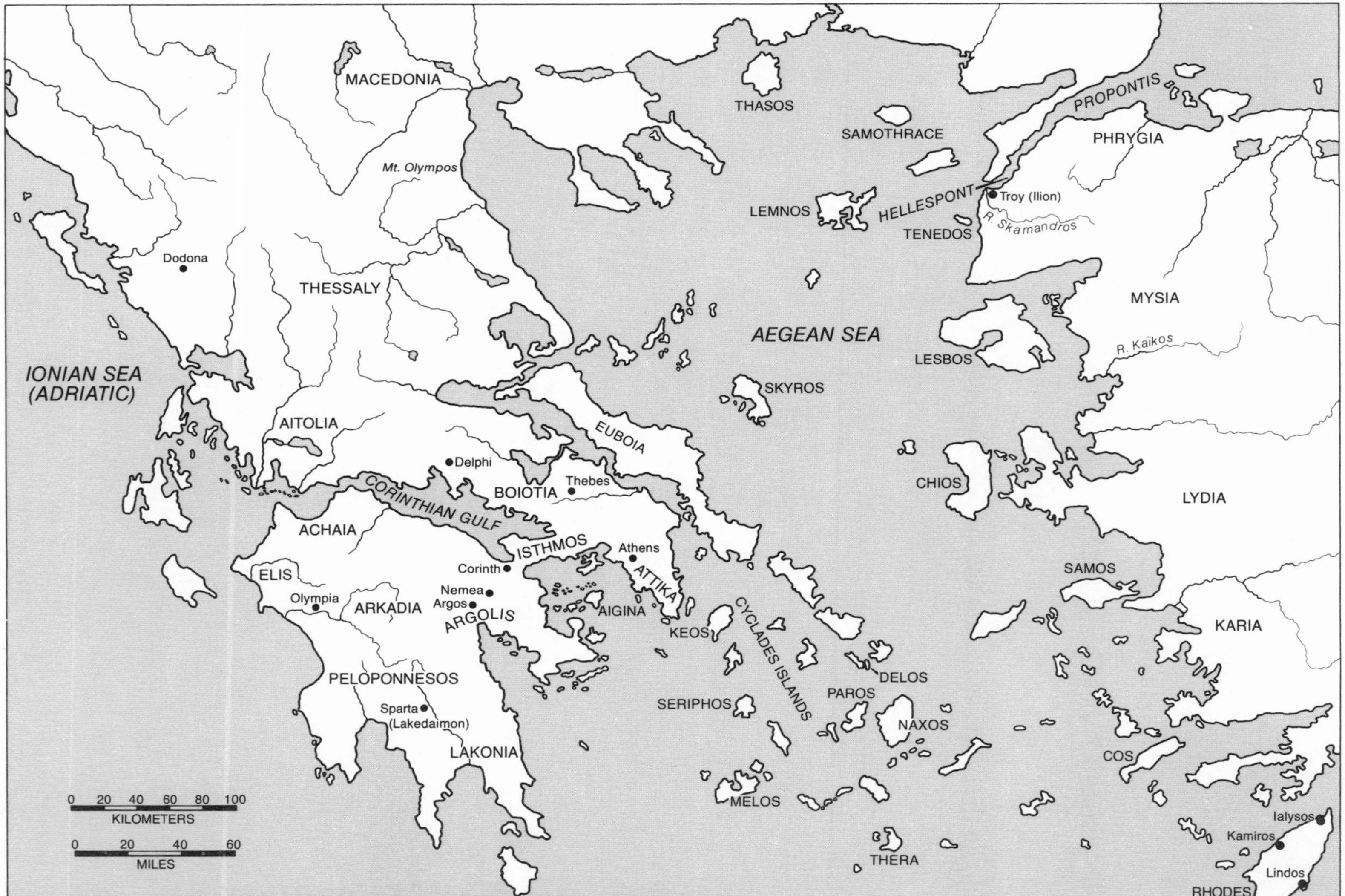

GREECE, THE ISLANDS, AND ASIA MINOR

scene of celebration, he would have provided the victor with a fair copy of the ode itself. At other times, when he did not accompany the victor back from the games, he must have composed the ode at home. He would then send it, complete with directions for performance, to the victor, or he would send it together with a chorus leader who saw to its performance.

None of this is very familiar in modern poetry. The idea that a poet should be hired to celebrate an important event scarcely occurs to anyone. More important, over the last two and a half millennia the link between poetry and music has been severed. Lyric poetry, once a matter involving musical instruments and, in its choral form, intricate dance steps, now involves only a solitary audience reading in silence what the poet wrote without anyone's asking him to write it. Pindar's odes have been reduced from their original splendor to the bare minimum with which all poetry must now make do. But if the only strength of Pindar's odes lay in their instrumentation or in their choreography, they would not have survived. We may feel nostalgia for the missing dance and musical accompaniment, but the essential power of the poetry is still there, in the words.

Pindar's Life and Times

Pindar was born in Thebes, the main city of Boiotia, in 518 B.C. His earliest extant ode, *Pythian 10*, was composed in 498, when he was twenty; his last datable poem, *Pythian 8*, was written in 446, when he was seventy-two. (See Appendix I.) Thus his career as a writer of victory odes spans at least fifty-two years.

During the course of his long, productive career, Pindar traveled from one end of the Greek world to the other, celebrating the triumphs of aristocrats and kings. He lived during momentous times and wrote for men who played both large and small roles in the unfolding of events. For this reason it is advisable that a reader have some awareness of historical background. The Persian invasions of the first quarter of the fifth century and the gradual changes that occurred in the Greek world in the twenty-five years or so that followed, mainly as a result of the growing power of Athens, are the two principal developments to keep in mind.

The most famous and powerful patrons of Pindar's art were the Sicilian dynasts Hieron and Theron, both of whom Pindar visited in 476. He had praised Theron fourteen years previously, in *Pythian 6*, which celebrates the victory of Theron's brother Xenokrates in the chariot race at Pytho in 490. It is addressed to Xenokrates' son, Thrasyboulos, Theron's nephew, whom Pindar commends by reference to his more famous uncle (line 46). Even while Thrasyboulos and his friends were enjoying Pindar's song at Delphi, a Persian army was on its way to the shores of Greece. Not long afterward the Athenians pushed

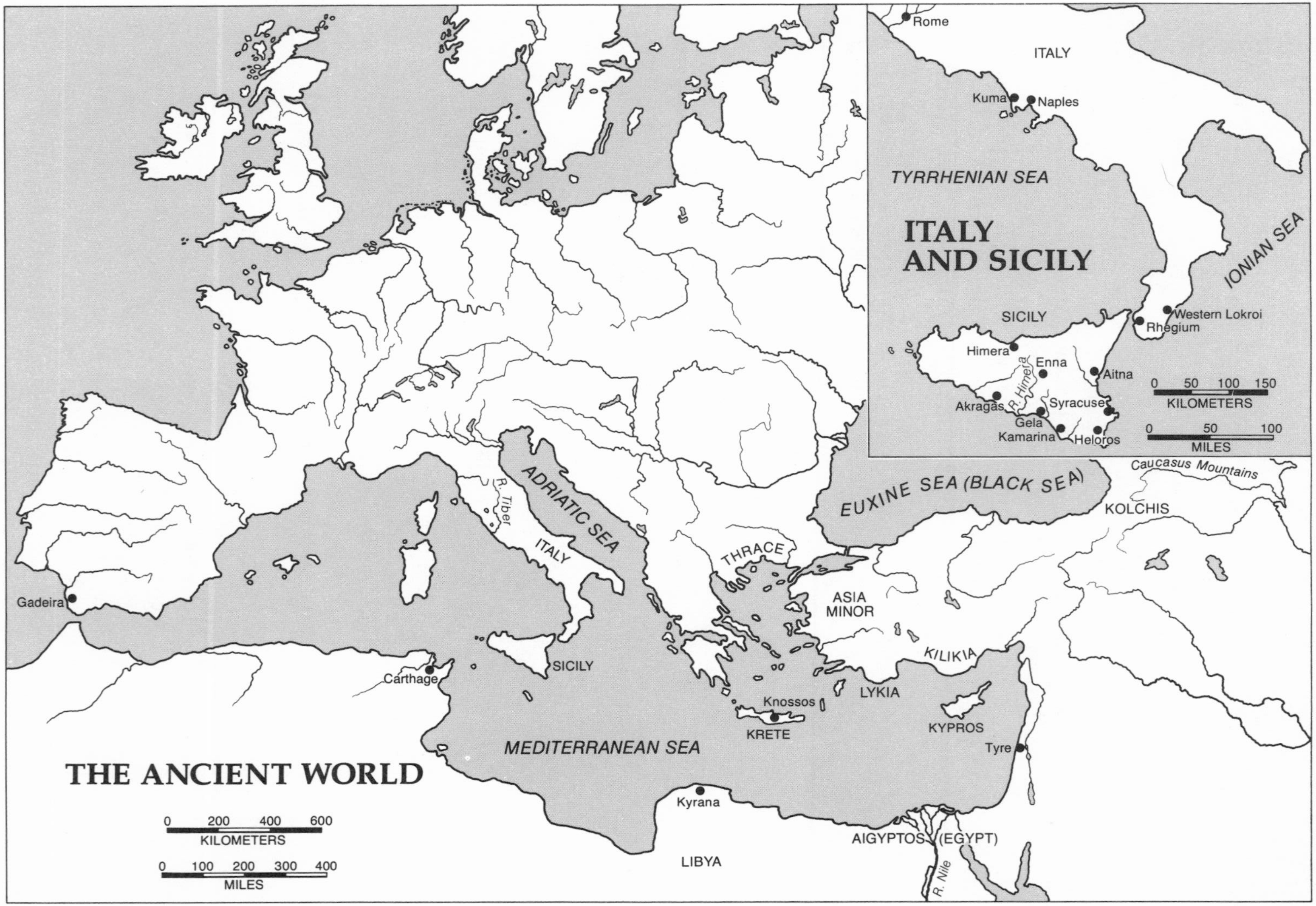
THE ANCIENT WORLD
0 200 400 600
KILOMETERS
0 100 200 300 400
MILES
Gadeira
Carthage
SICILY
R. Tiber
ITALY
ADRIATIC SEA
MEDITERRANEAN SEA
THRACE
Knossos
KRETE
Kyrana
LIBYA
ASIA
MINOR
LYKIA
KILIKIA
KYPROS
Tyre
AIGYPTOS (EGYPT)
R. Nile
EUXINE SEA (BLACK SEA)
KOLCHIS
Caucasus Mountains
ITALY
AND SICILY
Rome
ITALY
Kuma
Naples
TYRRHENIAN SEA
IONIAN SEA
SICILY
Western Lokroi
Rhegium
Himera
R. Himera
Enna
Aitna
Akragas
Syracuse
Gela
Kamarina
Heloros
0 50 100 150
KILOMETERS
0 50 100
MILES

the invaders into the sea at the battle of Marathon. But by the time Pindar went to Sicily, fourteen years later in 476, the Persians had come again, and Greek Sicily itself had faced an equally ominous threat from another quarter.

A decade after Marathon a second, more formidable barbarian invasion was launched against Greece. In the east, Xerxes attacked by land and sea. In the west, Carthage sent an army against the Greek cities in Sicily. In all likelihood, the two invasions were coordinated. Athens and her allies defeated the Persian fleet at the battle of Salamis. At almost the same time, Theron of Akragas and Gelon of Syracuse, Hieron's older brother, met and defeated the Carthaginian army at the battle of Himera in Sicily. In the following year, a Greek army under Spartan leadership defeated the Persian army at the battle of Plataia.

The battle of Salamis took place in September 480. Some time after that, Pindar was commissioned to write an ode honoring Phylakidas of Aigina for a victory in the *pankration* (see Appendix V) at the Isthmian games. The poem, *Isthmian 5*, mentions the battle of Salamis by name. We can guess with some confidence why Pindar mentioned the battle in this particular ode, written for a citizen of Aigina. After the battle, the Greeks who had fought in it singled out the Aiginetan contingent for its bravery. The allusion to the battle in which his countrymen had distinguished themselves is designed to please the victor.

A similar design accounts for Pindar's mention of the battle of Himera in the first Pythian ode, written for Hieron in 470. Hieron's older brother Gelon had defeated the Carthaginians at Himera in 480. By the time Pindar wrote *Pythian 1*, Salamis and Plataia had become examples of Greek bravery for all to emulate. It is to Pindar's credit that he perceived the importance of the battle of Himera, for it determined the survival of Greek culture in Sicily, as the other two battles ensured its survival in the mother country. In *Pythian 1*, Pindar places all three battles on a par. Plataia was fought "beneath (Mt.) Kithairon"; Himera was won by the "Deinomenidai" (sons of Deinomenes), Gelon and Hieron:

I will earn
the praise of Athens by singing of Salamis,
and of Sparta by making my theme
the battles beneath Kithairon
where the curve-bow Persians strove and were crushed.
But when I come to the rivery field of Himera
I will sing of the Deinomenidai, conquerors of the foe. (75–80)

Pindar is said to have gone to Athens in his youth to learn song and music. In the above lines from *Pythian 1*, he praises Athens for her part in the battle of Salamis. Some years later, he wrote a dithyramb for the Athenians. The poem (fragment 76), apparently recalling the role

Athens had played in saving Greece from the barbarian enemy, hails her as "the bulwark of Hellas." Pindar's own city Thebes, an enemy of Athens throughout the fifth century, on this occasion reportedly fined Pindar for praising her. Eustathius records the sum of 1,000, Isocrates of 10,000, drachmas. Isocrates adds that the Athenians voted Pindar 10,000 drachmas in recompense for the fine. We hear of another instance of Athenian affection for Pindar from Pausanias, who tells us that the Athenians erected a bronze statue of Pindar seated with his lyre beside him. Exactly when the Athenians erected the statue we cannot tell, nor do we know if it had anything to do with the alleged rivalry between Athens and Thebes—Thebes anxious to punish and Athens to reward Pindar for his Athenian sympathies.[1]

There is probably a trace of historical fantasy operating in much of this, a result of the natural tendency to wonder what Pindar must have felt and experienced, being both a pan-Hellenic and a Theban poet. Thebes had disgraced herself during the invasion of Xerxes. She had capitulated to the invader before the battle of Salamis, and Theban forces had fought alongside the Persians against the Greeks at Plataia. In the course of his career, however, Pindar the Theban poet was called upon to sing of Athens and of at least two Athenian athletes. He also sang, possibly during the period of Theban disgrace, of Thebes and of at least four Theban athletes. (See Appendix II.) Enmity between Thebes and Athens was as intense as it has ever been between any two states. Though it is hard for us to imagine a prominent citizen in one country ever asking a poet from an adversary country to celebrate an event of national significance, that happened in Pindar's case, and not merely because he had acquired a reputation for tact. The great games in which his patrons competed took place during times of declared sacred truce, when all hostilities between Greek states were suspended and the Greeks vied with each other in pursuit of glory, as if they were a single nation, not a hodgepodge of cities ever embroiled in territorial and ideological disputes. The pan-Hellenic character of the games affected the poetry they produced. "One man at a people's bidding" is Pindar's way of describing himself, a private individual with a Hellenic message (*Olympian 13.* 49).

The war against Persia did not end when Xerxes' vast armies were beaten back. In 478, the Greeks formed a league to guard against yet another threat from the East and to carry on the struggle. Athens became the dominant member of this alliance, known today as the Delian League, because, in the beginning, its headquarters were located on the island of Delos. But as Athens began to use her control over the League to further her own ambitions, what had been a mutual defense alliance of Greek states turned into an Athenian empire. The treasury of the League was eventually transferred from Delos to Athens and used to finance the rebuilding of the Acropolis, pillaged by the Persians.

Membership in the League, at one time voluntary, became compulsory. One of the states that wanted out was Aigina, long a rival, at times an open enemy, of Athens. Hostilities between the two date from the end of the sixth century. In 459, war broke out between them again. Aigina was defeated, her fleet dismantled, and she was forced to pay a yearly tribute of thirty talents.

Behind this struggle for power and independence an equally important and bitter ideological struggle was being waged. Athens was a vigorous young democracy. Aigina, visible from the port of Athens and dependent, like her, on the sea for commerce, was ruled by a small number of ancient noble families whose claims to power were hereditary and who traced their ancestry back to the great heroes of the Trojan War and beyond them to Zeus himself. Other Greek cities were ruled by similar if less illustrious oligarchies. The struggle between them and Athens became a struggle not only among cities but also among forms of government and ways of life. When Athens succeeded in imposing her will, she uprooted institutions that displeased her and replaced them with democracies on whose loyalty she felt she could rely. More traditional, conservative states like Thebes, Sparta, and Aigina considered her an aggressor and exporter of revolution. Approximately twenty years after Pindar's death, the Peloponnesian War erupted between Athens with her allies and Sparta with hers. The seeds of destruction had been sown long before.

Already in his last years when the Athenians put an end to Aiginetan independence in 458, Pindar did not live to see the outbreak of the Peloponnesian War in 431. His last poem, *Pythian 8*, celebrates an Aiginetan victory. Indeed, a fourth of his odes celebrate victors from Aigina, a fact that must indicate a bond of mutual affection between the poet and the island. His own city, Thebes, suffered with Aigina in the struggle against Athens, but not as much. For a brief period between 456 and 447 Boiotia was under Athenian domination; Aigina lost her freedom in 458 and did not recover it for over fifty years. Meanwhile her citizens continued to intrigue against Athens, with the result that when war broke out in 431, the Athenians removed them from their homes and brought in a new population. The Aiginetans returned at the end of the war in 403, but they were never again prominent in the life of Greece. Only the magnificent ruins from the temple of Aphaia and the odes of Pindar remain to tell us what they were.

The odes, however, give us a very different view of Greece from what we find in historical descriptions of the fifth century. Even when Pindar names what we would call an historical event it seems to have become no longer a simple event but a paradigm, a model, something to which he can appeal in illustration or defense of a truth whose relevance he wants to press home. At such moments we may feel that history has melded into myth. A more accurate way of describing it would be to say that myth and history are not as distinct from each other in Pindar's mind as they are in ours. The political and ideological sympathy between Thebes and Aigina, for example, appeared to Pindar as a reflection of their mythological relationship: Aigina and Theba, nymphs for whom the two places were named, were both daughters of the river god Asopos in Boiotia, where Thebes was located. Zeus had fallen in love with Aigina and had taken her from her original home in Boiotia to the island of Oinona, which thereafter bore her name. There he made love to her and there she bore him a son, Aiakos, founder of the Aiakid line. Thus when Pindar sang of Aiakid heroes, he could think of them as his remote ancestral cousins, descended from Aigina, sister of Pindar's "mother" Theba. Pindar speaks of these relationships as if they were actual, while we can only take them metaphorically. To Pindar, however, the Aiginetan warriors were what they were at the battle of Salamis because of their descent from the sons of Aiakos, the Aiakidai, who were even imagined to have fought beside them against the Persians.[2] Similarly, a figure like Patroklos belongs, in our view, to a category utterly separate from that in which we place the Greek warriors who died fighting the Persians at the battle of Plataia; the funeral games of Patroklos in the *Iliad* and the funeral games conducted every fifth year in honor of those who fell at Plataia[3] inhabit two different realms in our minds, the one belonging to mythology, the other to history. It was not so for the Greeks. For them, a living and apparent connection existed between what happens now and what happened in the remote past, between history in our sense of the word and myth in the Greek sense—not what was imagined to have happened or was now over, but what had happened and had also become, through poetry, part of a living tradition.

Almost from the moment of their first appearance, then, Pindar's odes have belonged both to poetry and to history. Written in order to preserve the memory and interpret the significance of certain real events, they have an historical emphasis not usually present in poetry. The further we have come in time from the original celebration that gave them birth and of which they were a part, the more their historical aspect has come into prominence. The passage of time has made it easy for us to forget that Pindar's odes are poems; it is tempting to treat them as documents. But, unlike most forms even of occasional poetry, a Pindaric ode did not begin its life as a document until sometime after Pindar had entrusted it to its patron. Up to that moment it was less an interpretation or a recollection of events than an event in and of itself. Because the odes were written for performance, we have in each of them not a record of fifth-century life, but an actual piece of it.

The History of the Text[4]

Pindar was confident that his odes would become well known. The opening lines of *Nemean 5* contain his most vivid boast on this theme: his song, he tells us, will not stand still, like a statue fixed to its own base. It will travel on every ship, carrying its message everywhere. We may well wonder what kind of cargo a poem could have been in Pindar's day. Was there a more or less extensive trade in books flourishing? Were companies of scribes on hand for the performance of a Pindaric ode, ready to reproduce it for sale, even for export abroad? The materials for such publication were available, papyrus having been used in Greece for writing since the seventh century. Homer's epics had been committed to writing at Athens in the sixth century. In the fifth century, the works of other famous poets, Pindar included, probably enjoyed some form of circulation, in addition to being quoted from memory by different people in different places. Aeschylus, Sophocles, and Euripides echo Pindar's words from time to time. The earliest author to quote him directly is Herodotus (III.38). By the end of the fifth century, the works of Anaxagoras, the Ionian philosopher, were on sale in the Athenian market place, where editions of Pindar could probably be purchased as well. When Aristophanes more than once delighted in parodies of Pindar's lofty style, he was counting on members of his audience to enjoy the joke, which depended on some familiarity with the poetry being mimicked. Whether they had acquired that familiarity from books or from hearing Pindar sung is impossible to say. In all likelihood it was due, in some measure, to both.

In the earliest period of their existence, Pindar's odes depended for their preservation on the interest of the person or group for whom they were written. This is true, at least, of the two poems about whose preservation at the earliest stage we have some evidence. The ancient commentary to *Olympian* 7 informs us that that ode was inscribed in gold letters in the temple of Athena in Lindos, a Rhodian city. The victor who commissioned the poem from Pindar surely had something to do with this, but he need not have acted alone. The ode is a monument to the artistic greatness of the people of Rhodes. It enshrines the signal events of their island's history, paying tribute to the glory of its past. It was in their interest that it survive, that it be read by others and be known by as many as possible. The second poem about whose early preservation we have some evidence is Pindar's hymn to the god Ammon, which Pausanias saw inscribed on a triangular pillar in the god's temple.[5] The priests of the god and the Rhodians both had a stake in the survival of the poetry Pindar had composed for them. We can imagine a similar solicitude on the part of others who had engaged Pindar to write for them. In addition, Pindar himself probably kept copies of his odes. What happened to these after his death is unknown, but his native city Thebes, proud of her poet's reputation, was probably a place where copies of his works could be obtained.

When Pindar died, he left behind a large number of poems preserved in different places throughout the Greek world. Selections of them had probably been made and distributed during his own lifetime, especially once his fame had become worldwide. But not long after his death he seems to have gone out of favor, at least in Athens. The old man Strepsiades in Aristophanes' *Clouds* complains that the younger generation no longer appreciates choral lyrics. Eupolis the comic poet laments that Pindar's poems have been silenced "by the crowd's hostility to beauty." He and Aristophanes both record the low popular esteem for the nondramatic choral lyric toward the end of the fifth century: to sing it is to be *archaic*, old fashioned.[6]

What was true at Athens need not have been the case everywhere, but it does indicate that by the fourth century Pindar's work had entered a new phase in its history. His odes were now being read, not performed. On one hand, this made for their more faithful transmission: numerous corruptions crept into the texts of dramas that were presented again and again on stage, while Pindar's odes, being unperformed, remained comparatively pure. On the other hand, understanding of Pindar must have suffered from the demise of choral song. Once the odes had ceased to be a living part of Greek social and public life, they became more and more remote and difficult. What had been a poetry involving music and dance, and civic and religious pride, gradually became a poetry for the sophist to utilize[7] or the curious to decipher. Or so it seems.

There are some indications that even during this period Pindar's odes exerted more than a mere historical or philological fascination. When Alexander the Great destroyed Thebes in 335, one building he ordered his troops not to level was the house of Pindar. There were many famous buildings in that ancient city, including many sacred to the gods. Alexander's reverence for Pindar does not seem to have sprung from passive acceptance of a great reputation: the conqueror who slept with a copy of the *Iliad* under his pillow must have kept a copy of Pindar within reach as well.

The admiration of Alexander the Great is mirrored in the mythology that grew up around Pindar's name. Men imagined that as a boy he had fallen asleep by the roadside, and while he slept bees came and distilled honey on his lips.[8] But there is also evidence that Pindar's reputation inspired intellectual curiosity as well as fanciful awe. Not long after Alexander had spared Pindar's house, Chamaeleon the Peripatetic wrote a book about him. Nothing of it survives, but the fact of its existence indicates that Pindar was still being read and that editions of his works, more or less complete, were available toward the end of the fourth century.

By the end of the fourth century, Pindar's odes had come a long way from their original performances. His musical notation and choreographical directions had most likely begun to disappear from copies of his works. There would be no point in taking the extra pains to preserve them if no one understood them anymore, or if, as in fact was the case, their inclusion served no practical purpose, since the odes were no longer performed. This is how one generation unconsciously deprives future generations of things they will sorely miss. Meanwhile, the odes had been traveling from place to place. Because men like Hieron and Theron attracted attention by their wealth and power, the odes Pindar addressed to them found an early audience beyond the confines of their Sicilian homes. In the last quarter of the fifth century, Athenian political and economic interest in Sicily (with its tragic consequences later) created a demand for information about the island and possibly a market for Sicilian odes like *Olympians 1* through *6*, *Pythians 1* through *3*, *Nemean 1*, and the dance-song Pindar wrote for Hieron and Aristophanes parodied in the *Birds*.[9] Across the water from the port of Athens, the island of Aigina in the last half of the fifth century was a veritable museum of Pindaric manuscripts. When the island fell under Athenian domination, Athenians with an antiquarian interest or a touch of greed or both probably treated these venerable relics as the Romans were later to treat their own incomparable works of art: the odes left Aigina for private Athenian collections or for sale in the marketplace. Precisely which of the other odes, if any, circulated in written form individually or in collections at this time we do not know. In addition to odes for Sicilians and Aiginetans, Pindar had written at least two for an Italian Greek, two for a king of Kyrana (Cyrene) in north Africa, one for a private citizen there, five for athletes from his native Thebes, nine for victors from various other cities in mainland Greece, and one for a Rhodian. (See Appendix II.) One,[10] and probably several, of these odes were familiar, at least in part, to the Greek world at about the time of Pindar's death and must have continued so during the century that followed. By the time Alexandrian scholars of the third century set to work on what became our edition of Pindar, they probably had to do some traveling in search of texts, but many of Pindar's songs had already come to them.

The Alexandrian Edition. The earliest critical edition of Pindar's poems was the work of Zenodotus, first head of the library at Alexandria (c. 284 B.C.) We cannot tell to what extent Zenodotus had to sift the material before him, deciding which of the odes really belonged to Pindar and which were spurious. In fact we know very little about his edition. Some of the odes before him were still written in the old Attic script. These he would have had to transliterate into the new Ionian alphabet adopted at Athens in 403 and elsewhere in Greece during the fourth century. He would have had to make decisions of orthography from time to time, since there were three different "E" sounds and three different "O" sounds that were not distinguished from each other in the old alphabet. In addition, Zenodotus would have had to devise a uniform presentation of all the poems collected from different sources. The ancient commentaries to the victory odes mention three instances where Zenodotus altered his received texts. In one the comment reads: "Instead of *drenched*, Zenodotus writes . . . ," but Zenodotus' suggested reading (at *Olympian 6*. 55) has been lost. At line 4 of *Olympian 2* he preferred a spelling that would have violated Pindar's metrical scheme. A more serious metrical blunder is recorded in the ancient commentary to *Olympian 3*. 29. It is clear that Zenodotus had an imperfect understanding of the meters of lyric poetry.

Another Alexandrian who dealt with Pindar was the scholar-poet Callimachus. In his massive *Pinakes*, a catalogue of works preserved in the library at Alexandria, Callimachus classified the poems of Pindar and the other lyric poets, arranging Pindar's odes for athletic victors according to the place where the victories were won, the arrangement adopted later by Aristophanes of Byzantium and still adhered to in editions of the Greek text and in most modern translations. Callimachus is also the earliest in a long line of scholars who have contributed to the controversy over the occasion and meaning of *Pythian 2*. Allusions to Pindar in Callimachus' own poetry show that he had a poetic as well as a scholarly interest in Pindar. Unfortunately, the poems of Callimachus are mostly in fragments now, so it is difficult to estimate the full extent of his debt.

The man who did most for Pindar's text was Aristophanes of Byzantium, head of the library at Alexandria from about 194. The two areas where he had most effect were in colometry, or line-division, and the arrangement of the books and the poems within them. Until Aristophanes worked on the text of Pindar, the lines had been written out continuously like prose. Aristophanes divided these continuous lines into shorter units. He also divided the odes into stanzas labeled strophes (turns), antistrophes (counterturns), and epodes (stands). Due to a basic misunderstanding of Pindar's verse, Aristophanes broke the long Pindaric line into units that were actually too short, often ending in mid-word. These short, seemingly irrational Pindaric lines remained standard in Pindar's text down to modern times, with the result that Pindar's verse has seemed disorderly to some, "free" and inspired to others. More than one Pindarizing poet of the Renaissance mistakenly thought he was following Pindar when he wrote in brief, staccato measures. In spite of this shortcoming, Aristophanes understood principles of metrical responsion ignored by Zenodotus. His text, reflecting awareness of the meter of the poetry in its format, marked a major advance over all previous editions.

Aristophanes, as we have seen, had some help from his predecessor

Callimachus in the arrangement of the odes. Like Callimachus, he chose to group the odes according to the place where the victory celebrated in each had been gained. But there was more to deal with than the odes for victors. In the course of his career, Pindar had been called on to write a variety of songs, sometimes for individuals, sometimes for religious occasions. Among the poems he wrote for individuals were epinician or victory odes (*epinikia*), songs of praise unconnected with athletic victory (*enkomia*), and dirges (*thrênoi*). Among the poems he wrote for religious occasions were *hymns* to various gods, *paians* or songs to Apollo, *dithyrambs* or songs for Dionysos, and *prosodia* or processional songs to be sung on the way to an altar or temple. He also wrote dance-songs (*hyporchêmata*) and songs for maiden choruses to sing (*parthenia*).

Aristophanes divided this large collection of extant poetry into seventeen books, placing the religious poetry first (six books), the poems for individuals last (six books), and the poems of indeterminate character in the middle (five books):

Sacred Poems	Hymns	(1 book)
	Paians	(1 book)
	Dithyrambs	(2 books)
	Prosodia	(2 books)
Poems of Indeterminate Character	Parthenia	(3 books)
	Hyporchêmata	(2 books)
Secular Poems	Enkomia	(1 book)
	Thrênoi	(1 book)
	Epinikia	(4 books)

Of this considerable body of poetry only the last four books remain, the *epinikia* or victory odes. Even they are incomplete. Bits and pieces from the thirteen other books have been collected by scholars from various sources—some from quotations, paraphrases, and summaries of Pindar in ancient authors; others, more recently, from papyri recovered from the sands of Egypt. These bits and pieces are the fragments of Pindar's work, bearing the numbers given to them by various modern editors.

Within the four books of victory odes themselves, Aristophanes adopted principles of arrangement that might seem peculiar to a modern editor. The four books appear in the order of the relative antiquity of the games for which they were labeled, beginning with the Olympian, the most ancient. Within the books, however, no attention whatever is paid to chronology. The earliest poem of all, *Pythian 10*, is not placed first, even in its own book; and the latest, *Pythian 8,* is not placed last. The odes are gathered into books according to the games they commemorate, but they are arranged within those books in accordance with the prestige of the athletic contest involved, the chariot race being the most prestigious, followed by the mounted horse race, the mule-car race, and then the various gymnastic contests: pankration, wrestling, boxing, pentathlon, and the foot races: the race for men in armor, the long race, the double-lap race, the single-lap race. Last of all was the musical competition, celebrated by Pindar only once, in *Pythian 12*, the last of the Pythian odes. (See Appendix V.)

Aristophanes adhered to these principles of arrangement, but not rigidly. He placed *Olympian 1* first in the collection, though it celebrates a victory in the horse race, while *Olympian 2* celebrates a chariot victory. His reason for doing so was the majestic opening of *Olympian 1*, called by Lucian the most beautiful of all lyric poems.[11] Aristophanes may have been moved by its beauty to place it first, or, more likely, by its theme, the supremacy of the Olympian over all other contests. He dealt freely with the first three Pythian odes as well. *Pythians 1* and *2*, for Hieron, celebrate chariot victories. *Pythian 3* does not, and yet it comes before *Pythian 4*, which does. The reason for the discrepancy is not hard to find: *Pythian 3* is for Hieron, like *Pythians 1* and *2*. It would have been foolish to destroy the effect of a Hieronic sequence merely to keep an arbitrary scheme intact.[12]

Such was Aristophanes of Byzantium's Pindar. Emended from time to time, expounded in various ways, Aristophanes' text was not superseded until August Boeckh in the early nineteenth century discovered the secret of Pindar's meter.

After Aristophanes, scholarly activity on Pindar in the ancient world continued. There is evidence of the existence of a large number of studies devoted to Pindar and his poetry. All these have perished, though not without leaving their mark. As the text was transmitted from age to age, the opinions of famous Pindaric scholars gradually began to be written in the margins. The monographs, perhaps even excerpts from the lectures, of ancient Pindarists were abbreviated and incorporated into their place in the text itself. No mere idle curiosity was at work in this process: the comments became more and more necessary to the elucidation of Pindar's meaning. He was a difficult poet to begin with. The loss of appreciation for the genre in which he composed made him seem at times incomprehensible. The inexpert would have grasped at straws often enough, and often enough the opinions to be found in the margins were not worth much more than straw, for all their antiquity. At other times they were extremely valuable. Though they can be misleading in the interpretation of Pindar, primarily due to their biographical-historical emphasis, they have much to tell us about the history of the text and about the ancient world. In modern times, they are no longer printed with the text but separately under the title of *Scholia*—notes, interpretations, commentary.

The Second-Century Selection. The first and second centuries A.D. witnessed a decline of Greek studies in the eastern provinces of the Roman Empire. Among the casualties suffered by literature then were the first thirteen books of Pindar's poems. The text we have today, comprising only the last four books of the Aristophanean collection, dates from this period, when an unknown scholar, for whatever reason, selected only the victory odes for presentation and prepared a new commentary to suit the needs of the time.[13] How desperate a time it was for Pindar may be gathered from the treatment of his text. The anonymous editor based his commentary on the work of the first-century scholar Didymus, but he interspersed it with a running prose paraphrase of the odes, as if they had to be translated from one form of Greek into another in order to make sense to their readers. It was at this time also, or shortly before, that the text of Pindar's four books of victory odes was transferred from four papyrus rolls, the ancient form of publication, into a single *codex* or book with pages. Aristophanes of Byzantium had arranged the four books of victory odes in order of the relative antiquity of the games celebrated in each. The Olympian games date from 776, the Pythian from 582, the Isthmian from 581, and the Nemean from 573, and the books were arranged accordingly. But when the four papyrus rolls containing the four books were written into a single codex, the order of the last two was mistakenly reversed, so that the Nemeans occupy third place and the Isthmians are last. The old arrangement, however, was appropriate in another way, which seems to have escaped the anonymous editor responsible for the change. The last three Nemean odes have nothing to do with the Nemean games. When the Nemean collection formed the final section of the victory odes, it made sense for Aristophanes to attach to it these three odes that belong among Pindar's victory songs but to none of the great festivals commemorated in the rest of them. The last three Nemeans, then, were a kind of appendix to the original edition. Their attachment to the Nemean collection now, in the middle of the book, makes no sense.

By the middle of the third century A.D. Pindar ceases to be quoted except from his epinician or victory odes, a sure sign that by now the selected edition had become standard and the old collection of all seventeen books had gone out of circulation. We may contrast the practice of Plato in citing Pindar five centuries earlier: of the sixteen Pindaric citations in Plato's work, only four come from the victory odes,[14] the other twelve derive from poems published in the thirteen lost books. We may lament the loss, but it is also probable that if the selection had not been made, if Pindar's work had not been reduced and adapted to the changing times, it may well have perished altogether.

The Surviving Manuscripts. Pindar can be read today thanks to the survival of 142 manuscripts.[15] These manuscripts fall into two groups:

those that go back more or less uninterruptedly to an ancient archetype (the ancient manuscripts) and those that were edited during the fourteenth century by three Byzantine scholars[16] (the interpolated manuscripts). Both groups derive ultimately from the same archetype, the selected edition of Pindar made by the unknown scholar of the second century A.D.[17]

The second-century edition was copied an unknown number of times between its first appearance and sometime in the second half of the fourth century, the approximate date of the copy from which the manuscripts belonging to the Ambrosian recension of it derive. They are named for the manuscript that best represents them, Ambrosianus C 222 inf., a thirteenth-century manuscript preserved in the Ambrosian Library in Milan.

Toward the beginning of the fifth century, another copy of the archetype was made. The manuscripts that go back to this recension are named after a manuscript dating from the twelfth century and preserved in the Vatican Library in Rome. The ancient manuscripts, then, belong to two different recensions, the Ambrosian and the Vatican.

A number of manuscripts belonging to the Ambrosian recension contain only the Olympian odes, or the Olympian odes together with the Pythians. Similarly, the Vatican recension contains manuscripts with all four books and manuscripts with the Olympians and Pythians only. The practice of publishing one or two books of odes together with learned commentary goes back to antiquity and continues today.

The front and back of ancient books were exposed to wear and tear. Thus the manuscript in the Ambrosian Library that gives its name to the entire recension has suffered the loss of *Olympian 1* and *Olympians 13* and *14*—the first poem and the last two poems of the original volume, which contained only the Olympians, with scholia. Fortunately, the odes missing here are abundantly represented in the other manuscripts. The situation was far more perilous for the concluding lines of *Isthmian 8*, our last complete Isthmian ode. Its final lines are preserved in one manuscript only, Laurentianus 32, 52—a manuscript that also contains our only copy of what is left of a ninth Isthmian, probably the whole of its first stanza.[18] When the Isthmians were displaced from third to last position in the codex, they were exposed to danger of loss. In addition to the ninth Isthmian ode, which perished except for its first stanza, we hear from a scholiast to Lucian of a possible tenth, written for a Rhodian named Kasmylos.[19] And among the fragments of Pindar's poems are broken remains of several other Isthmian odes apparently included in the original collection before its displacement to the back of Pindar's works.

In spite of blemishes and shortcomings, Pindar's text is well preserved, containing only three or four places where we are never likely to be certain of the correct reading—an enviable situation compared with that in most other Greek texts.

We may now consider the nature of what has come down to us in the text of Pindar.

II. Pindar's Victory Songs

Pindar's odes come to us from that nebulous period in the history of Greek literature called The Archaic Age, falling roughly between the epic of Homer and the drama of Aeschylus. In lyric poetry its chief and almost sole representative is Pindar. His contemporary and rival in the art of the victory ode, Bacchylides, was known only from scattered pieces of his poetry until 1897, when the publication of a papyrus discovered in Egypt gave us a substantial portion of his work. Bacchylides' uncle Simonides is the earliest poet who we know wrote victory odes. Of Simonides' work in this genre there remain some titles, a few lines, but nothing complete. One or two of the other poets who composed lyric in the Archaic Age enjoy more renown than the pitiful remains of their work would lead us to expect. Sappho, the most famous, is little more than a ghost. Anacreon's fame is due more to his reflection in later poetry than to the slender substance of his own. The bitter voice of Archilochos speaks with such telling effect at the beginning of the archaic period that he has been called the inventor of personality. Archaic poetry would be more apprehensible to us if it were not mainly in ruins.

Pindar's work, the one edifice left standing among those ruins, is not easy to enter. It would be wise to remain outside a moment, studying its external characteristics. First is the surrounding landscape: the archaic period itself. A working notion of the fundamental habits and predilections of archaic poetry is essential preparation for reading Pindar. Second is the language in which his odes are written. We cannot go into much detail here, but awareness of a few facts will afford the view needed to appreciate the peculiar character of Pindar's work and to assess the degree to which it can be represented in English. This is even more the case with regard to the third external characteristic, the meter of the odes. If there were any way to experience the odes of Pindar as choral poetry, it would be through their rhythmical patterns. The complexities of these are too enormous to permit of anything beyond a brief description of major facts. The facts, however, are exciting in themselves, not only because Pindar was a consummate artist in metric but also because his meters and their laws are mainly a modern rediscovery. The same can be said of the fourth external characteristic, the conventions of the genre. It is only in the last half century that these have come into the light again. Like the meter, they have much to tell us about the original nature of choral song. But they are more important, for while we can forget the original meter when reading a translation, or keep it in the back of our minds as a silent reminder of what has been lost, if we do not recognize the presence and respond to the operation of the conventions of the victory song from moment to moment, we shall miss not only the sound but also the sense of Pindar's poetry. Finally, the more difficult aspects of Pindar's style must be considered, for their misinterpretation, perhaps more than anything, has contributed to the development of a Pindaric tradition in literature that has very little to do with Pindar as he actually was.

The Archaic Period: Patterns of Thought and Style[20]

There is a scene in the *Iliad* that sets the tone for Pindar and other poets of his era perhaps better than any other: the scene in Book 24, where Achilleus consoles the aged Priam for the death of his son Hektor, killed in hand-to-hand combat by Achilleus himself. To Achilleus, there seems to be very little sweetness or light in human life, and he advises Priam not to miss the little that there is. The temptation to mourn forever must be resisted:

> We'll probe our wounds no more but let them rest,
> though grief lies heavy on us. Tears heal nothing,
> drying so stiff and cold.

The uselessness of sorrow is one reason for putting a limit to it. Another is that its causes lie beyond our control. What has happened to Priam is not singular, it is the rule. Achilleus sees what lies behind his own grief, behind Priam's, behind everyone's:

> This is the way
> the gods ordained the destiny of men,
> to bear such burdens in our lives, while they
> feel no affliction.

We may observe two tendencies in the way Achilleus proceeds: he does not dwell for long upon the particular but almost immediately sees in it the manifestation of a general truth, and he cannot think of the human condition without at the same time imagining its opposite. His observation, that the gods who feel no sorrow themselves send it in abundance to us, is not a complaint. The phrase "while they (the gods) feel no affliction" has almost the force of a defining epithet. Of course they feel no affliction, for they are gods. The thought of human misery automatically conjures the thought of divine bliss, and vice versa. He goes on:

> At the door of Zeus
> are those two urns of good and evil gifts
> that he may choose for us; and one for whom

the lightning's joyous king dips in both urns
will have by turns bad luck and good. But one
to whom he sends all evil—that man goes
contemptible by the will of Zeus; ravenous
hunger drives him over the wondrous earth,
unresting, without honor from gods or men.[21]

The argument Achilleus is making, that the gods are responsible for everything that happens to us, immediately takes on concrete expression. Achilleus speaks both as a teacher and as a storyteller. What he has to say he says in two ways at once, assertively and mythologically. A little later, when he is urging Priam to eat, he appeals to the example of Niobe in order to strengthen his persuasion. All these tendencies—to see the general behind the particular, to grasp one thing by contrast with its opposite, to trace human vicissitudes to the will of the gods, and to explain, appreciate, or find the right response to a present situation through reference to myth or proverb—remain as dominant forms of thought and style in archaic poetry.

Achilleus does not imagine Zeus sending mortals nothing but good. Some good, yes, or all bad—but never good unalloyed with evil. This too is a dominant feature of archaic poetry: it is steeped in profound pessimism. Like Achilleus, Pindar sees the gods dispensing more evil to men than good, and he urges the man to whom he is speaking to bear up under the circumstances:

If, Hieron, you understand,
recall the proverb now:
the deathless gods
dole out to death-bound men
two pains for every good.
Fools make nothing of either.
The noble turn both to advantage,
folding pain within,
and showing beauty without.

(*Pythian 3.* 80–83)

Ancient and modern commentators on this passage have accused Pindar of misunderstanding Homer: Homer's two jars, one good and one bad, have apparently become three jars, two bad and one good. Pindar, however, is adapting a traditional image to his own purposes, as he often does. In his lines, the evil is exactly twice the good. The impression of a finer distinction carries over into a much more precise and succinct bit of advice than that given by Achilleus to Priam. Pindar urges Hieron to respond to reality as a wise man would. The conscious decision to suppress what is painful and to put on display what is not takes wisdom to conceive and strength to execute. It involves an acceptance of, and triumph over, pain. And it has an artistic emphasis that is typical of Pindar: Hieron, in arranging the happy and the unhappy elements of his life, is similar to Pindar arranging the light and dark elements of his poem. The artist in words counsels the king to be an artist in character.

Still, we may wonder why this pessimism, characteristic of Homer and early Greek poetry in general, should make so strong an appearance in Pindar's odes, which are written, after all, in order to celebrate a happy event, a success. The answer is that Pindar's odes also *evaluate* success. Pindar sees success against the background of failure and death, as Achilleus saw the happiness of the gods against the background of mortal sorrow and affliction. Though Pindar has been hired to rejoice in someone's behalf, he knows that a simple shout for joy makes little impression in the world and that one man's fortune may provoke another's resentment. The traditional poetic wisdom to which he is heir also puts a very slight premium on human happiness, a still slighter one on human power and understanding. Most happiness is foolish, most understanding unhappy, and those who pride themselves on either may discover that the gods have deceived them. For happiness, finally, is the gods' prerogative. In a world where the gods may take offense at human exultation, it is *dangerous* to exult. Such attitudes come, as it were, to bear on Pindar's poetry from without: they are in the wind, they are the milieu, the ethical assumptions that govern archaic poetry. Sometimes they become explicit, sometimes they remain in the background. But they are always there.

All these habits of mind affect Pindar's style too. If one thing leads him to think of its opposite, he may do so immediately: we will miss the kind of grammatical linkage to which we are accustomed. The figure of litotes is very common: instead of stating something positively ("this man is brave"), Pindar will give us the negative of its counterpart ("he is no coward"). Moments of high emotion will suddenly yield to moments of cautious restraint. The audience would have had to adjust to a dramatic shift, but not to a disconcerting one, for they and the poet shared in the traditional distrust of human happiness. They expected the poet to remind them of it. As the Muses' representative, he should wield authority, interpreting both the present occasion and the myth he has chosen to tell. In addition, the poet's assumption of the role of moral instructor would be a signal to his audience. They would know, for example, that a myth has been concluded when suddenly the poet speaks in his own voice, pronouncing a maxim or even a series of maxims, while we at such moments are liable to feel jolted by an irrelevant intrusion. We do not appreciate, let alone expect, the poet's sage advice or wise counsel, for with us he has lost his ancient authority. Pindar's audience would anticipate his teaching. They would look forward to it, wondering how much he would extract from the occasion in the form of memorable utterances. These might come singly or in clusters of seemingly independent ideas. What is in fact an argument or development of themes will appear as a series of conclusions in several arguments to which we never hear the proofs. The effect is confusing to the eye that scans the page. On the ancient audience, it probably made the double impression of massiveness and speed: massiveness in the juxtaposition of ideas, speed in the omission of the logical steps leading to them.

Pindar, indeed, composes with a maximum of compression. We may remember what Ezra Pound observed about the German word *dichten*, "to compose poetry." Pound gave it a Latin gloss: *condensare*, to condense, to compress.[22] It makes for slow reading, inviting contemplation. If we had the benefit of seeing and hearing a Pindaric ode performed, the connections between its various parts might be more apparent. If we were familiar with the range of truths taken for granted in this kind of poetry (some of them are described above), we would be more adept at supplying the connections that the poet, in his sovereign will to forge ahead, has omitted to spell out. Most important, if we were schooled in the special grammar of the victory ode, its conventions, we would recognize the various signs Pindar employs in moving from theme to theme. But if we were in such command of the genre, we would feel the compression, not the omission, of the thought. It would still be true, however, that archaic poets, and Pindar in particular, place greater emphasis on moving ahead than on smoothing the transitions between one section of the poem and the next. The net effect in Pindar is one of his most distinctive qualities, the pleasing ruggedness described by Dionysius of Halicarnassus.[23] It is due both to Pindar's disposition and to the nature of the victory ode. The meters and the language, as we shall see, are composite things; the same is true of the ode itself: it consists of a number of parts that the poet combines into a whole. Pindar seems to have preferred placing masses solidly together. His rival Bacchylides achieves a greater fluidity in his verse, but also less grandeur.

Another composite entity is the poet's own personality. He is both a private and a public figure. The Archaic Age is an age of wandering bards, itinerant choir-masters hired by towns, tribes, and individuals to conduct choruses of youths or maidens in the celebration of gods and of great events. The earliest remains of choral poetry show us the poet giving a voice to the different members of his choir. In the maiden song composed by Alcman in Sparta during the seventh century, we overhear the girls praising each other's beauty, their talent in the dance, their grace in song. As far as we can tell, the poet's personality has merged with that of his chorus. There is a similar authorial anonymity in one of Pindar's fragments, a *paian* written for the people of Keos. Here the choral voice belongs not to Pindar, but to the island of Keos and its people.[24]

The situation is more complex in the victory ode, which is a choral performance and therefore a more or less public event; but it is composed in honor of an individual. Praise of a god or even of a city invites no one's resentment. Except, perhaps, in unusual political circumstances, there are no problems attending it. But praise of an individual in a public setting is another matter. The introduction of the victor into a choral ode has consequences for the poet too—indeed, especially for him. He and the victor must face the potential resentment of other men and of the gods. By its very nature, then, the victory ode will demand tact. At the same time, it is the duty of the poet to see the significance of the present occasion in all its facets, and to exult for the victor. He should balance exultation with advice, warning both his audience and his patron not to offend the gods. For all this he will need the authority of the Muses who have instilled the power of song in him. The clearest evidence of its presence in him will be his poetic skill. In the victory ode that skill is often taxed most by the composite character of the song itself. It is no accident that Pindar often draws attention to his poetic role and mastery just at those moments when he is making a transition from one section of the ode to another.

The reader will notice, finally, that Pindar is proud of his art and does not hesitate to say so. No doubt his willingness to sing his own praises expresses something about his character, but it is also part of his heritage as a choral poet of the Archaic Age. Alcman, Ibycus, and Bacchylides also proclaim their power in song, and it is not mere egotism for them to do so. Their art, choral poetry, is first of all an event. There is much more involved in it than pen and ink. Indeed, the participation of the chorus, the practice sessions, the execution of dance patterns to express the ode, the playing of music to accompany it, and, not least, the gathering of the audience to hear and see it—that is, the entire occasion, with its various formal and ritual components—all these things make such an impression on the poetry that it tends to merge with them: the medium of the song becomes its subject. The poet will invite the audience to share with him in the genesis of the poem. His skill and inspiration, after all, place a guarantee of permanence on all these things, the only guarantee possible. Hence, the greatness of the poet is not an offensive theme to his audience—it is a legitimate subject of his verse. In Pindar's odes, we have the fullest surviving expression of an age that valued poetry as a gift from the gods.

Pindar's Language: The Dialects of Art[25]

In ancient Greek literature, genre determines dialect. The various literary genres keep the dialect of the people who first developed them. Even prose is no exception. Historical and scientific prose was first cultivated in Ionia. The history of Herodotus and the medical treatises attributed to Hippocrates, a Dorian from the island of Cos, were written in the Ionian dialect. There is more diversity in the case of the lyrical monody, the most subjective of the genres. Yet even here the Aiolian dialect of Sappho and Alcaeus, with its strong admixture of epic diction, exerted its influence on other forms of lyric, while the Boiotian dialect of Corinna remained provincial. Choral poetry, the genre of Pindar, was a creation of the Dorians. Our earliest examples come from Sparta, but the poet who composed them, Alcman, though his language is heavily Dorian, was no Dorian himself.

Dialect, then, was part of the craft of poetry: the ancient Greek poet had to learn it. An Athenian dramatist, for example, composed his dialogue passages in Attic, his dialect and that of his audience. Not so the choral odes that come between the passages of dialogue: choral poetry is a Dorian genre. Consequently, Aeschylus, Sophocles, and Euripides, who were Athenians, gave a Dorian color to the lyrical passages sung and danced by the chorus in their plays. This would involve, among other things, substituting the long Doric alpha for the Attic-Ionic eta in many a word. The audience would still recognize the word, but it would have an alien, exotic, perhaps lofty tone. They might hear the same word a few moments later in a dramatic interchange between the actors, only now it would have its familiar sound again.

The poet, the audience, and the scribes later responsible for writing down the plays in manuscript knew these general requirements sometimes a little better than they knew the dialects. There came into existence as a result the odd phenomenon known as a "hyperdorism," a word too Dorian to be genuine. Not every Attic eta was in fact alpha in Dorian; and there are other improprieties as well.

A recent study of Pindar's language reaches the impressive conclusion that neither he nor his scribes were guilty of hyperdorisms.[26] It is possible that the very difficulty of Pindar's poetry inspired its transcribers, almost from the beginning, with an unusual respect for the text before them. It is also possible that Pindar's native speech enabled him to master the Doric of choral lyric better than an Athenian could. The dialect spoken in Thebes during Pindar's lifetime was a mixture of Aiolic and a strain of West Greek. The Boiotians of Pindar's day were descended, in all likelihood, from a northwest Greek tribe that had overrun the Aiolic inhabitants of Thessaly, only to be driven out themselves later by other West Greek invaders. During the period of their sojourn in Thessaly, the West Greek dialect they spoke came under the influence of the language spoken by the original inhabitants. That language was Aiolic. Hence, Pindar's native speech was composite, a blend of Aiolic, the language of Sappho and Alcaeus, and West Greek, the family of dialects to which Doric, the dialect of choral poetry, belonged. Pindar's heritage, so to speak, was the language of subjective and objective lyric.

But like all poets composing in Greek, Pindar was also heir to the language of Homer, a composite of Ionian and Aiolic elements. So pervasive is the epic coloring of the odes that several scholars have described Pindar's dialect as fundamentally Homeric, with one or two Dorian elements added and a large strain of Aiolic. The basic mixture, then, would be a blend of epic and lyric language. Others describe it as having a Dorian base, with a large strain of Aiolic and a strong Homeric coloring.[27] The point on which all are agreed is that the language is composite, and the one rule governing what could or could not go into the composition was a rule against everything offensively provincial. Pindar, in other words, composed in a Dorian genre and a pan-Hellenic dialect with a strong Dorian color appropriate to that genre. Locutions from the Homeric poems were as welcome in it as they were in all Greek poetry. And the sounds of Aiolic, already present in Homer's dialect, would have had another avenue into choral lyric because they were the sounds of lyric monody.

We may now consider some of the poetic qualities of this highly artificial language. What particular effects did it make available to the poet who composed in it?

In the first place, the mixture of the dialects gave the poet a certain metrical advantage. As we shall see in a moment, he composed in meters of great complexity, observing the schemes he imposed on himself with all but invariable strictness. No wonder, then, that he would appreciate being able, for example, to use different words that had the same meaning, choosing one or the other as the meter dictated. The ubiquitous modal particle *an* and its dialectal equivalent *ke* are a good example of this. Pindar uses them interchangeably. Since one begins with a vowel and ends with a consonant, while the other begins with a consonant and ends with a vowel, the poet could choose one or the other as the requirements of the verse demanded. *ke* might have had a Dorian flavor or it might have seemed, at least, less Attic-Ionic than *an*. But it is virtually impossible for us to pinpoint the poetic effect of these variations on the audience. Obviously, they were not offensive, for they are common practice in choral lyric. At the very least, they must have impressed the audience with the exoticness of what they were hearing.

An effect perhaps more audible to us would be Pindar's dialectal play with the name of Zeus, chief god of the Olympian pantheon. In the majority of Greek dialects, his name is declined *Zeūs, Dĭŏs, Dĭĭ̆* (*Dī*), *Dĭă.* In Homer, we find the variation *Zeūs, Zēnŏs, Zēnĭ, Zēnă*. Pindar uses one declension or the other as he pleases. The second as the rarer might have added a certain color to the poetry, a Homeric tinge, but we cannot be certain. The two declensions give the poet different syllabic quantities to work with, so his choice of one or the other will be determined largely by the demands of the quantitative meter from moment to moment.

But not all Pindar's dialectal variations are due to meter. In his native dialect, the great sea god Poseidon was *Poteidaon.* In Pindar's odes we find, generally, the epic form *Poseidaon* or the Aiolic *Poseidan. Poteidan,* a Dorian form of the name attested in inscriptions from Corinth, appears in one ode only, but it appears there twice, and in neither instance is it metrically motivated. The ode, *Olympian 13,* was composed in honor of a victor from Corinth. The unique instance of a Dorian Poseidon seems to be a complimentary gesture to the victor's Dorian city. If it were Pindar's practice to vary his dialect according to his audience in this way, we could be certain about it. Unfortunately, there seem to be only isolated cases of such variation.

A similar example occurs in *Pythian 8.* In two very prominent places in that ode Pindar uses the verb meaning "to fall." It is the first word in the first line of the second triad, and, in a compounded form, the main verb in the first line of the last triad. In the earlier occurrence, the victor's city, Aigina, is the subject, and the verb is negated. Pindar says, literally, that Aigina has not fallen far from the Graces' favor.[28] In the second occurrence, the verb is affirmative and the victor is the subject. There is further modulation in a change of person: Pindar speaks directly to the victor: "you fell upon (your opponents)." The modulation from negative to positive and from third to second person would be normal enough. What is remarkable is the modulation in dialect: the third-person instance is in a form common in Homer and elsewhere in Pindar; the second-person instance is in a rare Dorian form. Thus we have the same verb appearing in the same ode in two very prominent positions and in two different dialects. Since the victor was an Aiginetan, hence a Dorian, he might have sensed an emotional modulation in the dialectal change: the poet was, literally, speaking to him in his language.

But at this distance it is impossible to be certain of such poetic effects, secured by Pindar's play with the dialects in his repertory. Their duplication, even their approximation, is virtually a lost cause in English, where dialect, in most forms of poetry, plays a very different role, if it plays a role at all. Even students of Pindar's Greek are at a disadvantage when it comes to dialect. In all likelihood, they began their study of the ancient language with Attic Greek for their model. They will forever be referring dialectal variations to that model. The ancient Greeks, even those whose dialect was Attic, had no sense of such a standard. To them the variations were of the very essence of poetry. Poetry was not composed in Greek, but in a special form of Greek, a *Kunstsprache* or art language. The basis of that language was the fund of poetry already created. From it a poet could draw at any time, either simply adorning his own work with beauties taken from elsewhere or putting them to new uses, with transformations appropriate to the genre in which he was composing. The poet's freedom to draw on past poetry and to blend dialects in the process naturally led him to the creation of new words. There are new words in every one of Pindar's odes—words, that is, which make their first recorded appearance in Greek via Pindar's text.

Pindar enjoyed some of his linguistic freedom simply because he was a writer of choral lyric. One of the licenses permitted in choral poetry was the choice to use or not use the augment by which Greek verbs formed their past tenses. By the time Pindar composed his odes, augment had become fixed and regular. But in Homer the use of augment to form past tenses is not fixed. The poet does or does not employ augment, at his own convenience, and this is the case in Pindar. On one hand, it is a license: it simplifies the poet's metrical problems. On the other hand, because it harks back to an earlier time, it is by nature poetic. It has the sound of a different, a remoter, a nobler speech than that employed from day to day. Thus the dramatist enjoys the freedom to employ or not employ augment only in his choral passages, but in dialogue he must retain the practice of normal speech.

A similar situation obtains for the definite article. Homer does not even know of it: it has not yet come into existence. It is, in Homer, still a demonstrative or relative pronoun. Gradually, over a period of centuries, it begins to appear until, in Pindar's day, it is a regular part of the Greek language. But a reader of Pindar's first Olympian ode in Greek will notice that of the twenty nouns appearing in the first stanza only two have the definite article. The opening stanza of *Olympian 1* was famed for its grandeur. Does the omission of the article have anything to do with that grand quality? Apparently, yes: almost anything ancient was, to the Greeks of Pindar's audience, poetic. The article was more or less recent in development. To omit it habitually, as Pindar does, would be to suggest the time in the history of the language before it appeared, the time when the language of poetry came to birth. The archaic and the poetic in Greek are often synonymous.

The conservative impulse that characterized, indeed dominated, Greek poetry and made it imperative for the poet to keep to the dialect in which his genre had originated did not condemn him to stale repetition. If he could give a new place to an ancient truth, a new ring to an old phrase, he added authenticity to his verse, he gave it the right sound, the sound of poetry. The connoisseur of Greek lyric would not have understood Wordsworth's insistence that poetry resemble speech. Speech was heard every day, speech was ephemeral. It was not so with the language of poetry. Poetry combined the sound of the past with the vital concerns of the present in such a way that the present reembodied the past and was ennobled by it. At the same time, once the language of poetry had been lifted out of the daily stream in which language forever continues on its course, it became subject to a new set of laws. The poet's creative will replaced linguistic regulation; the laws of language were suspended in his favor. But he needed that extra freedom, that dialectal license, to help him with another set of laws, a system of rhythmical patterns more complex and unbreakable than any in the history of literature.

Pindar's Meters: The Music of His Words[29]

Ancient Greek poetry was quantitative: its various poetic rhythms resulted from the alternation of syllables that took more time to pronounce with syllables that took less. Knowing from our own experience that music imposes quantities on syllables, we can infer that all Greek poetry originated as sung, not spoken, rhythm. When Pindar and other Greek poets used the word "sing" to describe the poetic process, they were speaking the literal truth: lyric poets were also composers. The chorus that performed Pindar's odes sang them to the musical accompaniment that he wrote for them. It is clear from the complexity of the metrical patterns that this musical accompaniment was just that—an accompaniment: a metrical pattern so intricate would not have been fashioned merely to be set aside in performance for the sake of a dominant instrumental or vocal melody. It is also clear for the same reason that the chorus sang the ode together, line by line, one line at a time, not in polyphony.

The simplest meters to describe and appreciate are stichic meters, those that repeat themselves a definite number of times per line, line after line, without admitting rhythms of a different character. Such are the dactylic hexameter (the meter of Homer) and the iambic trimeter (the meter of dramatic dialogue). Meters are far more complex in choral lyric. Here it is better not to speak of individual meters, because choral poets habitually composed stanzas of such complexity that naming the different elements of which they consist results in a tangle of terminology that is not helpful and is in fact misleading. It is unlikely, for example, that Pindar would have conceived the opening line of *Olympian 1* as a "glyconic" plus a "pherecratean." The names were not applied to the meters until long after Pindar, while the meters themselves had been in use well before him.

Within the line, the relationship between the metrical structure and the syntactical structure is not one to one. Syntax, the movement of thought, and rhythm, the movement of sound, are two separate systems working together, now diverging, now coinciding, with no regularity governing the interplay between them. In the opening two lines of *Olympian 1,* the first syntactical pause (*ariston men hudor*: "best is water") occurs within a larger metrical unit (line 1):

> ariston men hudor, ho de chrusos aithomenon pur

The words that follow *ariston men hudor* and fill the rest of the metrical unit initiate a statement that is not syntactically complete until the end of the next metrical unit (line 2):

1 ariston men hudor, ho de chrusos aithomenon pur
2 hătĕ diaprepei nukti meganoros exocha ploutou.
1 "Best is water, and gold, a fire burning
2 as it were at night, is conspicuous beyond mighty wealth."

Thus the first metrical pause (end of line 1) occurs within a second, larger syntactical unit (lines 1–2), and meter and syntax come to a simultaneous pause at the end of line 2. Line 3 initiates a dramatic new development in theme. The metrical units suddenly shorten for three lines:

3 ei d'ăēthla garuen
4 eldeai, philon ȇtor,
5 mȇket' āĕliou skopei

while the syntax stays incomplete, as if in suspense:

3 "But if to sing games
4 you yearn, my heart,
5 no longer look than sun . . ."

Line 6 expands into a metrical unit longer than lines 3, 4 and 5 together, but the thought is not completed until line 7:

6 ". . . for another star shining in day through deserted ether warmer (than sun, line 5),
7 nor shall we sing a contest mightier than Olympia."

Our expectations for the syntactical structure of a sentence beginning with "if" are fulfilled at line 6, but there is something odd in the statement "If you want to sing of games (3–4), don't look for a star brighter than the sun (5–6)." The point of the comparison is expressed by line 7: "nor shall we sing a contest mightier than Olympia." The two systems of syntax and meter work simultaneously and separately throughout the seven lines, coinciding only twice, at climactic moments (end of lines 2 and 7). The sense, then, is not contained in a line, but runs on from one line to the next.

This interlocking of meter and sense is called *enjambment.* If there were no enjambment, there would be exact correspondence at all times between metrical units and syntactical ones. But exact correspondence at all times would be monotonous. Enjambment of sense and meter is one of the major principles of Pindar's metrical art.

If we look again at the opening line of *Olympian 1*, this time paying attention to the alternation of long and short syllables, we find either one or two short syllables enclosed between two longs: either – ⏑ – or – ⏑ ⏑ – :

ărīstōn mĕn hŭdōr, hŏ dē chrūsŏs aīthŏmĕnōn pūr

A. M. Dale calls the enclosure of either one or two shorts between two longs "the primary formula for a rhythmic sequence."[30] A poet may combine these units in various ways, either in a series, that is, side by side: – ⏑ – – ⏑ –, – ⏑ ⏑ – – ⏑ ⏑ –, or by the method characteristic of choral song, prolongation, which may be single: – ⏑ – prolonged to – ⏑ – ⏑ –, or double: – ⏑ – prolonged to – ⏑ – ⏑ – ⏑ –. It may also be mixed: prolonging – ⏑ – by – ⏑ ⏑ – gives – ⏑ – ⏑ ⏑ –. The opening line of *Olympian 1* is formed by such a mixed prolongation:

ărĭstōn mĕn hŭdōr, hŏ dē chrūsŏs aīthŏmĕnōn pūr

There are three exceptional places in the line: at the opening, where the poet is free to start on a short rather than a long syllable;[31] at the close, where he is free to employ either a long or a short syllable that is extrametrical; and, sometimes, within the course of the line where two different units, either – ⏑ – or – ⏑ ⏑ –, come together, and the poet places an extra or "link" syllable between them. When two units come together without a link syllable between them, we have what is called "blunt juncture."

The first line of *Olympian 1* opens with ⏑ – and closes with –. Since any line may open with a "headless" measure, ⏑ – at the opening of *Olympian 1* may be considered – ⏑ –, with the first element omitted: ‸ ⏑ –. If so, there are two blunt junctures in the line and, possibly, a third, before the last syllable: ‸ ⏑ – / – ⏑ ⏑ – ⏑ – / – ⏑ – ⏑ ⏑ – / –. There are no link syllables within the line. The frequent intermingling of – ⏑ – and – ⏑ ⏑ – within the same line and the omission of link syllables between the units are two characteristics that distinguish Aiolic, the metrical system in which *Olympian 1* is composed, from Doric, or dactylo-epitritic, rhythm.

All but two of Pindar's odes (*Olympians 2* and *5*) are written in one or the other of these two systems: 20 in Aiolic, 23 in Doric. The Aiolic rhythms are so named because of their frequent appearance in the Aiolic lyric of Sappho and Alcaeus. The Doric or dactylo-epitritic system first appears in Stesichorus, who worked at Sparta. Its prominence in the choral poetry of Pindar and Bacchylides and in the choral odes of drama is a likely indication that it was invented for choral poetry specifically.

Dactylo-epitritic offered the poet a means of creating highly complex but readily appreciable rhythms. The basic elements of which it is composed are only two: dactylic (usually – ⏑ ⏑ – ⏑ ⏑ –) and epitritic (usually – ⏑ – –, but sometimes – ⏑ – ⏑: the last syllable, being a link, is variable in quantity).

Aiolic, on the other hand, exhibits some fifteen different combinations of these units.[32] When link syllables do occur within Aiolic systems, they are often short, with the result that the distinction between one unit and the next is blurred. The freedom to resolve a required long syllable into two shorts is very frequently employed in

Aiolic, almost never in Doric. Doric rhythms tend, as already mentioned, not to intermingle – ⏑ – and – ⏑ ⏑ – in the same line, while it is characteristic of Aiolic, as we have seen in the first line of *Olympian 1*, to mix them frequently. For all these reasons, Doric gives the impression of greater regularity and slower movement than Aiolic. It is, indeed, much easier for us to appreciate rhythmically.

If we were to scan line 2 of *Olympian 1*, we would find it metrically different from line 1. Line 1 and line 2 are both in Aiolic rhythm, but the components are arranged differently in each. Line 3 is considerably shorter than line 2. It also exhibits its own particular arrangement of the elements of Aiolic verse. The same is true of line 4, and so on to line 11, the last line in the ode's first stanza. All the lines of the stanza are in Aiolic rhythm, but each differs from the one before it. As we enter the second stanza, we find its first line metrically identical with the first line of stanza one, and so on to the end of the stanza, each of its lines being metrically identical with the corresponding line in the first stanza. This relationship is reflected in the traditional names given to the stanzas: stanza one was called a *strophe* or "turn." The stanza answering it was called an *antistrophe* or "counterturn." In the third stanza, however, we notice a change. The first line is Aiolic, as before, but it is not metrically identical with the first line of the turn and counterturn. The same is true of the remaining lines in the third stanza. The first three stanzas together make up what is called a "triad": two stanzas in exactly the same metrical pattern followed by a third stanza in the same type of meter, but with a different arrangement of the metrical components. This third stanza was called an *epode* or song sung standing still, a "stand."

Apparently, the chorus sang the turn while executing a dance pattern moving to the right, the counterturn while executing the same dance pattern to the left, and sang the stand while standing still. All the turns and counterturns in *Olympian 1* are identical in meter and all its stands with each other. Pindar, in other words, adheres rigidly for the duration of the ode to the pattern created in its first triad. This is always his practice in odes where he composes more than one triad.

If we were to scan *Olympian 4*, the next ode in the collection written in Aiolic meter, we would not find it metrically identical to *Olympian 1*. In fact, none of the Aiolic odes is written in the same meter as any other. This is also true of the Doric odes: all are written in the same metrical system (dactylo-epitritic), but the arrangement of the metrical components in each is different. Pindar, then, always creates a new metrical pattern for each of his odes.[33]

Not all the odes are triadic in form. *Olympian 14, Pythian 6, Pythian 12, Nemean 2, Nemean 4, Nemean 9,* and *Isthmian 8* are written in stanzas that are simply repeated for the duration of the ode, without changing the rhythm in the third stanza to form a triad. For most of these, evidence within the ode suggests that it was not meant to be danced by the chorus, but sung in procession. All the "processional" odes are, like the triadic ones, unique in meter.

Turn, counterturn, and stand derive from choreography: triadic odes were danced as well as sung by the chorus. The literal truth of this can be felt in Pindar's phrase at *Isthmian 1.* 7, where he speaks of "dancing" the god Apollo on the island of Keos. This means performing a choral ode whose theme is the god, but as soon as we rephrase it that way we lose the immediacy of Pindar's expression. Pratinas, another choral poet, uses a similar phrase: "listen to my Dorian dancing."[34] The visual component of the performance, a dancing chorus, is inseparable from its auditory component, a singing chorus. Pratinas' phrase, at any rate, is not an example of synaesthesia. He is not asking us to experience song as dancing: for him the two are identical. There is, perhaps, no more striking instance of the unity of the two arts than Pindar's phrasing at *Pythian 1.* 2, where the dance step is said to *hear* the music of the lyre. A literal translation would suggest a foot with ears. Again, we are not dealing with poetic fusion of the senses, but with linguistic traces of an original unity. Having no choral poetry, we do not instinctively identify dance and song.

Our difficulties here are minor compared with the problem we face trying to appreciate Greek quantitative metric at all. We can conceptualize it, we can spread it out before us in a maze of longs and shorts, but we cannot experience it physically, as it actually was for the Greeks. This is so because our language pays no attention to the duration of syllables in the structuring of verse. Rhythm and sense together are articulated by the stress accent. It is exactly the opposite in ancient Greek metric: accent is totally disregarded and the sense plays no part in the articulation of the meter. Though we can derive a great deal of pleasure from reading Greek verse aloud and observing, while we do, the intricate patterns of longs and shorts created and maintained by the poet, we will not be able to pronounce them as longs and shorts: on our lips they become stressed and unstressed syllables. Without that conversion, our reading dissolves into something indistinguishable from prose.

It should be some consolation to us that even ancient students of Pindar's meters could not fully understand them. When Aristophanes of Byzantium undertook to edit Pindar, it is likely that he was able to appreciate the quantitative rhythms of the poetry, for it was not until the first century A.D. that quantitative rhythm began to vanish "not only from the literature, but from the speech of Europe."[35] To that extent, Aristophanes of Byzantium was in a better position than we are: he could enjoy the poetry in a purely physical way that is no longer open to us. However, choral poetry had ceased to be composed by the time Aristophanes edited Pindar. He may have witnessed choral odes performed in drama, but these are different in metrical structure from Pindar's odes. Dramatic choral poetry tends to fashion its lines from single metrical units, while Pindar fuses such units into lines of greater length and intricacy.

Aristophanes of Byzantium and the other ancient metricians did not grasp the principles by which Pindar articulates his massive stanzas. Failure to do so caused them to overlook the stanzaic structure of *Olympian 14*: they saw it as a single stanza instead of two identical ones. They also failed to see the triadic structure of *Olympian 5*: to them it appeared as three matching stanzas instead of three triads. Perhaps most telling of all, they did not recognize that more than half of Pindar's victory odes, the dactylo-epitritic or Doric odes, are written in the same type of meter. The ancient metricians constantly analyzed these odes into the discrete meters they knew from other types of poetry. Focusing on naming these smaller units, they failed to perceive that all the odes in question, though differing in the arrangement of the components, belonged to the same class of meters.

These are isolated blunders. The most noticeable legacy of ancient ignorance is in the colometry, or line-division, of Pindar's odes. In ancient editions of Pindar, the first line of *Olympian 1* was written

ariston men hudor, ho de

and labeled a "glyconic." The second line appeared as

chrusos aithomenon pur

and was labeled a "pherecratean." The third line broke off in mid-word:

hătĕ diaprepei nuk-

and was labeled an "ithyphallic with initial trochee resolved." Line 4 began with the fragment of a word left over from line 3:

-ti, meganoros exocha ploutou

and was labeled "anapestic dimeter catalectic."[36] The mixture of glyconic, common in the Aiolic meters of Sappho and Alcaeus, with ithyphallic and anapestic elements betrays little awareness of metrical contexts. ⏑ ⏑ – in a choral march is anapestic; ⏑ ⏑ – at the start of a Pindaric line may be – ⏑ ⏑ –, with first element omitted. To call them both anapests is like saying that the word "start" is a noun in the phrase "at the start" and in the clause "they will start soon." Identical in form, the two words are completely different in function. It takes an anapestic *context* to identify an anapestic unit. But since the ancient metricians did not know how Pindar composed his lines, they broke the lines into units they recognized and were unable to see the larger whole.

The situation was not rectified until August Boeckh published his monumental work on Pindar in the early nineteenth century. Boeckh's basic insight was that Pindar did not compose in the short metrical units known as *cola*, but in combinations of them. These combinations are called *periods*, and the division of Pindar's odes into periods gives us their true line-division, the line coinciding with the period. Occasionally, Pindar fashions a period out of a single recognizable colon, such as a glyconic or pherecratean; more often he builds his period of two, three, or even more cola. The major sign by which we determine the length of these Pindaric periods is word-end. A period will not end in mid-word. Words are divided in modern texts not to indicate period-end, but because the long Pindaric period sometimes cannot be accommodated on the page.

By itself, the principle that a period must end with a word and not in the middle of one would not be enough to establish Pindar's colometry. But Boeckh discovered two other tools to aid us. One is the observation of hiatus. If one word ends with a vowel and the next begins with a vowel, there is a "gap" (in Latin, a *hiatus*), a perceptible pause in forward movement. Such pauses define the ends of metrical units. The second tool is the observation of what is called in Latin *syllaba brevis in elemento longo:* a short syllable occurring where we would expect a long. When the poet takes this liberty, he may not be acting arbitrarily. The short element may be *equivalent* to a long, because there is a pause at that point: that is, we may have reached the end of the period, and we pause before going on to the next. Hiatus and *brevis in longo* at the end of a colon, then, are probable indications of a pause in forward movement, or, in other words, they may indicate that the end of the colon is also the end of the period. Together with the occurrence of word-end, we have in them an almost infallible means for determining the length of Pindar's lines.

There are one or two places where the technique fails us, and one editor will disagree with another as to the precise colometry. But these are instances where the poems are too short to allow complete certainty. It must always be remembered that word-end, hiatus, and *brevis in longo* would be of no help to us if Pindar did not observe the principle of *responsion.* If, using the tools at our disposal, we decide upon a certain length for a Pindaric line, the correctness of our decision will be verified by the exact replication of that line in the corresponding places of the ode. The more correspondences, the stronger the case for our choice. The shorter an ode, the harder it is to be certain of its colometry down to the last syllable.

The longest period in the victory odes is the sixth line of the turns and counterturns in *Pythian 1.* It is thirty syllables long. Yet, according to modern colometry, it comprises a single rhythmical unit of Doric or dactylo-epitritic verse. It would have been danced and sung by the chorus and felt by the audience as such. How do we know this? Here is its first occurrence, at line 6:

aienaou puros. heudei d'ana skaptô Dios aietos, ôkei-
an pterug' amphoterôthen chalaxais

The line as printed in Snell's text is too long to be accommodated on the page. Let us see if we can shorten it:

aīĕnăoū pŭrŏs. heū-

This would be a recognizable dactylo-epitritic colon. It cannot be a dactylo-epitritic period, however, because it ends within a word. So we enjamb the metrical unit with the next one, and try to find the next logical place to pause:

aīĕnăoū pŭrŏs. heūdeī d'ănā

Here, again, is a possible stopping place. We have a recognizable dactylo-epitritic unit and word-end.[37] The same thing occurs in the corresponding line of the counterturn (line 12):

kō̂mătĭ, kē̂lă dĕ kaī daīmŏnō̂n

But the pattern is broken in the corresponding line of the third triad (line 46):

eī găr hŏ pā̂s chrŏnŏs ōlbōn mĕn hoū-

The metrical unit we thought we had perceived in lines 6 and 12 comes to an end here, in the corresponding line 46, *within* a word (*hou-tô*). So the line does not end there after all. We continue lengthening it:

aīĕnăoū pŭrŏs. heūdeī d'ănā skāptō̂ Dĭos̆ aīĕtŏs ō̂keī-
ān ptĕrŭg' āmphŏtĕrō̂thēn chălāxaīs.

If we try to stop it before *chalaxais,* something sets it in motion again. Pindar, for example, often completes a metrical unit in this system with an extra syllable. The first syllable in the word *skaptô* might be such a syllable, if only it fell at word-end. But it does not: the extra syllable, falling within the word, is a link rather than a termination, and the line proceeds to grow. Another recognizable unit in this system would be at the link syllable where Snell has broken the line in order to fit it on the page. If a word ended with this syllable, as it does in the corresponding place in line 26, the line too might end. But it does not coincide with word-end here, so the line continues to expand. The segment *-ān ptĕrŭg' āmphŏtĕrō̂thēn chălāxaīs* would be a dactylo-epitritic period if only it opened with the beginning rather than the end of a word. It does open with word-beginning in the corresponding lines 26, 52, and 66, but in all the other corresponding lines it is enjambed with what precedes it. It is, then, a colon, not a period.

In this way, observation of metrical responsion and word-end is enough by itself to determine what Pindar meant the rhythmical duration of his sixth line to be. The same principles determine the length of line 3: it has nine syllables. Line 6 has thirty. Thus the longest line in the stanza is more than three times the length of the shortest, and the shortest is not unusually short for this type of meter. Both lines are governed by the same internal and external rules. The freedom with which Pindar creates units so different in size and so uniform in kind is one of the most impressive demonstrations of his metrical skill.

Pindar's metric is only partially open to our enjoyment, even when we read him in Greek. Because of the absolute distinction between quantitative and dynamic rhythms, virtually nothing of the original *sensory* experience of hearing and seeing Pindar's odes performed is left behind in the Greek text for our appreciation. To compensate for the loss, there is the *mental* delight of observing the relation between meter and meaning, perceiving the alternation of the rhythmic and syntactic pulses of the ode. But as with all appreciation of this sort, it does not come naturally or easily to us: we have to work for it. It takes time before the basic cola of Doric and Aiolic rhythms become familiar to us. Only then can we experience the peculiar oscillation between stopping and going, restraint and impetuous forward movement, that is the hallmark of Pindar's style. When the syntax makes us pause, the meter pulls us further on; when the individual colon comes to an end within the period, the unfinished word causes the movement to continue. When one period is over, the unfinished syntax draws us into the next. The conflict between retardation and momentum within and between periods and stanzas is resolved and begun again on a grand or small or medium scale, over and over until the end.

As with dialect, so with meter: Pindar is a master of fusion. To notice the ways in which he combines cola into periods is to notice his metrical craftsmanship at work.[38] Unfortunately, Pindar's specifically metrical effects are rarely suggestible in translation. One place where an effect can be approximated occurs in the final stand of *Olympian 2.* The first word of that stanza is *Thērōnos*, Theron's name in the genitive case. The meaning is "than Theron." While it is the first word in the new stanza, it is also the last word in its own sentence. Thus there is a full syntactical stop with its utterance, before the movement of thought, impelled by the uncompleted rhythm, begins again with the conjunction "But . . .". It is easy to keep Pindar's dramatic placement of Theron's name here, at the start of the final stand, but what can a translator do to suggest its original effect? He can only advise the reader ahead of time to remember that Pindar's dancing chorus would have uttered the name after coming to a stand. The music too would have stopped or modulated dramatically. The metrical phenomena we have been describing were not created for their own sake. They participate in a larger activity. They too are only part of Pindar's craft, part of a poetry that is composite not only in language and rhythm but also, as we shall see now, in its general form.

Pindar's Genre: Conventions of the Victory Song

In all probability, Pindar's audience had a basic notion of the form an epinician ode might take. They knew its basic elements and probably also had an idea of the order in which the elements would occur. In spite of complex exceptions to the rule, the parts of the victory ode and their usual order of appearance in Pindar can be briefly described.[39]

Every ode contains a proclamation of the victor and of the victory being celebrated. The victor's name and the place where the victory was gained are the two most important items in the proclamation, and they tend to occur together. In close proximity to them we usually find the name of his city and the name of his father, as they would have been announced by the criers at the games. The event in which the victor had competed is either mentioned together with his name and the site of the victory, or not far from them.

Another feature of the victory ode is the myth. Not all the odes contain a myth, but the majority do, and even those that do not contain a full myth may have some mythical material.

The odes without a myth amount to little more than an elaborate proclamation of the victory. Because the proclamation is the essence of the poem and the poem itself is short, Pindar tends to delay the proclamation in such odes until late in the poem, thus giving it a climactic position. Elaborate prayers, traditional examples, or statements on the relationship between victory and song precede the proclamation and prepare the way for it. Sometimes the reason for the particular method of preparation is readily apparent. In *Olympian 14*, the fact that the victor comes from Orchomenos, home of the Graces, explains Pindar's opening prayer to the Graces. In *Olympian 12*, the vicissitudes of the victor's career account for the opening hymn to the Goddess of Chance.

Odes with a myth are more complex. There are two types, those that begin directly with a myth and those that have the myth more or less in the center.

Odes that open directly with a myth have the peculiarity of being little more than myth. In them the victor may appear in the beginning, almost as an excuse for telling the myth; or he may not appear until sometime in the course of the ode, after the opening myth has been told. Then he will receive some attention before the start of yet another myth, with which the ode concludes.

The majority of odes with myth tell only one myth, and they tell it after the opening proclamation of the victor, and before the end, with its renewed praise of him. Pindar often tells the myth as illustration of a truth he observes being fulfilled in the victor's own life, or he may take the myth from the legendary material furnished by the occasion itself—either from the legends that belong to the victor's homeland or even his family, or from ancient traditions associated with the site of the games or the religious festival of which they are part. In this type of ode Pindar also adheres to a basic form in telling the myth. He will summarize the story briefly, then go back in time, dwelling on single aspects of the story at greater length and, finally, return to the point where he began, thus suggesting a ring or circle.

The odes written for victors from Aigina follow a pattern of their own. The majority of them have catalogues of mythical subjects from which Pindar selects one to tell at length. In a few there is no catalogue, but instead a first myth that is then set aside in favor of a second. Special treatment of the myth and of the victor's homeland in Aiginetan odes suggests that the people of Aigina cultivated their own style of victory ode and expected a visiting poet like Pindar to adhere to it.

In addition to the victor's proclamation and the myth, readers of Pindar will notice the occurrence of gnomic or proverbial statements and of prayers throughout the odes. Gnomic statement is the most variable part of the victory ode: it may occur anywhere—in the beginning, in the middle, or at the end. Prayers tend to occur at the beginning or at the end, depending on the type of prayer. Invocations naturally come at the start; prayers for the future welfare or success of the victor tend to appear at the end, though they may also occur just after the victor's proclamation early in the ode. In this latter position, they often serve as transitions from the victor to a gnomic section, which in turn leads to a myth.

The most unpredictable section of the ode is its conclusion. The only thing certain to occur is renewed praise of the victor in some form. It may include a catalogue of his previous victories. The end of the ode is also a likely place for gnomic statements elaborating on the poet's credentials or illustrating the victor's character, or both. Some odes end with prayers for the victor's future success, others with warnings that the future cannot be counted on.

The basic parts of the victory ode all derive from the occasion being celebrated. The proclamation of the victor, the most fundamental part, occurs in every ode and is modeled on the victor's actual proclamation at the games.[40] The presence of prayer and hymn is also universal and should not be surprising: the odes celebrate victories in sacred games, solemn religious occasions attended by representatives from the entire Hellenic world. Successful competition in them was proof of divine favor, for which the poet and the victor would show gratitude in hymns of praise. The myth is not as closely related to the occasion, but it is none the less important, for it is the poet's chief means of exalting that occasion.

The poet begins as a kind of master of ceremonies at the victory celebration, but he ends as its interpreter. He must not only set the mood and join the festivities; he must also point out the special significance of the occasion and make it memorable, not only to the victor, but to the rest of the audience. His poetic role is principally one of mediation between past, present, and future, between the victor's proclamation at the games and the world of gods and heroes: between the parts of the ode that concern the victor and the present moment only and those that have a more universal application. The main vehicle for the expression of these interconnections and for forging links between the different parts of the odes is the poet's own voice, speaking in gnomic or proverbial tones. Whenever the poet enunciates a general truth or uses the pronoun "I," we may be sure that the ode has reached a transitional point. A new subject is coming; an old one is being left behind.

The special character of occasional poetry gives these moments of transition added importance, for often moving from one section of the ode to another involves the blending of ephemeral events with permanent realities. The poet's ability to bring out what is of enduring significance in the occasion is his proudest possession, the only thing separating the victor's achievements from oblivion. Poetry can bestow immortality. That is its chief contribution. Without it, the victory celebration is hollow, the poet a mere master of ceremonies.

While the parts of the victory ode are usually simple in themselves, understanding how they fit together is another matter. The subject is too vast for anything like complete discussion here. What is possible instead is a brief description of various methods and techniques Pindar uses at the opening of the ode and at key points of transition within it. On the way, we can observe some of the major conventions of the epinician ode and one or two essential thought patterns. We may also notice from time to time the manner in which Pindar carefully adapts the ode, with its general form and its usual parts, to the particular circumstances of each occasion. To accomplish this, let us take a look at some particular passages.

O lady Muse, my mother!
        Come, I beseech you,
                in the sacred Nemean month
        to Dorian Aigina, island haven
of the wide world:
                        by the waters of Asopos
the young men wait,
        builders of sweet revel-songs,
            eager for your voice.

So begins Pindar's third Nemean ode, with a prayer to the Muse. Similar prayers for inspiration open the *Iliad* and the *Odyssey*, but in neither of those grand poems does the poet go so far as to call the Muse his own mother. Here, at the start of the ode, Pindar is proudly presenting his credentials. But he does not allow us to dwell on the bold claim he has just made for himself. There is an air of urgency:[41] twelve, fifteen, perhaps twenty young men are waiting, eager for a song. One of their friends has triumphed in the Nemean games, and their enthusiasm for him is infectious: Pindar cannot avoid feeling as eager as they feel. The ode has its origin in enthusiasm, warmth, and love.

Readers unfamiliar with Pindar may follow the train of thought and catch the tone of the above lines, but they will probably not appreciate everything in them until they have acquired a basic sense of the kind of poem they are reading. This poetry is occasional, tailored to a specific situation. Certain things have to be mentioned, some to be singled out for more expansive treatment. For this reason, at least in the beginning, it is helpful to separate the *meaning* of Pindar's words from their *function*. For example, the occasion here is a victory in the Nemean games. Instead of its simple announcement, we have a phrase telling us that the ode is being composed "in the sacred Nemean month." The sacredness of the time adds something to the statement and goes well with the invocation to the Muse who is, after all, a goddess. But behind its meaning is its function in a poem of this kind: once the phrase is uttered, there can be no doubt that the ode will celebrate a triumph in the Nemean games. An essential item of information has been transmitted obliquely. In the next phrase, Pindar tells the Muse where to journey. We have not heard the victor's name yet, but once we hear the words "to Dorian Aigina," we know where he was born. Another essential item of information has been transmitted obliquely.

Thus Pindar accomplishes two things at once: he announces his theme and presents his credentials. The idea that the Muse is his mother is one way of laying claim to supreme poetic ability: the son of the Muse will inherit her nature—he will have a talent for poetry. And there is another force at work, another indication that the poem about to begin will be good: the poet is inspired; he will not have to cudgel his brains for ideas. Both these notions—the poet's inborn talent and the richness, the attractiveness of his theme—will occur again and again in the odes.

The main purpose of the odes is to glorify the victor, and one of the main challenges in reading them is to develop a sense of the manifold ways in which Pindar fulfills that basic task. Even his frequent claim to poetic supremacy, for all its apparent egoism, enhances the victor's prestige, for it implies that the victor, in choosing Pindar to celebrate his deeds, shows a certain good taste and understanding. He knows that all the values of his life, particularly those expressed in his athletic career, come to fulfillment in poetry. Without poetry they will be confined to a single period of time, a single region of space; and being parochial, they will perish in oblivion. This understanding frees the victor from the pettiness and narrowness that blind most men. It makes him *generous* toward the poet, toward his own city, his friends, his family, and, above all, toward himself. When the glow of success is still warm, he will not chill it by thrifty restraint. He will spread the feast for his friends and enjoy the moment to the full. And he will make the one investment that will never cease to pay him returns. He will hire a poet of the rank and caliber of Pindar.

This nexus of ideas is extremely important to keep in mind while reading the odes, for it appears constantly and may not always be instantly recognizable for what it is. Pindar's audience apparently knew so well how epinician poetry functioned that a hint was often enough to alert them to the presence and operation of complex ideas. They would not lose the train of thought when, for whatever reason, the poet chose to condense or abbreviate standard topics. We, who are not conditioned to the reading, let alone the performance, of this kind of poetry, are apt to lose our way when the signs are not, so to speak, lit up in flashing lights. Man is utterly subject to death. Poetry alone offers him some means of escape from his mortality, provided he has done something worthy of tribute in song. A wise man who has put energy and devotion into achieving something noteworthy understands that death awaits not only his body but also his deeds. Having this understanding, he will not think of the financial cost of engaging a poet who might provide him with some measure of immortality. The whole complex of ideas is clear enough. Now let's see how it appears in a Pindaric ode:

> For great deeds of strength, if they lack songs
>   are sunk in deep obscurity,
> and we know
>   of only one
>   mirror
>   for noble achievements:
>   if Mnamosyna
> in her shimmering veil consents
>   to let a man find
> reward for toil
>   in the song of verses, givers of glory.
>
> And men of discernment, aware that the wind will rise
> on the third day, are not hurt by the thought of gain.
> Rich and poor alike fare onward to the tomb
> of death. (*Nemean* 7. 12–20)

The first thing we notice about our complex of ideas is what happens to it in the transition from prose to poetry. Everything becomes allusive and intricate. Instead of poetry itself, Mnamosyna is the agent. Her name means "Memory" and she is, from the religious and mythological point of view, the mother of the Muses. She would call to mind the Muses and with them the art of poetry. But memory, the first thing necessary for the preservation of deeds, exists only in the mind. The mirroring, the immortalization of the victor's achievements, must come about through the song itself, the very song now being sung. The claim, however, is not explicitly made. Nor is death, the catalyst for all these thoughts, immediately mentioned. We hear of obscurity, and then of a wind that will rise on the third day. Today, tomorrow even, we are happy. But the day after tomorrow is unknown, ominous. Men with understanding, we hear next, "are not hurt by the thought of gain." The expression is an example of the ubiquitous figure of litotes: the archaic tendency to think in terms of paired opposites is so natural to Pindar that he repeatedly makes positive assertions by stating the negative of their counterparts. Here he *means* that men of discernment spend accordingly; but he *says* that they are not hurt in the long run by short-term savings. He does not even spell it out that clearly, for in addition to litotes he employs condensation of expression, making ideas into kernels or nuggets that have to be cracked open or polished clean before they show their actual content and value. In the next phrase, the shadow of death materializes into the thing itself: the rich man will not differ from the poor man when both arrive at the tomb. Saving money makes no sense if the proper investment can deprive even death of its power to level all things and blot out all distinctions. The commodity in which such an investment is made must be something tremendous. We expect Pindar at this point to name it openly and celebrate its power. Instead we get:

I even suspect that Odysseus' fame
was greater than his worth, through the sweet words of Homer.

The subject of praise, poetry and its power to immortalize, suddenly shows a darker side. The reference to language and to Homer keeps it before us, but it is no longer the subject of a straightforward encomium. Poetry is so powerful that it can sometimes make even those who do *not* deserve it immortal. For a moment the dependence of poetry on achievement is shattered. But Pindar's disapproval in the very next lines (22–23):

For in his lies and in his winged devices
there is an awesome power

keeps us from assuming that he has embarked on a celebration of immoral art. The first concrete example of the power of poetry in the ode is negative. Against it, as against a foil, Pindar's own poetry will appear and make its unique claims. Litotes, working in the single phrase, is complemented by *negative illustration*, working in the stanza, the triad, or the ode in its entirety.

The celebration of the poet's greatness and of the victor's intelligence go hand in hand. The one implies the other, and both are, in a sense, expressions of the bond between poet and victor. The best word for that bond is the Greek noun *xenia*, hospitality, friendship. *Xenos* originally denoted a stranger, someone from another place. It has the special meaning of "host" or "guest" and the general sense of "friend," with the connotation that at some point in the past the friendship began in the host-guest relationship. It is difficult for us to appreciate the importance and the intimacy of this particular relationship in ancient Greece. In this regard, reading the *Odyssey* might be the best preparation for reading Pindar. Pindar was a traveling poet. The exercise of his art depended not only on the fee paid to him personally but also on the generous outlay for a chorus to perform the ode; and, if a banquet was involved, there would have been all the difference in the world between a host who was close-fisted and one who was lavish in the entertainment of guests and friends. Conditions of travel are also relevant. A journey from Olympia to Syracuse was not a matter of a day or two, but of weeks. It was dangerous and expensive. And when Pindar arrived on the scene, he would not finish his task in a day. How warmly he was received, how generously he was put up, might have no small influence on the creativity he could muster in his host's behalf. The strength of the feeling between a generous host and a grateful guest may be judged from the durability of the bond. Glaukos and Diomedes in the sixth book of the *Iliad* refrain from fighting each other when they realize that their grandfathers had once met as host and guest. They themselves had never met before. In Pindar's tenth Nemean ode, the fact that a remote ancestor of the victor once entertained the divine twins Kastor and Polydeukes guarantees that they will have a special feeling for the victor himself. *Xenia* is the foundation on which Pindar's odes are built. Without hospitality and generosity there could be no victory celebration, and though it needs poetry if it is to be complete, poetry is still only a part of it. Pindar constantly praises the victor and his city for their *xenia* toward himself and toward poetry, just as he constantly demonstrates the genuineness of his own *xenia*, his concern for the victor.

One indication of the concern Pindar felt toward the victor is the extent to which he adapts the ode to his circumstances, his station in life, his achievements, aspirations, hopes, and dreams. The men for whom he wrote were victors in the athletic games of Greece. All had cities to be glorified, families to be given their due of praise, hopes and wishes to be addressed by Pindar in appeals to the gods. These things are common to them all. Yet the odes of Pindar show a remarkable variety, a lively range of differences. The principle that binds them together is their basically laudatory intent. The means Pindar employs to fulfill his basic purpose are the conventions of the victory ode.

We have already considered some purely stylistic conventions in the sections on dialect and meter. More crucial to understanding Pindar in translation are certain conventions of theme and structure. The theme of immortality, for example, occurs in poetry of all languages and periods, but it has a peculiar force in the victory ode, where it does double duty as a celebration of the poet's greatness *and* the victor's intelligence, and where it is connected, as we have seen, with the theme of generosity.

The structural conventions, on the other hand, are more alien to us because they derive from the requirements of choral poetry, an ancient genre for which there is no true modern parallel. One of its requirements is the need for brevity. The limitations of performance do not allow the poet to spell out all his meaning. Instead of dwelling, for example, on the significance of a particular myth for the present occasion, he may simply bring its narration to an end by praying to the gods or by making a general observation on man's fate or even by stating a personal preference or abhorrence. In this way prayers, proverbs, and personal utterances come to serve a transitional function. By drawing attention to the poet's personality or to the mood of the chorus, they prepare the way for a change of subject. Their transitional function should be kept in mind, for while it will not solve every problem in reading Pindar, it will help prevent mistakes. First-person statements in particular have been the source of misunderstandings. A single example may suffice to show what can happen when the laudatory purpose of an ode is forgotten, or when its reliance on epinician conventions is overlooked.

The eleventh Pythian ode celebrates the victory of Thrasydaios of Thebes in the foot race for boys at Delphi.[42] The poem opens with an elaborate prayer bidding the goddesses and heroines of Thebes to come join the victor in an act of public homage. It quickly modulates into the telling of a myth of murder, intrigue, and tragedy, the story of the House of Atreus—of Agamemnon and Kassandra killed by Klytaimestra, of her in turn killed by her own son. Once the myth is told, Pindar returns to the victor and his family. We come upon them at the start of the last triad, the conclusion of a catalogue of their triumphs in the games:

and at Pytho, stepping down
        stripped for the races, they silenced
            all Hellas by their speed.

In the next phrase, Pindar speaks in the first person, as if inviting us to take his words at face value. It is at points like this that we should pause to separate the meaning of his words from their function:

May I pray for noble
favors from the gods, seeking
what is possible in my time,
for, having searched
into the city's ways, and having learned
that moderation blooms
with a longer happiness,
I have no fondness for the tyrant's lot.

If one forgets that each of Pindar's odes is meant for a specific occasion, one is troubled by the gap between the sentiments expressed above in *Pythian 11* and these, from *Pythian 3* (84–85):

You have a share of happiness—on you,
if on any man, great destiny has smiled,
for you are master of a people.

In *Pythian 11*, Pindar is speaking for a boy who lived in Thebes; in *Pythian 3*, he speaks to the most powerful man in the Greek world, Hieron, tyrant of Syracuse. Long before Pindar wrote *Pythian 11*, the poet Archilochos had expressed his disagreement with the popular notion that the pinnacle of human happiness is attained by the tyrant of a city, unlimited in power, with boundless wealth at his disposal. Hieron of Syracuse actually could fulfill that popular ideal. Would it be appropriate for Pindar to devalue it, belittling Hieron's status in a poem written to honor him? On the other hand, in a poem written for a boy and his family (who, though they probably belonged to the Theban nobility, were surely not in a position to command a city or an army), would it have been tactful of Pindar to praise the blessings of tyranny? The thing to do would be to find something of special value in the victor's way of life. Pindar does this by telling us not only what Thrasydaios of Thebes is but also what he is not: he is not exposed to the kinds of peril that plagued the great House of Atreus, subject of the myth told in the second triad of *Pythian 11.* Because Thrasydaios concentrates on achievements that benefit rather than oppress his fellow citizens, he reaps their gratitude rather than their hatred:

Striving instead for prizes
that promote public good,
I keep resentment at bay.
If a man, gaining the summit
and living in peace,
has also shunned
dread arrogance,
he may encounter
a nobler end in dark death

because he leaves his kin
the most valuable possession, grace of a good name.

The first-person statement here (lines 53–58) is in the voice of the bard, publicly declaring an authoritative moral code. Such is the sound it would have in a choral poem. It is ancient wisdom, a borrowing from the treasury of Greek proverbs, a variation on the theme that the heights are dangerous, the mountain peaks bear the lash of the lightning, human arrogance invites divine retribution. The proverb, however, is not uttered for its own sake. The proverbial theme is spun out at such length that it becomes, in effect, no longer a proverb: it is adapted to the praise of Thrasydaios and his family. The poet has seen something in their way of life that is of universal import. Members of the audience would have sensed the complex character of these words. Because the proverb suits the victor's status in life and is adapted to the ode in his honor, the blend of personal and universal is not incongruous.

It is only rarely that we can tell why Pindar chose to develop a particular theme more extensively than he does elsewhere, or in a unique fashion. There must be an element of guesswork, for example, in our view of Thrasydaios, whose personal wealth and political importance are virtually unknown to us. We may at least take it for granted that Pindar did not *insult* him with his stated preference for moderation over the tyrant's life. The statement itself reads like the poet's reaction to the myth told earlier; and the myth, with its impious crimes and its emphasis on secrecy, is in direct opposition to the opening of the ode, where we see Thrasydaios engaged in a public act of piety and patriotism, virtues that have their expression also in his athletic career, for his success in the Pythian games brings glory to Thebes and is a direct manifestation of divine favor. The section in which Pindar declares his preference for the middle way thus shows a certain logic when viewed against the background of the ode in its entirety.

But if we assume that the first-person pronoun of the passage designates Pindar the man speaking in his own voice rather than Pindar the bard voicing the values that sustain and motivate his patron, the passage loses its connection with the previous parts of the ode. Pindar turns into a poet capable at any moment of disrupting a formal occasion in order to spout his own biases. It would have to be something very compelling, very urgent, to stir him to such drastic measures. Thus scholars have imagined that Pindar in *Pythian 11* faced a Theban audience distrustful of his loyalty after his return from Sicily and the courts of Hieron and Theron, *tyrants* for whom he wrote proud poems of praise. To understand what Pindar says in *Pythian 11*, these scholars have had to supply a background of inaudible mutterings, the citizens of Thebes whispering to each other against Pindar, even as the people in the myth of the ode murmur against their overlords:

For the people
are prone to speak evil, and high prosperity
fosters more resentment, while the man
whose breath hugs the ground grumbles unheard. (28–30)

The noise in the background is, then, stifled by Pindar's antityrannical outburst.[43] This is what can happen if the first-person pronoun is taken for a simple entity, designating Pindar the man.

And there are other consequences of this approach. It ends by finding the meaning of Pindar's words outside the ode itself. If we could do so and at the same time make the other parts of the ode fit together in a coherent way, it would be less damaging to Pindar's image. If Pindar speaks for himself in *Pythian 11*, what does he intend to impart by telling the myth of the House of Atreus? Perhaps he is representing his own plight among his suspicious fellow citizens by Klytaimestra's plight among her people, since he tells us specifically that she was the victim of scandalous whisperers (lines 25–30). Or is Pindar Kassandra? He and she are voices of the gods, she as prophetess and he as poet. Is Pindar warning his enemies not to assassinate him, as Klytaimestra had murdered Kassandra? Was not Klytaimestra punished by the gods for having killed their representative? All these interpretations have been put forward,[44] but those who proposed them did not pause to consider how the young Thrasydaios would have felt, having his solemn victory celebration turned into an opportunity for Pindar's symbolic self-defense. Coherence and propriety go out the window together once the ode ceases to be studied as a single example of a general type of poetry, employing standard topics and conventions in varying ways to suit changing contexts.

Pindar says one thing to Hieron, another to Thrasydaios. It matters immeasurably to whom he is speaking. *Tact* is the essence of his art. Yet he does not hesitate to bring up matters which we would expect him to leave unmentioned, such as his financial arrangements with the victor. *Isthmian 2*, for example, begins with an ironical devaluation of epinician poetry on the grounds that it is paid for. In that complex opening passage, Pindar invites us to convict his Muse of insincerity because she is hired, like a prostitute.[45] There is a similar, if less complex, instance in *Pythian 11*. After the conclusion of the myth of the House of Atreus and just before the second celebration of his patrons' victories, Pindar suddenly pretends to have forgotten what his patrons were paying him for:

Truly, friends, I have been whirled along
ever since
the road divided—
all was well till then;
or was it a sudden gust

blew me off course
like a boat at sea?
It is your task, Muse,
if you have taken
silver for your voice,
to let it run shimmering from theme to theme—

now to the father Pythonikos
and now to Thrasydaios, the son—
their liberality
and reputation burn bright for all to see.

Here, midway through the second triad (37–45), Pindar's voice irrupts for the first time into the ode. Taken at face value, his words suggest a poet who does not know what he is doing. But to take his words at face value is to read the poem in isolation, without awareness of the kind of poem it is. If we do not know that a sudden shift from third person into the poet's own voice is conventional, a calculated way of changing the subject, all sorts of irrelevancies may besiege our minds. Pindar may emerge from the barrage resembling the champion of incoherence apostrophized by Voltaire: "Divine Pindar . . . you who possess the talent of saying much without saying anything, you who skilfully composed verses that no one understands and everyone must admire."[46] But the impression of befuddlement, of a poet carried away by his material and clumsily recovering from his inspiration, wears away on closer examination. The myth of the House of Atreus, with its darkness and power, has ended. Suddenly the poet who told that myth assumes the mask of someone light enough to be blown off his course. The subject is changing, and the tone changes with it. If the poet is light-headed, we note a certain cunning in his foolery: the mention of his fee coincides with a celebration of his patron's liberality. The audience knew that the poem had been paid for. Drawing attention to it compliments the patron for generosity: everyone in Thebes benefits from it. The immediate stimulus for the whole transaction is this family's athletic prowess, most recently demonstrated by a win at the Pythian games. The dark myth of the House of Atreus, or at least the manner of its telling, is Pindar's invention, his personal poetic contribution to the occasion, not an item that could have been predicted simply because *Pythian 11* is a victory ode. Now follows a list of things that were traditional in victory odes. Thus the mention of the ode itself and the financial transaction behind it helps the poet back into the specifically epinician theme. It is humorous, useful, and relevant.

Pindar, then, may talk about the kind of poetry he composes, even about the conditions under which he works. In *Nemean 4*, he makes the victory ode itself, with its special forms and limitations, into a foil for his own poetic performance. The epinician ode becomes, for a moment,

Pindar's antagonist: it is not enough for a poet with his burning enthusiasm. He *will* be excessive. First, he bows to the necessary limits of time and convention:

But the laws of the song and passing time
forbid dwelling on a theme at length.

The previous stanza (25–32) had told a myth about Herakles and Telamon. The sudden attention paid to the poem itself in the above lines (33–34) might signal a shift from myth to the victor. Since it is only the fifth stanza, there is the possibility of a rather brief ode. Instead, Pindar insists that he is not yet done:

And yet I feel a spell steal over me now—
the charm of this new-moon festival. (35)

The festival is that of the Nemean games. Pindar's language suggests an almost sexual attractiveness in it: it moves him. His enthusiasm will carry him beyond ordinary limits. Nothing can stop him, not even the sea:

Come then! Though the deep salt sea
grip your waist, fight against conspiracy!

Conspiracy? Who is conspiring against Pindar? The temptation to go in search of his personal enemies may again invite us away from the text of the poem itself. These are the enemies of the victor, anyone who might not think him worthy of the majestic song being sung in his behalf, who would bring it to an end. But such men are no match for the poet:

Mightily will we seem to enter the lists,
in daylight, superior to our foes,

The ode honors a wrestling victor. The poet faces the victor's enemies (and the sea itself—note "grip your waist") as the victor had faced his opponents at Nemea—in a wrestling bout. Pindar responds to the victor's triumph with praise. His poetic rival does the opposite:

while another fellow looks about him
with envy in his eye, fumbling
in darkness at an empty thought
that tumbles to the ground.

Pindar's opponents, the dispraisers, are lost in thought. He himself moves with the swiftness and sureness of inborn grace and power. Let others reflect. He has faith in his ability:

Whatever talent
sovereign Destiny has given to me,
I have no doubt

oncoming time will bring
to its due fulfillment.

For three stanzas (7–9) he then celebrates the heroes of his patron's native island.

Pindar often pretends in this way that he does not follow the rules, that acquired techniques are for the man of mean abilities. The pretense, of course, is a technique. It gives the illusion of enthusiasm breaking with orderliness, of inspiration refusing restraint, of genius not needing the guidance of education. In this, as in so much else, the poet's tendency to strengthen the momentum of his poem by inventing dualities, contrasts, and antagonisms is remarkable. Its aesthetic function comes out if we press Pindar on almost any topic. For example, his repeated insistence that talent is everything does not mean that he puts no emphasis on work or can see no value in it. Elsewhere he expresses the idea that all human achievement results from a combination of inborn gifts, divine favor, and determined efforts. In one place, as we have seen (*Nemean* 7. 21–30), he condemns Homer for lionizing Odysseus; in another (*Isthmian* 4. 39–41) he salutes Homer for redeeming Aias' glory through the power of magic words; in both he is celebrating the greatness of poetry. There are a number of passages where he tells a myth because a false version of it is current among men—or so he would have us believe. In fact, he is highlighting his own version by making it the antagonist of another, less accurate one. The procedure is similar in the above passage from *Nemean 4*, where Pindar's extended treatment of Aiginetan mythology is set against a limited treatment of it. Here, however, the choice between one way of telling the myth in a victory ode and another almost instantaneously becomes a fight between Pindar the poet enchanted by his theme and some "other fellow" who has different feelings. To search for the actual identity of that less poetic fellow is to miss his poetic function in the ode itself. He is a foil for Pindar.

There is, however, an obvious danger in calling him a foil. It gives the impression that Pindar proceeds by constantly defeating straw men, correcting false myths, discarding rigid technical rules—in short, by fighting battles easy to win because the terms of conflict are laid down by the poet himself. We cannot tell what was happening in Aigina at the time *Nemean 4* was composed. We do not even know for certain when that time was (see Appendix I). Perhaps there was local opposition to the victor, perhaps there were people who would have preferred a modest recognition of his achievements and would have resented linking them, in the grand manner, to the heroic deeds of the Aiakidai. We can only guess about details such as these: about the generalities, we can be more certain. Our own personal and literary experience tells us that praise is a difficult thing to carry off. We listen with a more sympathetic ear to satire than to eulogy. In archaic Greece, it was even dangerous to praise a man. If he happened to be powerful enough to disdain the ill will of his fellows, he could not disdain that of the gods. Every time Pindar struck his lyre in praise of a mere human being, he had to be careful, both for himself and for the object of his praise. This formidable negative power must be reckoned with, for it threatens the foundations of Pindar's poetry. The poet deals with it by asserting against it the victor's *rightful* claims. There is something of the scapegoat technique in his manner: he takes that part of the resistance that he can overcome, the natural jealousy of men, and attacks it, not only defeating it but also proving his own worth as poet. The part that cannot be overcome is taken over and made into a reminder to the victor of his mortality. The line is drawn between divine and human in such a way as to place the victor at the summit of human greatness—just below the heroes and far beneath the gods.

Such considerations as these are important, but they are not all. Within *Nemean 4* itself there are forces working to shape Pindar's imaginary struggle against the victor's enemies. The wrestling imagery in which it is envisioned comes from the occasion, a victory in *wrestling* at Nemea. Occurring just after a stanza describing the conflict between Herakles and Alkyoneus, it picks up a previous battle theme, so that Pindar's own poetic struggles are a continuation, not an interruption—a change of focus, not of subject. The conspiracy against which Pindar fights has its complement later in the myth of the ode, in the conspiracy of Hippolyta against Peleus (stanzas 7–8). Pindar must have known ahead of time what myth he would tell. Perhaps the victor had requested it. Whatever the case, the choice of myth and the diction of the ode influence each other.[47]

But there is always the possibility that mysterious passages, whose import cannot be agreed on, may in fact result from lapses in the poet's power. It would not be all that surprising. The metrical complexity of the odes alone might lead us to expect it once in a while. In a system of precise responsions, usually involving thousands of syllables, an occasional vague choice of words, a too abrupt transition, may well occur. How much time did Pindar have to compose the odes? A few—*Olympian 11* and *Pythian 6* are fairly certain examples—seem to have been composed before the victor left the scene of victory: in a day or two, perhaps in a matter of hours. But when one problem after another yields to analysis, when passages that seem difficult to us at first become clear through comparison with similar passages elsewhere in the odes, we begin to suspect that our own lack of familiarity with this kind of poetry is at fault, not the poet.

The conventions of the victory ode are only part of a modern reader's problem with Pindar. Even if we could claim mastery of the conventions—perfect, spontaneous familiarity with them in all their shifting guises—a complete understanding of Pindar's poetry would still not be within our grasp. We would always wonder about the appropriateness of a particular myth, the suitability of a particular proverb, to the victor's achievements or the moment when the ode was written. If Pindar had written with no one but the victor in mind and with only the moment of celebration before him, he would have excluded us entirely. The victor would have been displeased with such a treatment of his success, for he wanted a poem that would reach beyond its immediate time and place. By the same token, an ode that paid no attention whatever to the ephemeral circumstances of the victory and the actual feelings of the victor would have been a failure, at least as a victory ode. For better or for worse, the victory odes are the only evidence by which we can determine the accuracy of the ancient description of Pindar as "first by far among the nine lyric poets."[48]

Style and the Pindaric Tradition

Pindar's genre is not the only problem facing a modern audience. His style is also difficult. The way in which he says things can puzzle the reader, if only because Pindar is often terse to the point of being cryptic. In addition, Pindar tends to express ideas in concrete terms. While this is often described as a virtue in poetry, indeed as one of the main features of a poetic as distinct from a prosaic style, the blend of ideas and images in Pindar poses a unique problem for the translator, because in Pindar image often almost submerges idea. The apparent suppression of the thought holding the words together may suggest that there is no thought, that images come to Pindar's mind in a frenzy of inspired utterance.

A student of Pindar, trying to perceive how one thing follows another in the Greek, is constantly frustrated by Pindar's use of the particle *de*, a word that can drive the translator to the brink of despair when it is not coordinated with the particle *men*, to give the meaning "on the one hand (*men*) . . . on the other (*de*)." Since the word is often mildly adversative, a translator's first inclination is to render it "but" or, to avoid monotony, "yet." This gives the impression that Pindar is constantly correcting himself. Even worse, it reduces half of what he says to nonsense. Sometimes the word means "and." The reader with no knowledge of Greek may imagine the plight of the translator faced with an ubiquitous little word capable of being taken in two completely different senses. Add to this the fact that it can also be translated "for" (explanatory), and the enormity of the problem will begin to be appreciated. At times, finally, it is no more than a sign of something being added to something else—neither "but" nor "for," and not quite "and" either: it expresses simple relationship, possibly nothing more than sequentiality. In this latter usage, its actual meaning is often best translated by omitting it altogether. Many a passage in Pindar makes no sense until the translator decides which of these renderings is the right one.

A typical example occurs at the opening of the second triad of *Olympian 10.* The second word of that triad is *de.* Pindar has just dealt in some detail in the previous lines with the debt a boxing victor owes his trainer. Even Herakles, he observed, had to retreat once, in combat against Kyknos. There is a feeling of struggle and uncertainty in the preceding stanza. Hence, when the second triad begins with the word "effortless" coupled to the preceding triad only by the particle *de*, it seems sensible to render "*But* a few men have won joy without effort." Such is one's first inclination: but there is another *de* two lines later. In this later occurrence, *de* introduces an expression indicating that the song has taken a new turn in its thematic development. The logical rendering here, then, would be "but." We now have two sentences starting with "but." Further, rendering the first *de* adversatively has unfortunate implications: the victor had to toil for his final satisfaction, *but* some people have won joy without having to work for it. This would be bad enough, but Pindar then adds that such effortless joy is "a radiance on life outshining every achievement." Under these circumstances, a reader would feel that Pindar is for some reason demeaning the victor's hard-won accomplishments. If not "but," maybe "and" is more suitable. But this would connect the new triad with the preceding stanza in all too simple a fashion. The English word "and" suggests that the argument is continuing in the same manner. What could Pindar mean by saying that the victor owes his trainer gratitude *and* some have won joy without effort? The only rendering that cancels itself out immediately is the explanatory one. Clearly, the victor did not need his trainer's help *because* a few men have won joy without effort.

I decided that *de* is mildly adversative here and that it puts the opening word, not the opening sentence, in opposition to the preceding stanza. The second *de* then narrows the focus of Pindar's concern in this ode: he will deal with another class of triumphant heroes and men, those who had to labor for their triumphs. Herakles, founder of the Olympian Games, and Hagesidamos of Western Lokroi, winner in boxing at Olympia, belong to this class, and it is they who occupy Pindar's attention from now to the end. To avoid confusion with the second *de*, I left the first untranslated:

A few have won joy without effort,
        a radiance on life
                outshining every achievement.
                        But Zeus' sacred right moves me to sing
                Of his favored contest,
        which Herakles established . . .

What makes this example significant is its occurrence at a moment of transition in *Olympian 10.* It is not simply a matter of one line, or the connection of one word with another: the second triad is being joined to the first. Such major linkages tend to be effected in Pindar in exactly this way: without the use of subordinating conjunctions or adverbial expressions making immediately clear how we are to see the new material in relation to the old. In the above example, the triad-break helps us to get our bearings. The gnomic character of the new sentence alerts us that we are witnessing a transition. The second *de* then helps us to interpret the first: going with a sentence that states the ode's new theme, it is clearly the adversative one; the previous *de*-clause is a foil for the new material. So much is taking place in the passage, so little is being stated overtly: no wonder Pindar has acquired a reputation for haste, for sovereign indifference to the requirements of normal, logical discourse!

These remarks might give the impression that Pindar is a primitive stylist, that he places the elements of his sentences together and utters sentence after sentence without indicating the relationships among them. The technical description of such a style is *parataxis.* Its opposite is *hypotaxis*, the construction of complex sentences and paragraphs in which the principal and subordinate components are clearly marked as such by the use of conjunctions and adverbial expressions.

Pindar employs both styles, and both entail special problems for the reader and the translator. In complex examples of Pindaric hypotaxis, however, the problem is more peculiarly the translator's. It was easier for Pindar to construct expansive sentences in Greek than it is for us to preserve their structure in English, mainly because Pindar's language is inflected and ours is not. A pronoun or a participle or an adjective in Pindar may occur at a great distance from the noun it modifies without creating any problem in comprehension because its gender, number, and case are marked in the way it is spelled. The paucity of such means for immediate recognition in English makes it necessary either to break Pindar's long constructions into brief units, or to repeat the noun when its distant modifier appears. Except in rare instances, only repetition and punctuation are available to indicate that a single unified sentence is in progress, as opposed to a group of sentences merely strung together. English syntax does not have the elasticity of Greek. The result in translation is the impression that Pindar's vast sentences hang together very loosely on dashes and colons and repeated words. The sentences seem inflated; their author gradually acquires the reputation of being out of control.

Uncontrolled inspiration and indifference to logic are the salient features of Pindar's style, at least according to the Pindaric tradition in poetry—the tradition created by the translators and imitators and critics of Pindar from antiquity until now. Nothing would seem more likely to account for these two characteristics of the tradition than Pindar's use of imagery, a subject too large to admit of anything more than brief treatment here. To facilitate discussion, I shall consider only one type of passage, that in which appreciation of the genre helps us to see what Pindar's imagery is doing.

A rather simple and yet notorious example occurs in *Pythian 10*:

> No miracle is too great
> for my belief, when the gods
> bring it to pass.
> Stay the oars now!
> Heave the anchor overboard
> before we splinter
> on the bristling reef.
> For the song of praise
> darts from theme to theme, like a bee. (48–54)

The poet's sudden reference to himself signals a transition. The mythical portion of the ode has just concluded. The ode is now a ship, the poet its helmsman. There is a treacherous reef to be avoided, not by steering the ship in a different direction, but by halting its progress altogether. Pursuing the myth any further would be a mistake. But the poem has not ended yet—it is not only time to stop but also time to move on to a different theme. The latter idea is then expressed by a different image: the "song of praise" that was a ship moments before is now a bee flitting, we assume, from flower to flower. We may feel that we are confronted with a mixed metaphor. Actually, two sides of the same idea, the necessity of transition back to the victor, are being expressed in two different ways, each way figured in a different image. For the stopping, coming to the end of one section of the ode, there is the anchor; for the new forward movement, the bee. Possible disaster is embodied in the reef; fresh attractiveness in the coming theme is implied by the suggestion of flowers. We must keep the two sides of the idea separate: the images are not mixed, but shifting rapidly, carrying a different message each time.

A far more complex and difficult passage—perhaps the most vexing example in Pindar—occurs in the sixth Olympian ode. If it were not clearly a transitional passage, a reader of the Greek would be hard put to make any sense of it at all. On first glance, it seems to involve an outrageous confusion of images. The problems are best illustrated by starting with a literal rather than a finished rendering:

> I have a certain image upon my tongue of a shrill whetstone, which steals upon me in my eagerness with lovely-streaming blasts. My maternal grandmother is a Stymphalid, blossoming Metopa . . . (82–84)

The sudden reference to the poet himself alerts us to a shift in focus. Since the previous lines had dealt in detail with the victor for the second time, we might expect the ode to conclude in a series of statements presenting the poet's credentials. This, it turns out, is the case. Meanwhile, we must make sense of the above medley of images. How does it prepare the way for the poet's new claims in his own behalf? The words themselves—an image, a tongue, a shrill whetstone, lovely-streaming blasts—do not suggest anything coherent, and we are disappointed if we expect much help from the grammar. The relative pronoun introducing the verb "steals upon" is feminine singular. Grammatically, it could refer to the image, or the whetstone, or even the tongue. The latter is the least likely, but the choice between the other two is not obvious. Since an image is more likely than a whetstone to "steal upon" someone, it ends by being our choice for the subject of the verb in the relative clause. But to have an image "upon one's tongue" is rather odd; perhaps it resembles our expression, to have something "on the tip of one's tongue"—that is, to be about to say something. Is Pindar about to make a comparison between sharpening his instrument, speech, and sharpening a metal instrument, such as a knife? If so, he leaves the comparison unfinished. This is hard enough, but what are we to make of the "lovely-streaming blasts" that we meet next? In what way does the image of a whetstone come over the poet "with lovely-streaming blasts"? Clearly, someone is not sharpening a knife within Pindar's hearing. The sound he hears must be that of the flute playing to his ode. The shrill note of the flute reminds him of a whetstone. The concept, one sound reminding Pindar of another, is distracting all by itself. Fortunately, we have Pindar's state of mind to help us identify the process being described: he is "eager" or "enthusiastic." Since the previous lines had celebrated the victor, we may assume that the poet's warm feelings are directed toward him, or caused by him. Under the spell of his enthusiasm, Pindar has had a sudden insight and is about to make a bold claim, which turns out to be that he and the victor are actually related. There are a number of logical steps involved in reaching such a conclusion, a veritable Gordian knot of interconnections. Pindar cuts right through to the conclusion with the sharp instrument of his poetic speech: "My maternal grandmother's a Stymphalid, blossoming Metopa, mother of horse-driving Theba, from whose delightful springs I drink as I plait the intricate song for spearmen."

Metopa is a nymph from Stymphalos, the victor's Arkadian home. Her daughter is Theba, the nymph for whom Pindar's city Thebes was named: hence Pindar is the grandson of Metopa, his own city being, metaphorically, his mother. This, of course, puts logic to work in the service of mythology. It is a daring statement, prepared for by the expectation that the poet will use his tongue incisively. The entire passage is doing two things at once: drawing attention to Pindar's poetic skill and forging a link between himself and the victor, thus enhancing the impression of genuine feeling. The tightness of expression is extraordinary, even for Pindar. The poet's speech is being applied to the whetstone at the same time the image of a whetstone is on the tip of his tongue. We hear of the image before we hear of what brought it to mind, the sound of the flute. And the flute is not overtly mentioned: we have to infer it from other passages where its streaming sound or shrillness are named; or from our awareness that, indeed, the flute was playing while Pindar's chorus sang, and probably while Pindar composed the ode. "Divine Pindar . . . you who skilfully composed verses that no one understands and everyone must admire": one can see the reason, if not the justice, of Voltaire's opinion.

Voltaire had no appreciation of Pindar's genre or of his meter. Neither had been rediscovered yet, and both were lost for centuries. When one adds to the effect of their loss the effect of Pindar's density, his tendency to express ideas through images, and his stated disdain for the laborious processes of poetic technique, it is easy to see how the traditional image of Pindar as either the vatic or the vapid bard has evolved. The basic misconception in this traditional image is that Pindar is always sublime. The trouble with such a poet is that his translators and imitators must be equally sublime, and sublimity all the time is impossible to sustain. Pindar himself admitted other moods into his verse; his sublimity, also, has nothing to do with incoherence. The meaningless excitement attributed to him is apparently validated by the experience of one of his most famous translators, Abraham Cowley, who observed "If a man should undertake to translate Pindar word for word, it would be thought, that one madman had translated another."[49] Even worse is the fault attacked in William Cowper's *Ode: Secundum Artem,* a satire on verse with Pindaric pretensions:

Shall I begin with *Ah*, or *Oh*?
Be sad? *Oh*, yes! Be glad? *Ah*, no!
Light subjects suit not grave Pindaric ode,
Which walks in meter down the strophic road . . .
    Come, placid Dullness, gently come,
    And all my faculties benumb.[50]

True inspiration may at times pass beyond the bounds of strict rationality; fragmentation of logic may occasionally be beautiful. When carried to extremes, both lead to monotony and the result is boredom, the dullness Cowper made into the Muse of Pindaric verse. "More bad poems have been written in the intention of rivalling Pindar than in any other sphere of classical imitation" is Gilbert Highet's sad but accurate description of the Pindaric tradition in literature.[51] Pindar, more than anyone, is an author whose reputation gets in the way of understanding him. The real difficulties he poses are, as we have seen, considerable; the problem of a poetry with nothing to communicate but the poet's afflatus belongs not to Pindar, but to the tradition unfairly named after him. Neither insipid nor wild, Pindar will continue to appear so in translation if the problems discussed above, and others to be mentioned now, are not dealt with effectively.

III. The Translation

Diction, dialect, and word-order make up no small portion of Pindar's stylistic resources. Of the three, only diction is at least partially suggestible in English. Dialect and word-order often have little to do with the basic meaning and so their representation in English is virtually impossible. Since Pindar's dialectal practice often involves archaism, it would be appropriate to give the rendering an archaic color. But the *significance* of archaism in Pindar will either be missing in English or, even worse, misleading. Pindar echoed ancient poetry musically *and* contextually. Homeric cadences or allusions or both were at home almost anywhere in Pindar because Homer's poetry was in the bones of his audience. We have no similar heroic tradition to echo. Occasionally a biblical or Shakespearean sound will work, but almost never exactly where Pindar himself is alluding to ancient poetry.

To preserve or even reflect Pindar's word-order is impossible. Here the ancient and the modern languages simply part company, as they do in their metrical nature. Greek is inflected. The syntactical relations among the words are signaled not only by their position but more so by their inflections. This allows the poet, within certain limits, to place words in patterns of varying complexity, sometimes making their position reinforce their meaning, at other times simply weaving intricate designs that have little direct connection with the sense. Often it seems, when all the words are translated, that there are too many of them, and the temptation to cut is very strong. At moments like these, the translator who wants to include everything must envy Pindar the almost tactile quality of words in Greek, the plastic power available to him simply because his language was inflected: those words whose naked rendering adds nothing in English form, in Greek, part of a metrical and verbal mosaic that all by itself, independent of any meaning, is very impressive. When we designate a word or a phrase as "decorative," we are liable to be speaking pejoratively. Decoration in Greek is a basic aesthetic principle.

The situation is slightly more hopeful in regard to Pindar's use of diction, his verbal artistry from ode to ode. He manages to make the occasion or the myth of each ode into a special context in which certain words, images, and ideas take on added force because of their interrelationships with each other and with the ode in its entirety. The usual sign for this is repetition, either of the words themselves, the words themselves in altered form, or the ideas and images they convey. As in the case of Pindar's verbal mosaics (whose beauty and intricacy of pattern often exist in their own right, without any perceptible reinforcement of meaning), repetition of words may have an impact on the mind and senses of the audience without necessarily contributing to the meaning of the ode. To put a particular interpretation on such effects is often to go too far, to make something basically musical semantic. The relationship between these effects and the meaning of an ode is like the relationship between its meaning and its meter: there is occasional convergence amid general divergence.

But a poetic translation of Pindar should communicate the experience as well as the meaning of a Pindaric ode. The purely musical effect of repeating sound patterns is essential to all poetry. It is only occasionally that it can be transferred from Greek into English. Mechanical use of the same word or the same root in translation to reflect repetition in the original almost always comes out strange, for the Greek words in question usually have other meanings that come to the fore in repeated use, requiring the substitution of synonyms in English if the sense intended in each new context is to be preserved. Use of exactly the same English word throughout would keep the effect of repetition, but at the cost of distorting, if not destroying, the meaning.

When the repetition seems purely musical and unattainable in English, I have generally tried to compensate for its loss by creating sound patterns of my own. But when the musical effect of repetition and the overall meaning of an ode certainly converge and reinforce each other, it is incumbent on a translator to try for the effect in English. A good example is *Nemean 11*, a poem in which Pindar places unusual emphasis on psychological motivation.[52] The relationship between this theme and the diction of the ode readily transfers into English everywhere except one place, line 40, where Pindar says, literally, that the trees "do not want" to put forth their flowers in equal abundance year after year. But the literal meaning of negative volition, thematically related to the rest of the ode, is only suggested in the original Greek, for the phrase in question, *ouk ethelei*, can be taken literally or idiomatically, depending on the context, and here the immediate context demands the idiomatic sense "are not accustomed to." If there were not an additional context, that of a poem containing repeated instances of negative volition, the idiomatic *denotation* would be the only meaning a translator would have to reckon with. But under the circumstances, the literal *connotation*, secondary from the point of view of the immediate context, is primary from the point of view of the ode as a whole. But to translate the phrase literally would be to force the personification of the trees into the foreground, when Pindar leaves it in the background—a suggestion, not a statement. Is there any way to do both things in

English? Ideally, what is needed is a phrase that sometimes has one meaning, sometimes another. Both meanings have to be sufficiently strong to survive when one is immediately meant, and the other only implied. To solve the problem, I decided to use the word "will" as future auxiliary (denotation) and as a synonym for "consent" (connotation). To say that the trees will not flourish every year with the same abundance is almost the same as saying it is not their custom to do so, and it also suggests that they refuse to do so.

The reader may now have some idea of the difficulties faced by a translator trying to preserve Pindar's craftsmanship in words, his use of diction from ode to ode. The effects described above come under the general heading of Pindar's *logopoeia.* According to Ezra Pound,[53] who coined the word, *logopoeia,* "the dance of the intellect among words," is not translatable. Neither, in general, are the purely musical effects of rhythm and cadence, the effects of a poet's *melopoeia.* The only facet of a poet's art that can readily show itself in another language is the art of imagery, *phanopoeia.* These three types of poetry provide a good framework for an essay on translating Pindar.

Melopoeia

Melopoeia consists of two things: the rhythm of words and their quality of sound. Both aspects come out clearly in the following lines from Pindar's first Pythian ode (21–26):

> tâs ereugontai men aplatou puros hagnotatai
> ek muchôn pagai: potamoi d' hameraisin
>   men procheonti rhoon kapnou
> aithôn': all' en orphnaisin petras
> phoinissa kulindomena phlox es bathei-
>   an pherei pontou plaka sun patagô.
> keino d' Haphaistoio krounous herpeton
> deinotatous anapempei: teras men
>   thaumasion prosidesthai,
>   thauma de kai pareontôn akousai,

Pindar has imitated the sound of the awesome event he is describing, the eruption of Mount Aitna. The 6 lines explode with 21 plosive consonants—21 "P," "B," and "F" sounds to suggest the bursting and hissing of the volcano's activity. In addition, there are 14 guttural consonants, "K's" and "G's", to punctuate the explosion with a suggestion of internal rumbling, belching, and crackling. It is, in brief, an acoustic *tour de force.* It cannot help but make a strong impression on anyone who reads the ode in Greek. A translator, even if he does not pause to count the plosives and the gutturals, knows from the sheer energy of the description that here Pindar is at his best: here, literally, we have some Pindaric pyrotechnics. It is not often that a reader gets to enjoy the sight and sound of a volcano erupting. In my translation, I rendered it as follows:

> Within her secret depths
> pure springs of unapproachable fire
> erupt—her rivers in daytime pour forth
> billows of glaring smoke,
> while at night the blood-red
> rolling blaze whirls boulders crashing
> onto the flat plain of the sea.
> It is the monster beneath,
> spewing torrents of fire—
> a wondrous portent
> to behold, a wonder
> even to hear of
> from those who have seen

For Pindar's 21 plosives, I was able to find 14. For his 14 gutturals, I produced a mere 5. So much for the sounds, the individual units that make up the total acoustic impression; what of their rhythm, their movement? "It is practically impossible," Pound wrote, "to translate (Melopoeia) from one language to another, save perhaps by a divine accident, and for half a line at a time." Here, I believe, is my one divine accident. I had a great deal of trouble, not with the whole stanza, but with the line and a half in which Pindar describes the eruption of Aitna at night. For some reason, when I started to change my literal prose version of the words into poetry, I decided that Pindar meant to picture the volcano streaming in the dark with molten lava. So I introduced lava into my version, but when I came to revise it I felt that something was wrong, not with the lava so much as the sound it made—the movement, the rhythm was wrong. For a long time I tried to make my lava move with a little more energy, but it remained true to its nature—it stayed sluggish and so did my stanza, to my great chagrin because I knew that Pindar's was anything but sluggish. When, finally, as a last resort, I looked again at the Greek text, lo and behold, there was no lava at all. I revised my lines to read

> while at night the blood-red
> rolling blaze whirls boulders crashing
> onto the flat plain of the sea.

There is a minimum of readjustment here: the translation is almost literally faithful to Pindar's Greek. But none of this is accident, still less divine. It might seem foolish not to have done it that way from the start. But the accident and the blessing came later, when I asked myself *why* the sound of the line and a half was better now than it was before.

Looking at its metrical pattern I found, to my great delight, that it could be scanned in a facsimile of dactylo-epitritic meter, the Dorian measure in which the ode itself is composed.

Such occurrences are, however, accidental. To try to make a pattern of stresses and nonstresses in English consistently correspond to the metrical pattern of long and short syllables in the Greek would be suicidal. And yet the translator should do something about Pindar's Melopoeia, since it is, as we have seen, a feature of colossal magnitude in his poetry. It cannot be represented on its own terms in English, but there is another aspect of Pindar's choral art that, in a special way, is related to his Melopoeia. In fact, I am tempted to make this element a fourth category in addition to Pound's three, and to say it comprises at least half of Pindar's music. I am thinking of his *Choro*poeia, the fact that all his triadic odes are *dances* as well as poems. Attention to Choropoeia can make a large part of Pindar's musical workmanship appreciable to a modern reader without sacrificing the translator's life or sanity.

I have paid attention to it, first by labeling Pindar's turns and counterturns and stands, so that readers will always be aware of when they are reading one or the other. Then, since all of Pindar's triadic odes are metrically unique, I have devised a unique shape for each, and I have tried to make them all look to the eye like dance-patterns on the page. This may seem at first mere play, or, worse still, pedantic subservience. Why should readers always know where the chorus is in its dancing if they cannot see the chorus? The answer is that they often *can* see the chorus, if they know how to look for it.

We know very little about ancient dance, but one thing is fairly certain: it was mimetic. It involved not only movement, but expressive movement, and not of the body only but also of the hands. The chorus, in other words, danced the ode in three senses, not just one: it moved in patterns of its own that would appear beautiful even without the music or the poetry; it moved with the music of the ode as the poet composed it; and it moved in such a way as to suggest visually what the ode was about. Once we have had our attention drawn to these facts of ancient choreography, and once it is as easy for us as it was for the original audience to distinguish turn from counterturn and stand, we begin to notice other things as well: we begin to appreciate the architecture of the odes, and architecture is music articulated spatially.

Let me illustrate what I mean from a rapid glance at the first Pythian ode. The stanza quoted above in transliterated Greek and in my own version is the second turn of that ode. In the first turn, Pindar had called the thunderbolt of Zeus "the lancing bolt of everflowing fire." It was with that spear of lightning, as the ancient audience knew, that Zeus had overthrown the monster Typhon, and hurled him into the terrible prison where he is now, beneath Mount Aitna. In the first turn, we have the lightning-spear of ever flowing fire; in the second, we have the victim of that spear of fire, Typhon beneath the volcano, *throwing* boulders into the air, a fountain of fire. Then, in the third turn, we find Pindar speaking of his own desire to praise the victor of this ode, Hieron of Aitna. He uses a simile: "and I, yearning to praise this man, hope not to cast my bronze-tipped javelin with whirling hand off the field, but to fling it far beyond my rivals." The lightning-spear of the first turn, *thrown* by Zeus when he pleases, the rocks and torrents of fire *thrown* by Typhon in his writhing beneath Mount Aitna in the second turn, are both recalled in the third turn by the vision of Pindar in peaceful competition, hoping not to *throw* his javelin amiss in his enthusiasm. In the fourth turn, Pindar describes the Dorian peoples settling in their new home at the foot of Mount Taÿgetos in the Peloponnese, where "the fame of their *spear* bursts in blossom." If we go to the fifth and last turn of the ode, we find Pindar advising Hieron: "forge your speech on the anvil of truth." The first audience of this ode would have remembered that the smith god Hephaistos had his smithy beneath Mount Aitna. In fact, the torrents of fire in my rendering of the second turn are torrents of "Hephaistos" in the original Greek. The fire of the weapon-forging god and, implicitly, the weapons he forges, among them the spear, recur in the fifth and last turn as a figure for the power of speech, the power that has articulated the complex unity of this ode. What gestures the chorus executed each time it did the turns we can only imagine. The patterns of movement would have been the same, reinforcing the similarity in the more variable patterns of word, imagery, and idea. The counterturns and stands show a similar tendency to repeat and vary the same images and ideas. We miss the appreciable music of this ode and others if we are oblivious to such patterns. But if the turns and counterturns have identical shapes and are labeled as such, only the inattentive reader will miss the patterns, and with them much of Pindar's melody.

Phanopoeia

These are some of the ways in which a translator can preserve the music, the Melopoeia, of Pindar's odes. Their Phanopoeia, the poetry of their imagery, is more accessible because it is by nature translatable. The translator can see the picture present in the Greek and transfer it into English far more readily than he could ever transfer a cadence or a quality of sound. "When the Phanopoeia is good enough," Pound wrote, "it is practically impossible for the translator to destroy it save by very crass bungling." In Pindar, the Phanopoeia is not only good enough, it is almost overwhelming. If the translator bungles it, he would do so, it seems to me, in two ways: by simply not taking care to render it as vividly in English as Pindar had in Greek; or by not making certain beforehand that the particular image is, in fact, something that *can be seen* in English. This last precautionary measure is sometimes omitted in practice, with ludicrous results.

The ancient Greek language is a garden where images grow in slightly wilder profusion than they do in English. Their rank transplantation into English sometimes gives an exotic effect that is pleasing, but at other times it makes the garden of the poem seem as if it had been grown on Mars, and the strangeness is not something an earthling will ever get used to.[54] The transplanter of Pindar's Phanopoeia, in other words, must use the pruning knife from time to time. There are some images in the Greek text that can be shown in English only at the price of spoiling the rest of the show.

To take a single example: "Forge your speech on the anvil of truth," Pindar, as we have seen, advised King Hieron. Suppose I had rendered it literally: "Forge your tongue on the anvil of truth." "Ouch!" I can hear the reader say. What a picture: the king with hammer and tongs, the blazing fire whipped by bellow-blasts, and the tongue ringing, or writhing, under the blows. The translator is saved from so torturing the reader's sensibilities by the fact that the word "tongue" in Greek—*glôssa*—can also be used by metaphorical extension for what the tongue does: it speaks. Hence, "tongue" in Greek also means "expression," "speech," "language," "saying." But the first meaning, present at the back of the mind, is "tongue," and Pindar—perversely, from our point of view—often seems to relish suggesting the concrete image, when he should limit what he is saying to the metaphorical extension.

Beside more or less intractable images such as this, there are a host of others that a translator will escort from Greek poetry into English with sheer joy. I think of the infant Herakles, with his bare hands strangling the two serpents sent by his stepmother Hera to devour him on the day of his birth (*Nemean 1*); or of the infant Iamos, lying on a bed of yellow and purple violets, abandoned in the woods, to be fed honey by green-eyed serpents (*Olympian 6*); or of the three ominous and gigantic serpents that sprang hissing against the newly built ramparts of Troy (*Olympian 8*); or of the tangle of snakes drooping from the heads of Medusa's two sisters as they grieve for her death (*Pythian 12*); or of the serpent, bigger than a ship, looming up over the Golden Fleece (*Pythian 4*). There is Jason prodding a pair of fire-breathing bulls in the ribs as he guides them up and down the furrow (*Pythian 4*); or Athena appearing in a dream to Bellerophon, to give him the newly invented bridle (*Olympian 13*); or Bellerophon falling from the sky, tossed by Pegasos down to earth after having tried to gallop into the company of the gods (*Isthmian 7*). One sees Poseidon with his gleaming trident come up out of the sea at night, summoned by his former lover Pelops (*Olympian 1*). The island of Rhodes blooms from the depths of the sea, like a flower (*Olympian 7*). Queen Klytaimestra with two strokes of her bronze sword sends the souls of Agamemnon and Kassandra hurtling to the dark shores of Acheron (*Pythian 11*); Aias falls on his own sword in the dead of night (*Isthmian 4*). Apollo strides through the flames of the funeral pyre to seize the unborn Asklepios from the womb of his dead mother (*Pythian 3*). Pindar's Phanopoeia, his imagery, is, in a word, the poet-translator's richest and most usable resource. The presence of mythical narrative in many of the odes also challenges the translator's ability to show images in motion, to be a dramatic as well as a lyric poet.

But the opportunity and the challenge of Pindar's imagery is not without its price: the translator must take extreme care not to let the imagery stand out as the only successfully rendered part of the ode. He must evoke and sustain the *thought* within and behind the ode, the shaping and moulding power that has not only created the imagery and the narrative but also set them in motion for reasons beyond themselves. They are not purple passages, but parts of an integral unity; their beauty increases when we observe them participating in the articulation of the ode as a whole. To bring this participation out vividly is the most difficult problem facing the translator of Pindar, the problem least often solved. Even accomplished Greek scholars may satisfy themselves as to the meaning of all the phrases in a Pindaric ode and still not understand what they are saying together. One can translate Pindar and then have to translate one's translation. There are many reasons why this is so. Chief among them is the dominance of Logopoeia in Pindar's art.

Logopoeia

The victory ode is a context within a context—a special system of meanings within a larger system, the Greek language itself. The conscious poetic manipulation of special meanings that attach to words in certain contexts but not in others belongs to the third type of poetry as defined by Pound: Logopoeia, the poetry of the thought inseparable from the words in which it is expressed. In addition to the poetry heard by the ear, there is a poetry seen and heard and felt by the mind. We listen to a series of words and take delight in their sound. We also sense within and behind them certain semantic resonances—double meanings, echoes, associations that contradict or intensify or exist independently of the associations immediately evoked by the actual words we are hearing. Logopoeia is the poetry of language itself.

There are many varieties of Logopoeia in Pindar. One type of it comes to the fore in Pindar's manipulation of conventions: here the poet avails himself of a peculiar freedom in the treatment of standard topics and traditional thoughts—abbreviating, expanding, even overthrowing them. He enjoys this freedom because he has an audience familiar with the kind of poetry being presented. They expect it to move in certain ways. They recognize the signals that mark movement from one topic to another. Hence, they will enjoy *departure* from the expected as much as they will appreciate *fulfillment* of it. They are, in a word, sensitive to the varying contexts that appear only in this genre. The poet can depend on certain associations to arise within those contexts; he can play with them as he wills. I have already dealt with this kind of Logopoeia in the previous sections on genre and style; the reader will find further help with it in the prefaces to the individual odes.

Other types of Logopoeia in Pindar have less to do with his genre than with his language. Certain poetic effects arise from the nature of the language in which they are attained. Ancient Greek, for example, does not avail itself of rhyme—at least not deliberately or for very long. It does, however, rely a great deal on an effect which is as peculiar to it as rhyme is to English. I am referring to the suspension of sentences over periods of varying length, an effect that is possible and attractive because Greek is an inflected language. A Greek poet can give us an adjective or a participle without its noun. He can then keep us waiting for the noun until it is opportune to reveal it. Because the language is inflected there is no real loss of clarity. The simple utterance of the definite article, for example, carries a world of grammatical information that keeps us oriented as we wait to find what specific noun belongs with it. An impressive example of this technique in Pindar is from the twelfth Olympian ode, lines 5–6a. In Greek it reads:

hai ge men andrôn
poll' anô, ta d' au katô
pseudê metamônia tamnoisai kulindont' *elpides.*

The sentence starts with the definite article (*hai*). But notice the difference between "the" in English and "*hai*" in Greek. "The" in English is almost completely uninformative: will the noun attached to it be singular or plural, masculine or feminine, subject or object? We do not know until we hear the noun, and for that reason we hear it immediately: "The hopes" (*hai . . . elpides*). But with translation the original poetic effect has evaporated. In Greek, "the" (*hai*) tells us a great deal more: as soon as it is uttered, we expect a plural noun, feminine in gender, nominative in case, therefore subject of the whole sentence. With this information we are equipped to watch the subject go through the sentence before we know what it is. Our curiosity is aroused, but we are not mystified; nor are we kept in suspense merely for the sake of suspense. We wait for the subject of the sentence, we expect it and when it comes, at the very end, it means "expectations," "hopes" (*elpides*). Pindar has made the placing of the word in the sentence reflect its lexical meaning. The original poetic effect of this is unattainable in English because it relies on a quality peculiar to Greek. A translator can only try for a different poetic effect, hoping to be, if not poetic in the same way, at least *as* poetic.

Another type of Logopoeia is the pun. The translator of Pindar faces a considerable difficulty when it comes to his author's puns. He is in a position to neglect some of them, but others he cannot escape. In *Olympian 9*, for example, Pindar is engaged in an elaborate compliment to the victor's family. The victor belongs to the noble stock of the town of Opous. It was there that legend said Deukalion and Pyrrha came down from Mount Parnassos after the flood had drowned everyone else. They consulted the oracle to find out how they might repopulate the earth and heard the enigmatic answer: "By throwing your mother's bones over your shoulders." It took them a while to guess that the earth was their mother, her bones were rocks, and so the oracle's prescription need not involve them in an act of filial impiety. Pindar does not go into any of these details; he assumes his audience's familiarity with them:

> Sing instead (he says) of Protogeneia's town,
> where by decree of Zeus, dazzling in thunder,
> Pyrrha and Deukalion stepped down
> from Parnassos
> and built their first home.
> They sowed a singular folk, born of no embrace—
> *people*, they were called,
> from the *pebbles* thrown.

This is one solution for the problem here: the similarity in sound between the Greek word for "people" (*laos*) and the Greek word for "stone" (*laas*). To do nothing about the pun is to leave the reader wondering what necessary connection there might be between stones and people.[55]

Other puns whose operation affects the meaning of the ode but whose incorporation into English I found more or less impossible are elucidated in the prefaces to the odes where they occur. Major puns in *Olympians 6*, *7*, and *10* are examples. Puns that do not seem to have major significance and yet are striking in themselves also tempt the translator. A famous one appears in the last stand of *Pythian 2*. There Pindar is rebuking envious people whose envy is an expression of greed, the desire to keep all to oneself. Pindar uses the image of a land purchase to express his idea. The land is measured off by a line at either end of which there is a sharp stake. The first stake is driven into the the ground. The line is then pulled to its limit, the second stake is driven into the ground, and thus the boundary is marked. Envious people in their greed pull the line as tightly as they can in order to make it include as much land as possible. They pull on it so hard that the other stake comes loose and the stake they are pulling toward themselves stabs them in the heart. In Greek Pindar says that, pulling (*helkomenoi*), they plant a wound (*helkos*) in their hearts. The similarity in spelling between the participle (*helkomenoi*) and the noun (*helkos*) is purely fortuitous from a linguistic point of view. Pindar, however, is serious about such coincidences: he believes that they express causality. All this is interesting, but can the pun itself be suggested in English? I tried to suggest it, but I could only make the attempt by changing Pindar's imagery. Instead of the greedy land purchasers, I thought of fishermen who let their lines out further and further, allowing their nets to keep on filling until, when they attempt to retrieve their catch, it proves too heavy, snaps the line, and so breaks their hearts:

Yet even that fails to appease the envious
who pull on a line *unwound* to the limit
until it snaps: a *wound* to their own heart
before they compass their desires.

A pun like this could have been neglected in translation, for it does not seem to have any major significance in the poem where it appears. And yet a translator must look with regret on other puns he could do nothing about, for the total effect they have on the reader of Pindar is, in fact, significant. For one thing, they reveal a sensibility quite different from ours. We still feel a little of the impatience with punning displayed by Samuel Johnson in his *Preface to Shakespeare*: puns seem perversely clever. They may be so, but they also exemplify a different attitude toward language. In Pindar's case, they are an isolated example of a much more constant and important feature of style: the poet has a way of letting individual words and images take over and guide the development of the ode. In the above example from *Pythian 2*, the similarity between two words controls the formation of thought for a few lines only. In *Pythian 1*, as we have seen, the imagery and diction associated with the act of throwing recur throughout the ode. To notice this is not to isolate the single unifying principle that gives *Pythian 1* its coherence, but it is to isolate one of the principles and to see the ode as a unity in at least one regard.

Pindar's tendency to play with conventions and with language gives his odes a kind of coherence that is unique in western literature. Its uniqueness has led to its being overlooked, with the result that Pindar has seemed incoherent. Scholarship has made progress toward correcting that view, but scholarship speaks mainly to the specialist. The translator still must find a way of making Pindar coherent in English—no easy task, when Pindar's unity is often buttressed by effects peculiar not only to Greek, but to Pindar's way of using it.

"There is no Muse of translation"

Seeing how a Pindaric ode makes sense from beginning to end is the hardest thing for a modern reader. Nothing in a Pindaric ode seems to conform to our notions of logic or of what to expect. Time is often disregarded. Statements in the past lead immediately to statements in the present, with no perceptible passage of time intervening. The very irrelevance of things may be what makes them relevant. Joy leads to sorrow. The happiness of the present moment provokes thoughts of the uncertainty of the future. The virtues of the victor are seen by contrast with the vices of his enemies or of those who do not resemble him. *Isthmian 1*, for example, ends with the sudden portrait of a miser. He appears just after we have seen the victor preparing to try his luck at Olympia, which will cost *money.* The point is that the victor is not a miser, *unconsciously* condemning himself to *obscurity* by refraining from competition or by failing to engage a poet's services. None of these connections is explicitly made by Pindar: the ideas are present in abbreviated form; the whole expression is a condensed, implied litotes. The victor, through the negative example of the miser, is being praised for his wisdom and generosity.

This kind of compression is only one of many factors making the literal translation of a Pindaric ode often result in a kind of nonsense. We have to impose on it the logic of the genre if we are to see the sense of it. To notice the recurrence of words and images is to get a slightly different impression: where logic seems to fail, picture and music may come to our aid. The major problem here is that it is impossible to make diction and imagery alone account for an ode's coherence. We can say, for example, that *Pythian 1* is about throwing, or *Isthmian 6* about drinking, or *Pythian 2* about gods and men and animals, but if we do not go further, we give the impression that Pindar anticipated surrealism by two and a half millennia. Still, there is a measure of truth in each of the above statements. The elusive logic of an ode becomes less elusive as we begin to experience its coherence in other ways than the strictly logical ones to which we are accustomed. The eruption of Aitna in *Pythian 1* is more than an impressive opening: the basic imagery of it continues to appear throughout the ode. The ideas that are developed in the ode do not seem to coincide with this imagery at any point, at least not rigidly. However, Typhon comes into the ode as an example of a being who has a specifically hostile reaction to music, the art of Pindar. Pindar's poetic hurling of the javelin later in the ode places him in counterpoint to Typhon: there is the same general activity of throwing, but its motivation is entirely different. This does not explain the ode, but it does afford a view that at least partially satisfies our need to find sense, unity, coherence, in what we read.

The coherence of a Pindaric ode also is hard to perceive because a host of particular details are involved in it. One needs to know facts about the victor, about his family, his ancestral past, his city, his athletic specialty, for the linguistic transformation of these facts in the ode is one of the most poetic things about it. It would be convenient if we could dispense with the facts, but that would be to violate the very nature of the poetry. Long before Ezra Pound declared it the translator's duty to "make" the poem he is translating "new," Friedrich Nietzsche, in *The Gay Science*, spoke with enviable abandon of the freedom enjoyed by Roman poets "making new" the works of the Greeks:

> . . . What was it to them that the real creator had experienced this and that and written the signs of it into his poem? As poets, they had no sympathy for the antiquarian inquisitiveness that precedes the historical sense; as poets, they had no time for all those very personal things and names and whatever might be considered the costume and mask of a city, a coast, or a century: quickly, they replaced it with what was contemporary and Roman. They seem to ask us: "Should we not make new for ourselves what is old and find ourselves in it? Should we not have the right to breathe our own soul into this dead body? For it is dead after all; how ugly is everything dead!" They did not know the delights of the historical sense; what was past and alien was an embarrassment for them; and being Romans, they saw it as an incentive for a Roman conquest. Not only did one omit what was historical; one also added allusions to the present and, above all, struck out the name of the poet and replaced it with one's own—not with any sense of theft but with the very best conscience of the *imperium Romanum.*[56]

The translator of Pindar, like the translator of any poet, must "make it new"—he must find a way of making Pindar modern; but he must do so within the limitations that are binding for Pindar alone. To disregard the names and places that Pindar took care to weave into the fabric of his poetry would be to destroy it, not to translate it. Similarly, to tamp down Pindar's enthusiasm for his subject, to mute his belief in the significance of human life might be to adapt his poetry better to our own times, but it would also be to betray it. The temptation may be great, for of all the poetry we know, there is none more alien to the modern spirit than that written in the so-called Pindaric tradition. And yet that tradition is mostly counterfeit. Centuries of misunderstanding have caused Pindar to be criticized *and* admired for the wrong reasons. Because his language is as majestic as his meaning is hard to follow, he has gradually come to be a byword for the mysterious or the monotonous sublime. Sublimity in Pindar's Greek is tempered by conciseness and austerity, qualities he should also have in English if he is to resemble himself in his new guise.

Translating Pindar, then, has its special problems; but there is also a sense in which translating Pindar is no different from translating any poet: translating poetry at all seems to involve an inevitable frustration, felt by anyone who tries it. "There is," Walter Benjamin observed, "no Muse of translation."[57] What, then, moves the translator to undertake his ultimately impossible task? It has occurred to me that there is a Muse of translation. If I had to give her a name, I would call her Eurydice.

The poetic translator is a kind of Orpheus who descends into the underworld in search of something lost, something he hopes to bring back with him into the light of day, the light of the language he speaks, the language his contemporaries will understand and respond to. Down in the underworld of the foreign language, Eurydice appears to him in all her original beauty. She then follows him in his poetic labors step by step toward the living world, but just at the moment of reentry he looks back at her and loses her again. All that is left of her is a memory, only an impression that he can convey to others—his version, his translation.

Notes

1. For the 1,000 drachma fine, see Eustathius, *Prooemium* 300.12, in A. B. Drachmann, *Scholia Vetera in Pindari Carmina* III (Leipzig, 1927). For the 10,000 drachma fine, see Isocrates, *Antidosis* 166. For the bronze statue of Pindar, see Pausanias I.8.4. The tradition that Pindar studied at Athens may be based on the remark in the *Vita Thomana* 4. 13 that he was the pupil of Lasos of Hermione, which may in turn be a fabrication: see Sir Arthur Pickard-Cambridge, *Dithyramb, Tragedy, and Comedy* (Oxford: Oxford University Press, 1962), p. 14. The *Vita Thomana* appears in A. B. Drachmann's edition of the *Scholia*, Volume I (Leipzig, 1903), pp. 4–7. For recent disenchantment with the biographical-historical interpretation of Pindar and other ancient poets, practiced both in antiquity and in modern times, see Mary R. Lefkowitz, "Pindar's Lives," *Classica et Iberica* (Worcester: College of the Holy Cross, 1975), pp. 71–93; "The Influential Fictions in the *Scholia* to Pindar's *Pythian 8*," *Classical Philology* 70 (1975), pp. 173–85; and "The Poet as Hero," *Classical Quarterly* 28 (1978), pp. 459–69.

2. See *Isthmian 5*. Of the Greeks at Salamis, Plutarch wrote: "Others believed that they saw apparitions, in the shape of armed men, reaching out their hands from the island of Aegina before the Grecian galleys; and supposed they were the Aeacidae, whom they had invoked to their aid before the battle." Plutarch, *The Lives of the Noble Grecians and Romans,* translated by John Dryden and revised by Arthur Hugh Clough, 1864 (reprinted by Random House, Modern Library), p. 143. On the Aiakidai at Salamis, see also Herodotus, VIII. 64; 83–84.

3. Thucydides III. 58; Plutarch *Aristides* 21.

4. In this section, I rely heavily on Jean Irigoin, *Histoire du Texte de Pindare* (Paris: C. Klincksieck, 1952), pp. 1–111.

5. Pausanias IX. 16. 1. Pindar's fragment 36.

6. Eupolis 139K, *Clouds* 1357–58. Contrast the situation in the time of Alcman (and, most likely, Pindar), as described by Hermann Fränkel, *Early Greek Poetry and Philosophy* (New York: Harcourt, Brace, Jovanovich, 1975), p. 160, with note 3.

7. For example, Callicles in Plato's *Gorgias* (484b).

8. Drachmann, *Scholia Vetera in Pindari Carmina*, I. 6–9; 8. 11–13; Pausanias IX. 32. 2. The same miracle occurred to Plato: Lefkowitz, "Pindar's Lives," p. 73, note 8.

9. The dance-song (fragment 105), quoted by Aristophanes (*Birds* 926–30) and by Plato, and *Olympian 1*, quoted by Plato and by Aristotle, may well have formed part of an edition of Pindar published in Athens at the end of the fifth century: Irigoin, *Histoire du Texte de Pindare*, pp. 19–20. See below, note 14.

10. *Olympian 13*, a phrase of which is echoed in Herodotus VIII. 77. See Lewis Richard Farnell, *The Works of Pindar, II: Critical Commentary* (London: Macmillan and Co., 1932), p. 90.

11. *Dream*, Ch. 7.

12. Principles of arrangement in the *Pythians, Nemeans,* and *Isthmians* are discussed by Aimé Puech, *Pindare* (Paris: 1922–23), II: 12–13; III: 10–11; IV: 11–12.

13. Ulrich von Wilamowitz-Moellendorff first proposed the theory in his edition of *Herakles* (Berlin, 1895), I: 185; it is accepted by Farnell, *Critical Commentary*, p. xviii, and others.

14. *Olympian 1*, in *Euthydemus* 304 bc; *Olympian 2*. 30, in *Protagoras* 324 b; *Pythian 3*. 54–58, in *Republic* 408 b; *Isthmian 1*. 2, in *Phaedrus* 227 b. The first three of these are for Sicilian tyrants. Plato may have known them from an edition published at Athens: Irigoin, *Histoire du Texte de Pindare*, p. 18. See above, note 9.

15. The manuscripts are listed in O. Schroeder, *Pindari carmina* (Leipzig, 1900), pp. 6–7.

16. Moschopoulos, Thomas Magister (author of the *Vita Thomana*), and Triklinios.

17. Wilamowitz, *Herakles,* I: 184.

18. Puech, *Pindare,* IV: 11.

19. Ibid.

20. In this section, I rely heavily on Hermann Fränkel (above, note 6). The major ideas are developed in my article, "The Leaves of Triumph and Mortality: Transformation of a Traditional Image in Pindar's *Olympian 12*" in *Transactions of the American Philological Association* 107 (1977): 235–64.

21. *Iliad* 24. 522–33, translated by Robert Fitzgerald (New York: Anchor Press/ Doubleday, 1974), p. 585. Reprinted with the permission of Robert Fitzgerald.

22. *A B C of Reading* (New York: New Directions, 1960), p. 36.

23. *De Compositione Verborum* xxii.

24. *Paian 4*. See Mary R. Lefkowitz, "ΤΩ ΚΑΙ ΕΓΩ: The First Person in Pindar," *Harvard Studies in Classical Philology* 67 (1963): 183–85.

25. In this section, I rely mainly on Bernhard Forssman, *Untersuchungen zur Sprache Pindars* (Wiesbaden: Otto Harrassowitz, 1966).

26. Ibid., pp. 83–85.

27. Epic and lyric: Basil L. Gildersleeve, *Pindar. The Olympian and Pythian Odes* (New York, 1890), p. lxxvii; C. A. M. Fennell, *Pindar. The Olympian and Pythian Odes* (Cambridge, 1893), p. xxxii; Antoine Meillet, *Aperçue d'une Histoire de la Langue Grecque* (Paris: C. Klincksieck, 1975), pp. 208–13; Ulrich von Wilamowitz-Moellendorff, *Pindaros* (Berlin, 1922), pp. 101–3. Basically Dorian: Forssman, *Untersuchungen zur Sprache Pindars*, p. xi; Jacqueline Duchemin, *Pindare. Pythiques* (Paris: Presses Universitaires de France, 1967), p. 11.

28. On the diction of *Pythian 8*, see Mary R. Lefkowitz, "Pindar's *Pythian 8*," *Classical Journal* 72 (1977), pp. 209–21. The first occurrence of the verb is metaphorical (the metaphor taken from the falling of lots).

29. In this section, I rely on A. M. Dale, "The Metrical Units of Greek Verse, I-III," *The Collected Papers of A. M. Dale* (Cambridge: Cambridge University Press, 1969), pp. 41–97.

30. Ibid., pp. 48–50.

31. The chorus may have "set down a foot to a silent long element before these headless initial units." Ibid., p. 68; cf. also p. 77.

32. They are listed in Paul Maas, *Greek Metre,* translated by Hugh Lloyd-Jones (Oxford: Oxford University Press, 1962), p. 54.

33. The one exception is the duplication of meter in *Isthmians 3* and *4*. See the prefaces to these odes.

34. Pratinas in Denys L. Page, *Poetae Melici Graeci* (Oxford: Oxford University Press, 1962), 708.16 (p. 367).

35. Maas, *Greek Metre*, p. 4.

36. Drachmann, *Scholia Vetera in Pindari Carmina*, I: 12. 6–13.

37. But not the kind of word-end permissible before a pause: see Maas, *Greek Metre*, p. 135.

38. *Nemean 8* opens with an Aiolic measure (a pherecratean) and then modulates into dactylo-epitritic for the rest of the ode (Maas, ibid., p. 55). *Olympian 13* begins in Aiolic, modulates into dactylo-epitritic at line 6 of the turn; the stands are in dactylo-epitritic. Pindar thus at times fuses the two systems together. See Dale, "The Metrical Units of Greek Verse," pp. 63–64.

39. In my description of the parts of the victory song and the order of their occurrence, I am much indebted to Richard Hamilton, *Epinikion. General Form in the Odes of Pindar* (The Hague and Paris: Mouton, 1974).

40. See my article, "*Olympian 1.* 8–11: An Epinician Metaphor," *Harvard Studies in Classical Philology* 79 (1975): 59.

41. Readers will note similar expressions of urgency or necessity throughout the odes of Pindar. Victory calls for song, success deserves or demands poetry. Often the word *chreos* (it is *necessary*) occurs in such passages, whence the critical term "*chreos*-motif." It is hard to avoid the implication of constraint or external compulsion in English, but it is lacking in Greek.

42. In my discussion of *Pythian 11*, I follow the lines laid down by David C. Young, *Three Odes of Pindar. A Literary Study of Pythian 11, Pythian 3, and Olympian 7* (Leiden: E. J. Brill, 1968), pp. 1–26.

43. Wilamowitz, *Pindaros*, p. 263 is responsible for popularizing this view. For others who adhere to it, see Young, *Three Odes of Pindar*, p. 7, note 1.

44. Wilamowitz, *Pindaros*, p. 263; Jacqueline Duchemin, *Pindare, Poète et Prophète* (Paris: Société d'Édition Les Belles Lettres, 1955), p. 252, note 1.

45. For a complete reading of this ode, see my article "Convention and Occasion in *Isthmian 2*," *California Studies in Classical Antiquity* 10 (1977): 133–56.

46. *Ode 17*, stanza 1, quoted by Wilamowitz, *Pindaros*, p. 5, and by Gilbert Norwood, *Pindar* (Berkeley: University of California Press, 1945), p. 240.

47. On this entire subject, see Mary R. Lefkowitz, *The Victory Ode* (Park Ridge: Noyes Press, 1976).

48. Quoted by Rudolf Pfeiffer, *History of Classical Scholarship from the Beginnings to the End of the Hellenistic Age* (Oxford: Oxford University Press, 1968), p. 205.

49. *Pindaric Odes*, Preface. Samuel Taylor Coleridge put Cowley's dictum to the test and found it wanting. See *Biographia Literaria*, chapter xviii.

50. Cowper's ode is conveniently printed in *English Augustan Poetry*, edited and introduced by Paul Fussell (New York: Anchor Books, 1972), pp. 561–63.

51. *The Classical Tradition* (New York: Oxford University Press, 1949), p. 242.

52. See Mary R. Lefkowitz, "Pindar's *Nemean 11*," *Journal of Hellenic Studies* 99 (1979).

53. "How to Read," *The Literary Essays of Ezra Pound* (New York: New Directions, 1968), p. 25.

54. A. E. Housman's *Fragment of a Greek Tragedy*, though not a translation, gives a good idea of what can happen when Greek phrases are rendered literally. See *Yale Review* 17 (1928): 414.

55. Pindar only alludes to the pun, as if it were too undignified to be incorporated into his ode: "They founded a stony (*lithinon*) race; and they were called people (*laoi*)." Pindar's disdain of the pun reflects his disdain for the people. I owe my English pun ("people" from "pebbles") to my former teacher, Professor Joseph Fontenrose, *The Classic Myths: A Syllabus* (Berkeley: A. S. U. C. Store, 1964), p. 9.

56. Friedrich Nietzsche, *The Gay Science*, translated, with commentary, by Walter Kaufmann (New York: Vintage Books, 1974), pp. 137–38. Reprinted with the permission of Random House, Inc.

57. Walter Benjamin, "The Task of the Translator," *Delos* 2 (1968): 88. Conveniently available now in Walter Benjamin, *Illuminations*, edited and with an introduction by Hannah Arendt (New York: Schocken Books, 1969).

"to win from her Pisan father the girl Hippodameia."
—*Olympian 1*, 70–71

Red-figured amphora, showing Pelops and Hippodameia. Courtesy, Istituto Centrale per il Catalogo e la Documentazione, Rome.

THE OLYMPIAN ODES

OLYMPIAN 1

Hieron of Syracuse, race for single horse, 476 B.C.

Hieron won the horse race at Delphi in 482 B.C. and again in 478, the year he succeeded to the tyranny of Syracuse. Two years later, at Olympia, he won the same event, with the same horse, Pherenikos ("Victory Bringer"), whose name Pindar mentions early in *Olympian 1.*

The principal theme of the poem appears in its famous opening lines: in every sphere, there is one thing that is supreme. Of the elements, water is best; when it comes to wealth, gold, compared with other possessions, resembles fire at night; in athletic competitions, an Olympian victory will eclipse all others, even as the sun blots out the stars in daytime. The mention of Olympia brings Pindar to another sphere of activity, epinician poetry, which takes its greatest inspiration from the Olympian games. Among Olympian victors, Hieron stands for the highest type, since he is a king. Among poets, Pindar will prove himself the supreme example.

Pindar's claim to distinction in poetry becomes explicit for the first time in the ode with the introduction of the myth. At the opening of the first stand, he refers to Olympia, site of Hieron's victory, as "the land of Pelops." From here it is only a step to the myth of Pelops, the story of his arrival at Olympia and how he came to be tutelary hero there. But Pindar hardly embarks on the myth before he stops, expressing incredulity with regard to at least one feature in the traditional version: Pelops' fabulous ivory shoulder. The original audience of the ode would have known what it was; they might also have felt some alarm at its mention, for it is associated with a grim episode in the legend, the story of how Pelops was dismembered, boiled, and set before the gods at a banquet. Pindar first gives a psychological explanation of how this ugly story came into existence; he then replaces it with a myth of his own making.

The ode concludes with a prayer that Hieron win the chariot race at Olympia. Pindar, who visited Hieron in 476, was probably present at the performance of the ode.

Turn 1

Water is preeminent and gold, like a fire
burning in the night, outshines
all possessions that magnify men's pride.
But if, my soul, you yearn
to celebrate great games,
look no further
for another star
shining through the deserted ether
brighter than the sun, or for a contest
mightier than Olympia—
where the song
has taken its coronal
design of glory, plaited
in the minds of poets
as they come, calling on Zeus' name,
to the rich radiant hall of Hieron (1–11)

Counterturn 1

who wields the scepter of justice in Sicily,
reaping the prime of every distinction.
And he delights in the flare of music,
the brightness of song circling
his table from man to man.
Then take the Dorian lyre
down from its peg
if the beauty of Pisa
and of Pherenikos
somehow
cast your mind
under a gracious spell,
when by the stream
of Alpheos, keeping his flanks
ungrazed by the spur, he sped
and put his lord in the embrace of power— (12–22)

Stand 1

Syracusan knight and king, blazoned
with glory in the land of Pelops:
Pelops, whom earth-cradling Poseidon loved,
since Klotho had taken him
out of the pure cauldron, his ivory shoulder
gleaming in the hearth-light.
Yes! marvels are many, stories
starting from mortals somehow
stretch truth to deception
woven cunningly on the loom of lies. (23–29)

Turn 2

Grace, the very one who fashions every delight
for mortal men, by lending her sheen
to what is unbelievable, often makes it believed.
But the days to come
are the wisest witness.
It is proper for a man
to speak well of the gods—
the blame will be less.
Pelops, I will tell your story
differently from the men of old.
Your father Tantalos
had invited the gods to banquet
in his beloved Sipylos, providing
a stately feast in return
for the feast they had given him.
It was then Poseidon seized you, (30–40)

Counterturn 2

overwhelmed in his mind with desire, and swept you
on golden mares to Zeus' glorious palace
on Olympos, where, at another time, Ganymede came also
for the same passion in Zeus.
But after you had disappeared
and searchers
again and again
returned to your mother
without you, then one of the neighbors,
invidious, whispered
that the gods had sliced you
limb by limb into the fury
of boiling water,
and then they passed
morsels of your flesh
around the table, and ate them. (41–51)

Stand 2

No! I cannot call any of the blessed gods
a savage: I stand apart.
Disaster has often claimed the slanderer.
If ever the watchlords of Olympos
honored a man, this was Tantalos.
But he could not digest
his great bliss—in his fullness he earned the doom
that the father poised above him, the looming
boulder which, in eternal
distraction, he strains to heave from his brow. (52–58)

Turn 3

Such is the misery upon him, a fourth affliction
among three others, because he robbed
the immortals—their nektar and ambrosia,
which had made him deathless,
he stole and gave
to his drinking companions.
But a man who hopes
to hide his doings from the gods
is deluded.
For this they hurled his son Pelops
back among the short-lived
generations of men.
But when he grew
toward the time of bloom
and black down curled on his cheeks,
he thought of a marriage there for his seeking— (59–69)

Counterturn 3

to win from her Pisan father the girl Hippodameia.
Going down by the dim sea,
alone in the dark, he called on the god
of the trident, loud pounding
Poseidon, who appeared
and stood close by.
"If in any way,"
Pelops said to him,
"the gifts of Aphrodite
count in my favor,
shackle the bronze spear of Oinomaos,
bring me on the swiftest chariot
to Elis, and put me
within the reach
of power, for he has slain
thirteen suitors now, and so he delays (70–80)

Stand 3

his daughter's marriage. Great danger
does not come upon
the spineless man, and yet, if we must die,
why squat in the shadows, coddling a bland
old age, with no nobility, for nothing?
As for me, I will undertake this exploit.
And you—I beseech you: let me achieve it."
He spoke, and his words found fulfillment:
the god made him glow with gifts—
a golden chariot and winged horses never weary. (81–87)

Turn 4

He tore the strength from Oinomaos and took
the maiden to his bed.
She bore him six sons, leaders of the people,
intent on prowess.
Now in the bright blood rituals
Pelops has his share, reclining
by the ford of Alpheos.
Men gather at his tomb, near the crowded altar.
The glory of the Olympiads
shoots its rays afar
in his races, where speed
and strength are matched
in the bruise of toil.
But the victor,
for the rest of his life,
enjoys days of contentment, (88–98)

Counterturn 4

as far as contests can assure them.
A single day's blessing
is the highest good a mortal knows.
I must crown him now
to the horseman's tune,
in Aiolian rhythms,
for I believe
the shimmering folds of my song
shall never embrace
a host more lordly in power
or perception of beauty.
Hieron, a god is overseer
to your ambitions, keeping watch,
cherishing them as his own.
If he does not abandon you soon,
still sweeter the triumph I hope (99–109)

Stand 4

will fall to your speeding chariot,
and may I be the one to praise it,
riding up the sunny Hill of Kronos!
The Muse is tempering her mightiest arrow for me.
Men are great in various ways, but in kingship
the ultimate crest is attained.
Peer no farther into the beyond.
For the time we have, may you continue to walk on high,
and may I for as long consort with victors,
conspicuous for my skill among Greeks everywhere. (110–16)

OLYMPIAN 2

Theron of Akragas, chariot race, 476 B.C.

Olympian 2 contains Pindar's longest and most explicit reflections on the fate of the soul after death. The passage, which describes the soul's reincarnations, begins in the third stand and occupies the whole fourth triad. The sentence introducing it is left incomplete. Pindar seems about to draw the conventional conclusion that a man of wealth and success who understands human fate will invest in poetry (see the Introduction, *Pindar's Genre*), but instead the thought of death leads him in another direction.

Theron, tyrant of Akragas, came to power in 488. In 482, he subdued the neighboring town of Himera, whose former ruler appealed to the Carthaginians for help. Two years later Theron, in alliance with Gelon of Syracuse, inflicted a massive defeat on the Carthaginians at the battle of Himera (see the Introduction, *Pindar's Life*). Enormously enriched by the booty of war, Theron set about glorifying Akragas with new buildings whose ruins today are among the most impressive surviving from antiquity. Among Pindar's patrons, Theron was second only to Hieron of Syracuse in wealth and power.

Theron belonged to the clan of the Emmenidai, who traced their descent through Thersandros, son of Polyneikes and Argeia the daughter of Adrastos, all the way back to Kadmos, who founded the city of Thebes and brought the alphabet to Greece. Kadmos' son Polydoros was the father of Labdakos, father of Laios, whose "tragic son," as Pindar refers to him in this ode, was Oedipus, Attic drama's most famous character. Kadmos' daughters were also renowned: Semela became the mother of Dionysos by Zeus; Ino acquired immortality in the sea. Pindar mentions these two in the course of the ode as salient examples of the theme that human life is subject to uncertainty and vicissitude, for both of them suffered before their exaltation.

The poem is dominated by this theme of alternation between good and bad, blessing and disaster, both in the individual's experience of life and in the experience of successive generations. The theme itself may have occurred to Pindar from reflection on the checkered destinies of Theron's forebears, but it is also possible that recent troubles between Theron and Hieron brought it to his mind. See the preface to *Olympian 12.*

The ode begins in typical fashion, with the grand announcement of the victor's name and homeland and the victory to his credit. The opening phrases, echoed by Horace and others, are famous among Pindar's lines: "what god, what hero, what man/shall we celebrate?"

Pindar's triple question immediately receives a triple answer. The last item in the series announces the subject: Theron is the man. He and his ancestors and the vicissitudes of their lives take up the first three triads of the ode. Counterturn 3 contains a reference to the victories of Theron's brother Xenokrates, celebrated by Pindar in *Pythian 6* and *Isthmian 2.*

Turn 1

Songs, lords of the lyre,
what god, what hero, what man
shall we celebrate?
Pisa belongs to Zeus.
Herakles founded the Olympian Games,
firstfruits of war.
And Theron must be proclaimed
for his chariot victory—
Theron, true host of strangers,
bulwark of Akragas, exalter of his city,
noblest scion of noble ancestors (1–7)

Counterturn 1

who suffered much
to win their sacred home
by the river, and they became
the light of Sicily,
their fated course
bringing wealth and honor
to match their inborn greatness.
But O Kronian son of Rhea,
lord of Olympos' throne,
of Alpheos' crossing and the greatest of contests:
moved by my song, preserve their native land to them (8–14)

Stand 1

and their posterity.
What has been done
with justice or without
not even time the father of all
can undo.
But with good luck
oblivion may come, for malignant pain
perishes in noble joy, confounded (15–20)

Turn 2

whenever a fate from the gods
raises
happiness on high.
So the royal daughters of Kadmos
suffered greatly,
but their sorrows
fell before mightier blessings.
Long-haired Semela, dying
in the thunder-roar,
lives among the Olympians, beloved of Pallas and Zeus
and ever beloved of Dionysos, her son, (21–27)

Counterturn 2

and they say that in the sea
with the daughters of Nereus
for all time
imperishable life embraces Ino.
Truly, mortals have no way
of knowing the bounds of death,
nor even whether we shall finish
a day, a sun's child,
with cheer unblemished.
The shifting tides of good and evil
beat incessantly upon mankind. (28–34)

Stand 2

Thus the fate that guards the ancestral fortune
of these men, bringing them happiness secured
by the gods,
has also sent them affliction, sure
to abate in its turn,
from the moment
Laios' tragic son, crossing his father's path,
killed him
and fulfilled the oracle spoken of old at Pytho. (35–40)

Turn 3

And sharp-eyed Erinys saw and slew
his warlike children
at each other's hands.
Yet Thersandros survived
fallen Polyneikes and won honor
in youthful contests
and the brunt of war, a scion of aid
to the house of Adrastos;
and his seed lives on
in Theron, son of Ainesidamos, who deserves
to enjoy the lyre and the song of praise. (41–47)

Counterturn 3

For he himself took the prize at Olympia,
while at Pytho and Isthmos too
kindred Graces brought his brother,
paired with him in destiny, garlands
for the four horses driven
twelve times around the post.
A man forgets the strain of contending
when he triumphs.
And wealth, uplifted by nobility,
gives scope for actions of every kind,
kindling the heart with zeal for achievement, (48–54)

Stand 3

a star far-seen, a man's truest beacon-light.
And if, possessing it, one knows what must befall—
that of those who die here, the arrogant
are punished without delay,
for someone under the earth
weighs transgressions in this realm of Zeus,
and there is iron compulsion in his word. (55–60)

Turn 4

But with equal nights
and equal days,
possessing the sun forever,
the noble enjoy an easy existence, troubling
neither earth nor the sea's waters
in might of hand
for an empty living,
but with the gods they honored, all
who delighted in oath-keeping
abide free of affliction, while the others
go through pain not to be looked at. (61–67)

Counterturn 4

And those who have endured
three times in either realm
to keep their souls untainted
by any injustice, travel
Zeus' road to the tower of Kronos,
where ocean-born breezes blow around
the island of the blest
and sprays of gold flower
from the earth and from the sea—
with these they wreathe their hands
and crown their heads, (68–74)

Stand 4

obeying the high decrees of Rhadamanthys,
who sits, a ready companion, beside
the great Father, consort of Rhea throned on high.
Among them dwell the heroes Peleus and Kadmos
and Achilleus, whom Thetis, moving Zeus' heart with prayer,
brought to their company, her son (75–80)

Turn 5

who smote Hektor to the ground, Troy's
invincible, unyielding bastion,
and consigned to death
Kyknos and Memnon, child of the Dawn.
There are in my quiver
many swift arrows, striking
to the wise, but the crowd need interpreters.
The man of discernment
knows much by nature.
Let those who have acquired their knowledge
chatter in vain, unruly jackdaws bickering (81–87)

Counterturn 5

at the majestic eagle of Zeus.
It is time we took aim, my heart:
whom are we hitting
again, letting fly
the arrows of glory
from the string of gentle thoughts?
Aiming at you, Akragas,
I swear with true mind,
no city in a hundred years
has reared a man more liberal in thought
or lavish of hand (88–94)

Stand 5

than Theron.
But praise falls in with surfeit
and is muted, not in justice
but because of boisterous men, whose noise
would obscure beauty,
for sands cannot be counted,
and how many joys
this man has brought his fellows,
who can say? (95–100)

OLYMPIAN 3

Theron of Akragas, chariot race, 476 B.C.

Olympian 3 celebrates the same occasion as *Olympian 2.* The ode is dominated by the presence of "the sons of Tyndareus," worshipped as heroes among the Dorian peoples in antiquity. Today they are best known as the Twins, the Gemini of the Zodiac. They were not precisely "sons of Tyndareus," since Tyndareus was the father of only one, the mortal brother Kastor; Polydeukes, the immortal twin, was sired by Zeus. Their mother, Leda, gave birth to them together. Their place in this ode is due to the honor they still enjoyed at Olympia in Theron's day. According to Pindar, Herakles, founder of the Olympian games, had entrusted the care of the games to the "sons of Tyndareus" as he passed on his way to Olympos to become a god. As tutelary heroes at Olympia, they have had something to do with Theron's success there.

In the opening lines of the ode, Pindar prays to please these "sons of Tyndareus" and their sister Helen by his discovery of a new mode of song. We cannot tell exactly what newness is meant. Almost immediately, Pindar moves to the glorification of the victor. He dwells on one of its most important features, the crowning at the games. Nowhere else in the odes does Pindar render this event so clearly and in so much detail, and he has a reason for doing so here: the Olympian victor's triumphal garland of olive leaves is the starting point for the myth of this ode, which tells how Herakles brought the olive tree to Olympia from the far north.

Most of Herakles' labors took him far and wide. On one of them, according to Pindar, he had gone all the way to the land of the Hyperboreans, Apollo's people who lived, as their name implies, "beyond Boreas," the north wind (see *Pythian 10*). At the time he journeyed there, Herakles was in pursuit of a golden-horned doe sacred to "Leto's child," Artemis. It had been dedicated to the goddess by the girl Taÿgeta. Herakles' pursuit of it brought him to the region of the Danube, where he saw for the first time a forest of olive trees, and marveled at their beauty. Later, when he had founded the Olympian games, he remembered that beautiful olive forest far to the north, for the field at Olympia had as yet no forest of its own. So Herakles undertook a second journey to the north and returned with the olive whose leaves now shade Olympia and decorate the brows of its victors.

The only potential difficulty for the reader in the mythic portion of this ode is the chronological sequence followed by Pindar. He moves backward in time from a fixed moment, and then suddenly returns to it, bringing the story full circle.

The ode concludes with praises of Theron and his family, the Emmenidai. In particular, Pindar singles out their lavish hospitality and their devotion to the gods. The gods in question are, again, "the sons of Tyndareus." There is an echo here of the opening of *Olympian 1*, with its focus on water and gold.

Turn 1

I pray that I may please Tyndareus' gracious sons
and lovely-haired Helen
as I sing of glorious Akragas,
raising the Olympian victory hymn
in honor of Theron and his thunder-hoofed horses.
For so the Muse stood at my side
when I discovered this new mode of song,
the shine still in its fabric:
voice and Dorian sandal fitted together for the dance (1–5)

Counterturn 1

of splendor. For the garlands placed on Theron's brow
have put me under a spell
of sacred obligation, to make
the lyre's varied voices,
the chorus of the flutes,
and the rhythm of my verses harmonize,
and Pisa also
moves me to sing, Pisa
where song, the gift of a god, comes to men (6–10)

Stand 1

whenever the Aitolian judge, performing
Herakles' ancient behests,
raises his unerring hand
over a man's head
and places on his hair the silver-gray
adornment of olive
that Amphitryon's son
once brought from shadowy springs
of the Danube, to be the most
beautiful trophy of contests at Olympia: (11–15)

Turn 2

Herakles, who had won Apollo's men,
the Hyperboreans,
by his appeal, requesting,
in devotion to his father,
a gift for Zeus' grove, open to all:
an olive shoot to shade the crowds and crown the winners.
Already had the Moon at midmonth
made the whole eye of evening
shine upon him from her golden car, (16–20)

Counterturn 2

and he had set up the sacred judgment of the contests
and the five-year festival
upon the hallowed banks of Alpheos—
but the ground in the valley
of Kronian Pelops had not yet put forth
its radiant forest, and naked of that
the garden seemed to him
defenseless against the sun's sharp rays,
and his heart stirred to convey him (21–25)

Stand 2

back to the Danube
where Leto's daughter,
driver of horses, once had received him
when he came from Arkadia's cliffs
and from its winding recesses
under compulsion from Zeus
and Eurystheus' dispatches, to catch
and bring away the golden-horned doe
that once Taÿgeta had dedicated
Sacred to Artemis Orthosia. (26–30)

Turn 3

And in pursuit of her he saw that land
behind the gusts of icy Boreas,
and stood in amazement at its trees.
Longing came upon him
to plant them around the post at the end
of his racecourse, circled twelve times
by the chariot-teams.
And now to this feast he comes in good cheer
with the twin sons of slim-waisted Leda. (31–35)

Counterturn 3

For to them he entrusted the care
of the contests of men
and the swift cars of the racing
as he went on his way to Olympos.
And so my heart moves me to say
glory has come to the Emmenidai and Theron
as a gift from those horsemen,
the sons of Tyndareus, whom they revere
more than any, at the tables of friendship, (36–40)

Stand 3

guarding the rites of the blest
with pious minds.
                    If water is preeminent,
if gold of all possessions
is most treasured, Theron has journeyed
to the world's end and grasped
the Pillars of Herakles
in his success.
                    What lies beyond
neither the wise nor the unwise can explore.
Let the fool attempt it. I will not. (41–45)

OLYMPIAN 4

Psaumis of Kamarina, chariot race, 452 B.C., or mule car race, 460 (?) B.C.

Psaumis has left virtually no other impression than the one recorded in Pindar's fourth and fifth Olympian odes, and even that impression is vague. His city was Kamarina; his father's name was Akron. These two facts alone emerge from the odes themselves; other essential details have to be guessed at. *Olympian 4*, for example, contains no clear indication of the victory being celebrated. Some ancient and some modern scholars have identified it as a chariot victory gained in 452. If this is the case, *Olympian 5* would seem to have been written for a later victory gained in the mule car. Others take both poems as celebrations of the same event, a victory in the mule car race in approximately 460 B.C.

The ode falls neatly into three divisions, corresponding to its triadic structure. The turn addresses Zeus, god of the Olympian festival and conqueror of Typhon (see the preface to *Pythian 1*). The counterturn introduces Psaumis, honored by Zeus with victory in the Olympian games. Pindar praises him for his hospitality and his civic virtue, expressed by his devotion to Hesychia, goddess of Concord. The stand illustrates by means of a brief myth the maxim with which the counterturn concludes.

The myth has to do with a certain Erginos, son of Klymenos. Erginos was an Argonaut, one of those who sailed aboard the fabulous Argo to fetch the Golden Fleece (see the preface to *Pythian 4*). The Argo had put in at the island of Lemnos, either when it was on its way to get the fleece, or when it was bound for home. While Erginos was with the Argonauts on Lemnos, he competed in athletic games, specifically, the race in full armor (see *Pythian 4*, 247–61). Before the race began, however, his gray hair evoked the ridicule of the Lemnian women, who were looking on. Erginos then won the race and claimed his crown.

Turn

Zeus, driver of thunder-hoofed horses
riding with ceaseless crash
across the sky, yours
are the Seasons
whose wheeling courses
send me abroad
with song, with intricate tunes on the lyre,
my theme the greatest of contests.
When friends succeed, good men hear the news
as a hound hears its master's step.
Son of Kronos, you who keep
dark-hearted, hundred-headed Typhon
trapped beneath the windy wrack of Aitna,
welcome this band of revellers
for the Graces' sake,
welcome their song of Olympian triumph, (1–9)

Counterturn

the long-enduring radiance
of mighty prowess.
For Psaumis' friends have come
praising him, the charioteer
crowned with Pisan olive
and eager to waken
glory for Kamarina.
May the gods favor his future prayers,
repaying his readiness
in raising horses, his delight
in hospitality to all,
and his regard
for Hesychia, guardian of cities.
I will not stain what I say
with a lie.
Performance proves the man. (10–18)

Stand

So the son of Klymenos silenced
the Lemnian women's laughter.
Victorious
in the race run in bronze armor,
he said to Queen Hypsipyleia
as he went for his crown:
"This is the man I am
for speed; my hands and my heart
are just as good.
Gray hair often grows
on young men too, belying their real age." (19–27)

OLYMPIAN 5

Psaumis of Kamarina, mule car race, 460 (?) B.C.

Kamarina, founded by colonists from Syracuse in approximately 600 B.C., was destroyed by her mother city for asserting her freedom some fifty years later. For approximately another half century, she lay in ruins (though there is record of an Olympian victor, Eponymos, presenting himself as a citizen of Kamarina at the games in 528 B.C.). Her second foundation, shortly after 492 B.C., she owed to Hippokrates, tyrant of Gela, one of Kamarina's more powerful neighbors, engaged at the time in a struggle with Syracuse. After his victory at the battle of the Heloros river (see the preface to *Nemean 9*), Hippokrates took the site of Kamarina from the control of Syracuse and set about rebuilding the city. But her new lease on life was not to last long. A few years later, when Gelon became tyrant of Syracuse, he determined to make his new seat of power as great as possible. He forced one-half the population of Gela to relocate to Syracuse. Two other Sicilian cities, Megara and Euboia, also had to contribute citizens to swell the population of the new center. Kamarina suffered even more: all her people were uprooted and transplanted. For the second time, in 485 B.C., she lay desolate. Some time after 461 she was restored again. Her restoration is alluded to in *Olympian 5.*

The ode consists of three triads. The first addresses Kamarina, the second Athena, and the third Zeus. The praises of Psaumis are fairly evenly distributed throughout. In the first triad, he appears as Olympian victor. His success has brought glory to Kamarina, whose varying fortunes are suggested by the phrase that concludes the triad: "his city, risen again." In the second triad, Psaumis arrives at Kamarina, praising Athena as Pallas Polias, the goddess who kept the city in her care. A number of Kamarina's local features are then enumerated: the river Oanos, the lake for which Kamarina was named, and then, as we enter the counterturn, the river Hipparis. Kamarina was situated on a hill between the mouths of these two rivers. The counterturn ends with a reference to the rebuilding of Kamarina and a phrase suggesting her restoration from ruin. In the final triad, Zeus the Savior is invoked and beseeched on behalf of the city and her victorious son.

Olympian 5 is the only ode among Pindar's surviving victory songs whose authenticity has been doubted. The dispute begins with a notice in the ancient commentaries, to the effect that *Olympian 5* did not appear in the *edaphia.* No one knows exactly what is meant by *edaphia*, the diminutive of *edapha*, manuscripts or the text of manuscripts as opposed to their margins. We are certain, however, that Didymus, a scholar who lived in the first century A.D., had *Olympian 5* in his text of Pindar.

Turn 1

Receive, daughter of Okeanos,
the fairest reward of lofty achievements
and of garlands gained at Olympia—
the gift of Psaumis and his mule car
drawn by undaunted hooves:
graciously receive it, (1–3)

Counterturn 1

Kamarina, whose town he exalted
at the greatest
of all festal gatherings, with sacrifice
at the six double altars,
and in the whirling races
of the fifth day, (4–6)

Stand 1

the chariot, the mules, the single horse.
Victorious, he has secured
luxuriant renown
for you,
having his father Akron acclaimed
together with his city, risen again. (7–8)

Turn 2

He comes from the lovely grounds
of Oinomaos and of Pelops,
singing, Pallas Polias,
of your sacred wood,
of the stream Oanos
and the lake nearby, (9–11)

Counterturn 2

of Hipparis, whose channels
bring pure water to this city;
raising her houses as a lofty grove,
he swiftly lifts his people
back into the light
from their ruin. (12–14)

Stand 2

Always, in the contest for excellence,
expense and labor
struggle to achieve an exploit
whose end
lies veiled in danger—though the public
thinks it sees wisdom in success. (15–16)

Turn 3

Zeus, savior in the high clouds,
dweller on the Hill of Kronos,
glory of broad Alpheos
and Ida's sacred cave,
        to the music of Lydian flutes
            I come, beseeching you (17–19)

Counterturn 3

to adorn this town
in the splendor of her brave men—
and may you, Psaumis,
who look with joy
        on the steeds of Poseidon,
            bring your life to completion (20–22)

Stand 3

in good cheer, with your sons
standing beside you.
If the wealth a man tends and cares for
be sound,
        his house ample, and his name renowned as well,
            let him not envy the gods. (23–24)

OLYMPIAN 6

Hagesias of Syracuse, mule car race, 468 (?) B.C.

Hagesias, son of Sostratos, was a Syracusan, friend and ally of Hieron. He also belonged to Stymphalos, a town in Arkadia. Through his maternal ancestors, he traced his lineage back to the Arkadian hero Iamos, son of Apollo. The Iamidai or descendants of Iamos were hereditary priests of Zeus' oracular altar at Olympia (see the opening of *Olympian 8*). Hence, Pindar refers to Hagesias at the opening of the ode as both a victor and a seer. This double praise reminds Pindar of the mythical hero Amphiaraos, famed warrior prophet who participated, with Adrastos, in the expedition of the Seven against Thebes. When the siege was over, Zeus caused the earth to open and swallow Amphiaraos before he could suffer disgrace in battle (see *Nemean 9*, stanzas 5 and 6). Later Adrastos described the virtues of Amphiaraos, honored as a hero in Thebes, with the formula "a good prophet, and a good fighter." Pindar applies the formula to Hagesias, who, according to the ancient commentary on the ode, saw many a military campaign in the service of Hieron, who is mentioned at the close.

At the start of the second triad, Pindar calls on Phintis, the man who drove Hagesias' mule car to victory. He bids him yoke the winning mules together for yet another ride, a poetic ride from the opening of the ode to its mythical section. The mule car race was the least prestigious event at Olympia. Pindar contrives to mention it less as an achievement in its own right than as a transition to something else. The place to which the poeticized mules take us is the town Pitana, connected, in the myth that follows, with the origins of the victor's clan. But the town quickly changes into the girl for whom it was named, and with that the myth begins.

The myth beginning with Pitana has a dual purpose: to trace the ancestry of Hagesias back to Apollo, and to explain how his clan, the descendants of Iamos, came to be seers of Zeus' altar at Olympia. In the course of the myth occur two puns on the name Iamos. In the third turn, Pindar says that the infant Iamos was fed "the blameless venom"—*io amemphei*—of the bees. The expression, a kenning for honey, is due to the similarity between the Greek word for venom, *ios*, and Iamos' name. A second, more important and less translatable pun derives from the Greek word *ia*, the violets among which Iamos is discovered five days after his birth. It is from these *ia* that he is called *Ia*mos.

With the birth of Iamos, Pindar has traced the ancestry of the clan of the Iamidai back to Apollo. The genealogy is as follows:

Pitana—Poseidon
|
Evadna—Apollo
|
Iamos
|
The Iamidai
|
Hagesias

One of the peculiarities of the ode is the manner in which Pindar involves himself in the victor's praises. He fashions a genealogical link between his own city, Thebes in Boiotia, and Stymphalos in Arkadia, seat of the victor's maternal ancestors. "My maternal grandmother's a Stymphalid," he says, relying on the connection between Metopa, a nymph from Stymphalos, and her daughter Theba, the goddess for whom Thebes was named. (See the Introduction, *Style and the Pindaric Tradition.*) Also, Pindar seems facetiously proud of his accomplishment in weaving the various strands of this ode together. In the last turn, he exhorts the chorus leader, Aineas, to say whether, by the truth of his words, he has once and for all escaped the proverbial slander against Boiotia as a place fit only for swine to inhabit.

Turn 1

As when we build a shining palace,
raising its portal on golden columns,
so now we must make radiant
the entrance to our song.
If it's to praise
an Olympian victor,
one of those who reared
illustrious Syracuse, a prophet
of Zeus' mantic altar in Pisa,
what glory will he miss,
if only he finds
his people open to delightful music? (1–7)

Counterturn 1

Let the son of Sostratos know
his is the foot
destined for this sandal.
A deed done without danger,
hand to hand
or aboard the hollow ships,
lacks glory, but men remember
if someone dares and wins.
Hagesias, yours is the praise Adrastos spoke
for Amphiaraos, Oïkles' prophet son,
when the ground
had swallowed him and his gleaming horses. (8–14)

Stand 1

The seven pyres had smouldered for the dead,
when the son of Talaos, later, in Thebes
spoke, saying: "I miss the eye of my army,
a good prophet, and a good fighter."
The same words fit
this triumphal Syracusan.
Though I am neither
quarrelsome nor fond of controversy, I will say it
clearly, swearing a heavy oath—
and the sweet-voiced Muses will allow me. (15–21)

Turn 2

But come, Phintis! bridle those mighty mules of yours
as fast as you can, so I may mount the chariot, drive
on the clear road, and reach,
at last, the source of this clan.
For they know the way
better than others,
having won
crowns at Olympia.
We must fling the gates of song
open before them
and arrive on schedule
today, at Eurotas' crossing, home of Pitana, (22–28)

Counterturn 2

who lay with Poseidon once and bore
Evadna, violet-braided girl.
Unwed, her mother had hidden
the pain in her womb
until the ninth month, then sent
attendants, bidding them give her baby
to Aipytos, son of Elatos,
lord of Arkadians in Phaisana,
with Alpheos in his dominion.
There Evadna was reared,
and there for the first time,
in Apollo's arms, she knew the sweetness of Aphrodite, (29–35)

Stand 2

but could not hide the fruit of the god's seed
until the end:
Aipytos saw and went to Delphi
to consult Apollo, suppressing with keen determination
the unutterable anger in his heart,
while she
unloosed her purple-threaded belt, put down
in the blue shade of the wood
her silver urn, and bore a godly boy.
Gold-haired Apollo made Eleithyia and the Moirai attend on her.
(36–42)

Turn 3

Without delay, in welcome labor, Iamos
came from her womb into the light.
In her distress, she left him there
on the ground.
A pair of gray-eyed serpents,
by the gods' will,
took care of him,
fed him the bees' inviolate honey.
And the king driving from Delphi's cliffs
returned,
asking all in the house
for the boy Evadna bore: "He is Apollo's son (43–49)

Counterturn 3

and will be a seer preeminent
for mortal men.
Never will his race fail."
So the king declared, but they
swore they had neither heard
nor seen
the five-days' child.
No wonder, for he lay hidden
amid tall grass and forbidding brambles,
his delicate body bathed
in the yellow
and deep blue rays of violets, from which his mother (50–56)

Stand 3

then named him Iamos, a name immortal forever.
And when Hebe downed his cheeks in gold
he waded midstream in Alpheos, called
through the clear night air on his grandfather Poseidon
and on Apollo, asking
an honor to sustain his race.
Quickly his father's voice replied: "Rise,
my son, and come this way
toward my voice, to a place open to all." (57–63)

Turn 4

They climbed the steep rock front of Kronos' Hill.
There Apollo gave him
a double share of prophecy:
to hear at that time
the voice of truth, and then—
when bold Herakles,
mighty scion of the Alkidai,
had come and founded
the Olympian festival, the games
that draw men in throngs—
he would become
priest on the height of Zeus' oracular altar. (64–70)

Counterturn 4

From that day, the descendants of Iamos
are famous throughout Greece,
and prosperity has followed upon them.
Pursuing honor, they walk in the light.
Their deeds bear them witness.
The envious censure of others
lurks on the sidelines, whenever
someone rounds the twelfth turn
in first place, and Grace sheds
the gleam of glory about him.
Yet if, in truth, Hagesias,
your mother's family dwells in Kyllana's foothills, (71–77)

Stand 4

if with frequent prayer and burnt offerings
they honor Hermes, god of contests
and prizes in heroic Arkadia: then he,
O son of Sostratos, and the thunder-father
secure your good luck.
The flute's whistling note
puts me in mind of a shrill whetstone that hones my speech
for what I'll say, pierced with enthusiasm:
the mother of my mother was from Stymphalos, blossoming Metopa,
(78–84)

Turn 5

mother of horse-riding Theba,
from whose delightful springs I drink
as I plait the intricate
song for spearmen.
Rouse your comrades,
Aineas, and sing first
of Hera Parthenia, and then say
whether by our words we thrust
that old insult *Boiotian sow*
aside,
for you're a trusty messenger, bearer
of the Muses' code, sweet bowl of thunderous songs. (85–91)

Counterturn 5

Pour out a word for Syracuse
and Ortygia, where Hieron is king,
with radiant scepter and straight counsels,
priest of red-sandaled Demeter,
of her girl
borne on white horses,
and of Aitnaian Zeus.
Harps and lyrics know him.
May time to come never disturb his bliss.
And may he welcome
to the feast
Hagesias' reveling friends as they come (92–98)

Stand 5

from home to home, leaving behind the walls
of Stymphalos, their mother Arkadia, nurse of flocks.
On a winter's night, two anchors
best secure the ship.
May the god in his favor
give glory to both these cities.
Lord of the sea, husband of Amphitrita
with her golden distaff, grant a safe journey
to them and new bloom to the song they carry. (99–105)

OLYMPIAN 7

Diagoras of Rhodes, boxing, 464 B.C.

The ancestors of Diagoras were Dorians who emigrated from Argos to Rhodes under the leadership of Tlapolemos, son of Herakles, through whom they traced their genealogy back to Zeus:

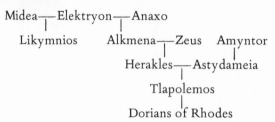

```
Midea—Elektryon—Anaxo
  Likymnios      Alkmena—Zeus    Amyntor
                   Herakles—Astydameia
                        Tlapolemos
                     Dorians of Rhodes
```

In the course of *Olympian* 7, Pindar tells a triple myth, each phase of which concerns events from the past of Rhodes. The progress of the story is backward in time: Pindar begins with the most recent event, the colonization of the island; he then recounts the birth of Athena, which had occurred there earlier; and finally he describes the birth of the island itself.

The myth is one of Pindar's deliberately corrected versions (see, for example, *Olympian 1*), differing in several details from the traditional story as we find it in Homer (*Iliad 2.* 653–70) and other sources. Among Pindar's alterations of the story perhaps the most significant are the mention of Tlapolemos' wrath as the specific reason for his murder of his grand-uncle Likymnios, son of Elektryon and his concubine Midea; and the role assigned to the oracle of Delphi in the colonization of Rhodes.

The Rhodians were famed for their artistic skill. Pindar praises them for it in the course of the poem, but in such a manner as to suggest that he is altering popular tradition here as well. He places all the emphasis on the heritage enjoyed by the Rhodians as descendants of Helios, the Sun God, and on the favor they enjoy from Athena, patroness of arts and crafts. Tradition, however, associated Rhodian artistic skill with the Telchines, mythical magicians who emerged from the sea together with Rhodes. They were wonderfully skilled in metal work and other crafts, but evil in character. Pindar alludes to them in his assertion that superior skill is guileless (stand 3).

In the section describing the birth of the island, the reader should bear in mind that the Greek word for Rhodes also means "rose." Pindar takes advantage of this double meaning, as indeed the Rhodians themselves seem to have done by stamping their coins with the device of the rose. The flower was an emblem of the island itself. "Rhodes" also designates the nymph who dwelled on the island, bride of Helios and mother of his seven children, the ancestors of the original Rhodians living on the island before the arrival of Tlapolemos and his Dorian settlers.

One or two details regarding Rhodes itself and the victor's lineage appear in the final lines. Atabyrion is a Rhodian mountain. In his concluding prayer, Pindar beseeches Zeus, god of Mount Atabyrion, not to obscure the seed of Kallianax, one of the forebears of Diagoras. The "sons of Eratos," mentioned next, are the clan to which Diagoras belonged.

Olympian 7 was dedicated in gold letters in the temple of Athena in the Rhodian city of Lindos. It was thus once literally worth its weight in gold.

Turn 1

Even as a man who takes a golden bowl,
his best possession,
brimming with the froth
of wine inside it,
and gives it
with lavish hand
to his new son-in-law,
toasting him from home to home,
honoring the party and the groom
and making him,
seated among friends,
enviable for the harmony of his bridal bed—
(1–6)

Counterturn 1

so I, sending a stream of nektar,
the gift of the Muses,
the sweet yield of my mind,
offer libation for Olympian
and Pythian victors.
Blest is the one
on whom such praises shower.
Grace that makes life blossom
shines now on one man,
now on another
as the lyre strums
in harmony with the flute's manifold voices. (7–12)

Stand 1

Listen! To the music of both instruments
I have come with Diagoras, singing
Aphrodite's sea-child, the bride of Helios,
Rhodes,
that I might glorify him for his boxing—
a man prodigious, eager for the fray,
who had himself crowned beside the Alpheos
and by Kastalia—
and glorify his father,
champion of Justice, Damagetos,
dwelling with Argive spearmen
on the triple-citied island
over against the cape of spacious Asia. (13–19)

Turn 2

For them, the descendants of Herakles
in their wide strength,
I will set right
the traditional story, going back
to the beginning,
with Tlapolemos.
They boast Zeus at their root
from the male stem,
Amyntor on the mother's,
Astydameia's, side.
Yet over men's minds
the clouds of countless errors hover— (20–25)

Counterturn 2

it is impossible to know what happens
for the best, now, or in the end.
In Tiryns once, this city's founder,
furious, with a club
of gnarled olive wood
battered to death
Alkmena's bastard brother
Likymnios, as he came
from Midea's room.
Disturbance of mind has turned
even a wise man astray.
He went for consultation to the god. (26–31)

Stand 2

From within the fragrant sanctuary,
Apollo of the golden hair declared
a voyage from Lerna's rugged coast
to a land
with the sea all around it,
where once the gods' great King
had drenched a city in snowing gold—
it was after
Hephaistos with the edge of his bronze axe
had tapped Zeus' brow and up
from her father's head Athenaia vaulted
with a huge shout.
The heavens
and mother Earth trembled before her. (32–38)

Turn 3

And then it was that the god, Hyperion's son
and carrier of light to men,
told his children how to claim for themselves
her future rites:
"Be first to build the goddess
a shining altar,
and burn a sacred offering
to gladden Zeus' heart
and hers, the spear-bolt
in her hand."
Care born of forethought puts
success and joy within men's reach
(39–44)

Counterturn 3

and yet, unlooked for, oblivion
comes, a cloud stealing
knowledge of the right way
from their minds—
and so it was with them:
they went up
but left the seed of blazing fire
behind—with flameless rites, then,
they founded her mountain grove.
Zeus gathered a blond cloud and rained
deep gold upon them,
and the bright-eyed goddess gave them (45–50)

Stand 3

all art, to outshine mankind in the yield
of their hands' skill.
Their avenues bore works that seemed to breathe and move,
and their glory was exalted,
for in the master-craftsman even
superior cunning has no guile.
Ancient stories tell us
that when Zeus and the gods
were allotting the world,
Rhodes was not yet visible on the ocean surface—
it lay hidden,
an island in the briny depths. (51–57)

Turn 4

And Helios was absent—no one assigned him a portion,
he was left without a place,
even he, the sacred god.
Then at his complaint
Zeus would have cast the lots
a second time,
but Helios forbade it,
saying he had seen
within the gray depths, growing
from the sea's floor, an island
that would be
rich in nurture for men and kindly to their flocks.
(55–63)

Counterturn 4

He told Lachesis, garlanded in gold, to raise her hands
and swear never to break
the gods' great oath,
but nod assent with Zeus
that once Rhodes
had broken through
to bright air,
it would be his prize.
He spoke, and what he said
came, in truth,
to fulfillment:
the sea's glittering furrows put forth (64–69)

Stand 4

the island,
and now the father, source of piercing light
and master of fire-breathing horses,
has her for his own.
He mingled in love with Rhodes
and sired seven sons
whose minds were subtler
than any of that day.
Of the seven, one sired Kamiros,
another Lindos, and a third Ialysos, the oldest.
These divided their paternal land in three
and ruled each apart,
and each seat bears its founder's name. (70–76)

Turn 5

Here Tlapolemos, fleeing Tiryns,
found redemption from his bitter sorrow.
Here to this day
in honor of him
sheep are sacrificed
as to a god,
and here his games are held,
in whose flowers
Diagoras has crowned himself twice,
winner at Isthmos too,
and time after time
at Nemea and rocky Athens. (77–82)

Counterturn 5

The bronze at Argos and the prizes
given in Arkadia and Thebes knew him,
the contests of the Boiotians,
Pellana and Aigina,
where he won
six times.
The stone tablets in Megara
tell no other story.
But O father Zeus,
who haunt the peaks
of Atabyrion,
honor this song of his, the Olympian victor's due,
(83–88)

Stand 5

the man who has found triumph in his boxing.
Grant him affectionate regard
from neighbors and strangers alike,
for he walks on roads of respect,
knowing well the counsels
his noble fathers pass on to him.
Hide not the seed of Kallianax.
When sons of Eratos rejoice
in victory, the whole city
rejoices too.
But in a single
interval of time, different winds
arise, disperse, and blow their ways. (89–95)

OLYMPIAN 8

Alkimedon of Aigina, boys' wrestling, 460 B.C.

The island of Aigina, off the Attic coast, was the seat of the richest mythical tradition in the Hellenic world, stemming from Aiakos, son of Zeus and the nymph for whom Aigina was named (see the opening of *Nemean 8*). Aiakos sired the illustrious line that included Achilleus and Aias, heroes of the Trojan War.

In the myth of *Olympian 8*, Apollo and Poseidon summon Aiakos to help them build Troy's walls. The invitation is an honor to Aiakos, but it has evil consequences for Troy. If she were to fall one day, it was necessary that mortal hands take some part in the building of her fortifications. There is in the *Iliad* (6. 431–39) a trace of the idea that Troy's walls contained a fatal weak spot. According to Pindar, a wondrous portent occurred after the walls were built. Apollo prophesies from it that Troy's walls would be breached in the place where Aiakos had worked; he goes on to say that Troy would fall through Aiakos' sons, and that the process of her destruction would begin in the first and end in the third generation after Aiakos. The genealogical chain is as follows:

Zeus — Aigina
Aiakos
1) Telamon — Peleus
2) Aias — Achilleus
3) Neoptolemos

Troy fell not once but twice. Telamon, in the first generation after Aiakos, sacked her the first time (see *Nemean 4*, stanza 4; *Isthmian 6*, triad 2). In the next generation, Telamon's son Aias participated in the siege against her, and Achilleus, hero of the *Iliad*, killed Hektor, the only force standing between Troy and final destruction. Achilleus, however, did not live to see the ruin of Troy. It was reserved for his son Neoptolemos to destroy the city forever.

In the opening triad, Pindar prays to the sacred grove of Zeus at Olympia, asking it to welcome the band of singers who come bringing the crown won by the boy victor, Alkimedon. The ode thus seems to have been written for performance at Olympia after the victory. The impression that the poem is being sung during an act of religious homage is reinforced at the close, where Pindar speculates on the power of ritual to reach even the dead in the world below. The religious thought is not without motivation: the young victor's father, Iphion, is dead. To him, and to another dead relative, Kallimachos, Pindar at the end of the ode sends the message of Alkimedon's triumph at Olympia. "Angelia," who bears the message and whose name literally means "Announcement," is an original personification created by Pindar. Pindar makes her the daughter of Hermes not only because Hermes is the messenger of the gods, their *angelos*, but also because he is the psychopomp who conducts the souls of the dead into the underworld (see also the close of *Olympian 14*).

Alkimedon's trainer, Melesias, praised at the close of the third triad, was an Athenian. Relations between Athens and Aigina were anything but friendly in 460 B.C., and this may have something to do with the peculiar emphasis on resentment in this part of the ode. Pindar praises Melesias in *Nemeans 4* and *6* also, but much more briefly than he does here. Four years after the date of *Olympian 8*, Aigina fell under the domination of the growing Athenian empire (see the Introduction, *Pindar's Life and Times*). Pindar seems to be aware of her danger at the end of the first and the beginning of the second triad, where he hails Aigina as a seat of commercial justice and prays that she may continue to be a column of refuge for foreigners of every land.

The ode was apparently commissioned by the victor's older brother Timosthenes, since it is to him, and not to Alkimedon, that Pindar speaks directly. Alkimedon and Timosthenes were members of the Blepsiad family. They traced their descent to Zeus through Aiakos.

Turn 1

Mother of contests for the golden crown,
queen of truth, Olympia,
where men of prophecy,
consulting Zeus' sacrificial fire,
probe his will!
God of the white-flashing bolt,
what has he to say
of the contenders, struggling
for glory, breathless until they hold it? (1-7)

Counterturn 1

Prayers are answered in return for reverence.
O thickly-wooded grove
above Alpheos, receive
this chorus and the crown it brings:
the fame your shining garland gives
is great and lives forever.
Yet there are other forms of fortune,
and many are the roads
success travels in a god's companionship. (8-14)

Stand 1

Timosthenes, it is your lot to have
Zeus in your ancestry.
He made you shine
at Nemea, and by the Hill of Kronos
he made your brother, Alkimedon, an Olympian victor.
Handsome in appearance, he cast no shame on his looks
in action:
he triumphed in wrestling
and had his home proclaimed—
Aigina,
haven of long-oared ships
and harbor of Justice, Lady of Salvation,
who sits by Zeus, god of strangers, and is honored here (15-22)

Turn 2

more than anywhere. For whatever has much weight
swaying in the balance
is hard to determine
with fair mind
and by strict standard.
Yet some divine decree—
may future time preserve it—
has reared this column
of light for every stranger, this sea-rounded land (23-29)

Counterturn 2

governed by Dorian folk since Aiakos' day:
Aiakos, whom Leto's child
and Poseidon,
lord of the tide,
summoned to help them
crown Troy with her ring of walls,
because it was her doom
to sink in the tumult of war,
gasping billows of black smoke. (30–36)

Stand 2

Serpents, three serpents with cold
green in their eyes, sprang
at her newly built tower.
Two fell down
stunned, spitting their life-breath out,
while the third landed hissing
upon it.
Apollo marked the wonder
and said to Aiakos:
"In the place
where your hands have worked
Pergamos is taken. So I read
this omen sent by Zeus the thunderer, (37–44)

Turn 3

and she will fall through battle-might of yours,
beginning with the first
and ending with the third
in your line."
So the god spoke, clearly,
and rode full-speed for Xanthos,
to the Amazons and the Danube,
while Poseidon steered for Isthmos,
bringing Aiakos to Aigina on golden mares, (45–51)

Counterturn 3

then on to Corinth, famed for its festival.
But nothing brings the same delight to all.
And if in my song
I have magnified
Melesias' glory
as a trainer of youths,
let no resentment strike me
with a foul stone, for I will also sing
of his triumph over the youths at Nemea, and mention next (52–58)

Stand 3

his victory against the men
in pankration.
To teach, then,
is easier for one who knows.
The man of no foresight
gives a fool's lesson,
for the thoughts of inexperience
have no weight.
Melesias will tell you
better than anyone how to train
a man bent on taking
glory from contests.
And now Alkimedon
is his pride, and his thirtieth triumph: (59–66)

Turn 4

with fortune from god and his own courage
he threw his four opponents
and laid upon their limbs
a hateful homecoming,
disgrace,
and secrecy,
while in his father's father he inspired
new strength against old age:
a man's noble deeds put Hades out of mind. (67–73)

Counterturn 4

But I must waken memory and tell
how the hands of the Blepsiadai
have flowered in victory:
the sixth crown
falls to them now
in contests for garlands.
And the dead, too, have a share
in a rite's due performance.
The dust does not hide their kinsman's glory. (74–80)

Stand 4

Iphion will hear the voice
of Hermes' daughter, Angelia,
and pass on her message
to Kallimachos, the shining adornment
Zeus gives his kin at Olympia.
I pray
that he give good upon good
and brush away sting of sickness
or any second thoughts in his bounty.
Let there be painless life for them
and sure exaltation for their city. (81–88)

OLYMPIAN 9

Epharmostos of Opous, wrestling, 466 B.C.

Olympian 9 opens with a comparison between the spontaneous singing of the victor and his friends immediately after an Olympian victory and the more elaborate song Pindar is about to begin now. The simple song to which Pindar alludes was composed by Archilochos and has come down to us: "Hail lord Herakles, handsome in triumph, you and Iolaos, spearmen both."

The second triad opens with a curious negative illustration of man's dependence on the gods: if men receive their power from the gods, how could it be true that Herakles, as Homer (*Iliad* 5. 395–400) and other sources (scholiast to *Iliad* 11. 690) would have it, ever battled against the gods themselves? The story of Herakles' combat against Poseidon, Apollo, and Hades is unacceptable to Pindar. He rejects it not only because it is incompatible with his belief in the dependence of man on the gods but also because it would involve the gods in unseemly conduct: we meet here another example of Pindar the editorial poet, who corrects popular tradition in favor of a higher concept of the nature of the gods and of man's relationship with them.

The main myth of the ode begins early in the second counterturn, where Pindar turns away from violent tales unworthy of the gods and relates instead a popular myth connected with the town of Opous, the victor's home. The myth of Deukalion and Pyrrha would give the victor and his ancestors a lowly origin, the stones of the earth (for the myth and the pun "people" from "pebbles" see the Introduction, *Logopoeia*). But there is another problem in the local mythology, the tradition that Opous, the hero for whom the town was named, had quarreled with his father Lokros. Lokros was eventually driven out and went to found the city of Lokroi in the west, leaving his estranged son behind to rule over the city now named for him. Pindar solves both these problems with a single stroke: he introduces Zeus into the pedigree of the Opountian noble families who, as he claims, are descended on the one hand from the stock of the Titan Iapetos through Deukalion and Pyrrha (stand 2), and on the other hand from Zeus himself, who was the real father of Opous, Lokros being his adopted father.

According to Pindar (third triad), Lokros had been childless until Zeus, in order to supply him an heir, brought him a young bride already pregnant with Zeus' own seed. In gratitude to this girl, Lokros named his adopted son after her father, Opous, and this second Opous, grandson of the first, inherited Lokros' town and people. In this peaceful fashion, not in the unseemly manner of the local myth, the name of the town and the power over it passed from Lokros to Opous, ancestor of Epharmostos. Thus Pindar removes a blot from ancestral memory and guarantees to Epharmostos an unbroken line of descent far more prestigious than the lapidary one that the popular story would give him. He goes all the way back to the Titan generation, picking up Zeus himself on the way:

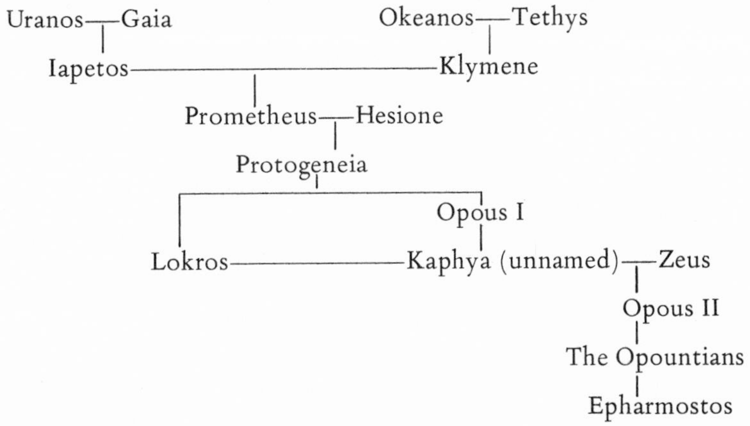

Pindar has invented Opous I to be the maternal grandfather of Opous II. He tells us that this older Opous lived in Elis, and in fact there was a town there called Opous. And though he does not name her, Pindar hints at the identity of the girl whom Zeus spirited away and lay with. The hint is in the mention of Mount Mainalos, on whose slopes was the town of Kaphyai, named for Kaphya who was, according to Plutarch, the wife of Lokros and the mother of Opous. Her introduction into the family tree of Epharmostos adds something special to it, since she came from Elis, where Olympia was located, and where Epharmostos, her descendant, was later to be victorious. These alterations in the traditional story seem to be what Pindar means by his promise, in the second stand, to sing a *new* song.

The most famous Opountian hero was Patroklos, beloved comrade-in-arms of Achilleus. His father Menoitios was among the heroes who came to join Opous in the town that now bore his name (third counterturn).

We learn in the first counterturn that Epharmostos had also won at the Pythian Games. In the fourth triad, Pindar lists his minor victories. Patroklos and Achilleus form a fitting prelude to this part of the ode, since it begins not with Epharmostos alone, but with him and his friend Lampromachos, who triumphed with him on the same day in the Isthmian Games. Now come some reminiscences of Epharmostos' very early career. It seems he had such a prodigious physique that even though entitled to compete in the boys' division at Marathon, the judges took him for a man and made him fight against his elders. His splendid physical endowments and their concomitant courage bring Pindar back to the theme sounded earlier in the ode, the theme of natural talent aided by divine favor. These avail a man more than sheer will and training.

In the final lines, we learn that Epharmostos has placed his triumphal garlands on the altar of the local hero Aias, son of Oïleus (not to be confused with the Salaminian Aias, son of Telamon).

Turn 1

When the song of Archilochos,
Handsome in triumph! filled the air
in triple refrain—it was at Olympia,
and Epharmostos led the way
with his friends singing around him
up the Hill of Kronos.
But now
let the long-range bow of the Muses aim
at Zeus himself, lord of crimson lightning,
and let its arrows rain upon
the sacred height of Elis, won
by Lydian Pelops when he took
Hippodameia for his bride. (1–10)

Counterturn 1

The arrow's honeyed shaft lights on Pytho next—
my words will not fall to the ground
when I pluck the strings
in honor of this man, a wrestler
from the radiant town
of Opous:
praise her
for her inheritance of Justice and Law,
for her triumphs
bursting in bloom
by Kastalia's stream and by the river
Alpheos, whose gathered crowns
exalt her, bright-leaved mother of Lokrians! (11–20)

Stand 1

So I make this city blaze,
fuel to my impetuous song,
this town I love.
Faster than keen stallions
or ships speeding with wing-light oars
I will send this message everywhere
if, with god-given skill,
I cultivate choice flowers in the Graces' garden.
They are the ones who give delight
and we receive it, strong or wise (21–28)

Turn 2

as the gods determine. Who, then, could believe
Herakles once brandished his cudgel
against Poseidon's trident, when the sea-god
moved on him at Pylos, and Apollo
moved against him, menacing
with his silver bow,
and Hades
shook the wand with which he leads
doomed bodies down death's hollow ways?
Away with such a story!
It is an evil art
that vilifies the gods.
Ungainly boasting is the prelude (29–38)

Counterturn 2

to delusion: no such babble now.
Let war and turmoil never taint the deathless gods!
Sing instead of Protogeneia's town,
where by decree of Zeus, dazzling in thunder,
Pyrrha and Deukalion stepped down
from Parnassos
and built their first home.
They sowed a singular folk, born of no embrace–
people, they were called,
from the *pebbles* thrown.
Let us, in their honor, raise our voices
and reopen the song-road!
But we praise wine for its age, and songs (39–48)

Stand 2

for the fresh bloom upon them.
The story goes
that water's strength had glutted the black earth
but then, by Zeus' skills, a sudden ebb-tide
drained the flood away.
From Pyrrha and Deukalion,
through the daughters of Iapetos' stock
and the mightiest sons of Kronos,
your bronze-shielded forebears descend,
kings in the land from time immemorial (49–56)

Turn 3

until Olympos' chief, lifting
the daughter of Opous out of Elis,
lay with her at ease on the slopes of Mount Mainalos
and brought her to Lokros' house
lest age overtake and leave him childless,
for his bride
carried the god's seed.
Gladness overcame him
to see his adopted son,
a wonder of beauty and strength.
He called him Opous,
his mother's father's name,
and gave him town and people to rule. (57–66)

Counterturn 3

And they came to see him, strangers
from Argos and Thebes, Arkadians, Pisatans:
of them he prized Aktor's and Aigina's son the most,
Menoitios, whose child went with the Atreidai
to Teuthras' plain and stood alone
at Achilleus' side
when Telephos turned
the strong Danaans back
and hurled them on their beached sea-prows.
Men of understanding
recognized then the mighty spirit
that was Patroklos.
And from that day Thetis' son (67–76)

Stand 3

made him promise
never to take a stand
in murderous battle
apart from his own man-breaking spear.
Now may I find words
at my finger-tips,
now may boldness and power attend me
into the Muses' chariot.
Loyal in my friend's success
I went to Isthmos and vouched
for Lampromachos' crowns—he and Epharmostos both (77–84)

Turn 4

triumphed on that one day.
And twice again Epharmostos found battle-joy,
by Corinth's gates and in Nemea's lap.
At Argos, he won glory in the men's division.
At Athens, he competed as a boy;
at Marathon, they plucked him
from the boys' ranks,
but how he bore the brunt of full-grown men
contending for the silver trophy!
His swift cunning moves tossed them over
without a slip: what a shout, as he walked
amid the circle of onlookers, young
and noble in achievement as in looks! (85–94)

Counterturn 4

At Lykaian Zeus' festival, throngs of Parrhasians
admired him, others too the day
he won the cloak, a warm remedy
against chill blasts, at Pellana.
Iolaos' tomb will bear his splendors
witness
and Eleusis by the sea.
Always strongest is the strength inborn.
Many try to win glory
with talents gained by instruction,
but a venture in which the gods
have no part is none the worse
when silence envelops it. For one road (95–104)

Stand 4

leads farther than another, and the same
endeavor will not support us all.
The ways of art are steep.
But in this instance simply declare,
with a shout to heaven:
"The gods gave this man
sure hands, lithe limbs, the face and brow of power.
Aias, son of Oïleus, he has triumphed.
Now, at the feast, he wreathes your altar
in his triumphal garlands." (105–12)

OLYMPIAN 10

Hagesidamos of Western Lokroi, boys' boxing, 476 B.C.

Verbal play inspires more turns of thought in *Olympian 10* than in any other ode of Pindar. The punning begins immediately, with Pindar's admission that he has forgotten his obligation to the victor, his promise to compose an ode for him. The Greek word meaning "I forgot" is *elathon.* The Greek word for truth is *alatheia*, literally "nonforgetfulness." The fact that these two words are formed from the same root (*lath-*) accounts for Pindar's subsequent worry that he may appear as a *liar* to his friends. We may suppose that a man who makes a promise and then does not keep it lied when he made it, but in Greek the connection is more immediate: if truth is memory, forgetfulness is a kind of lying.

Pindar begins to recover from his remorse in the counterturn, where he expresses the thought that the interest he will pay on his debt will put him back in the victor's graces. This is clear enough in English, but in Greek it works on two levels, thanks to the double meaning borne by the Greek word for "interest." It is literally the "child" of the debt, what the debt has produced in the meantime, its progeny. This double meaning has significance for the conclusion, where Pindar compares the ode itself to a child born to a man in old age.

At the end of the first counterturn, the ode is imagined as a wave washing over a pebble. In Greek, the pebble is also a counter used to keep track of a debt's amount. As the pebble is washed away by the wave, so the debt will be erased by the ode. Very little, if any, of this linguistic playfulness can be suggested in English.

In the first stand, the poet's indebtedness to the victor becomes the gratitude that the victor owes to his trainer. This in turn reminds Pindar of the debt of gratitude owed by Patroklos to Achilleus. Patroklos, like Hagesidamos the present victor, is a Lokrian, which also accounts for Pindar's brief mention of him here.

The main myth of the ode (triads 2–4) also deals with indebtedness. King Augeas, for example, had refused to pay Herakles for a service rendered (the cleansing of the Augean stables). For this Herakles destroys him and his city. On the other hand, Herakles did not forget to express his thanks to his father Zeus for victory over Augeas: he dedicated the Altis, the sacred precinct at Olympia, to Zeus, and founded the Olympian Games in Zeus' honor. The story is complicated somewhat by the introduction of the sons of Molione, Kteatos and

Eurytos, who had ambushed Herakles' army. Herakles had to defeat them before he could avenge himself on their uncle Augeas.

There are two additional references to mythology in the ode, one near the beginning and one at the end. In the first, Pindar alludes very briefly to an adventure of Herakles, his encounter with Kyknos. Herakles had turned away from it. This is all Pindar tells us, and at first glance it appears to be part of his apology: "Allow me a lapse of memory. Didn't Herakles back down once?" But the allusion occurs just before Pindar's tribute to Ilas, the victor's trainer. The victor did not win alone. In the first encounter with Kyknos, however, Herakles was alone, and Kyknos was not: the giant stood against him with his father, Ares, at his side. Herakles retired and came back with Athena, and this time he carried the day. Pindar does not go into any of this, but the poet Stesichorus, who came from Matauros in the vicinity of Western Lokroi, had sung of the conflict between Herakles and Kyknos. Perhaps Pindar could expect his audience to catch the allusion, for they were, by reputation, lovers of poetry (stand 1). Pindar also does not force the association between Ilas and Hagesidamos on one hand, Herakles and Athena on the other. Each pair exemplifies teamwork in achieving victory.

The other mythical allusion appears in the last line, where Pindar compares the beauty of Hagesidamos to that of Ganymede. Ganymede's good looks had attracted no less a lover than Zeus himself. With Aphrodite's help—the Greek way of saying through sexual attraction—Ganymede's beauty moved Zeus to bear him off to Olympos and immortalize him. Likewise the love inspired in Pindar by the beauty of Hagesidamos results in immortality, the kind of immortality a poet can bestow.

Turn 1

The son of Archestratos, winner at Olympia:
read out his name,
tell me where it's written
in my heart's ledger.
I forgot, and I owe him
a honeyed song.
O Muse and Zeus' daughter,
Alatheia, look to the oversight:
redeem me from the charge
that I'm a liar, a hedger with my friends! (1–6)

Counterturn 1

For the time ahead is suddenly here,
and I am deep in arrears
and embarrassment.
And yet payment
with interest
can alleviate
the sting of discredit.
As the white wave washes
the spinning pebble under,
so I'll sweep my debt away gladly. (7–12)

Stand 1

For Honesty rules in Western Lokroi,
and they cultivate Kalliopa there
and the bronze God of War.
Even champion Herakles
recoiled once, in battle with Kyknos.
Let Hagesidamos, winner in boxing at Olympia,
pay his trainer Ilas gratitude
as Patroklos paid Achilleus.
With a god's favoring hand, one man
may whet another's ambition, inspire him
to prodigious feats,
if glory's in his birthright. (13–21)

Turn 2

A few have won joy without effort,
a radiance on life
outshining every achievement.
But Zeus' sacred right moves me to sing
of his favored contest,
which Herakles established
to be held in six events
near Pelops' ancient barrow.
It was after he had cut down
Kteatos, Poseidon's unblemished son, (22–27)

Counterturn 2

and Eurytos—willing work for his hand,
to make proud Augeas pay
unwilling wages for a slavish task.
In the wood beneath Kleonai,
Herakles waited, and when
Molione's arrogant sons
passed along the road,
he slew them, avenging
the destruction they had wrought
on his Tirynthian army, as it lay encamped (28–33)

Stand 2

in the deep vales of Elis.
And not long after,
their Epeian king, deceiver of strangers,
saw his wealth-laden country
bow beneath the sword-stroke
and remorseless fire,
his own city sinking
into the torrent of ruin.
Strife
against one's betters
is doomed.
He too, last of all,
fell in chains for his foolishness
and did not escape precipitate death. (34–42)

Turn 3

Then Zeus' warlike son drew his entire host
together in Pisa,
all the booty skimmed
from the heap of battle.
He marked out a precinct sacred
to his father,
fenced the Altis apart in the clear
and made the plain around
a place for feasting,
honoring the ford of Alpheos (43–48)

Counterturn 3

and the twelve lordly gods:
he called it Kronos' Hill,
for in former times,
when Oinomaos ruled,
it had lain beneath deep drifts
of snow, without a name.
Now, at its first birth rites,
the Moirai stood by, and next to them
the one
who alone proves Truth true, (49–54)

Stand 3

Time,
and Time moving onward
has made it manifest:
how Herakles set war's firstfruits
aside for sacrifice and ordained
the five-year festival
with the first Olympiad
and its triumphs.
Say, then, who won the new crown—
praying for victory in his thoughts
and seizing it by his deeds
in boxing, in running, in the chariot race? (55–63)

Turn 4

Running the straight dash, Oionos was the best,
Likymnios' son,
who came from Midea
at the head of a host.
For wrestling, Echemos
had his home Tegea'
proclaimed to the throng.
Doryklos of Tiryns took away
the boxing prize.
And with the four-horse team (64–69)

Counterturn 4

it was Samos out of Mantinea, Halirothios' son.
With the javelin,
Phrastor struck the mark.
In distance, Nikeus sent the stone
spun from the whirl of his hand
past them all, and as it passed
his comrades-in-arms
sent a shout roaring after it.
And then the radiance
of the moon's beautiful eye made evening shine. (70–75)

Stand 4

All the precinct rang with music, sung at the feast
in the mode of praise.
Following those beginnings,
let us even now
sing the song named for victory,
our theme
Zeus' thunderbolt,
the spear of fire
flung from his fist, cleaving
heaven with its din, the blaze
of lightning paired with all power,
and the song's movement, swaying to the flutes,
will join the lyrics that have come (76–84)

Turn 5

at last from famous Dirka.
But as the child
he has longed for
warms a father's heart
with love, even
as he leaves his youth behind—
for wealth
abandoned to another's keeping,
someone from outside,
is most hateful to a dying man— (85–90)

Counterturn 5

so when a man has triumphed
and vanished in death's bourne,
Hagesidamos, without a song
to accompany him, he has won
for his hopes and his toil
a brief delight.
On you the lyre rains sweet words,
the flute showers grace,
and Zeus' daughters, the maidens of Pieria,
ensure the growth of your glory. (91–96)

Stand 5

And I have lent them a hand
in my zeal, embraced
the Lokrian people
                    and bathed their heroic town
in music.
          I praised
Archestratos' good-looking son, whom I saw
in his might, by the Olympian altar
the day he won, handsome in build
and blessed with the youthfulness
that once, through Aphrodite's favor,
warded ruthless death from Ganymede. (97–105)

OLYMPIAN 11

Hagesidamos of Western Lokroi, boys' boxing, 476 B.C.

Pindar's other poem for Hagesidamos' Olympian victory appears where it appears in the manuscripts because it was taken by ancient scholars to be the "interest" referred to in the proem of *Olympian 10.* Hence it follows the tenth Olympian ode as if it were an appendix or extra song. Modern scholars have tended to reverse this relationship, making the eleventh earlier than the tenth. They base their arguments on the brevity of *Olympian 11* and on a couple of future tenses that appear in its final stanza. The brevity of the poem would indicate that Pindar composed it on site at Olympia immediately after the victory, and the future tenses would mean that Pindar will go to Western Lokroi sometime later and celebrate Hagesidamos' victory on a grander scale, as he eventually did with *Olympian 10.* But this interpretation has been rejected in its turn by Elroy L. Bundy in the first of his *Studia Pindarica.* Bundy argued that the future tenses do not refer to anything outside the ode in which they occur. "I will sing" in Pindar means simply "I am singing now." Bundy's argument is basically that the poem ought to be taken on its own merits, by which it must stand or fall.

It opens with a catalogue of the various needs men feel at various times. This prepares the way for a standard epinician topic, that victory is incomplete without song. Once Pindar has reached this point, he is only a step from announcing that it is an Olympian victory he will sing of, and then come the particulars.

Turn

Sometimes men need the winds most,
at other times
waters from the sky,
rainy descendants of the cloud.
And when a man has triumphed
and put his toil behind,
it is time for melodious song
to arise, laying
the foundation of future glory,
a sworn pledge securing proud success. (1–6)

Counterturn

For Olympian victors, such acclaim
is laid in store
without limit, and I
am eager to tend it with my song.
For a man flourishes
in wise understanding,
as in all things,
through a god's favor.
Know now, son of Archestratos,
Hagesidamos, because of your boxing victory (7–12)

Stand

I will sing, and my song will be
an added adornment
to your gold olive crown,
shining with love for Western Lokroi.
Go there
and join the revels, Muses.
By my bond,
you will not find a people indifferent to strangers
or blind to beauty, but men of keenest discernment
and courage in war.
For the crimson fox
and thunderous lion cannot change their inborn ways. (13–20)

OLYMPIAN 12

Ergoteles of Himera, long foot race, 466 B.C.

The twelfth Olympian ode shows perhaps more clearly than any other the closeness of the relationship between the victor and his city. The poem is addressed to the goddess Tycha—Chance or Lady Luck. Both the victor and his city were particularly indebted to her favor, for both had passed through a series of frightful vicissitudes on their way to safety and success.

The victor, Ergoteles, was not born in Himera. He emigrated there, driven by civil strife from his birthplace, Knossos in Krete. His departure from Krete is directly responsible for his arrival in Himera, and for his journeys to the great games, where he won several triumphs. The Kretans, though famed for their speed of foot, were not frequent competitors at Olympia. They did their racing at home. Pindar at the close of the ode contrasts Ergoteles in this regard with the fighting rooster who stays in his own yard. Ergoteles would never have won the garlands whose leaves Pindar mentions here, if he had not suffered exile.

Himera owes whatever fame she enjoys to the great battle named for her (see the Introduction, *Pindar's Life and Times*, and also the preface to *Olympian 2*). After the battle, Theron put his son Thrasydaios in charge of the government of Himera. From 480 to 478 B.C., Thrasydaios so alienated the Himeraians that they were ready to intrigue for their freedom when the opportunity came. As troubles between Theron and Hieron neared open war, the people of Himera made overtures to Hieron. But Hieron settled the differences between himself and Theron without a battle, and in the process he betrayed the Himeraians to Theron. Theron, a mild prince in his own city, punished Himera with mass executions. So many perished that the city had to be replenished with new citizens from abroad. One of those who came to Himera at about this time was Ergoteles.

Himera was again under the control of Thrasydaios. In 470, some time after the death of Theron, Thrasydaios had the temerity to make war on Hieron. His own people rebelled against him and he lost on the field of battle. Thus, he was overthrown, and Akragas, along with Himera, came under the sway of Syracuse. Approximately four years later, Hieron died and his brother Thrasyboulos (not to be confused with the son of Xenokrates, whom Pindar addresses in *Pythian 6* and *Isthmian 2*) came to the throne at Syracuse. The cities under his dominion rose in rebellion against him, Himera among them. He was defeated, Syracuse became a democracy, and Himera gained her freedom at last. The opening reference to Zeus the Deliverer is probably due to these events.

Through all these vicissitudes Himera and Ergoteles have been under the favor of Tycha. Pindar prays to her in the opening turn. He goes on in the counterturn to reflect on the blind ignorance of men, who have no way of knowing what lies ahead. In the stand, he turns for the first time to the victor, who thus enters the ode as a particular example of Tycha's power over the lives of men.

In the last lines of the ode, we find reference to a local feature: Ergoteles now bathes in the warm springs in the neighborhood of Himera. These, represented on Himera's ancient coins, have left their trace in the modern name for the city, Termini, "Baths."

Turn

Hear me,
daughter of Zeus the Deliverer:
watch over Himera,
gird her with strength,
O savior Tycha.
Under your guidance,
swift ships pilot the seas,
wars veer over the earth,
assemblies pass their motions.
Men's hopes,
in endless undulation,
soar and plummet,
borne on falsehoods
that heave and tumble
in the wind. (1–6a)

Counterturn

No earthbound mortal man
has ever encountered
a sure sign
of future events
sent him by the gods.
The eyes that look ahead
are blinded already.
Things often fall out
unexpectedly, capsizing
one man's pleasure,
while another's sorrow,
beating upon him
in the storm of pain,
suddenly changes
to a surge of joy. (7–12a)

Stand

Son of Philanor! your honor too
(like that of the cock who fights
in his own yard) would have no glory—
the leaves won by your speed
would stream to the ground
and vanish
had not dissension,
pitting man against man,
deprived you of your home in Knossos.
You went to Olympia and won its crown.
At Delphi twice, and Isthmos too, the same.
Now when you bathe by your new fields, Ergoteles,
the nymphs in the warm springs mingle with fame. (13–19)

OLYMPIAN 13

Xenophon of Corinth, foot race and pentathlon, 464 B.C.

Olympian 13 celebrates an unusual athletic feat: the victory of one man in two events in the same Olympiad.

The ode opens with praises of Corinth, which Pindar imagines to be the home of the Horai (Seasons), daughters of Zeus and Themis. They are Eunomia (Law), Dika (Justice), and Eirena (Peace). In the counterturn, they are depicted as the enemies of Hybris (Pride) and of Koros (Ambition).

The introduction to the mythical section (third and fourth triads) briefly mentions two figures renowned for their cunning, Sisyphos and Medea, both of whom are connected with the traditions of Corinth. Sisyphos is said to have built Corinth. He is best known from Homer's account of his punishment in the underworld, but Pindar only mentions him, counting on his audience to be familiar with the salient features of his story. His outstanding trait is his cunning, a cunning that enabled him to outwit death, not once but twice. Odysseus saw him in the underworld, punished for his audacity by having to roll an enormous boulder uphill. Once up, it comes crashing down and must be pushed back up again (*Odyssey* 11. 593–600). Of all this Pindar says nothing, and of Medea he says little more, perhaps because a similar darkness hovers in the background of her story. Medea's children were buried at Corinth.

Pindar moves from Corinthian astuteness, exemplified by Sisyphos and Medea, to Corinthian bravery. The warriors of Corinth, he tells us, played their part in the battle for Troy. He is thinking of Glaukos, who appears in Book 6 of the *Iliad*, but Glaukos, like Medea and Sisyphos, is only a step in the progress toward the main hero of the myth in this poem, Bellerophon, whom Glaukos introduces. The genealogical connections permitting these narrative leaps are as follows. Sisyphos sired a son, Glaukos, who in turn sired Bellerophon. Bellerophon's son was Hippolochos, father of the Glaukos who appears in the ode, boasting of his ancestral relationship to Bellerophon. The latter is the real subject of the myth, uniting in one character the dual celebration of the ode, Corinth's inventive and martial brilliance.

Bellerophon's main claim to glory for inventiveness is his discovery of the bridle. Pindar tells the story of the bridle's invention simultaneously with the story of Bellerophon's attempt to tame and ride the winged horse Pegasos. As in the case of Sisyphos and Medea, there is darkness in the background of Bellerophon. Pindar alludes to it by expressly refusing to talk about it. He is less reticent in the seventh Isthmian ode, where he says that Pegasos had thrown Bellerophon when the hero insanely attempted to ride into heaven itself. Bellerophon fell to earth and spent the rest of his life roaming in the Eleian fields, lame and crazed (see Milton, *Paradise Lost*, VII, 17–20). The hero's fall is, in *Isthmian 7*, a clear warning against too bold a confidence. In *Olympian 13*, it is an ominous complement to the caution Pindar expresses by praying to Zeus and by reflecting on the need for restraint.

The ode concludes with a catalogue of victories, those won by the sons of Oligaithos, members of the clan to which Xenophon belonged. In counterturn 5 the reference to Enyalios, god of war, seems inspired by the necessary element of strife in athletic competition.

The meter of the ode is an unusual blend of Doric and Aiolic. The turns and counterturns are in Aiolic meter. From their sixth to their ninth lines, they begin to modulate to dactylo-epitritic, which then becomes the meter of the stands.

Turn 1

Praising a house
that has won
three times at Olympia,
a house
gentle to citizens
and thoughtful of strangers,
I will glorify
Corinth, the blest,
doorway to Poseidon's Isthmos,
brilliant in her young men,
home of Eunomia
and her sisters—
Dika, unshakable foundation of cities,
and Eirena, preserver of wealth:
golden daughters of sagacious Themis. (1–8)

Counterturn 1

They are eager to repel
Hybris, brash-tongued
mother of Koros.
Yet there is beauty
to tell of here,
and boldness moves me
to tell it.
Who can hide
the nature with which he was born?
Sons of Alatas, on you
the Horai rich in bloom
have often showered
bright petals of victory
in the sacred games, and often
in the hearts of your men they cast (9–16)

Stand 1

the seeds of ancient inventiveness: the glory
of every work goes to its maker.
Who first framed the dithyramb of Dionysos, sung
on the way to the altar where the ox is felled?
Who added the bit to the horse's gear
or set the eagle, king of birds, above
the temple pediment, at either end?
In this town,
the Muses breathe sweetly, and Ares
bristles in the young men's deadly spears. (17–23)

Turn 2

Father Zeus,
ruling with wide sway
from Olympia's height,
harbor no envy
against my words
now or ever.
Guide this people
away from harm,
and swell the sails
of Xenophon's luck.
Welcome the revelry
due him for his crowns.
He comes from Pisa's plain, winner—
as no mortal before him—
in foot race and pentathlon too. (24–31)

Counterturn 2

And twice
in the Isthmian games
plaited leaves of triumph
shaded his brow,
nor will Nemea
smart to hear him praised.
His father Thessalos
enjoys glory for speed
where Alpheos flows,
and honor at Pytho for taking
the single and the double race
within a single day,
and three times within a month
in rocky Athens, the day's
swift running gave him garlands, (32–39)

Stand 2

and seven times Athena flung him wreaths
in her Corinthian games,
and in the rites
of Poseidon on the sea-fringed fields
his kinsman Ptoiodoros won, followed by
his sons, Terpsias and Eritimos: too long
a song will follow if I tell their deeds
at Delphi, or how many times they beat
opponents on the lion's pastures. Why try
to reckon all the pebbles of the beach? (40–46)

Turn 3

In every matter
measure is the thing–
to know it
is all tact.
I have set sail,
one man
at a people's bidding.
Singing the mind of the ancients,
singing war,
I will not betray Corinth,
rich in heroic legend,
with Sisyphos, shrewd in devices
like a god, and with Medea,
who put her love before her father
to save the Argo and its crew. (47–54)

Counterturn 3

And in the test of battle
around Troy's walls
on either side
Corinthian warriors appeared
to determine the outcome–
those who strove
with Atreus' dear sons
to bring Helen home and those
who beat them back.
Danaans trembled
at Glaukos coming out of Lykia.
Before them he boasted
of Corinth
where his seat of power lay,
the hall and splendor of his father (55–62)

Stand 3

Bellerophon, who once had suffered much
beside Peirana's spring, deluded
in his need to catch and master Pegasos,
the son of snaky Gorgon–
until Athena
brought him the golden bridle, a dream at first
and then no dream: "Asleep, Aiolian king?
Here is a drug to calm a stallion's mood.
Rise, and when you've killed a silver bull
in honor of Damaios, show him this." (63–69)

Turn 4

The maiden,
with the deep blue aegis
before her in the dark,
appeared
to speak these words.
From the depths of slumber,
he jumped to his feet
and found
the marvel lying there.
In joy he went to Polyïdos,
seer of the land,
and showed him the bridle,
explaining all that had happened,
how he lay night-long as the seer instructed,
and how Athena came and gave him (70–77)

Counterturn 4

the spirit-taming gold.
"Obey the dream,"
the seer replied,
"and when you've slain
a bull for the Earth-Shaker,
build an altar to Athena,
goddess of horses."
The power of the gods
brings to fulfillment—
as if it were a trivial thing—
even the deed
no man would promise
or expect.
Strong Bellerophon hastened,
slipped the soothing bridle over the cheeks (78–85)

Stand 4

of winged Pegasos, and rode him
in maneuvers of war, mounted
in full bronze.
Then from the chill
folds of hollow heaven he let fly
the bolts of death, sweeping serried ranks
of Amazons, women armed with bows.
He killed
Chimaira, breathing fire, and the Solymoi.
His fall I won't recount, but Pegasos
entered Olympos and Zeus' ancient stables. (86–92)

Turn 5

Now I must put strength
   in the throw,
      and let go
a whirl of javelins
   straight at the mark,
      for I have come
a willing ally
   to the Muses
      and the sons of Oligaithos.
I will make their multitudes of victories
   at Isthmos and Nemea
      manifest in few words:
sixty times they won at both.
   The crier's voice
      will vouch the truth of what I claim. (93–100)

Counterturn 5

It seems I have
   already named
      their triumphs at Olympia.
Those that will come
   I would praise
      when they come.
I have my hopes,
   but the end
      is with the god.
If the family's luck endures,
   Zeus and Enyalios will do the rest.
      They won beneath Parnassos' brow,
at Argos and at Thebes,
   and in Arkadia the regal altar of Lykaian Zeus
      will testify to the host of their successes. (101–8)

Stand 5

Pellana, Sikyon, and Megara,
the Aiakian grove of Aigina,
Eleusis, shiny Marathon, the towns
beneath high Aitna that abound in wealth,
Euboia too:
            search the whole of Greece
and you will find they've won too many times
to calculate.
            Come, then! swim out with agile strokes
and Zeus, Perfector, grant them reverence
and good fortune's sweet delight. (109–15)

OLYMPIAN 14

Asopichos of Orchomenos, boys' foot race, 488 (?) B.C.

We know very little about Asopichos, the victor of this ode. He competed in the boys' division at Olympia; he lived in Orchomenos; his father, Kleodamos, was dead at the time. All this emerges from the ode itself. Though it is one of Pindar's briefest poems, it is favored for its beauty, which it may owe to the Charites, the Three Graces, whom it invokes.

The Three Graces are familiar in western literary tradition. Milton summons one of them near the opening of *L'Allegro*:

> But com thou Goddes fair and free,
> In Heav'n ycleap'd *Euphrosyne*,
> And by men, heart-easing Mirth . . .

And yet in order to appreciate Pindar's prayer to these divine beings, it is best to divest oneself of post-Pindaric literary history and to think of the Three Graces as they originally were in the ancient town of Orchomenos: real goddesses with a real temple and a real cult devoted to them. They were, in the beginning, associated with the powers of growth and fertility, an association that is still clear from the name of one of them, Thalia ("Bloom"). Pindar also names Aglaia ("Brilliance") and Euphrosyna ("Festivity") in the opening of the second stanza, but he sets Thalia apart, praying for her favor and attributing the victory of Asopichos specifically to her. As a growing boy, Asopichos was especially under her protection.

The religious reality of the Three Graces is reflected in the occasional setting of this ode, composed for a chorus of boys to sing as they marched in procession to the temple of the Graces. Remains of a temple of theirs have been found on the banks of the river Kaphisos, named in the first line.

The mythical king Minyas, son of Poseidon, founded Orchomenos. Apart from this, we know almost nothing about him. His descendants play a role in various mythological traditions. When Pindar calls the people of Orchomenos "Minyans born of old," he is honoring them by an evocation of ancient glory.

In the last lines of the ode, Pindar asks Echo to go to the house of Persephone, Queen of the dead, to tell the victor's father the good news of his son's triumph. Echo, like the Graces, was a living part of local tradition. She had fallen in love with Narcissus, son of the river Kaphisos, and therefore she was connected in mythology with the victor's city. As a reverberation of the ode itself, and as a mythological figure, she is the ideal messenger to the victor's father in the underworld.

This is the first of the odes in the collection intended to be sung by a chorus marching in procession rather than dancing, and therefore it is nontriadic in form. See the Introduction, *Pindar's Meters.*

1 You who dwell by the waters of Kaphisos,
in the country where bright colts are bred,
ladies whose tuneful voices
haunt the lanes of glittering Orchomenos
and who guard the Minyans born of old,
hear me, Graces, for I pray:
if anything sweet or delightful
warms the heart of any mortal man,
whether he has beauty, or skill,
or the light of victory shining upon him,
it is your gift.
Even the gods depend on you
and would renounce
ordering the dance and feast
without your favor.
Of all that is done in heaven you have charge.
Seated beside Pythian Apollo,
god of the golden bow, your worship makes
the Olympian father's glory stream forever. (1–12)

2 O lady Aglaia! Euphrosyna, lover of song!
Daughters of the strongest god, hear me,
and hear me, Thalia, who delight in music:
look with favor now upon this chorus
stepping lightly.
In Lydian measures and chosen phrases,
I come singing of Asopichos,
because his home,
the city of the Minyan people,
by your blessing
has triumphed at Olympia.
Now go, Echo, go
to the dark walls
of Persephone's house,
bearing the proud announcement to his father,
and when you've found Kleodamos, tell him
how his boy, in the cleft of Pisa's hills
where glory begins its flight, has wreathed his hair
with the radiant wings of victory. (13–24)

"having despoiled the head of beautiful Medusa."
—*Pythian 12*, 16

Red-figured hydria, showing Perseus and Medusa. Courtesy of the Trustees of the British Museum, London.

THE PYTHIAN ODES

PYTHIAN 1

Hieron of Aitna, chariot race, 470 B.C.

In 470, when Hieron, King of Syracuse, won the chariot race at the Pythian Games, he had himself proclaimed as an "Aitnaian" in honor of Aitna, the new city he had founded for his son Deinomenes to rule as king. The most striking feature of the new city is the volcano for which it was named, and one of the most impressive features of *Pythian 1* is the description of Aitna's eruption in the turn and counterturn of the second triad (on the imagery, see the Introduction, *Melopoeia*). Pindar attributes the cause of the eruption to the giant Typhon, who lies pinned beneath the mountain, punished for his attempt to usurp the throne of Zeus. Typhon's character, as an enemy of order and a champion of chaos, was already clearly established in Hesiod (*Theogony* 820–868), and Pindar inherited it. But he added his own special emphasis by introducing Typhon into the poem as a creature who cannot bear the sound of music. Music in this poem is a symbol of the ordering powers in the universe of man and nature.

Hieron and his older brother Gelon—the "Deinomenidai" or sons of Deinomenes—had inflicted a momentous defeat on the Carthaginians ("the Phoinikian," as Pindar calls them in the ode) at the battle of Himera in 480. At the end of the fourth triad, Pindar ranks Himera with the two great battles in which the mainland Greeks had stemmed the advance of the Persians: the Athenian naval victory at Salamis and the Spartan land victory at Plataia. Both battles took place in 479. In 474, Hieron had put an end to the expansion of the piratical Etruscans ("the Tyrsanoi") in a naval engagement off the coast of Kuma. Pindar mentions Kuma twice in the course of the ode: once in the first stand, where, together with Mt. Aitna, it designates the site of Typhon's imprisonment; and again in the fourth counterturn and stand, where it designates the site of Hieron's victory over the Etruscans.

In the third triad, Pindar compares Hieron as a warrior to the hero Philoktetes, son of Poias. The Greeks had abandoned Philoktetes on their way to Troy because he had a noisome festering sore on his leg. Ten years later, with Troy still untaken, they learned that the city would not fall without the aid of Philoktetes' bow. They went to get him from Lemnos, where they had left him, and with his help they finally succeeded in conquering Troy. The basis for Pindar's comparison between Philoktetes and Hieron seems to be Hieron's poor health. All Pindar tells us in *Pythian 1* is that Hieron took to the field like Philoktetes: in bad health, but with fate on his side. Pindar also mentions that someone with a proud heart was compelled to bow and sue for Hieron's favor, but we cannot tell who is meant. Possibly it is Akragas, a city that had almost gone to war with Hieron in 472. (See the preface to *Olympian 12.*)

The people who colonize Aitna are Dorians and they are to keep their Dorian ways of life. In the fourth turn, Pindar compares them with the Dorian invaders of some six hundred years before, who, under the leadership of Hyllos, son of Herakles, and Pamphylos and Dymas, sons of Aigimios, came down from the north, subdued the city of Amyklai, and founded Sparta, the chief power in the Peloponnesos. Just as these builders of a new city had remained faithful to their ancient institutions even though they had left their native land, so Pindar prays that the people settled by Hieron at Aitna will retain their Dorian constitution. He also wishes them a similar glory.

The last triad consists of a series of proverbs which are at first equally applicable to Hieron and to Pindar himself, but which then modulate into the poet's advice to the king. Pindar counsels Hieron to continue as he has. His eminence is due not only to his success in the games but also to his patronage of song, the vehicle of fame and immortal honor. Men who live nobly enjoy good fame after death, thanks to song; those who live otherwise have no poetry to protect them from oblivion (see the Introduction, *Pindar's Genre*). The ode concludes with an example from each category. The mild and generous king, Kroisos, is remembered in song; but there is no poetry of praise for his counterpart, the cruel Phalaris, tyrant of Akragas about a century earlier. Phalaris, according to tradition, roasted his enemies alive in a bronze bull.

Turn 1

Golden lyre, rightful possession of Apollo
and the bright-haired Muses,
to you the dancers listen
as they begin the celebration,
and the singers
follow the rhythm
plucked on your trembling strings
in prelude to the chorus;
it is you that quench
the lancing bolt
of ever-flowing fire and lull Zeus' eagle
perched on his scepter
with folded wings— (1–6)

Counterturn 1

the king of birds: over his bowed head
you shed a darkening cloud,
a soft seal upon his eyelids.
His supple back rises
and falls as he dreams, locked
in the spell of your music.
Even harsh Ares
drops his brutal spear
and soothes his heart.
Your shafts cast enchantment
on the mood of the gods
through the skill of Apollo
and the deep-breasted Muses. (7–12)

Stand 1

But all who feel Zeus' loathing are routed
when they hear the Muses' voice ring out
on earth and raging sea,
even he who sprawls
in the dark pit of Tartaros, hating the gods—
hundred-headed Typhon, whom the cave in Kilikia,
known by many names, once reared:
now the sea-beaten crags
off Kuma's coast, and Sicily's mountains
crush his shaggy breast.
He's pinned beneath
the pillar of the sky: white-capped Aitna, nursing
all year long her brood of stinging snow. (13–20)

Turn 2

Within her secret depths
    pure springs of unapproachable fire
        erupt—her rivers in daytime pour forth
            billows of glaring smoke,
                while at night the blood-red
            rolling blaze whirls boulders crashing
        onto the flat plain of the sea.
    It is the monster beneath,
spewing torrents of fire—
                                        a wondrous portent
to behold, a wonder
        even to hear of
            from those who have seen (21–26)

Counterturn 2

how he thrashes in bonds beneath
    the black-leaved peaks
        and sloping sides of Aitna,
            and his bed, scraping all his back,
                goads him as he writhes upon it.
            But let it be our lot
        to please you, Zeus, who haunt this mountain,
    brow of a fruitful land, and the city
named for it,
                        whose famed founder glorified her
in the Pythian Games
        when the herald proclaimed her,
            together with him, Hieron, (27–32)

Stand 2

victor in the chariot race.
                                        For men who embark on ships,
the first blessing is a breeze to fill their sails
and waft them on their way, for with it comes
omen of a safe return.
                                    And so it is with Aitna:
with such grace as this at her inception,
she must retain high fame for her crowns and horses
and the music of her triumphs.
                                            Lykian Phoibos, lord
of Delos and lover of Kastalia's spring upon Parnassos,
may you lay all this to heart willingly,
and make this city flourish. (33–40)

Turn 3

For all resourcefulness descends to mortals
only from the gods—
if men are skilled or mighty
or gifted in speech,
it is from them.
And I, yearning to praise this man,
hope not to whirl
my bronze-tipped javelin
off the field, but to fling it
far beyond my rivals.
May all time continue bringing Hieron
wealth, bountiful gifts,
and joy of his struggles. (41–46)

Counterturn 3

Well may he recall battles
where he stood steadfast
and took with the gods' help
honor no Hellene plucked before,
a lordly prize to crown his riches.
And just now he led his army forth
like a second Philoktetes:
a man proud of heart
felt compelled to beg his friendship.
So legends say
the heroes came, seeking
Poias' archer son, worn
by his festering sore (47–52)

Stand 3

in Lemnos: Philoktetes, who stretched
Priam's city in the dust and put an end
to the pains of the Danaans, though he walked
with broken strength—
there was fate in it.
So may the god watch over Hieron through coming time
and give him due season for reaping his desires.
Muse, obey me now: sing also at Deinomenes' side,
reward this four-horse chariot victory,
his father's triumph, and a joy to him no less.
Come then, a loving song for Aitna's king, (53–60)

Turn 4

for whom Hieron founded this city
to abide in freedom
by the rule of Hyllos.
So the sons of Pamphylos and Herakles,
though dwelling under Taÿgetos' crags,
keep the ways of Aigimios,
Dorians forever: they left Mount Pindos
and took Amyklai, happy men!
Today they are far-famed neighbors
to the twin Tyndaridai,
riders of white horses—
and the fame of their spear
bursts in blossom. (61–66)

Counterturn 4

May fortune such as they enjoy
fall also to the kings and citizens of Aitna
in the true report of men—through you, Zeus,
their prince may follow his father,
revering the people, leading them
in the harmonies of peace.
But I beseech you, son of Kronos,
keep the Phoinikian at home,
stifle the battle-shout
of the Tyrsanoi—
let them rue
their pride at Kuma
that burst into wailing for their fleet. (67–72)

Stand 4

Such was the anguish the Syracusan king
inflicted on them, when he hurled their youth
from the swift ships into the waves, saving Hellas
from the iron yoke of slavery.
I will earn
the praise of Athens by singing of Salamis,
and of Sparta by making my theme
the battles beneath Kithairon,
where the curve-bow Persians strove and were crushed.
But when I come to the rivery field of Himera
I will sing of the Deinomenidai, conquerors of the foe. (73–80)

Turn 5

Praise spoken in due season,
theme after theme set down
in quick succession, reaps
less blame from men, for tedium
dulls their keen attentiveness,
and hearing others extolled
rouses secret hatred.
Yet do not give up your noble ways:
better men's resentment
than their pity.
Govern the people with justice.
Forge your speech
on the anvil of truth. (81–86)

Counterturn 5

Even a trivial spark will start a blaze
if it fall from you
who are steward of many, and many
will be your witnesses, for good or ill.
But if indeed you yearn to hear
your name forever sounded
in the tones of praise,
abide in these high spirits,
go on being lavish.
Unfurl your sails.
Don't be deceived
by cunning thrift:
glory follows a man, (87–92)

Stand 5

glory alone, when he is dead, reveals
his manner of life to the lords
of song and story.
Kroisos' mild-minded ways
perish not, but in all lands hateful speech
oppresses Phalaris, pitiless burner of men
in the brazen bull.
No lyres in hall
welcome him to the soft embrace of boys' voices.
Success is the first of prizes.
To be well spoken of is second.
But he who finds them both and keeps them
wins the highest crown. (93–100)

PYTHIAN 2

Hieron of Syracuse, chariot race, date uncertain

Pythian 2 shares with *Nemean* 7 the dubious distinction of being one of the obscurest and most difficult of Pindar's odes. It commemorates a chariot victory, but when and where it was won is not clear. There is a tantalizing historical allusion, but it proves, on examination, to offer little if any real help in determining the date or occasion. In the first stand, Pindar says that the "West Lokrian maiden" owes her current security to Hieron. Hieron came to the aid of Western Lokroi not once but twice: sometime between 478 and 476 B.C., and again sometime between 471 and 470. The former date would be too early for either of Hieron's chariot victories; the latter would accord well with the Pythian triumph of 470.

The West Lokrian maiden appears as a specific example of gratitude toward a benefactor. Hieron saved her, she pays him back not only with gratitude, but with gratitude expressed in song, in poetry. Here is the principal theme of the ode, illustrated positively at the start and negatively later: the West Lokrian maiden with her songs for Hieron, the people of Kypros with their songs for their king-benefactor Kinyras (counterturn 1), and Pindar himself, with his song for Hieron, all share in a single virtue: they recognize their indebtedness to others, they are grateful.

The reverse of the Lokrian maiden, of the Kyprians, and of Pindar is Ixion, whose story and punishment illustrate ingratitude and its consequences (stand 1–stand 2). Ixion had lured his father-in-law Deïoneus into a pit of burning coals, thus becoming the first example of violence against one's kindred. Zeus had cleansed him of his blood-guilt and had welcomed him into the company of the gods on Olympos. In return, Ixion attempted to seduce Hera, Zeus' wife. Pindar mentions both of Ixion's crimes, but he deals in detail only with the latter part of his story, which is clear enough to follow as Pindar tells it. Its significance, however, is enhanced by the symbolic meaning of the wheel on which Ixion turns.

There are two clues to the special nature of Ixion's wheel. Pindar says that it is "winged" and that it has four spokes. A four-spoked wheel with wings upon it would have called to mind a word Pindar does not actually use in *Pythian 2*, the word *iunx*. The wings referred to are those of a bird, the *iunx* or wryneck, whose habits in mating apparently intrigued the ancient Greeks enough to result in their use of it for magical rites designed to procure sexual satisfaction from a reluctant partner. The bird was pinned to a four-spoked wheel and the wheel was spun with appropriate incantations uttered over it, to draw the desired partner into the spell. "*Iunx*, bring that man of mine home to me," the lovelorn Simaitha repeats again and again as she spins her magic wheel in Theokritos' second Idyll. The love charm, then, was called an *iunx*, and it was certainly known to Pindar, for in the fourth Pythian ode (213–17) he attributes its invention to Aphrodite, who brought it to Jason to help him seduce Medea. In *Pythian 2*, Pindar tells us that Ixion's punishment was his own doing, suggesting that Ixion was responsible not only for the punishment itself but also for the form it took. Ixion, in other words, employed his own *iunx* in his abortive wooing of Hera. There would be poetic justice in Zeus' punishment of him: the small *iunx* becomes gigantic, the bird on the wheel is replaced by a man.

The myth of Ixion concludes with a brief account of his progeny. Zeus had duped him into embracing an image of Hera fashioned of cloud. This cloud-Hera became pregnant and bore a son whom she named Kentauros. Kentauros then mated with the wild mares on Mt. Pelion, and from that union was born the race of Kentaurs (Centaurs), creatures half-man, half-horse, who ever after showed their ancestry by their inordinate sexual appetites and bad behavior. The scholar Peter Von der Mühll has shown that Pindar is here creating an etymology for the name Kentauros, from the verb *kentein*, meaning to goad, stab, or prick, and the noun *aura*, meaning air: the son thus bears a name recalling the generative act that produced him; his own progeny bear it ever after.

Pindar leaves the myth of Ixion behind at the start of the third triad, with a hymn to the greatness and power of the gods. The only peculiarity in this section of the ode is the way Pindar introduces the poet Archilochos, who lived some 200 years before. Of Archilochos' poems we have fragments only, but enough to know that he commanded an exceptionally vehement style. It is as a poet of invective and abuse that Pindar introduces him here. Invective and abuse are the precise opposites of praise, which is Pindar's poetic task. Ixion and Archilochos are both, in a sense, rejected by Pindar: Ixion is the opposite of the virtues commended in this poem, and Archilochos is no poetic model for Pindar to follow. Pindar's criticism of Ixion reminds him of his real task, praise of Hieron.

Hieron's athletic achievements form the subject of the opening praises of the ode. In the third triad, Pindar commends him for his military glory, his wealth, and his intelligence. The latter makes a bridge to the difficult final triad, where Pindar begins by paying tribute to Hieron's astuteness as a king and as an appreciator of words. The "Kastor-song" mentioned at the close of the third triad is in all likelihood this very ode, called by Pindar a Kastor-song because the ode celebrates a chariot victory: Kastor was the patron of all equestrian activities (see *Pythian 5*).

The fourth triad resembles the second: it is negative illustration. Pindar disavows an envious response to Hieron's greatness. "I will not envy you" is equivalent to "I will praise you as you deserve." The triad is phrased throughout in the first person (see the Introduction, *Pindar's Genre*). Pindar speaks here as a poet voicing the values of an aristocratic society, and he speaks in traditional riddles. The ape that children are so fond of is merely an imitation of a man: Hieron will not be fooled by appearances. With this we enter the royal court, where intrigue is always flourishing and where evil, if not utter chaos, will ensue if the king himself cannot tell the difference between truth and falsehood.

The closing stand contains a succinct lesson in Greek ethics. The realization that *all* human happiness is transitory makes envy not only undesirable but unreasonable as well. In this way, Pindar dismisses the envy men might feel toward Hieron, even while reminding him of the more dreadful divine resentment of which he must, and will, beware.

For the pun in this section (on *helkos* - *helkomenoi*), see the Introduction, *Logopoeia.*

Turn 1

Great city of Syracuse,
the war god's sacred ground,
divine support of men
and horses flashing iron,
to you I come, bringing a song,
an announcement from shining Thebes:
the chariot Hieron drove
over the echoing earth has won.
He has crowned Ortygia,
where Artemis is enthroned,
the goddess
who joined him
when he tamed those mares,
she and the man together,
gently lifting the intricate reins. (1–8)

Counterturn 1

For the maiden of showering arrows
and Hermes, god of contests,
together make a radiance
glisten about him
when he yokes his powerful team
to the burnished chariot,
takes the reins in hand,
and calls on Poseidon,
the trident-wielding, wide-dominioned god.
Men have praised
other kings, too, for their virtues,
and the voices
of the Kyprians
often sing of Kinyras—
whom Apollo gladly cherished (9–16)

Stand 1

and Aphrodite loved, her favored priest,
hymned by his people, surely, in return
for his kindness.
So the West Lokrian maiden
sings of you before her house, O son of Deinomenes!
Thanks to your power, she looks forth, free
from the hopeless stress of war.
But they say that Ixion,
spun every way upon a winged wheel, proclaims,
under command of the gods,
his lesson to mankind:
Repay your benefactor honor's kind return! (17–24)

Turn 2

And he had learned it well—
life among the gods had been his
to enjoy, but he could not
enjoy it long, when he yearned
in his frenzied thoughts
even for Hera, the great bliss
allotted to Zeus' bed.
But Ixion's arrogance thrust him into
infatuation, and soon enough
he got what he deserved,
a unique punishment.
Two crimes brought his doom upon him.
He was the first to pollute mankind
by shedding kindred blood,
not without treachery; (25–32)

Counterturn 2

and then, in the great dark inner chambers,
he reached for Zeus' wife.
But it is always necessary
to know one's limits.
Ixion's clandestine love
hurled him into disaster.
It turned upon him too,
fool, who lay with a cloud,
fondling a sweet illusion:
in shape she resembled Hera,
proudest of Uranos' children;
but it was Zeus' hand that formed
and placed her there,
a lovely affliction, to beguile him.
The four-spoked wheel (33–40)

Stand 2

was his own doing, destruction brought on himself:
tumbling in immovable fetters, he embraced
the lesson he proclaims to all.
But she, alone,
apart from the Graces, bore him a child,
arrogant and solitary,
without honor among men or gods.
Reared by his mother, who called him Kentauros,
he mated
with Magnesian mares on the spurs of Mount Pelion
and sired a monstrous brood, resembling
both parents: the father above, the mother below. (41–48)

Turn 3

God achieves his every aim exactly as he wills—
god, who overtakes the eagle flying
and passes by the dolphin
skimming through the sea.
And he curbs the man
whose thoughts soar on high
and gives to others ageless glory.
But I must shun the crowding bite
of bitter speech,
for in the distance I have seen
bilious Archilochos often in distress,
swollen with harsh words of wrath.
To prosper
in accord with heaven's will,
is wisdom's finest flower, (49–56)

Counterturn 3

and such is yours to display
with a free mind,
lord of an armed host,
ruler of cities draped in garlands.
If a man today should claim
that any in the past of Hellas
had wealth and honor to eclipse your own,
his vain thoughts would wrestle with the wind!
I will take ship now,
my sails festooned with flowers,
and sing of your success.
Boldness bolsters youthful strength
in the dread clash of arms,
and there too, I say,
you have achieved unending glory, (57–64)

Stand 3

fighting among horsemen and on foot.
And the counsels of your riper years
afford the means to sing your praise on every theme
without risk.
I wish you joy.
Like precious goods from Tyre, my melody
comes to you over the gray sea.
Hear it gladly,
the Kastor-song on Aiolian strings, gladly
for the seven-toned lyre's sake.
Listen, and become
what you are.
Children prattle that the ape is "pretty"— (65–72)

Turn 4

pretty indeed! But Rhadamanthys prospers
in the perfect yield
of his good sense:
he takes no joy in subterfuges
that always stalk a man
where whisperers are scheming.
The dealer in slander
is an evil to himself
and to others, intractable,
an utter fox.
But what's the net of all his cunning?
Like a cork above the brine,
I stay afloat
while the rest of the gear
toils in the depths of the sea. (73–80)

Counterturn 4

A crafty politician will not impress
the noble with his speeches—
and yet, fawning on everyone,
he weaves delusion to its end.
I have no share in his boldness.
May I love my friend, and move
against my foe, as a foe—
tracking his shifty spoor
in the wolf's way, now here, now there.
In every sphere,
the just and well-spoken man
wins respect, whether in a tyranny,
or where the noisy crowd hold sway,
or the wise keep watch.
But one must not strive against a god (81–88)

Stand 4

who lifts up this group now, and soon
gives another its turn of glory.
Yet even that fails to appease the envious,
who pull on a line unwound to the limit
until it snaps: a wound to their own heart
before they compass their desires.
It is better
to take the yoke upon one's neck and bear it lightly.
Kicking against the goad makes the pathway treacherous.
Be it mine to dwell among the noble, and please them! (89–96)

PYTHIAN 3

Hieron of Syracuse, race for single horse, 474 (?) B.C.

Pythian 3 puts unusual emphasis on two themes: human mortality and the power of poetry to transcend it. The first theme is articulated in the beginning by a two-part myth spanning the first three triads. The double myth is presented in the form of an elaborate *recusatio*: the characters whose fates are portrayed in it exemplify an attitude that Pindar rejects.

In the first part, Pindar tells the story of the girl Koronis who, though pregnant by Apollo, fell in love with a stranger and lay with him. The defilement involved is hinted at, but Pindar seems more interested in Koronis' impatience, her inability to wait until after giving birth to Apollo's child. Apollo, having sent Artemis to punish Koronis, takes pity on her unborn child and rescues it from its mother's body on the funeral pyre.

The child is Asklepios, whom Apollo entrusts to the centaur Chiron to be raised as a physician. Pindar enumerates the accomplishments of Asklepios as a healer of pain and disease down to the moment when he raised a man from the dead, a fatal transgression of the limits of nature, for which Zeus punishes him.

Asklepios and his mother Koronis are both examples of the human tendency to be unsatisfied with necessary limitations. Koronis could not wait for her wedding day, Asklepios tried to overcome the human condition itself. Pindar almost yields to the same tendency at the opening of the ode, where he comes close to expressing the wish that Chiron, teacher of Asklepios, were still alive. It is not until the third stand that we learn why Pindar desiderates Chiron's return to life: he would have persuaded Chiron to raise another healer, like Asklepios. He would then have brought this gifted physician to Syracuse, where Hieron, in ill health, had need of him.

In the fourth counterturn, Pindar pulls back from these impossible wishes and does, instead, what he can do. From this point to the end of the ode, its second theme, the power of poetry to transcend mortal limitations, comes to the fore. Pindar had begun with the wish that he could supply Hieron with a wonder-working healer; he ends by dispensing to him the balm of immortal verse.

In the final part of the ode, Pindar consoles Hieron much in the manner Achilleus had consoled the aged king Priam in Book 24 of the *Iliad* (see the Introduction, *The Archaic Period*). Hieron resembles Peleus and Kadmos in having attained the highest bliss available to mortal man. Yet not even they were free from sorrow. Pindar briefly describes the high points in their lives. Kadmos married Harmonia in Thebes, Peleus married Thetis on Mt. Pelion. The gods attended both ceremonies, and the Muses provided the music. But Kadmos lived to be ruined by his three daughters–Ino who leaped into the sea with her child Melikertes, Autonoê and Agave who participated in the brutal killing of Pentheus. The fourth daughter offered some compensation for these disasters: Pindar calls her Thyona here. Her more familiar name is Semela. She was the mother of Dionysos by Zeus.

The son of Peleus and Thetis was Achilleus, hero of the *Iliad*. The last counterturn contains a brief description of his death and funeral at Troy. The Muses had sung at the wedding of his parents. We know from the twenty-fourth book of the *Odyssey* that they joined Thetis at his funeral and sang the dirge. Pindar does not mention this, but his audience would have remembered it.

The last stanza of the ode contains a series of statements in the first person, but it is clearly the first person indefinite that is speaking here, not Pindar personally. The language is general and wholly in keeping with sentiments expressed on similar themes elsewhere (see the Introduction, *Pindar's Genre*). One who has wealth has the opportunity to compete in the national athletic festivals, to show generosity to his fellow citizens, and, most importantly, to hire a poet like Pindar.

The date and occasion of *Pythian 3* are mysterious. The only victories named in the ode are the two won by Hieron's horse Pherenikos at the Pythian Games in 482 and again in 478 B.C., but there are good reasons for dating the ode later. Since it dwells at length on Hieron's illness, it has been called a letter of consolation to him. Form and meter, however, indicate that it was intended to be sung and danced in the regular epinician fashion.

There is, finally, a hint that Pindar is correcting an earlier version of the myth of Apollo and Koronis. According to Hesiod, Apollo learned of Koronis' infidelity from a raven. In anger, he changed the bird, formerly white, to black. Members of the original audience who knew Hesiod's version of the story would have sensed an allusion to the raven in Pindar's mention of a "watcher" whom Koronis did not elude (turn 2). Pindar, stressing Apollo's omniscience, implies that the god would have had no need for an informer.

Turn 1

If I were permitted
to utter the prayer
in everyone's mind,
I would wish that Chiron,
son of Philyra and sovereign Kronos,
a friend of mankind,
now dead and gone,
were living still
and that he ranged
the ridges of Pelion,
even as he was
when he raised Asklepios,
the gentle hero, craftsman
in remedies for the limbs of men
tormented by disease. (1-7)

Counterturn 1

Before his mother,
daughter of Phlegyas the rider,
could bring him to birth,
before Eleithyia could ease her pangs,
she sank to the house of Death,
stricken in her chamber
by the gold arrows of Artemis
at the urging of Apollo:
the wrath of gods
finds fulfillment.
In her folly,
she had slighted him, consenting—
without her father's knowledge—
to another union
though she had lain before with Apollo (8-14)

Stand 1

and bore the god's pure seed within her.
She did not wait for her marriage feast,
the high cries of *Hymen! Hymen!*
such as girls of her age, maiden companions,
echo in song, bantering the bride
with girlhood names on her wedding night.
No: like many another, she hungered
for things remote.
There are some, utterly
shiftless, who always look ahead,
scorning the present,
hunting the wind of doomed hopes. (15-23)

Turn 2

Eager Koronis, fond of gay clothing,
was wholly taken
with this infatuation—she lay
in the arms of a stranger
who came from Arkadia,
but she did not escape her watcher:
Loxias the king,
in his temple at Delphi,
heard what had happened,
informed by his surest confidant,
his all-knowing mind
impervious to lies,
beyond the reach of mortal
or immortal deception,
of fraud planned or perpetrated. (24–30)

Counterturn 2

He saw her then,
lying in bed with Ischys,
son of Elatos—
he saw her blasphemous deceit
and sent down Artemis
raging with anger
to Lakereia, for the maiden dwelled
on the banks of Lake Boibias.
An evil power
possessed and destroyed her
and many others
were involved in her ruin.
Though but a spark of fire
fall on the mountain,
the thick trees blaze and are gone. (31–37)

Stand 2

Only when her kinsmen had placed the girl
on a wooden mound and the grim glare of flame
ran crackling around her
did Apollo relent:
"I cannot kill my own child, trapped
in the doom of its ruined mother,"
he said, and strode into the blaze.
The fire hid nothing from him:
in one step
he found the corpse, tore the infant from it,
and carried it to Chiron in Thessaly
to be taught the art of medicine. (38–46)

Turn 3

And those who came to him
with flesh-devouring sores,
with limbs gored by gray bronze
or crushed beneath flung stones,
all those with bodies broken,
sun-struck or frost-bitten,
he freed of their misery,
each from his ailment,
and led them forth—
some to the lull of soft spells,
others by potions,
still others with bandages
steeped in medications
culled from all quarters,
and some he set right through surgery. (47–53)

Counterturn 3

But even wisdom feels
the lure of gain—
gold glittered in his hand,
and he was hired
to retrieve from death
a man already forfeit:
the son of Kronos hurled
and drove the breath,
smoking from both their chests—
savior and saved alike
speared by the lightning flash.
From the gods we must expect
things that suit our mortal minds,
aware of the here and now,
aware of our allotment. (54–60)

Stand 3

Do not yearn, O my soul, for immortal life!
Use to the utmost
the skill that is yours.
Yet if wise Chiron still haunted his cave,
if my singing had worked upon his mood
like a soothing drug, I would have moved him
to rear another healer, a son of Leto
or of Zeus, a hero to relieve good men
of the blaze of fever.
And I would have come,
cleaving the Ionian Sea on ship,
to Arethusa's fountain and my Aitnaian host (61–69)

Turn 4

who holds the throne of Syracuse,
a king gentle to his citizens
and generous to his nobles,
a father to arriving strangers.
If I had stepped from ship
bringing this double grace to him,
golden health and a revel-song
to brighten his triumphs,
the Pythian garlands
Pherenikos took at Kirrha once,
beating all contenders:
I say I would have crossed
the deep sea
like a radiance reaching
farther than a heavenly star. (70–76)

Counterturn 4

But I wish to make my prayer
to the sacred Mother Goddess
whom Theban maidens celebrate
all the night through,
singing of her and of Pan
not far from where I dwell.
If, Hieron, you understand,
recall the proverb now:
the deathless gods
dole out to death-bound men
two pains for every good.
Fools make nothing of either.
The noble turn both to advantage,
folding pain within,
and showing beauty without. (77–83)

Stand 4

You have a share of happiness—on you,
if on any man, great destiny has smiled,
for you are master of a people.
Still,
no life was ever safe from falling:
not even Peleus,
the son of Aiakos, or Kadmos, the gods' double,
knew perfect bliss, though men account them
blest with the highest joy—
they heard the Muses singing
on the mountain and in seven-gated Thebes,
when Kadmos married dark-eyed Harmonia
and Peleus married Thetis, the glorious daughter of Nereus, (84–92)

Turn 5

and the gods feasted
in their company,
the children of Kronos,
kings on golden thrones:
they beheld them
and received their wedding gifts.
So Zeus blessed them with a change
from former troubles,
and their hearts were high.
But in time again
Kadmos lost his share of bliss:
three of his daughters destroyed it
and yet the fourth,
white-armed lovely Thyona,
welcomed Zeus to her bed. (93–99)

Counterturn 5

And the only child
of Peleus and immortal Thetis,
felled by an arrow in war
and leaving life behind,
stirred the lament of the Danaans
as he burned on the pyre.
It is proper that a mortal man,
knowing the way of truth,
prosper from the gods
when he has the chance.
Winds soar on high—
one is a blessing, another is not.
Happiness that wafts a man
in full sail
will not sustain him long. (100–106)

Stand 5

I will be small among the small,
great among the great.
The spirit embracing me
from moment to moment I will cultivate,
as I can and as I ought.
And if the gods bestow
abundant wealth on me, then I will hope
to find high glory in days to come.
We know of Nestor and Lykian Sarpedon
from resonant words, such as skilled craftsmen of songs
have welded together.
It is radiant poetry
that makes virtue long-lived,
but for few is the making easy. (107–15)

PYTHIAN 4

Arkesilas of Kyrana, chariot race, 462 B.C.

Pythian 4 is the longest of Pindar's odes. Most of its extra length is due to the expansion of the mythical section, in which Pindar tells the story of Jason's quest for the Golden Fleece. The ode is unique also in its clearly political purpose. It praises Arkesilas IV, but it also addresses an appeal to him on behalf of an exiled Kyranaian.

Arkesilas IV, king of Kyrana (Cyrene), a Greek city in North Africa, traced his ancestry back eight generations to the founder of the city, Battos I, who, on the urging of the Delphic Oracle, had led a colony from the island of Thera to Kyrana. Battos had consulted the oracle in hopes of finding a cure for his speech defect (the name Battos means "Stammerer"), but Apollo had taken the occasion to hail him as future king of Kyrana.

According to Pindar, the prophecy made to Battos at Delphi repeats a prophecy made seventeen generations earlier by Medea. Medea and the sailors of the Argo, on their way home from Kolchis with the Golden Fleece aboard, had reached the site of the future city of Kyrana in Libya; from there they sailed to Thera, called at that time Kallista Island. It was on Thera that Medea delivered the prophecy that Pindar quotes in the first three triads of the ode. Among those who heard it was a certain Euphamos, destined to be an ancestor of the people of Thera, future settlers of Kyrana. Euphamos' original home was Tainaros. Medea, in her prophecy, explains how it came about that his descendants colonized Kyrana not from Tainaros but from Thera.

At the end of the third triad, Pindar declares his intention to tell the myth of the Argo. The remote genealogical connection between Euphamos, one of the original Argonauts, and Arkesilas, present king of Kyrana, justifies the choice of this particular myth.

In the background is the story of Phrixos and Helle, the children of King Athamas by his first wife, Nephele. His second wife, Ino, conceived a deadly hatred for her stepchildren and plotted to destroy them. A golden ram appeared, the gift of Hermes to Nephele. On its back the children rode through the sky, escaping the cruelty of their stepmother. But Helle slipped and fell on the way, drowning in the sea that afterward bore her name: the Hellespont. Phrixos arrived safely in Kolchis, on the shores of the Black Sea. Here, in thanks for his safe passage, he sacrificed the ram and dedicated its golden fleece to Zeus. Aietas, king of Kolchis, son of Helios and father of Medea, placed the fleece in a grove sacred to Ares the god of war. There it remained, guarded by a terrible dragon, until Jason came aboard the Argo to fetch it home.

The greater part of the mythical narrative of the ode is taken up with the quarrel between Jason and his older second cousin, Pelias, usurper of the throne of Iolkos from Jason's father Aison. The fourth, fifth, sixth, and seventh triads dramatize this conflict. At the beginning of the eighth, Jason accepts Pelias' treacherous invitation to go in quest of the Golden Fleece. Triad 8 contains a list of the heroes who responded to his summons and sailed with him. In triad 9, they embark. Triad 10 brings them to Kolchis, where Jason must face the ordeals imposed on him by Aietas. These he could not pass without the help of Medea, whose passion for Jason leads her to betray her father. Aphrodite plays her part in this: she brings from Olympos for the first time the love charm described in the preface to *Pythian 2*, the *iunx* or wryneck, which helps Jason seduce the exotic princess. At the end of triad 10, Jason passes the first ordeal imposed by Aietas. In triad 11, Pindar breaks off just as Jason is about to confront the formidable dragon guarding the Golden Fleece. Pindar then rapidly enumerates certain important moments in the rest of the story, particularly the sojourn of the Argonauts among the Lemnian women, for it is here that Euphamos consummates the union from which his Theraian descendants will spring. Once we have reached this episode in the story, we have returned to the point where it began: here, in triad 12, Pindar repeats the prophecy of the colonization of Kyrana, now ruled by Arkesilas.

The ode contains in its closing triads an appeal to Arkesilas for the restoration of a certain Damophilos, living in exile. Pindar mentions him by name only once, but the entire poem seems to exist on his account. He may have commissioned it from Pindar as a means of ingratiating himself with Arkesilas.

Turn 1

Today, Muse, you must stand beside
a man beloved,
Arkesilas,
king of Kyrana,
and join him in celebration,
swelling the breath of songs
due to Apollo and Delphi,
where once the priestess, seated
by the gold eagles of Zeus,
foretold that Battos,
founder-to-be of fertile Libya,
would leave behind
his sacred island home and build
a city famed for chariots
on the gleaming white breast of a hill, (1–8)

Counterturn 1

and thus fulfill, seventeen generations later,
the prophecy Medea, Aietas' great-hearted daughter,
queen of Kolchians,
made on Thera,
speaking with immortal inspiration
to the spellbound seamen
who sailed with Jason:
"Hear me, sons of brave men,
children of the gods:
the day will come when Libya,
daughter of Epaphos,
in the temple of Zeus Ammon,
shall receive and have implanted in her
from this sea-beaten island
the root of cities dear to mankind. (9–16)

Stand 1

Instead of dolphins soaring through the waves,
they will see mares prancing,
and in their hands,
no longer oars, but reins to guide their dashing horses.
Thera shall be mother of great cities then,
when the portent of Euphamos
comes to pass:
he stepped from the ship's prow, where Lake Tritonis
surges into the sea,
and a god who seemed a man
offered him a piece of earth in welcome.
Father Zeus let crash a peal of thunder, for good sign— (17–23)

Turn 2

we were hoisting the bronze-fluked anchor,
the coursing Argo's bridle,
when he came upon us:
for twelve days
we had borne her over desert dunes,
having hauled her out of Okeanos
at my direction.
And then he came,
walking alone, a god
in the radiant likeness of a man,
deserving reverence.
And he began
with friendly words, such as a host will use
when greeting strangers, offering
refreshment from their journey. (24–31)

Counterturn 2

But we declined, eager to be on our way.
He said he was Eurypylos, son of Poseidon,
and he recognized
our longing to be off.
In his right hand then he seized
a clump of earth, the first thing
to present itself, and eagerly
sought to offer it
in token of hospitality.
And, just as eagerly, Euphamos
leaped onto the beach,
reached hand to hand,
and took the fateful gift.
But now I see that it has tumbled overboard
and skimmed in the ship's foaming wake (32–39)

Stand 2

nightlong over the bright main.
Indeed, I had warned
the sentries to keep close guard on it,
relieving one another at the watch.
But they forgot,
and now upon this island the immortal seed of Libya
has washed ashore before the time.
For if lord Euphamos—
son of Poseidon, Master of Horses, and of Europa,
Tityos' daughter, who bore him by the Kaphisos—
had brought this earth back home with him to sacred Tainaros
and cast it down where Hades' mouth gapes into the underdark,
(40–46)

Turn 3

then would his descendants in the fourth generation
have been destined to seize broad Libya,
together with the Danaans—
uprooted, in those days,
from great Lakedaimon,
Argos Valley, and Mykenai:
but instead he will found
a race of distinguished men
begotten on the women of a distant land;
and they will come, honored by the gods,
to this very island,
and in time produce among them
a man to be the future lord
of Kyrana's plains, veiled in clouds.
He will enter the Pythian temple (47–54)

Counterturn 3

and be told by Phoibos to transport cities
on shipboard to the rich precinct
of Zeus' Nile."
So Medea prophesied,
chanting in oracular verses.
The men listened, breathless,
stricken with awe by the words
from the depth of her mind.
It was you that she meant,
Battos, blest son of Polymnastos;
and you whom Phoibos' oracle later exalted,
speaking unbidden
in the cry of the Delphic priestess—
three times she bade you "Hail,
fated King of Kyrana!"— (55–62)

Stand 3

when you had come, asking the god to cure
the stammer in your voice,
eight generations ago.
And now it is the height of spring
for Battos' line:
Arkesilas his descendant is flourishing
like earth with crimson flowers.
To him Apollo and Pytho
gave glory of triumph in the chariot race.
Of him, then, will I sing,
and of the Golden Fleece,
for when the Minyan chiefs set sail to fetch it,
the gods sowed honor for his race and him. (63–69)

Turn 4

What, then, started them on that voyage?
What bound them with nails of adamant
to undertake the risk?
The gods had ordained
that Pelias would meet his death
at the hands of the proud Aiolidai,
or through their machinations:
an oracle had come to him
at Delphi, near the omphalos of mother earth,
and his shrewd heart froze
when he heard it:
"Keep close watch
against a man wearing a single sandal
when he comes from mountain lairs
to the sunlit land of famed Iolkos, (70–77)

Counterturn 4

whether a stranger or your countryman, beware."
In time, a man arrived,
with two awesome spears in his hand
and wearing
Magnesian hunting garb
wrapped about his powerful limbs,
and a leopard skin
to ward the rain's barbs off.
The bright curls of his hair
had not yet vanished under the knife,
but streamed down his back.
He went straight on,
exulting in his dauntless spirit,
and stood in the market place
where the crowd milled and thronged. (78–85)

Stand 4

They knew him not,
but said to one another, marveling:
"He wouldn't be Apollo—or do you think he is?"
"No, nor is he Ares, driver of the bronze chariot."
"I'd call him Otos, or even bold lord Epialtas,
had not those sons of Iphimedeia, as legend says,
died in shining Naxos."
"And the arrows of Artemis,
springing from her deadly bow,
hunted down Tityos, so that men might learn
to yearn for things that are within their grasp." (86–92)

Turn 5

So they spoke among themselves,
but Pelias arrived in haste,
driving his burnished mule car
at headlong speed.
He was amazed
when he saw that the stanger wore
a sandal on his right foot only.
But he hid the terror in his heart
and said: "What land do you claim
for your native country, stranger?
Who among earthborn women
cast you forth
out of her gray belly?
Speak, and do not dishonor your birth
with odious lies." (93–100)

Counterturn 5

And Jason, unintimidated, answered him
in gentle words: "This I have to say,
that I will show
my upbringing by Chiron.
Yes, I come from Chariklo and Philyra,
from the cavern
where Centaur's daughters reared me:
for twenty years I lived with them,
not once, in word or deed,
bringing them shame.
Now I have returned,
to claim the ancient honor
of my father, the gift of Zeus
to Aiolos and his children, no longer
theirs to enjoy in justice. (101–8)

Stand 5

For I have learned that the lawless Pelias,
pale with lust for power, stripped my parents
of their rightful rule.
On the day of my birth,
for fear of his brutal outrage, they pretended
a dark affliction had touched their house,
a death.
Under cover of night
and women's wailing, they sent me forth,
wrapped in purple swaddling bands,
a child for Chiron Kronidas to nurture. (109–15)

Turn 6

But now you know the highlights of the story.
Fellow citizens, point out to me clearly
the house of my fathers,
riders of white horses:
for I am he, the son of Aison,
a native of this country,
no foreigner in a foreign land;
Chiron the sacred centaur
called me by the name of Jason."
So he spoke.
And his father knew him
when he entered the house:
tears welled in the old man's eyes,
his soul brimmed with joy to see his son
the best, the handsomest of men. (116–23)

Counterturn 6

And at the news of his arrival
both Aison's brothers came
and joined them:
Pheres from nearby,
leaving the Hyperian spring;
and Amythan from Messana.
Admatos also came quickly,
and Melampos, wishing their cousin well.
And Jason, warmly receiving them
at a common banquet, gave them
gifts proper to the occasion,
and drew festivity out
to its full extent, culling
the delight of hallowed feasting
for five full days and nights. (124–31)

Stand 6

But on the sixth the man confided in his kinsmen,
set the whole affair in earnest down before them
and won their support.
Quickly from the banquet room
they rose and followed him in haste to Pelias' hall.
There they took their stand.
And Pelias himself,
born of Tyro careful of her braids, came before them
when he heard their clamor.
Jason, letting his words
fall in mild intonations, laid the basis of a wise appeal.
"Son of Poseidon who split the rock of Tempe, (132–38)

Turn 7

men are too quick to spurn justice
for treacherous gain, though they hasten
to a harsh reckoning after.
                                        You and I
should guide our passions rightly
    as we weave our plans for happiness.
        I believe you know what I mean.
            A single woman was mother
        to Kretheus and bold Salmoneus.
    In the third generation sprung from them,
we in our turn look upon
                                        the mighty gold of the sun.
May the Moirai turn away in disgust
    if any enmity between kinsman
        spoil their regard for one another! (139–46)

Counterturn 7

It does not befit us to let the blades
of brazen swords and spears make division
of our ample birthright.
                                        I leave to you
the sheep, the dun herds of oxen,
    all the fields
        you took from my parents
            and graze now, fattening your riches.
        It is nothing to me, if you
    and your house are glutted with these.
But the scepter of monarchy,
                                        the throne where Kretheus sat
when he rendered strict justice
    to his knightly people—
        both of these, without hurt to either of us, (147–54)

Stand 7

you must give up, or some newer evil
comes between us on their account."
                                        Thus Jason,
and Pelias answered, softly:
                                        "I will do
as you say, and yet
                                old age is upon me now
while you, in the flower of your youth, can appease
the wrath of the underworld.
                                        The spirit of Phrixos
cries upon us to bring him home from Aietas' realm.
And we must also fetch the deep-fleeced hide of the ram
upon whose back he rode to safety from the sea (155–61)

Turn 8

and from the deadly thrusts of his stepmother.
A wondrous dream has told me all this,
and I inquired
of the oracle at Delphi
whether I should go ahead with it.
The answer: an expedition by ship,
and no delays.
Do you, willingly, perform this task
and I swear that I will let you
rule as sole king here.
Zeus, our ancestor,
bear me witness,
and be a mighty oath between us."
They agreed, and parted company.
And Jason himself forthwith (162–69)

Counterturn 8

sent heralds to proclaim the voyage everywhere.
Soon three of Zeus Kronidas' sons arrived,
keen for battle:
the one dark-eyed Alkmena's child,
the other two
twin sons of Leda.
Also a pair of tall men,
sons of the Shaker of Earth,
Pylos and high Tainaros their homes:
Euphamos and you, mighty Periklymenos,
whose fame for noble deeds
is now assured.
And the father of songs arrived,
glorious Orpheus,
master of the lyre by Apollo's gift. (170–77)

Stand 8

And Hermes Goldenwand sent both his sons
to meet that high challenge:
Echion and Erytos,
clamorous in their youth.
Zetas and Kalaïs
were there at once, though they lived
far off among the foothills of Pangaion:
Boreas their father, the wind-king, willingly, quickly,
gladly dispatched them—
on both their backs
bristled a pair of purple wings.
And Hera kindled
in each of the demi-gods a sweet, all-conquering passion (177–84)

Turn 9

to sail aboard the Argo
and not be left behind
at his mother's side
coddling a life
free from danger, but to win,
together with his age-mates,
a cure for death itself
in his own renown.
So when that pick of sailors
had gathered in Iolkos,
Jason praised them one by one,
and Mopsos his seer
augured by birds and sacred lots
that it was time to cast off:
the anchors hung from the ship's ram, (185–92)

Counterturn 9

the captain, standing in the prow
with a gold dish in his hand, called
on Zeus who grips the thunder,
on the swift
pounding waves, the winds and nights,
the pathways of the deep,
days of bright calm,
and a final blessing in their return.
From the clouds a voice
bellowed in good omen
and rays of lightning
rained bursting down.
The heroes caught their breath,
moved by the god's signs,
and the seer shouted to them (193–200)

Stand 9

"Fall to the oars: our hopes are sweet!"
Under their swift hands then the oar blades
dipped insatiably,
and the South Wind bore them
to the mouth of the Inhospitable Sea.
Here they dedicated
a grove to Poseidon.
A herd of tawny bulls,
for use in the sacrifice, grazed nearby;
and on the altar they found, already fashioned,
a stone hollow to cup the blood.
Then, swept onward
into the peril of the deep, they called on the Lord of Ships (201–7)

Turn 10

to save them from the crash of boulders
rolling with a roar together:
two of them, rocks
instinct with life,
quicker than the winds' rumbling cohorts—
now they are still,
stopped when the heroes sailed between
and beached on the banks of the Phasis.
Here, in the very domain of King Aietas,
they joined in battle
with the swarthy Kolchians.
And Aphrodite came,
queen of swiftest arrows,
bringing from Olympos the dappled wryneck
pinned to four spokes on an inescapable wheel, (208–15)

Counterturn 10

to work on men for the first time, the bird
of madness: and she taught Jason
skill in prayers and charms,
to strip Medea
of all care for her parents,
that her longing for Hellas
might turn her mind, already burning,
and steer her with the goad of passion.
And quickly Medea revealed the means
of passing her father's ordeals:
in a base of olive oil she mingled
antidotes for pain,
and gave them to him, to anoint his limbs.
And they looked forward
to the sweet embrace of love. (216–23)

Stand 10

But now Aietas threw down before him
the adamantine plow, and brought out bulls
snorting streams of blazing fire through their jaws,
pawing the earth with brazen hooves.
Single-handed,
he led them to the yoke, tied them in, and drove them
plowing the furrows straight, digging a fathom deep
into the earth's brown back.
And then he spoke:
"Let the ship's master try his hand at this,
this first: and then the imperishable coverlet, (224–30)

Turn 11

the fleece fringed with gleaming gold."
So Aietas cast the challenge,
and Jason took it up.
Trusting in the gods,
he let his purple cloak drop to the ground.
Medea's skill in potions
kept the fire from his flesh;
he gripped the plow,
bound the bulls' necks to the yoke,
and, stabbing their stout-ribbed flanks
with a pointed goad,
he toiled through
his allotted measure.
Aietas, astonished at his power,
uttered a wordless cry. (231–38)

Counterturn 11

But his comrades stretched their hands
toward the man in triumph, raining
bayleaf garlands
and warm shouts upon him.
But grimly the son of Helios pointed the way
to the shimmering fleece,
where Phrixos with his blade
had flayed the ram and spread it out.
He had no inkling yet
that Jason would succeed,
for the fleece lay in a thicket,
and a dragon
loomed above it, foam
dripping from its cruel jaws, huger
than a fifty-oared, iron-bolted ship. (239–46)

Stand 11

But it's a long way by the main road,
and time presses.
I know a certain shortcut, for I am guide to many
in the turns of song.
Arkesilas, Medea's wiles
helped him past that green-eyed, speckle-backed serpent;
and she took part in her own abduction, she, Pelias' ruin.
And they sailed
over Okeanos' breadth and Red Sea waves
into the arms of the Lemnian women, murderers
of the male sex.
To them they showed their speed
in a contest with a cloak for prize, (247–53)

Turn 12

and then they led the women to their beds.
On that eventful day or in the nights of love
the seed of your greatness fell
                    in foreign furrows:
for then it was that Euphamos' race
  was sown to endure forever.
    In time, they came to dwell
      at home in Lakedaimon,
    whence they colonized Kallista Island;
  then Apollo joined the gods
to honor them again:
                    the plain of Libya
he gave to you, to make it prosper,
  and the city of Kyrana throned in gold,
    yours to govern (254–61)

Counterturn 12

by devising fruitful policies.
Observe, then, the wisdom
in Oedipus' proverb:
                    If a man
with sharp-edged axe
  hew away a tall oak's branches,
    spoiling its beauty,
      though it is ruined
    in fruit and foliage
  yet it will prove its worth
one day, when it comes at last
                    to the winter's fire,
or when it stands beneath a king's firm portal,
  enduring sad toil amid foreign walls,
    far from its native place. (262–69)

Stand 12

You, Arkesilas, are a healer with a sense of timing—
Apollo Paian's honor shines in you.
Put, then, a soothing hand to the wound's affliction
and tend it.
            Even men of no account
can shake a city, but to set her on her feet again
is hard,
      unless a god suddenly show the way.
I have spelled out these graces here for you
to be the author of them:
                    be bold, then,
and use all speed to win Kyrana's happiness. (270–76)

Turn 13

Versed as you are in the lore of Homer,
ponder this saying of his as well:
"A good messenger
furthers any enterprise."
And the Muse herself prospers
through a message rightly phrased.
Kyrana and the high bright hall of Battos
have had a chance to know and savor
Damophilos' just intentions.
He's young of heart when with the young,
but at the council table
he's as good as an elder
with a hundred years' experience behind him.
No evil tongue waits on his encouragement,
no arrogant man basks in his regard, (277–84)

Counterturn 13

he has no quarrel with the nobles,
nor does he dally with a project,
knowing opportunity
is brief among men.
And so he tends to it, a loyal servant,
not a reluctant drudge.
But men are agreed that this
of all things is most galling:
to know the right
but refrain from doing it, under duress.
He, a second Atlas,
still bruises his shoulder
against the sky, far from home and belongings.
But immortal Zeus let the Titans go,
and seamen change their sails (285–92)

Stand 13

as the wind falls.
All he prays for is to look one day
upon his home, having drained to the lees
his cup of affliction;
to let his heart
enjoy delights of youth, joining the symposium
beside Apollo's spring;
and to find his peace
playing the intricate lyre for cultivated friends:
causing no one any pain, himself unhurt by his neighbors.
Then would he tell you, Arkesilas, what a fountain
of immortal words he found, when lately entertained at Thebes!
(293–99)

PYTHIAN 5

Arkesilas of Kyrana, chariot race, 462 B.C.

Pythian 5 presents only a few difficulties to the modern reader, and these are basically historical. The ode commemorates the same victory as *Pythian 4*, won by Arkesilas. His brother-in-law Karrhotos, son of Alexibias, drove the winning chariot.

Arkesilas was a member of the royal house founded by King Battos I, who in 630 B.C. led a colony of Greeks from the island of Thera to the site of Kyrana and there founded the city. Battos I was originally named Aristoteles, and so Pindar calls him in the third stand. The use of both names in the poem would seem to draw attention to the meaning of the nickname: "Battos" means "Stammerer." According to Pindar, the sound of Battos' voice, with Apollo's help, put to flight a pack of lions.

Apollo plays a considerable role in the poem. To him Arkesilas is indebted for his triumph, since Apollo is patron of the Pythian Games. In addition, Apollo is the god of music: hence he takes delight in the performance of the present poem. But it is chiefly as a god worshipped in Kyrana that we see him in *Pythian 5.* The sons of Aigeus, ancestors of the Kyranaian chorus, had honored Apollo in Thera at a special feast called the Karneia, held in late spring. This custom came with them from Thera to Kyrana, where Apollo continued to be worshipped as Apollo Karneios.

Some 500 years before Battos I colonized Kyrana, the "Antanoridai," or sons of Antanor, were said to have arrived there from Troy, recently sacked by the Greeks. Between Kyrana and the sea there was, in fact, a hill called "The Hill of the Antanoridai." Pindar tells us that the sons of Antanor came "with Helen in their midst," meaning, apparently, that they accompanied Menelaos in his wanderings after the fall of Troy. Antanor was known for his disapproval of the marriage of Helen and Paris. The Greeks spared him and his family when Troy fell. The Antanoridai appear in *Pythian 5* as "guests" at Kyrana, honored with religious observances.

The most interesting feature of local religion touched on by Pindar in this ode comes at the end, where he speaks of the dead Battos in his tomb in the market place, and of the other kings buried outside the city. He tells us that they hear the song in which their descendant, Arkesilas, is honored, and that they too have a share in the glory.

The ode concludes with two prayers. One was granted: Arkesilas went on to win the chariot race at Olympia in 460 B.C. But the prosperity Pindar hopes will continue came to an end not long after Arkesilas' Olympian triumph: he lost his life in a popular uprising, and his dynasty died with him.

Turn 1

Wealth wields wide sway
when a mortal man,
receiving it from a god,
brings it into play, tempered
with his own pure excellence.
It supports him then, and many a friend
follows in its train.
Arkesilas, you have used it
gloriously, from your first steps
up the scale of renown, till now—
thanks to the favor
of golden Kastor
who has made
bright weather stream
over your blest hearth
after the winter's rain. (1–11)

Counterturn 1

Power bestowed by a god
works to even nobler effect
in a wise man's hands:
all around you
prosperity flourishes,
for you walk in the ways of justice,
king of mighty cities.
Prestige, the beacon
of inherited greatness,
burns all the brighter
when fed by thought like yours,
and today you are blest
because you have won
with your chariot
in glittering Pytho
and because you welcome this chorus (12–22)

Stand 1

to Apollo's delight.
To him you owe everything—
remember him, while they sing your name
around Aphrodite's garden in Kyrana.
And cherish
Karrhotos first among your friends: he has returned
to the royal house of the Battidai without Prophasis,
daughter of Epimetheus the wise-too-late, at his side.
No, for he was welcomed by Kastalia's waters, and he has placed
on your brow the crown for victory in the chariot race, (23–31)

Turn 2

having kept his reins intact
through all twelve turns
on the swift sacred course—
no trace of damage
in the sturdy rig
wrought for him by gifted craftsmen:
past the Krisaian hill
into the hollow of the god
he drove it
and hung it up in consecration.
The cypress chamber
enshrines it now,
beside the statue
hewn from the living wood,
which Kretan bowmen dedicated
in the Parnassian temple. (32–42)

Counterturn 2

Then let us welcome him eagerly,
our benefactor!
Son of Alexibias,
the long-haired Graces
light the flame of your glory.
Blest, to have memorial of peerless words
follow your prodigious exploit:
forty drivers wrecked
but you were unshaken,
you drove your chariot
directly through the melee
undamaged,
and now you have come
from the radiant contest
to the plain of Libya
and your native city. (43–53)

Stand 2

No man is, or ever shall be, without his share of troubles.
And yet the ancient prosperity of Battos—
a tower to the city,
a beacon to the wanderer—
endures, bringing its varied blessings.
Ancient Battos:
even roaring lions ran pell mell from him, in terror
of his exotic accent.
Apollo the Founding Father
inspired the brutes' sheer panic, lest
his oracles to Kyrana's steward come to nothing. (54–62)

Turn 3

He is the god who sends
mortal men and women
relief from grievous disease, Apollo,
who has given us the lyre,
who brings the Muse
to whom he chooses, filling the heart
with peace and harmony.
He holds the dark
chambers of prophecy,
whence he caused
the stalwart sons
of Herakles and Aigimios
to dwell in Lakedaimon,
Argos, and Pylos the august.
But the glory I delight in
boasts of its birth in Sparta, (63–73)

Counterturn 3

where ancestors of my own
had their beginning:
descendants of Aigeus,
they made their way
with the gods and fate leading them
to Thera, and the feast rich in sacrifice—
the prototype, Apollo Karneios,
of your banquet,
where we honor
strong-built Kyrana
held by her Trojan guests:
for the bronze-loving sons of Antanor,
with Helen in their midst,
once beached on these shores
after they had seen their city
billow with the smoke (74–84)

Stand 3

of war.
And here they are welcome still, received
at the sacrifice with gifts and faithful tendance
by the men Aristoteles brought in swift ships, opening
a deep path over the sea.
He widened the gods' sanctuaries.
He laid out a stretch of ground, level, cut straight
to be a road of hoof-clattered cobblestones:
Apollo's martial parades pass there,
by the edge of the market place,
where Battos lies entombed alone:
(85–93)

Turn 4

Battos, blest among men in life,
a hero revered in death.
Apart from him,
in front of their houses
dwell the other sacred kings
who have their lot in the undergloom.
Somehow, when high achievements
glisten with the dew
shed by song,
they listen
beneath the earth,
imbibing a share
of their son's happiness,
the grace Arkesilas deserves.
Well may he call on Phoibos
through the young men's singing, (94–104)

Counterturn 4

for he has earned at Pytho
the joyous chant of victory
that reimburses all expense.
Wise men commend him
and so will I, because
the mind and eloquence that sustain him
are mightier than his years.
His boldness has the wing-span
of an eagle among birds.
In a contest,
he is confidence itself,
a bastion of strength.
His musical gifts
were fledged in his mother's lap.
And he has proved himself
a master charioteer: (105–15)

Stand 4

in every local competition he has shown
his prowess.
A god lovingly gives him fulfillment now:
in time to come, O blest children of Kronos,
grant him the same, to keep in return for his deeds
and his counsels.
Let not the fruit-destroying blast
of winter wind savage the days ahead.
Zeus' vast mind
steers the fate of favored men.
I pray that he give
Battos and his race another triumph, at Olympia! (116–24)

PYTHIAN 6

Xenokrates of Akragas, chariot race, 490 B.C.

Xenokrates was one of the descendants of Emmenes and a member of the ruling family of Akragas. The ode celebrating his victory at Delphi, one of Pindar's earliest surviving poems, is addressed not to Xenokrates himself but to his son Thrasyboulos. The ancient commentaries inform us that Xenokrates had commissioned Simonides to write the official ode on this occasion. If this is correct, *Pythian 6* may have been an extra composition requested by Thrasyboulos to further enhance his father's glory. Composed to be sung in procession to the temple of Apollo at Delphi after the victory, it is written not in triads for choral performance, but in repeating stanzas for a processional. It opens with an appeal to the crowd for attention as the singing procession gets underway.

At the end of the first stanza and all through the second, Pindar imagines the poem itself in architectural terms, calling it "a treasure house of Pythian victory songs." He is alluding to the treasuries that lined the Sacred Way at Delphi, small temple-like buildings erected by the cities of Greece to contain the precious offerings they made to Apollo. The chorus would have passed these treasuries on its way to the main temple of the god and the *omphalos* or navel of the earth—a conical stone that, according to Greek popular belief, marked the location of the world's center.

The rest of the ode praises Thrasyboulos for his devotion to his father. He lives according to the moral code once taught to Achilleus by "Philyra's son," the centaur Chiron. Stanzas four and five illustrate the keeping of Chiron's precepts by another hero, Antilochos, son of Nestor. The poem then concludes with compliments to Thrasyboulos for his cultivation of poetry and for the delight he gives his friends at the banquet table. In munificence and good taste, he rivals even his splendid uncle, Theron, future tyrant of Akragas, for whom Pindar was to write the second and third Olympian odes fourteen years later.

Pythian 6 is not the only poem Pindar wrote for Thrasyboulos. We have a fragment of a drinking song that compliments him for conviviality:

> O Thrasyboulos! I am sending you this vehicle of delightful songs for singing after the feast. May it be, at your shared table, a sweet goad to your drinking companions, to the fruit of Dionysos, to the Athenian goblets: when the thoughts of men care-laden wander out of their hearts—and on a sea of wealth deep in gold we all sail together toward a false shore: the poor man is rich then, and

> the rich . . . lift up their hearts, smitten with the shafts of the vine . . . (fragment 124)

There is also *Isthmian 2*, which Pindar wrote for Xenokrates but, again, addressed to Thrasyboulos. It too opens with references to Aphrodite. The opening of *Pythian 6*, however, sounds a curious note of hesitation. Pindar declares that he is "plowing again" the field of Aphrodite, which would suggest a love song if it were by itself; but then he adds the phrase "*or* of the Graces," as if he were hesitating briefly between a love song and a victory song—but it is the love that comes first to his mind.

Only a few days after Xenokrates won the victory celebrated in this ode, the Athenians at Marathon defeated the Persian invaders led by Darius.

1 Listen! for we are turning over
dark-eyed Aphrodite's ground
or the Graces' furrows again,
on our way to the sacred
navel-stone of thundering earth:
there, in Apollo's valley glittering with gold,
the sons of Emmenes,
their city Akragas upon the river,
and even now Xenokrates
have built themselves
a treasure house of Pythian victory songs, (1–9)

2 which neither the winter's rain,
its pitiless plundering army
pouring from the thundering clouds,
nor wind
will ever batter down and drive,
smitten with all-carrying silt,
into the ocean's chasms. No,
its portal standing in pure light
will proclaim to mortal men
the glory of your father and your family,
Thrasyboulos, won in the chariot at Krisa. (10–18)

3 With victory at your right hand,
you abide by the precepts
men say Philyra's son once taught
the mighty Achilleus, Peleus' child,
left to his care in the mountains
far from home:
"Adore the son of Kronos,
lord of lightning and deep voice of thunder,
first among the gods,
and among men never deny
your parents first honor as long as they live." (19–27)

4 And long ago Antilochos the warrior
proved himself of such a mind:
standing against the killer of men,
Memnon, prince of the Ethiopian army,
he died to save his father.
For one of Nestor's horses, wounded
by an arrow from the bow of Paris,
had entangled the chariot, and Memnon
poised his deadly spear.
Whirling around in terror,
the old Messanian called on his son, (28–36)

5 and his cry for help did not fall to the ground:
godly Antilochos, standing firm,
purchased his father's rescue
with his own death
and won, by that prodigious feat,
fame for filial love
supreme among the youth of ancient times.
And so it was.
Of men alive today,
Thrasyboulos is the best example
of devotion to one's father, (37–45)

6 and in magnificence of display
he rivals his uncle, spending his wealth
with discretion, for he reaps
no brashness of youth, only the wisdom
that flowers in the Muses' garden.
To you, Poseidon Earth-shaker, lord of chariot races,
his thoughts are a delight,
while to his friends around the wine bowl,
his charm of mind and conversation
surpass in sweetness
even the latticed cellwork built by the bees. (46–54)

PYTHIAN 7

Megakles of Athens, chariot race, 486 B.C.

Pythian 7 is the briefest of Pindar's odes. Megakles, for whom it was written, was an uncle of Pericles, the famous Athenian leader. Both were Alkmaionidai or descendants of Alkmaion, a family that had been prominent in Athenian politics for a century and a half. The great-grandfather of Megakles had won the chariot race at Olympia in 592 B.C. This is the Olympian victory mentioned in the list concluding the counterturn. The list includes five Isthmian and two Pythian victories, one being the occasion of this ode.

Together with the athletic splendors belonging to the family, Pindar celebrates their renown as restorers of the temple of Apollo at Delphi after its destruction in 548 B.C. Although they had agreed to construct it of rough porous stone, they then went beyond the terms of the agreement to give the temple a resplendent marble façade.

Some four years before Megakles won the victory commemorated in this ode, his family had fallen under suspicion of having aided the Persian invaders before the battle of Marathon. Megakles himself, at the time he gained his Pythian victory, was in exile, a victim of the peculiar Athenian institution known as ostracism. This state of affairs must have added point to Pindar's reflections, at the end of the ode, on the resentment felt by men toward the greatness of others.

Turn

Praise of great Athens
is the noblest foundation
we can lay down as prelude
to a song honoring
a chariot victory
gained by the mighty sons of Alkmaion.
For what country will you dwell in,
what home will you inhabit,
telling all Greece it is more radiant than Athens? (1-8)

Counterturn

Familiar to every city is the story
of Erechtheus' townsmen
who made your temple, Apollo,
a wonder to behold
in sacred Pytho.
But five Isthmian triumphs inspire me now,
and one
flamelike in glory
at Zeus' Olympia, and two more at Kirrha, (9-16)

Stand

yours, Megakles, and your forefathers'.
No small joy do I feel
for this fresh success,
and yet I grieve
that envy pays back noble deeds.
This is exactly what is meant
in the saying of men:
Happiness
of abiding bloom bears
now and then a bitter fruit. (17-21)

PYTHIAN 8

Aristomenes of Aigina, wrestling, 446 B.C.

Pindar was seventy-two when he wrote *Pythian 8*. It is, as far as we can tell, his last poem.

The myth of the ode, taken from the traditions of Thebes, illustrates the theme of inherited greatness. Just as Aristomenes' victory bears out his noble ancestry, so, in the distant past, the warrior-prophet Amphiaraos could infer the greatness of the Epigonoi from the greatness of their fathers. The Epigonoi ("Those born after") were the sons of the ill-starred Seven against Thebes. Amphiaraos, an unwilling participant in the first siege against Thebes, had descended, at its disastrous conclusion, into the underworld (see *Olympian 6* and *Nemean 9*). From there he observes the progress of the second siege, noticing his own son, Alkman, among the other warriors. He also sees Adrastos, sole survivor of the first expedition, and makes a prophecy concerning him.

The ode opens with a prayer to "Hesychia." The Greek abstract noun, personified for the first time by Pindar, means, simply, Peace. In political terms it refers to internal peace, the peace enjoyed by the citizens of a city who may choose, while remaining on good terms with one another, to fight foreign enemies. This may help a modern reader resolve the apparent paradox of a goddess whose name means peace, but who also holds the keys to war, as Pindar depicts her in the opening turn. The counterturn shows her taking vigorous action against her enemies, mythologically represented by the king of the giants, Porphyrion, who tried, among other things, to rape Hera, and by Typhon, who strove to overthrow the sovereignty of Zeus. Pindar only goes so far as to mention their names and their defeats. The audience would have appreciated them for what they were—violent enemies of the universal order, creatures of chaos.

For relations between Athens, Thebes, and Aigina when *Pythian 8* was composed, see the Introduction, *Pindar's Life and Times.* Aigina had lost her independence to Athens some twelve years before. The Athenians had just recently withdrawn from Boiotia after the battle of Koroneia. Pindar's concluding prayer for Aigina's freedom must have moved an Aiginetan audience still oppressed by the yoke of Athens.

The victor Aristomenes was the son of Xenarkes and a member of the Meidylid clan.

Turn 1

Loving-minded daughter of Justice,
Hesychia!
source of the city's greatness,
keeper of the sovereign keys
to war and counsel,
welcome my song
honoring Aristomenes, victor at Delphi.
For you have mastery
in all the ways of kindness,
yielding to its sway
and showing it to others
with flawless instinct. (1-7)

Counterturn 1

But when a man has hidden resentment
deep in his heart,
he has you to contend with–
harsh against your enemy,
you plunge him thrashing
in the abyss,
you, whom Porphyrion all unawares
brashly moved to anger.
But gain is most valuable
when it comes
from the hand
of a willing giver. (8-14)

Stand 1

Violence has overthrown the violent in good time.
Kilikian hundred-headed Typhon did not escape it,
nor the King of the Giants.
They perished,
broken beneath the lightning bolt
and the shafts of Apollo,
who has gladly welcomed
the son of Xenarkes from Kirrha, crowned
with Parnassian laurel and Dorian song. (15-20)

Turn 2

His island home with her just city
has never fallen
from the Graces' favor:
the renown of Aiakos' sons
stays with her still,
and her name has kept
glory perfect from the beginning.
Many a singer praises her,
mother of heroes
who towered in the contest
and were beacons
in the flux of battle. (21–27)

Counterturn 2

And her people now bring her honor.
But I am without leisure
to set the whole story down
in melody and lyrics.
Tedium would surely come
and chafe my audience.
But here is something hastening to meet me.
I am indebted to you for it, my child—
the latest of your victories:
now watch it fly
upon the wings
of my devising. (28–34)

Stand 2

You follow in the footsteps of your mother's brothers,
champions in the art of wrestling:
Theognetos and Kleitomachos,
winners at Olympia and Isthmos;
and in glorifying the clan of the Meidylidai,
you prove the saying Amphiaraos uttered once,
when he beheld the sons
standing by their spears at seven-gated Thebes— (35–40)

Turn 3

the Epigonoi, the second army
to march out of Argos.
And thus he prophesied
while they were fighting:
"The spirit of the fathers
lives in their sons,
clear to see, implanted by nature.
I recognize him, Alkman—
a speckled serpent
blazes on his shield:
the first to assault
the gates of Thebes. (41–47)

Counterturn 3

And there stands Adrastos, the hero
who knew defeat
in his first attempt.
Now a bird of better omen
sends him on his way.
But grief at home
will cast a shadow on his triumph:
alone among the host of the Danaans
he will gather up
his dead son's bones, and go,
by the gods' will,
with his army safe, (48–54)

Stand 3

back to the spacious streets of Abas."
So spoke Amphiaraos.
And I too
crown Alkman with garlands and rain praises on him
gladly, for he is my neighbor,
the guardian of my wealth.
He met me
on the road to Delphi and prophesied to me
by the gift of truth that is his birthright. (55–60)

Turn 4

But you, Apollo, wielder of the bow
that strikes from afar,
lord of the gleaming temple
in Delphi's valley,
where the world assembles—
there you honored
Aristomenes with the best of prizes;
and at home in your festival
you gave him victory
in the pentathlon.
Now, I pray you,
with willing mind (61–67)

Counterturn 4

see me through the song, in harmony
each step of the way.
Justice stands beside
the celebrant chorus.
And I pray, Xenarkes,
that the gods
look with unjealous eyes upon your fortunes.
For many suppose
that a man who has triumphed
without great effort
must be a sage
in the midst of fools, (68–74)

Stand 4

arming his life with clever stratagems.
But all this lies beyond human calculation:
a god disposes it, hurling one man upward
and bringing another down to size.
Aristomenes,
you took the prize at Megara,
and in the glen of Marathon, and three times
you won the bout in Hera's local contest. (75–80)

Turn 5

And then you sprang with grim intent,
pinning the limbs
of your four opponents.
Not for them, as for you,
a sweet return from Delphi,
no light laughter
rising from their mothers' lips
in welcome. No,
they slink along back alleyways,
shunning enemy eyes
and nursing pain,
the bite of defeat. (81–87)

Counterturn 5

But he who has achieved a new success
basks in the light,
soaring from hope to hope.
His deeds of prowess
let him pace the air,
while he conceives
plans sweeter to him than wealth.
But the delight of mortal men
flowers,
then flutters to the ground,
shaken by a mere
shift of thought. (88–94)

Stand 5

Creatures of a day!
What is someone?
What is no one?
Man: a shadow's dream.
But when god-given glory comes
a bright light shines upon us and our life is sweet.
Dear mother Aigina, guide this city in the ways of freedom!
Zeus, join with her, with mighty Aiakos,
Peleus, Telamon the brave, and Achilleus! (95–100)

PYTHIAN 9

Telesikrates of Kyrana, race in full armor, 474 B.C.

Pythian 9 is distinguished by its erotic theme. There are moments of erotic feeling in other odes, notably *Pythian 6* and *Isthmian 2*, both addressed to Thrasyboulos of Akragas; and *Olympian 10* and *Nemean 8*, both written for youthful victors. But only in *Pythian 9* is the entire myth erotic in emphasis, and this is true not only of the long myth at the beginning, which fills almost three triads, but also of the briefer myth that concludes the ode. Even the victory catalogue preceding the final myth has an erotic overtone.

The myth of the love of Apollo for Kyrana follows immediately upon the opening lines of the ode, in which Pindar recalls, with poetic elaboration, the coronation and proclamation of the victor at the games. Because the city had shared the glory of coronation with the victor, Pindar imagines his own announcement of the victor and his city as a coronation of Kyrana, who is at that moment both the city and the goddess for whom it was named.

In the course of the myth, Pindar refers to Libya, where Kyrana was situated, as the "third root of the continent." This is the earliest example of the division of the earth's land mass into three sections, Europe, Asia, and Libya (Africa west of the Nile). Pindar also mentions a certain "island folk" who are to colonize Kyrana. These are the people of Thera (see the prefaces to *Pythians 4* and *5*). The child born to Kyrana and Apollo is Aristaios, who appears in the fourth book of Vergil's *Georgics* as the inventor of bee-keeping. The prophecy of Chiron in *Pythian 9* culminates in a list of the various names by which Aristaios was known to men: Zeus, Apollo, Agreus, and Nomios. The last two signify that he is a god of hunting and pasturing.

At the conclusion of the myth, Pindar returns to the triumph of Telesikrates ("Karneiadas' son") at the Pythian games. The fourth triad then begins with some general reflections on the need for brevity and for artful presentation of facts in an epinician ode. This is a prelude to the catalogue of minor victories about to begin.

Telesikrates had won in the Iolaia, local games at Thebes, in memory of the hero Iolaos. Pindar announces this victory by saying that the hero has honored the victor. The mention of the hero leads to a brief celebration of his most famous exploit: Iolaos had risen from the dead in order to kill Eurystheus, the persecutor of Herakles and his children. The Thebans then buried him again in the tomb of his grandfather Amphitryon, husband of Alkmena, who was the mother of Herakles by

Zeus. Pindar now praises Herakles briefly, along with his half-brother Iphikles. From here he passes to a rapid mention of three other victories gained by Telesikrates at Aigina and at Megara ("Nisos' hill"). These successes deserve recognition: even an enemy acting nobly deserves praise, as Nereus, the sea's Ancient, had said. At the end of the catalogue, we see Telesikrates winning in various minor games. We see him, however, not through Pindar's eyes, but through the eyes of the women who desire him.

The list of minor victories (one at the Iolaia, three at Megara and Aigina, one at Athens, one at the local Olympics, one at the games of Gaia or Mother Earth) continues into the final triad, where it concludes with the climactic phrase "all the regional games." At this point, Pindar mentions "someone" (possibly the victor or a member of his family) whose thirst for song is still unsatisfied. There is one further item to be sung of, an ancient victory belonging to the family past. Alexidamos, one of Telesikrates' ancestors, had competed in the race for the hand of Barkê, the daughter of Antaios of Irasa. The myth of that race brings the ode to an end. Within it Pindar tells the parallel myth of how Danaos married off forty-eight of his fifty daughters. Of the other two, Hypermestra had already married Lynkeus (see the preface to *Nemean 10*), and Amymone had borne a son to Poseidon.

Turn 1

Eagerly, with the blessing of the Graces,
I announce his name, Telesikrates,
proclaiming him fortunate, a victor
in the race at Pytho
for warriors clad in bronze;
and thus I place a crown upon Kyrana,
whom Leto's long-haired son once caught up
in the windy gorges of Pelion
and brought in his golden chariot,
a virgin huntress, to Libya:
there he made her queen
of a land teeming with flocks,
a land rich in harvest, the flourishing
third root of the continent,
hers to inhabit and delight in. (1–8)

Counterturn 1

And silver-footed Aphrodite,
touching the rail
of the god-built chariot
with delicate hand,
welcomed her Delian guest.
Over their bed she cast
alluring modesty and joined them
in love, union between a god and a girl—
the daughter of great Hypseus,
who was king at that time
over the rude Lapithai,
a hero second in generation from Okeanos:
Naiad Kreoisa bore him in delight
to Peneios
in the famed clefts of Pindos Mountain, (9–16)

Stand 1

she a daughter of Gaia.
And Hypseus reared his child
Kyrana,
a girl who cared nothing
for pacing back and forth at the loom
or for dining at home with her friends—
instead, fighting with bronze javelins and sword,
she slew beasts of prey, providing
security for her father's herds
but spending,
at dawn's approach, scarcely any time on sleep,
the bed-partner that comes most softly to the eyelids then. (17–25)

Turn 2

Once as she wrestled
alone and weaponless
with a mighty lion, Apollo
of the wide quiver and far-
ranging arrows came upon her.
Quickly he called Chiron from his den.
"Son of Philyra, leave your sacred cavern
to marvel at a woman's power, marvel
at her courage, how she struggles
with head undaunted,
a girl keeping her heart
above the battle:
no storm of fear ruffles her spirit.
Who is her father,
from whose house has she been reft away (26–33)

Counterturn 2

to haunt the lairs
of shadowy mountains,
putting her strength
to endless tests?
Is it permitted
to lay my hand upon her
and pluck the honeyed fruit of love?"
The inspired Centaur, with a knowing look
and an indulgent smile, immediately
imparted his thoughts:
"The keys to skilled persuasion
in the sacred rites of love
are secret, Phoibos: men and gods alike
hesitate
to go with open pleasure to the bridal bed. (34–41)

Stand 2

And so it is with you:
an amorous mood has made you
dissemble in this way, you whom no lie may touch.
Do you ask me, lord, this girl's identity?
You who know
the end that guides all things, and all the ways:
how many leaves the earth puts forth in spring,
how many sands, churned by waves
and blasts of wind, whirl in sea and river,
what is to happen, and why—
all is within your ken.
Yet, if I must contend with wisdom's very self, (42–50)

Turn 3

I will speak:
you came to this valley
to possess this girl,
and you will carry her overseas
to Zeus' choicest garden.
There you will gather about her
an island folk and make her
foundress of a city
on a hill surrounded by plains.
Even now Queen Libya
opens the doors of her golden palace
to your bride, and she will give her
a portion of the world to possess by right,
abounding in all fruits
and every beast of the wild. (51–58)

Counterturn 3

There she will bear a son
whom Hermes will take from his mother
and bring to the Horai and Gaia—
they will marvel at the infant on their lap.
Upon his lips they will distill
nektar and ambrosia
and make him immortal—
a Zeus and holy Apollo,
a joy to the men he loves:
the surest guardian of their flocks,
Agreus and Nomios,
and by others yet
he shall be called Aristaios."
So Chiron spoke,
and urged him to consummate the union. (59–66)

Stand 3

Swift is the doing and short the road
when a god sets his mind to a thing.
That very day
they were joined
in the gold chambers of Libya
where Kyrana has her city, renowned for triumphs.
Even now Karneiadas' son has put her
in the embrace of luck, having had her name proclaimed
to the throngs at Pytho.
And she will welcome him
in glory, home to his country, land of fair women. (67–75)

Turn 4

Great successes always come
with stories in great numbers—highlighting a few
brings delightful listening
to the wise, for a deft selection
captures the essence.
Seven-gated Thebes once saw
Iolaos honor him:
Iolaos, whom the Thebans laid to rest
when he had shorn away the head of Eurystheus
with the edge of his sword;
beneath the earth he lies
in the tomb of his father's father,
the Sown Men's guest, Amphitryon
who changed his home
to dwell in Thebes of the white horses. (76–83)

Counterturn 4

To him and Zeus at a single birth,
proud Alkmena bore
a brace of sons
mighty in battle:
dumb is the man who does not crown
Herakles with praise, or revere
the springs of Dirka
that nursed both him and Iphikles.
To them will I sing whenever good befalls me
and so fulfill my vow.
May the pure light of the Graces
abide with me, for I proclaim
you have glorified this city
three times now,
in Aigina and on Nisos' hill, (84–91)

Stand 4

where you escaped sullen obscurity.
Let others too—
friends or adversaries of the people—not ignore
a deed well done for all, but honor
the precept of the sea's Ancient:
Praise even a foe
when he deserves it.
And how many times
they saw you win at Athens:
girls who wished, in silence,
that you were their husband;
and women, Telesikrates,
who prayed that you might be their son, (92–100)

Turn 5

at the local Olympics,
  in the contest of Gaia,
    and at all the regional games.
      Yet someone still exacts a debt from me
        as I quench the thirst for song.
  He bids me stir to life again
    the ancient glory
of his forebears, those who went
to Irasa once, for a Libyan woman's sake—
  seeking the hand
                of Antaios' lovely daughter,
    for whom the contenders came
  in droves,
the best men
          from that country and abroad, drawn (101–8)

Counterturn 5

by her beauty, yearning
  to pluck the flower of her youth,
    budding in its golden crown.
      But her father planned
        still brighter glory
  for his daughter's wedding:
    he had heard of Danaos in Argos,
how he had found a match
for each of his forty-eight daughters, all by noon:
  he stood the whole troupe
                        at the finish line
    and bade the heroes,
  who had come as grooms, to race
and so decide
          which girl each man should marry. (109–16)

Stand 5

So too the Libyan:
                he placed his daughter
at the mark, arrayed in all her loveliness.
                              "Let the man
who first has touched the robes about her
lead her away."
            Alexidamos left the pack behind,
took the maiden by the hand,
and led her through the throngs
of Nomad horsemen.
                Many were the flowers
and garlands that were showered over him,
a champion, with many a crown of victory won before. (117–25)

PYTHIAN 10

Hippokleas of Pelinna, double race for boys, 498 B.C.

Pythian 10 has a special interest as the earliest of Pindar's extant odes, written when he was twenty years old. It was commissioned by Thorax of Larissa, the chief town in Thessaly not far distant from Pelinna, the victor's home. The victor's father, Phrikias, had already won two Olympian victories, both in the race in full armor, and one Pythian victory, in the sprint. In the last triad, we learn that the ode is being sung by a chorus of men from the neighboring town of Krannon, for Pindar here refers to a chorus of "Ephyraians," Ephyra being the ancient name for Krannon.

In the opening lines of the ode, Pindar connects Thessaly and Lakedaimon (Sparta) by recalling their common ancestor, Herakles. Thorax and his brothers were descendants of Aleuas, who traced their ancestry back to Herakles, and through Herakles to Zeus. The genealogy is as follows:

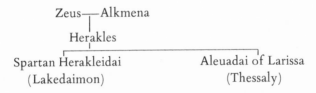

Zeus—Alkmena
Herakles
Spartan Herakleidai (Lakedaimon) — Aleuadai of Larissa (Thessaly)

The myth of the ode is framed by the adventures of another son of Zeus, Perseus, ancestor of Herakles, hence of Thorax and his brothers, the sons of Aleuas:

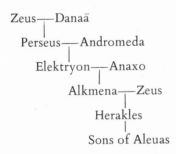

Zeus—Danaä
Perseus—Andromeda
Elektryon—Anaxo
Alkmena—Zeus
Herakles
Sons of Aleuas

The genealogical connection between Perseus and the patron of the ode, Thorax, adds a certain relevance to the myth, but its main subject is the Hyperboreans, whom Perseus visited on his way to fetch the head of the Gorgon Medusa. The Hyperboreans lived, as their name implies, "beyond the North Wind." They were a people favored by the god Apollo, in whose games the young Hippokleas has just been victorious.

Pindar introduces the blissful existence of the Hyperboreans into the ode in order to illustrate the limits of human achievement. The victor's father has attained as much happiness as a man could wish for. The Hyperboreans are happier still, but they are immortal. The only discord known to them is the noise made by the asses that they sacrifice to Apollo.

Pindar deals with the legend of Perseus again, and more fully, in *Pythian 12.* On the imagery in the transitional passage (stand 3), see the Introduction, *Style and the Pindaric Tradition.*

Turn 1

Lakedaimon is happy,
Thessaly is blest:
both have their kings
descended from one father,
Herakles, prince of battle.
Why am I declaiming
in this way?
Pytho and Pelinna exhort me,
and the sons of Aleuas, eager
that I bring to Hippokleas
the voices of the men
singing in glorious revel. (1–6)

Counterturn 1

For he enjoys the taste of victory:
the throng of surrounding people
heard Parnassos Valley
proclaim him best
of the youths in the double race.
The end and the beginning,
O great Apollo, ripen into sweetness for men
when a god urges them on.
He has done what he has done
in accordance, surely, with your plans.
But he has also walked
in the footsteps of his father. (7–12)

Stand 1

twice victorious at Olympia,
in the battle-worn gear of Ares.
And in the contest
in the deep meadow under Kirrha's crags,
Phrikias prevailed in speed of foot.
May father and son
behold their wealth's
proud flower bloom tomorrow as today. (13–18)

Turn 2

Having no small share
of the good things in Hellas,
may they encounter
no reversal of fortune
from the jealous gods.
The gods may feel no sorrow,
but a man
should be accounted happy
and worthy of song
if boldness and power have gained him
the greatest prize
for might of hand or speed of foot, (19–24)

Counterturn 2

and if he's also lived to see
his young son
duly crowned
with Pythian garlands.
The bronze sky is beyond
his reach forever, but he has found
all the happiness
our mortal race can come to.
For neither on shipboard
nor by any journey made on foot
would you ever discover
the miraculous way to the Hyperboreans.
(25–30)

Stand 2

With them Perseus, lord of the people, once feasted,
entering their houses.
He had come upon them
while they were offering
hekatombs of asses to glorify Apollo,
who delights in their perpetual feasts and hymns
and is amused
by the shrill impiety of their brutes. (31–36)

Turn 3

And the Muse has never traveled
from their midst.
To the strumming
of harp-strings
and the piping of oboes,
their maiden choruses
whirl, dancing everywhere.
They wreathe their hair in golden laurel
and regale themselves.
The cup of age and sickness
has not been poured for them.
Free of toil and battle (37–42)

Counterturn 3

they live, escaping the rigid
rule of Nemesis.
Into their blissful company
came the son of Danaä,
bold of heart,
for Athena was his guide.
He slew the Gorgon then,
and brought her head
decked in serpent curls,
a stony death
to the men of Seriphos.
No miracle is too great (43–48)

Stand 3

for my belief, when the gods
bring it to pass.
Stay the oars now!
Heave the anchor overboard
before we splinter
on the bristling reef.
For the song of praise
darts from theme to theme, like a bee. (49–54)

Turn 4

And I hope—while the Ephyraians
pour forth the honey
of my singing
along the banks of the Peneios—
that this music for his crowns
will make Hippokleas
still more admired
among his peers and elders and keep him
in the thoughts of young maidens.
Desire for one thing
moves one heart,
a different passion excites another: (55–60)

Counterturn 4

but if a man attains his wish
let him cling to it and not let it go
for something far off.
There is no telling
what will be
a year from now.
I put my trust
in the warm friendship of Thorax—
it is he who has yoked this four-horse chariot
of the Muses, eagerly tending my song,
loving one who loves him back,
each taking the other's hand. (61–66)

Stand 4

Gold and a straight mind show what they are
on the touchstone.
Let us praise
his brave brothers too, because
they bear on high the ways of Thessaly
and bring them glory.
In their hands
belongs the piloting of cities, their fathers' heritage. (67–72)

PYTHIAN 11

Thrasydaios of Thebes, boys' foot race, 474 B.C.

The victory celebrated in *Pythian 11* is the third in the family's possession. The other two are mentioned late in the ode, and rather vaguely: an Olympian chariot victory gained "long ago," and a second Pythian triumph.

The ode, written for a Theban youth, has a Theban setting. The whole first triad is a single-sentence invocation of various Theban heroines: Pindar summons them to the Ismenion, a temple of Apollo outside Thebes. The temple is named for Apollo's son by the Theban nymph Melia. Among those invited to join the celebration are two daughters of Kadmos and Harmonia: Semela, mother of Dionysos, and Ino Leukothea ("White Goddess"). Alkmena, the mother of Herakles, is also summoned to the temple for the ceremony, which takes place at nightfall together with the young victor's homage to Apollo. The triad concludes with a reference to Pytho as the land of Pylades, "friend of Lakonian Orestes." The mention of Orestes opens the way for the myth of the ode.

The myth begins with a tragic event in the childhood of Orestes, the murder of his father Agamemnon by his mother Klytaimestra; it concludes with an even more tragic event in his manhood, when he returned from Pytho and killed his mother. Between the descriptions of these two events Pindar tells the story of the House of Atreus and speculates on the causes of its disasters. The main characters in the myth are Arsinoa, the nurse who rescued Orestes from his mother's violence on the day of bloodshed; Klytaimestra, the wife and murderess; her husband Agamemnon, leader of the Greek expedition against Troy; his concubine Kassandra, daughter of Priam and priestess of Apollo; Aigisthos, Agamemnon's cousin, Klytaimestra's lover, slain with her by Orestes; and finally the old man Strophios, father of Pylades, to whose home the child Orestes fled for refuge when his father was murdered.

On the significance of the myth, the transition from the myth to the victor's praises in the third counterturn, and the meaning of Pindar's political utterances in the last triad, see the Introduction, *Pindar's Genre.*

In the fourth stand, Pindar's praise of the family takes the form of mythical parallels. Iolaos was best known for his devotion to the children of his uncle Herakles. He was also known as a great athlete, as a winner in the first Olympian Games, and as a patron hero of local athletic contests at Thebes, the Iolaia (see *Pythian 9*, turn 4). Much the same is true of Kastor and Polydeukes: they were renowned as athletes and as patrons of athletic festivals (see the preface to *Olympian 3*).

Pindar enumerates some of their athletic achievements early in the first Isthmian ode. Most importantly, they were famed for their devotion to each other. When Kastor was mortally wounded, the immortal Polydeukes, rather than lose his brother's company forever, consented to spend alternate days with him in his tomb at Therapna. The rest of the time they are together with the gods on Olympos (see *Nemean 10*).

Turn 1

Hear me, daughters of Kadmos!
Semela, in the company
of Olympian goddesses,
and Ino Leukothea, chambering
undersea
with the Nereids:
come with Herakles' mother
noblest in birth
and join Melia in the sanctuary
of golden tripods,
the treasury most honored of Loxias (1–5)

Counterturn 1

and called by him the Ismenion,
true seat of prophets.
O children of Harmonia!
come, where even now
the god bids his band of heroines,
dwellers in this country,
to gather in procession
at height of evening,
praising our sacred rites
and the great
justice of Pytho, center of earth. (6–10)

Stand 1

Come bringing grace to seven-gated Thebes
and Kirrha's contest,
where Thrasydaios
has had his home proclaimed, placing
a third crown upon his native hearth, victorious
in the rich plow-fields of Pylades,
friend of Lakonian Orestes, (11–16)

Turn 2

whose nurse Arsinoa saved him
from the murderous hands
and cruel treachery
of Klytaimestra
that day
she cut his father down
and, with stroke of gray bronze,
sent Kassandra—
Priam's Dardan daughter—
with Agamemnon's soul
to the dark banks of Acheron, (17–21)

Counterturn 2

woman without pity: and why?
Was it Iphigeneia
slaughtered
beside the Euripos,
far from home,
that set her wrathful hand in motion?
Or did lying at night
with another man
subdue and corrupt her?
This is an infamy
most hateful in young wives, impossible to keep (22–26)

Stand 2

others from talking about.
For the people
are prone to speak evil, and high prosperity
fosters more resentment, while the man
whose breath hugs the ground grumbles unheard.
He returned at last
to famed Amyklai, Atreus' hero son, only to die, (27–32)

Turn 3

and his captive prophetess
perished with him—he who had torn
Troy's towers from their pride
and put them to the torch
for Helen's sake.
His child Orestes
fled to old Strophios,
a loyal friend who lived
in Parnassos' foothills.
But Ares stood beside him at the last,
when he slew his mother and left Aigisthos in a pool of blood. (33–37)

Counterturn 3

Truly, friends, I have been whirled along
ever since
the road divided—
all was well till then;
or was it a sudden gust
blew me off course
like a boat at sea?
It is your task, Muse,
if you have taken
silver for your voice,
to let it run shimmering from theme to theme— (38–42)

Stand 3

now to the father Pythonikos
and now to Thrasydaios, the son—
their liberality
and reputation burn bright for all to see.
In their victorious chariots, long ago they caught
the glancing ray of fame from contests at Olympia (43–48)

Turn 4

and at Pytho, stepping down
stripped for the races, they silenced
all Hellas by their speed.
May I pray for noble
favors from the gods, seeking
what is possible in my time,
for, having searched
into the city's ways, and having learned
that moderation blooms
with a longer happiness,
I have no fondness for the tyrant's lot. (49–53)

Counterturn 4

Striving instead for prizes
that promote public good,
I keep resentment at bay.
If a man, gaining the summit
and living in peace,
has also shunned
dread insolence,
he may encounter
a nobler end in dark death,
because he leaves his kin
the most valuable possession, grace of a good name: (54–58)

Stand 4

such is the grace that spreads abroad
the glory of Iphikles' son,
Iolaos, worthy of song;
it carries the fame of mighty Kastor
and yours, Polydeukes,
sons of the gods,
who dwell one day in Therapna,
the other on Olympos. (59–64)

PYTHIAN 12

Midas of Akragas, flute contest, 490 B.C.

This is the only one of Pindar's odes that celebrates a victory in the musical competition at Delphi (see Appendix V). Apparently meant to be sung during a procession on the victor's return to Akragas, it opens with an elaborate prayer to the nymph of the city and to the city herself, bidding her to welcome the victor from Pytho. The invocation to Akragas includes mention of the goddess Persephone, who enjoyed special honor not only at Akragas, but in all of Sicily.

Pindar makes the invention of the flute, and of a particularly complex piece of music for the flute, the subject of his myth. According to him, the flute was invented by Athena. The inspiration came to her from the sound made by the two immortal Gorgons when they bewailed the death of their mortal sister, Medusa.

The Gorgons were the daughters of Phorkos and Keto, who were also the parents of three other daughters, the "Graiai" or "Gray Ones." Pindar refers to them simply as "the weird brood of Phorkos." And weird they certainly were: they had only one tooth and one eye, which they shared among them. They alone knew the way to the cave of the Gorgons, where Perseus had to go in his quest for Medusa. All Pindar says about this is that Perseus blinded them. Other sources tell us that he waited until the moment when they changed the guard, passing their sole eye from hand to hand. In the interval, when they were totally blind, Perseus leaped out of hiding and seized the eye, promising to return it if they would tell him the way to the Gorgons.

In the background is the story of Perseus' birth and childhood. His mother was Danaä, daughter of Akrisios, the king of Argos. Akrisios had heard that the son born to his daughter would supplant him as king. He therefore imprisoned Danaä in a tower, to keep her from becoming pregnant. But Zeus came to her in the form of a golden rain, and Perseus was conceived in this fashion. Some years passed and Akrisios, hearing the sound of a child in the tower, investigated, found the son born to his daughter, and, thinking to protect himself from fate, cast both mother and child adrift on the sea in a wooden chest. It alighted on the island of Seriphos, one of the Cyclades. Polydektas, king of Seriphos at the time, tried to force himself upon Danaä, who resisted his advances. When her son Perseus approached manhood, he wanted to free his mother from the threat of forced concubinage to Polydektas, who at this time announced a banquet to be held in honor of the wedding of Hippodameia. The guests at the banquet were required to bring a wedding gift. Perseus declared that he would bring Medusa as his contribution, and Polydektas eagerly accepted the promise, in the expectation that the young man would perish in the attempt. The mere sight of Medusa's face would kill a man by turning him instantly to stone.

With Athena's assistance, however, Perseus succeeded in his daring exploit. He returned to Seriphos with the head of Medusa in a sack. At an assembly of the people he lifted the head out of the sack. All the Seriphians who looked on it turned to stone (see *Pythian 10*).

Medusa had at one time been an attendant in Athena's temple, where she would have been expected to preserve her virginity. Her loveliness, however, attracted the god Poseidon, who ravished her in the temple. Athena turned away from her in disgust. Her hair, in whose beauty Medusa had particularly gloried, was changed to snakes. Pindar mentions the snake-hair of her sisters, the other two Gorgons, but he names only one of them: "Euryala," "Wide Leaper." The other was called "Stheno," "The Mighty." Their mourning for their sister moved Athena to invent the flute. The melody she played on that occasion was an instrumental imitation of the Gorgons' wail. Athena named it "the many-headed melody" from the numerous snakes that coiled in the Gorgons' hair.

At the end of the third and the beginning of the fourth stanzas, Pindar describes the flute and its functions. The playing of the flute marked the official opening of the Pythian contests. The crowd would respond to its music by gathering for the spectacle. The flute itself was composed of a bronze mouth-piece and of reeds that grew near "the city of the Graces," Orchomenos. The nymph Kopaïs, daughter of the river Kaphisos, had her sacred precinct there, where the reeds grew. Since the movements of the dancing chorus were in harmony with the flute's music, Pindar refers to the reeds as "witnesses" to the chorus.

The ode concludes abruptly with reflections on the uncertainty of human life (see the Introduction, *The Archaic Period*).

1 Most radiant of mortal cities,
lady of brightness on the height
above the sheep-nurturing banks of the Akragas,
among whose lovely buildings
Persephone has her throne—
on you I call:
welcome Midas and his coronal from Pytho.
Grant him the favor of men and of gods,
for he has conquered all Hellas by his skill
in the art Athena once invented,
when she wove
the grim death chant of the cruel Gorgons, (1–8)

2 which she heard pouring out
in streams of bitter anguish
under the maidens' repulsive serpent heads,
when Perseus cried out in triumph, bringing
the third of the sisters to Seriphos,
death to the people:
he had blinded the weird brood of Phorkos
and now, having despoiled
the head of beautiful Medusa,
he made that banquet a bane to Polydektas,
and made him rue his lust
to rape Danaä and keep her in bondage— (9–16)

3 Perseus, her son, who we say was sired
in a shower of streaming gold.
But when Athena had saved her favorite
from these dangers,
she fashioned the music of flutes
to imitate the piercing ululation
that came to her ears
from the fierce jaws of Euryala.
It was the goddess who invented it for mortal men
and called it *the many-headed melody.*
Now it woos
the people to attend the contest (17–24)

4 when they hear it stream through slender bronze
and through the reeds that have their home
by the city of the Graces,
on ground sacred to the daughter of Kaphisos—
faithful witnesses to the chorus.
If there is any bliss among men,
it does not appear without struggle.
Still, a god may bring it to pass this very day.
No man can avoid his fated end,
and in the time he has,
he will be struck with surprise
when one desire will succeed, but another will fail. (25–32)

"gripping both snakes by their throats,
one in each unshakable hand."
–*Nemean 1*, 44–45

Courtesy, Musée du Louvre, Paris. Photo by Chuzeville.

THE NEMEAN ODES

NEMEAN 1

Chromios of Aitna, chariot race, 476 (?) B.C.

Pindar wrote two poems in honor of Chromios, son of Hagesidamos: *Nemeans 1* and *9*. *Nemean 1* seems to have been written first, probably in 476, the year Pindar visited Hieron in Sicily. Chromios, Hieron's brother-in-law and trusted ally, was a man of wealth and power. In *Nemean 1* his princely hospitality occupies the foreground. He claimed descent from Hyllos, Herakles' son. This may account for Pindar's choice of Herakles for the myth of the ode. The ode falls into two almost equal parts, the first two triads dealing with Chromios, the last two with Herakles.

The opening turn is full of references to local features of Syracuse, Chromios' home. Pindar begins with Ortygia ("Quail Island"), just off the coast. According to legend, the river Alpheos in Arkadia had fallen in love with the nymph Arethusa and had pursued her under the sea from Greece to Ortygia where, finally, he burst from underground and mingled with her in what became the famous fountain of Arethusa. Pindar alludes to all this by calling Ortygia the place "where Alpheos breathes again."

Pindar's praise of Chromios for hospitality in the second turn is, on one hand, simple and direct: the banquet Chromios has prepared and the frequent arrival of guests from abroad both testify to his liberality. On the other hand, Pindar takes a brief sideways glance at people who choose to denigrate or find fault with such displays of wealth and festivity. These people are condemned, Pindar says, to carry water against smoke. The proverb suggests haplessness and futility. Chromios' achievements and his hospitality give Pindar the means to flourish in song. There is a similar if more direct preference for praise over blame in *Pythian 2* (turn 3). On Pindar's tendency to express his thoughts through negative illustration, see the Introduction, *The Archaic Period*. For the theme of generosity, see also the section on *Pindar's Genre*.

The last two triads tell the myth of Herakles' birth—how Hera had sent a pair of serpents to devour him and his twin brother Iphikles, both of them infants newly born. The prodigious feat performed by Herakles on this occasion caused his foster-father, Amphitryon, to summon the Theban prophet Teiresias to the scene. Teiresias prophesies the labors that lie in wait for Herakles. There is one rather mysterious episode among them. Pindar refers to "a certain creature, loathesome, lurching"—and scholars have wondered who this might be. Pindar obviously wants to keep whoever it is obscure, most likely for greater effect. But it may have been the giant Antaios, who always challenged passers-by to a wrestling match. The losers forfeited their lives, and Antaios heaped their skulls in front of his house. Pindar knew of this, for he mentions it at *Isthmian 4*, 70.

Turn 1

O sacred ground, where Alpheos breathes again!
Ortygia, scion of glorious Syracuse!
Bed of Artemis
and sister of Delos,
from you the music has its source,
sounding high praise of horses
with storm in their speed,
glory to Zeus of Aitna!
The chariot of Chromios
and Nemea
bid me harness deed to song
in praise of victory. (1–7)

Counterturn 1

The foundations have been laid—with the gods
and Chromios' inspired exploits.
The peak of perfect glory
appears in triumph,
for the Muse
loves to dwell on mighty contests.
Let her radiance
stream upon this island now,
Persephone's gift from Zeus,
lord of Olympos, who bent his brow
and promised to exalt her
over the fruitful earth, (8–14)

Stand 1

Sicily, teeming with cities supreme in wealth.
And the son of Kronos dowered her
with a people enamored of bronze war
and of horses,
a people often crowned
with the gold leaves of Olympian olive.
I have touched on a theme
rich in opportunity and founded in truth. (15–18)

Turn 2

At the courtyard doors of a liberal host, I stand
singing his noble deeds
here, where a brilliant banquet has been laid out for me.
Indeed, this house has often been
no stranger to guests from abroad.
For those who criticize the noble
are doomed
to carry water against smoke!
Different men have different skills.
One must take
the straight path:
fight with what one has by nature. (19–25)

Counterturn 2

Action is the way of strength;
stratagem the way of council, in those
endowed with the gift of foresight.
Son of Hagesidamos, thanks to you
I have a wide range of themes.
I love not to keep great wealth
buried deep in hall,
but to make good use of what I own
and be of good repute
among my friends.
For all men are alike
in expectation, (26–32)

Stand 2

born to endure.
But when I move among the heights
of triumph, Herakles comes to mind. I embrace him
eagerly, stirring to life again the ancient story,
how that child of Zeus,
having survived
the throes of birth and come with his twin brother
from his mother's womb into the sudden wondrous light, (33–36)

Turn 3

did not escape the notice of Hera
when he was laid
in purple swaddling bands.
Stung to the heart with wrath,
the Queen of the gods
dispatched a pair of serpents.
Through the open doors
into the wide inner chambers they glided,
to wind themselves around the babes,
eager to snatch them in their jaws.
But Herakles raised his head
and made first trial of battle, (37–43)

Counterturn 3

gripping both snakes by their throats,
one in each unshakable hand.
Moment by moment,
strangling,
the life-breath
fled their hideous coils.
Unbearable terror struck
the women in attendance on Alkmena.
She herself, leaping to her feet
just as she was, in her bed-clothes,
had tried
to keep the monsters at bay. (44–50)

Stand 3

And the chiefs of the Kadmeians arrived together
in haste, with a rattle of bronze arms,
Amphitryon among them, sword in hand,
shaken with anxiety.
For every man feels the weight
of sorrows at home, while troubles elsewhere
do not hold the heart for long. (51–54)

Turn 4

He stood there, wavering
between terror and delight,
for he could see the unearthly
strength and power of his son.
The immortal gods had turned
the messengers' report
from bad to good.
He summoned his townsman, great
prophet of Zeus on high,
unerring Teiresias, who told him
and the entire company
what lay in wait for Herakles— (55–61)

Counterturn 4

how many savage beasts he would slay
on land and sea, beasts
with no sense of justice;
how he would put an end
to a certain creature,
loathesome, lurching with perverse
glut of men.
And when the gods should face the giants
in battle on Phlegra's plain, he spoke
of bright hair fouled in the dust
beneath the arrows
sprung from Herakles' bow; (62–68)

Stand 4

and prophesied he would enjoy unbroken peace
for all time,
repose in the gods' blissful hall,
a perfect reward for his vast labors,
with lovely Hebe for his bride;
and that, having celebrated his wedding at the side
of Zeus, son of Kronos,
he would praise the sacred law. (69–72)

NEMEAN 2

Timodemos of Acharnai, pankration, 485 (?) B.C.

The second Nemean ode celebrates the return of Timodemos, victor in the pankration, from the Nemean games to his home in Acharnai, a suburb of Athens. The victor was the son of Timonoös and a member of the clan of the Timodemidai, praised by Pindar for their many athletic successes—four victories at Delphi ("beneath Parnassos"), eight at the Isthmos ("in noble Pelops' valley"), seven at Nemea, and countless others in local competitions. The Timodemidai were in fact a clan of Salamis, where Timodemos seems to have been born, or to have grown up. Hence Pindar links him with the most illustrious Salaminian hero, Aias, Hektor's opponent at Troy.

The ode was designed to be sung by a chorus in procession through the streets of Acharnai, either to the victor's home or to some local shrine. Pindar seems to have intended the ode to be repeated by the chorus as it passed along the way, for the last line is phrased in such a manner as to allow a return to the opening words almost without pause.

The "Sons of Homer" referred to in the opening line are professional rhapsodes, reciters of Homeric poetry, who began their recitations with a hymn, usually to Zeus.

1

Even as the Sons of Homer often begin
their interwoven lays
with a prelude to Zeus,
so has this man begun, laying down for himself
an earnest of triumph in sacred games
by winning at Nemea in Zeus' celebrated grove. (1-5)

2

Surely Timonoös' son in days ahead
will reap fair flowers of success
at Isthmos and at Delphi,
if in fact unerring destiny
has raised him to adorn great Athens
as his fathers have. For it is likely (6-10)

3

Orion will appear not far behind
the mountain Pleiades.
And Salamis is surely able to rear
a man of battle: Hektor at Troy
heard tell of Aias. O Timodemos,
your perseverance in pankration has exalted you. (11-15)

4

And, from of old, Acharnai rejoices in her people.
Her sons the Timodemidai
are acknowledged supreme in contests.
Four times they won in games
beneath Parnassos' awesome crest.
But the men of Corinth (16-20)

5

in noble Pelops' valley
have already crowned them eight times.
Seven times they won in Zeus' Nemean games.
Their triumphs at home cannot be numbered.
Sing, then, O fellow citizens, of Zeus
for Timodemos' glorious return. Lead off with sweet voice! (21-25)

NEMEAN 3

Aristokleidas of Aigina, pankration, 475 (?) B.C.

Nemean 3 opens with a prayer bidding the Muse come to the banks of the river Asopos; it closes with a reference to the lateness of the ode's delivery. The victor, Aristokleidas, son of Aristophanes, had some connection with the Thearion, the guild-hall of the sacred envoys sent from Aigina to Delphi. The ode may have been commissioned for performance in the Thearion at an official celebration. The two components of the victor's name, Aristo-kleidas, signify "superiority" and "glory." The second element in the name (-kleidas) accounts for Pindar's identification of the Muse of this ode with Kleo ("Glorifier"), later the Muse of History, here simply the Muse of Poetry, the vehicle of glory.

Superiority and glory apply even more impressively to the victor's homeland, which quickly becomes the theme of the ode: it is a place of superior athletes and glorious heroes, the descendants of Aiakos, in particular: Telamon, Peleus, and Achilleus, to whom Pindar turns after a brief celebration of the exploits of Herakles.

In the counterturn of the second triad, Pindar touches briefly on the story of Peleus' conflict with the city of Iolkos and his courtship of the sea-goddess Thetis, later the mother of Achilleus. Pindar returns to these episodes in *Nemeans 4* and *5*, where he treats them at somewhat greater length, each time dwelling on different aspects of the whole story, which may be conveniently summarized here.

Peleus reduced the city of Iolkos to servitude in retaliation against King Akastos. Hippolyta, Akastos' queen, had fallen in love with Peleus and had offered herself to him. Rejected, she told Akastos that Peleus had attempted to seduce her. Akastos then set an ambush for Peleus, who escaped and went on to capture the city. At the time Hippolyta approached him, Peleus was a guest in the house of Akastos. Because he had respected the claims of hospitality and chastity, Zeus, god of hospitality, rewarded him with the hand of Thetis. But before he could marry her, he had to endure the transformations she underwent in his arms. In *Nemean 4*, Pindar mentions two of the shapes she assumed: fire and a lion. In the second counterturn of *Nemean 3* he mentions only the process itself, which he seems to imagine as a wrestling match, with Peleus holding on to the goddess as she assumed one form after another.

On the opening of this ode, see the Introduction, *Pindar's Genre.*

Turn 1

O lady Muse, my mother!
Come, I beseech you,
in the sacred Nemean month
to Dorian Aigina, island haven
of the wide world:
by the waters of Asopos
the young men wait,
builders of sweet revel-songs,
eager for your voice.
Other deeds
have other thirsts, but victory
yearns for music,
the perfect attendant to its crowns and its valor. (1–8)

Counterturn 1

Let it tend upon us now, welling
from my mind: begin, daughter of Zeus,
the hymn of glory to the ruler
of the sky, deep in cloud,
and I will entrust the words
to the young men's voices
and to the lyre.
It will be a pleasant task
to adorn this country,
home
of the Myrmidons of old, whose fabled assembly
Aristokleidas did not disgrace—
with your help, he kept his nerve in the brutal (9–16)

Stand 1

pankration contest.
His triumph in the deep fields of Nemea
soothes the pain of blows endured.
But if
this son of Aristophanes—handsome in looks
and deeds to match—has reached the peak of manliness,
to go on from there is no light matter,
crossing
the pathless sea beyond the Pillars of Herakles, (17–21)

Turn 2

which that hero-god set up in glory
to mark the limits of our voyaging—
Herakles, who overcame
the monsters of the deep and, on his own,
explored the shallow straits,
his journey's end
and turning point: he had shown
the world's boundary. But O my heart!
to what foreign beach
are you blown off course?
I bid you summon the Muse to Aiakos and his race:
for though the essence of justice
appear in the maxim *Praise the noble,* (22–29)

Counterturn 2

longing for another's glory
is not the better way:
look closer to home.
Here you have honors
worthy of noble utterance:
lord Peleus
rejoiced in deeds of valor
long ago, when he cut his peerless spear.
He stormed Iolkos
alone, without an army,
and pinned down Thetis of the sea,
for all her struggles. And mighty Telamon
crushed Laomedon—he stood by Iolaos then (30–37)

Stand 2

and went with him once against the fierce Amazons
armed with brazen bows—
man-quelling terror never stopped him.
There is great weight in inherited glory,
while mere instruction leaves a man a thing of shadows:
puffing
here and there, he never comes down with sure foot
but savors endless exploits in his futile thoughts. (38–42)

Turn 3

Blond Achilleus, while still a child
at play about Philyra's house, performed
deeds of might: often brandishing
his iron javelin, swift as the wind,
he battled savage lions
to their deaths
and slew boars, dragging
their bodies, trembling
in the last gasp,
to Chiron the centaur;
this from the time he was six and ever after.
Artemis was amazed
and bold Athena marveled to see him (43–50)

Counterturn 3

killing stags without the help of hounds
or traps: he ran them down
on foot. And men of old tell how
shrewd Chiron raised Jason also,
in his house of stone,
and reared Asklepios,
whom he taught the mild-handed use
of salves and drugs.
And it was Chiron
who saw to the wedding
of Nereus' radiant daughter and brought up
her dread child Achilleus,
raising his thoughts in all things noble (51–58)

Stand 3

that he might go on the sea-winds' blast
to Troy of the clashing spears,
endure
the cries of Lykians and Phrygians, the shrill
Dardan battle-shout, and then,
hand to hand against
the spearmen of Ethiopia, determine that their prince,
fiery Memnon, cousin of Helenos, would never go home again. (59–63)

Turn 4

From Troy the fame of Aiakos' sons
burns like a beacon, seen
afar and forever. O Zeus!
it is your blood
in their veins, your contest
that the young men hail
as they proclaim Aigina's victory.
Aristokleidas deserves the jubilant
reception of song
for having bathed
this island in the speech of renown
and Apollo's Thearion in the brightness
of hopes. But trial alone reveals innate superiority (64–71)

Counterturn 4

in the youth among youths, the man
among men, the elder
among elders, each lot
as we inherit it, we—
a perishable race.
Yet our mortal life
brings with it four virtues also,
and bids us heed what lies at hand.
In these you are not lacking.
Hail, friend!
I send you this blend of honey and white milk
bubbling at the brim,
a draft of music breathed through Aiolian flutes, (72–79)

Stand 4

late, surely, and yet, among birds, the eagle
is swift:
though he swoop from afar, he has his prey,
spattered with blood, in his claws,
while the crows
chatter, grazing the lower air.
In you the brilliance
of a contending spirit, lit by Kleo's grace,
has shone forth from Nemea and Epidauros and Megara! (80–84)

NEMEAN 4

Timasarchos of Aigina, boys' wrestling, 473 (?) B.C.

Timasarchos also won at Athens and in the Games of Herakles at Thebes. His father Timokritos was dead at the time Pindar composed *Nemean 4*. Dead also were his maternal uncle Kallikles, an Isthmian victor, and, apparently, his grandfather Euphanes. The father Timokritos and the grandfather Euphanes were poets and musicians, to judge from what Pindar tells us about them at the beginning and at the end of the ode. The ode divides neatly into three sections: three stanzas dealing with the victor and his father, six stanzas dealing with mythological material, and a final three stanzas devoted, again, to the victor and his family. The nontriadic form of the stanzas would indicate that the ode was meant for a processional.

The six central stanzas celebrate the heroes descended from Aiakos. Like the ode in its entirety, this middle portion is divided into three parts. It begins with Telamon (stanza 4), modulates to a catalogue of Aiakid heroes (stanzas 5–7), and concludes with Telamon's cousin Peleus (stanzas 8–9). The beginning with Telamon develops from a reminiscence of the victor's triumph in the Games of Herakles at Thebes (stanza 3). Telamon, an Aiginetan, and Herakles, a Theban, were friends and partners in glory. Pindar himself was a Theban, Timasarchos an Aiginetan. In the background, then, is the mythological friendship of Herakles and Telamon; in the foreground, the actual friendship between the Theban Pindar and the Aiginetan Timasarchos.

On the transitional section (stanzas 5–6), see the Introduction, *Pindar's Genre.*

The catalogue of Aiakid heroes comes to end end in stanza 7. In stanza 8, Pindar relies on his audience to know the story (summarized in the preface to *Nemean 3*) of Hippolyta's attempt to seduce Peleus. When Peleus rejected her, she conceived a plan to avenge herself. It was her idea to steal the miraculous sword fashioned by Daidalos for Peleus and to set an ambush for him when he went to search for it in the mountain woods.

The last three stanzas of the ode contain Pindar's tribute to previous generations of the victor's family. Timasarchos was a member of the clan descended from Theandros. Stanza 10 briefly catalogues their triumphs in various contests. At its conclusion, Pindar speaks directly to the victor about his maternal uncle Kallikles, now dead. Kallikles had once triumphed at Isthmos. Pindar now bids him hear that triumph commemorated in this very ode (stanza 11). Here, as at the end of

Olympian 8, Olympian 14, and *Pythian 5*, Pindar imagines his song having the power to cross the border into the netherworld and be heard by the dead. In stanza 12, he adds another glory to the family's record: the memory of Timasarchos' grandfather Euphanes, who had once sung of Kallikles, even as Pindar is singing now.

The last lines of the ode summarize Pindar's attitude toward success and greatness. The diction with which Pindar here describes the relation between the poet and his duty is suggestive of a wrestling match. Thus Pindar pays the victor, a wrestler, and his trainer, Melesias of Athens, a final compliment.

1 Celebration heals a man's pain best
when the crisis of a contest is over—
and songs, wise daughters of the Muses,
ease him with their touch.
Nor does warm water
so soothe his limbs, as praise
wedded to the lyre's playing.
For the word lives longer than the deed,
whenever the voice
brings it from the depths of the mind
blessed by the Graces' favor. (1–8)

2 So would I raise to Zeus Kronidas,
to Nemea and the wrestling skill of Timasarchos,
the prelude of my hymn: may it be welcome
where Aiakos' sons dwell in towered Aigina,
a beacon to the world
for justice, the stranger's surety!
Your father Timokritos,
if he were still warmed by the sun's rays,
would incline to my music,
again and again plucking the intricate lyre
in praise of his son, handsome in triumph— (9–16)

3 who has sent a string of garlands
from the games at Nemea
and from shimmering, glorious Athens;
and at seven-gated Thebes
by the radiant tomb of Amphitryon,
the Kadmeians gladly decked him in flowers
for Aigina's sake: a friend among friends,
he arrived in their midst
and found them hospitable
and the doors opened to him,
into the blissful court of Herakles, (17–24)

4 with whom mighty Telamon
once subdued Troy, the Meropes,
and awesome Alkyoneus, huge and murderous,
who, before he fell,
crushed with a stone twelve four-horse chariots
and twice as many horse-mastering heroes
riding upon them.
Men who have seen battle
will know what I mean:
it befits the achiever
to suffer for achievement. (25–32)

5 But the laws of the song and passing time
forbid dwelling on a theme at length.
And yet I feel a spell steal over me now—
the charm of this new-moon festival.
Come then! though the deep salt sea
grip your waist, fight against conspiracy!
Mightily will we seem to enter the lists,
in daylight, superior to our foes,
while another fellow looks about him
with envy in his eye, fumbling
in darkness at an empty thought (33–40)

6 that tumbles to the ground. Whatever talent
sovereign Destiny has given to me,
I have no doubt
oncoming time will bring
to its fulfillment.
Come then, sweet lyre, make no delay!
Weave out the song in Lydian measure,
the song beloved of Oinona and of Kypros,
where Teukros, Telamon's son,
rules far from home,
while Aias keeps his native Salamis. (41–48)

7 Achilleus is lord of an island
gleaming in the Euxine Sea;
Thetis rules in Phthia; and Neoptolemos
sways the wide mainland grazed by herds,
lofty promontories sloping seaward from Dodona
down to the Adriatic coast.
But at the foot of Mount Pelion,
Iolkos bowed beneath the yoke
of slavery: Peleus, turning
his warlike hand against her,
bound her over to the Haimones, (49–56)

8 because her lord Akastos
had resorted
to the wiles of his wife Hippolyta,
using the sword of Daidalos
to plot Peleus' death by ambush:
but Chiron prevented it,
and the destiny decreed of Zeus
came to fulfillment:
Peleus, having withstood the blaze
of all-consuming fire,
the keen claws and dread fangs of ravening lions, (57–64)

9 married one of the Nereids on high
and saw, in a circle, the gleaming chairs
whereon the kings of sky and sea
offered him their wedding gifts
and revealed the power
that would spring from his race.
The darkness beyond Gadeira cannot be crossed:
sail back again to Europe,
back to land! There is no way
I could run through the whole
saga of Aiakos' sons. (65–72)

10 And I agreed to come
in behalf of the Theandridai,
an eager herald of limb-building contests,
of games at Olympia, at Isthmos, and Nemea—
where, having stood the test,
they returned with leaves of glory in their hands:
Nemea, where we hear
that your country, Timasarchos,
is devoted to songs of victory.
And if, for Kallikles, your mother's brother,
you also entreat me (73–80)

11 to raise a monument brighter than Parian marble:
gold in refinement puts forth all its quality,
and the song praising noble deeds
makes a man equal in destiny
to a king. May Kallikles,
dwelling by the River Acheron,
hear my voice, singing
of the Isthmos, where Poseidon,
lord of the pounding shore
and the mighty trident,
beheld him crowned with Corinthian garlands— (81–88)

12 and Euphanes your grandfather in old age
gladly sang of him once, my child.
Each generation has its contemporaries.
The deeds a man has witnessed himself
he hopes to speak of unforgettably.
How would he handle the struggle,
plaiting his sentences together
like Melesias, not to be thrown
in the match of words:
with gentle thoughts for the noble,
but a harsh antagonist awaiting the malignant! (89–96)

NEMEAN 5

Pytheas of Aigina, boys' pankration, 483 (?) B.C.

The first triad of *Nemean 5* concentrates on the victory for which the ode was commissioned, the last dwells on other family triumphs: Euthymenes, maternal uncle of Pytheas, had won in the Nemean Games, at Megara, and also at home in Aigina. The games at Aigina occurred during the month Delphinios, sacred to Apollo. The victor's trainer, Menandros of Athens, is praised at the end of the last counterturn. Pindar takes leave of Menandros with a play on the similarity in spelling between the words "athlete" and "Athens." Finally, Themistios–Euthymenes' father and Pytheas' maternal grand-uncle–is mentioned for his two victories at Epidauros, one in boxing, the other in pankration. Pytheas' younger brother Phylakidas later won two Isthmian victories, celebrated by Pindar in *Isthmians 5* and *6*.

The middle triad is devoted to the myth, taken, as usual for Aiginetan odes, from the legends of Aiakos' descendants. In this ode, there is a false start and a resumption. Shortly after announcing the victor's homeland, Pindar in the first counterturn recalls how the brothers Peleus and Telamon, sons of Aiakos and Endaïs, and their half-brother Phokos ("Seal"), son of Aiakos and Psamatheia ("Sand Goddess"), had prayed to Zeus Hellanios for the future prosperity of the island of Aigina, called in the first stand by its older name Oinona ("Vineland"). But the mention of the three brothers reminds Pindar of the tragedy that ensued: Peleus and Telamon, jealous of Phokos who was their father's favorite, killed him–deliberately, according to some sources; accidentally, according to others. Whatever the case, it was an instance of kindred blood spilled, and it necessitated the departure of Peleus and Telamon from Aigina.

Pindar shies away from dealing with the murder of Phokos, or even mentioning it specifically. There are other themes at hand, as he says at the start of the second turn: Aigina herself, and her heroes, give him ample inspiration. His audience would have known that Telamon went to Salamis after the death of Phokos, and that Peleus went to Thessaly, where he encountered Akastos and his seductive wife Hippolyta. That encounter becomes the subject of the myth, resumed in the second triad, where Pindar presents it as the theme of the song sung by the Muses at the wedding of Peleus and Thetis.

At the start of the last triad, Pindar alludes to the quarrel between Zeus and Poseidon for the hand of Thetis, a quarrel treated in greater detail in *Isthmian 8*. The allusion is contained in the statement that Zeus persuaded the brother-in-law of Thetis, Poseidon (see Glossary, **Amphitrita**), to allow her marriage to Peleus. Thetis and Amphitrita, the wife of Poseidon, were sisters.

Turn 1

I am no sculptor, fashioning statues
to stand motionless, fixed to the same base.
No, on every merchant ship,
on every boat I bid my song
go forth from Aigina,
spreading abroad the news
that Lampon's mighty son Pytheas,
his cheeks not yet darkened
by late summer, mother
of delicate bloom, has taken
the crown for pankration
in the Nemean games, (1–6)

Counterturn 1

bringing honor to the heroic spearmen
sprung from Kronos, Zeus,
and the golden Nereids:
the sons of Aiakos and their mother city,
a land dear to strangers,
destined to be strong
in her people and famed
for her ships, from the moment the glorious
sons of Endaïs stood at the altar
of Zeus Hellanios and prayed for her,
raising their hands to heaven
with Phokos lord of might, (7–12)

Stand 1

Phokos, whom the goddess Psamatheia bore
where the sea-waves break.
I hesitate to speak
of a fateful act, not ventured in justice—
how they fled the famous island,
and what god
drove those men of power from Oinona.
I will refrain:
not every truth, you know, is the better
for showing its face in the light,
and keeping silence
is often the wisest thing for a man to appreciate. (13–18)

Turn 2

But if praising wealth or might of hand
or iron war is the order of the day,
let someone dig me a wide jumping space
right here: there's a light
spring in my knees, and eagles
swoop beyond the sea.
Why, in honor of these people,
even the brilliant chorus of the Muses
sang eagerly on Mount Pelion.
And, as they sang, Apollo's
golden plectrum swept
the lyre's seven strings, (19–24)

Counterturn 2

leading the way through every hymn.
They began with Zeus and went on to sing
of sacred Thetis and of Peleus—
and how the wanton Hippolyta, daughter of Kretheus,
yearned to entangle him
in guile, persuading
her husband Akastos,
lord of the Magnetes, to join her
in her cunning plans: for she had framed
a false, fabricated story,
that Peleus had attempted
to embrace her in Akastos' own (25–30)

Stand 2

wedding bed.
The opposite was the case: repeatedly,
with all her will, she had entreated him,
but the mere
suggestion had roused his anger—he had spurned her,
dreading Zeus' wrath, god of guests.
And the lord
of the storm-cloud, king of the immortal gods,
took note of it on high, bending his brows
in promise to Peleus
that he would quickly win
a Nereid with golden distaff for his bride, (31–36)

Turn 3

obtaining the consent of her brother-in-law
Poseidon, who often goes from Aigai
to the glorious Dorian Isthmos,
where festal throngs receive him as a god
to the piping of flutes,
and hold the rugged contest
for might of limb.
Birth and destiny determine the outcome
of every deed. You, Euthymenes,
twice taken into the arms of Victory
at Aigina, have known the embrace
of elaborate song. (37–42)

Counterturn 3

Yes, Pytheas, even now your mother's brother
follows upon you, honoring the race
born in the line of Aiakos.
Nemea is true to him and the sacred month
Apollo cherishes.
He vanquished those of his age
who came against him, at home
and in the lovely arms of Megara.
I rejoice, that this whole city strives for honor.
Fortunate in Menandros' help,
you've won yourself a share
in the sweet (43–48)

Stand 3

recompense of toil.
It is only right
that a trainer of athletes hail from Athens.
But if you come to sing of Themistios, warm to the strain!
let loose your voice, unfurl the sails:
proclaim him a boxer;
add that he took a second glory,
winning in pankration at Epidauros,
and with crowns
of plaited grass and flowers in your hands, join
the shining Graces on their way to Aiakos' shrine! (49–54)

NEMEAN 6

Alkimidas of Aigina, boys' wrestling, 465 (?) B.C.

Alkimidas was one of the Bassidai, a noble Aiginetan clan with twenty-four victories in the sacred games to its credit. The victory celebrated in this ode brought that total to twenty-five.

The ode opens with an elaborate comparison between men and gods. The first counterturn reveals why the comparison came to Pindar's mind on this occasion: the vicissitudes and uncertainty governing human life in general are a foil for the experience of the victor's family, which has shown a certain rhythm from generation to generation. His father was not a victor, but his grandfather Praxidamas was; Praxidamas by winning at the games saved his own father Sokleidas, also not a victor, from the obscurity that would have enveloped him if it were not for the prowess of his three sons, all of them victors; and still further back there is Hagesimachos, father of Sokleidas, who, we may infer, had been a victor too. Thus, the family has produced victors in every other generation, and in this it resembles the earth itself, common mother of men and gods, that now is productive, and now lies fallow.

The first triad is concerned with the present occasion and with the thoughts it evokes in Pindar's mind. In the second triad, he dwells on the achievements first of Alkimidas' relatives, distinguished for their victories in boxing at the Isthmian Games, held in "the heart of Greece," and then of his fellow clansmen—Kallias, who won in boxing at the Pythian Games, and Kreontidas, victor in the Isthmian Games on "the bridge of the unwearying sea" (the Isthmos of Corinth) and at the Nemean Games "beneath the mountains of Phleious." The third triad celebrates Aigina, home of the Aiakidai. There follows a brief story taken from the fund of Aiakid lore: the myth of Achilleus' encounter with Memnon, son of the Dawn, in battle at Troy. From here Pindar modulates back to Alkimidas, with a brief and rather enigmatic reference to a near win at Olympia. It seems that Alkimidas and Polytimidas (a friend or relative) were unlucky in the drawing of lots, which cost them their Olympian crowns. The ode ends by praising Alkimidas' wrestling coach, Melesias of Athens.

Turn 1

There is one race of men,
one race of gods.
Yet from one mother
we both take our breath.
The difference
is in the allotment
of all power,
for the one is nothing
while the bronze sky exists forever,
a sure abode.
And yet, somehow,
we resemble the immortals,
whether in greatness of mind
or nature, though we know not
to what measure
day by day and in the watches of the night
fate has written that we should run. (1–7)

Counterturn 1

And now Alkimidas
gives clear proof
that the power
born in the blood
is like
the fruit-bearing fields
that now, in alternation,
yield mankind
yearly sustenance from the ground
and now, again, resting
withhold their strength.
See, he comes
from Nemea's joyful contest,
a boy contender, pursuing
the career that Zeus
has allotted him: he has shown himself
a hunter destined for success in wrestling, (8–14)

Stand 1

treading in the footprints of his father's father,
Praxidamas—
for he, victorious at Olympia,
first brought the Aiakidai garlands from Alpheos;
and having won the crown five times at Isthmos
and three times at Nemea,
he put an end
to the obscurity of Sokleidas, his father,
who proved to be
greatest of the sons of Hagesimachos (15–22)

Turn 2

because of his own three sons,
winners of prizes, who reached
the peaks of triumph
and had their share of toil.
But, with divine favor,
the contest
in the heart of Greece
has declared
no other house a steward of more
crowns for boxing.
I hope, with this boast,
to hit the target squarely,
like an archer:
come, Muse, direct
upon this clan
the glorious breath of song—
for when men have passed out of our midst (23–29)

Counterturn 2

poems and legends
convey their noble deeds,
and these are not lacking
to the Bassidai, a race
renowned of old,
who sail in ships laden
with their own triumphal songs
and can provide
the plowmen of the Pierides
with many a hymn
by their proud achievements.
For in the sacred ground
of Pytho, Kallias too—
a scion of this family—
having bound his fists
in leather thongs, found
favor with golden-distaffed (30–36)

Stand 2

Leto's children,
and shined by Kastalia at evening
in the Graces' attendance.
The bridge
of the unwearying sea honored Kreontidas once
in the biennial celebrations of the men thereabouts,
when bulls are slain in Poseidon's sanctuary;
and once
he decked his brow in the lion's leafage
beside the shadowy primeval mountains of Phleious. (37–44)

Turn 3

There are broad approaches
from every direction
that bards may take
to adorn this island—
for the Aiakidai,
by the display
of their great deeds,
have bequeathed to it
a glorious heritage, and their name
flies far over earth
and across the sea:
even into the midst
of the Ethiopians
it made its way, when Memnon
failed to return:
Achilleus had fallen upon them
heavily, stepping from his chariot (45–51)

Counterturn 3

the day he caught
the son of gleaming Dawn
on the point
of his raging spear.
Men of old have also
made these matters
into a high road of song,
and I myself, intent
upon my theme, follow them here.
But the wave rolling
nearest the ship's keel
is always a man's first concern.
I come,
a messenger gladly embracing
my double burden,
proclaiming that you,
Alkimidas, have provided this (52–58)

Stand 3

twenty-fifth triumph for your glorious clan,
from the games called sacred.
Near the holy grove
of Kronos' son a sudden lot deprived
both you, my child, and Polytimidas
of two Olympic garlands.
And I would add that Melesias
steered your hands and drove your strength,
a charioteer
equal in speed to a dolphin flashing through the sea. (59–66)

NEMEAN 7

Sogenes of Aigina, boys' pentathlon, 485 (?) B.C.

Sogenes and his father Theariôn were members of the Euxenid clan, descendants of Euxenos, whose name means "Good Friend." The theme of friendship between Pindar and his patrons, and between his patrons and the gods, takes up a great deal of space in *Nemean* 7.

The ode, one of Pindar's most difficult, opens with a prayer to the goddess Eleithyia, whose function it was to bring children safely to birth. She presided over the birth of Sogenes and over his subsequent career. That career has brought him athletic distinction and with it immortality through glorification in song. The victor and his countrymen fully understand the value of song and are willing to pay for it. This is the point on which Pindar dwells at the start of the first stand (see the Introduction, *Pindar's Genre*).

But the power of poetry to immortalize has a negative aspect. Poets are not always fair. Under Homer's influence the majority of men still think more highly of Odysseus than they should. Aias, a better man than Odysseus, committed suicide because the Greeks at Troy awarded the prize of Achilleus' armor to Odysseus instead of to him. Pindar was troubled by this injustice; he treated it in *Nemean 8* and *Isthmian 4* also.

Another hero who came to a tragic end was Neoptolemos, the son of Achilleus. Neoptolemos' story occupies the next three stanzas (counterturn 2–turn 3).

According to the ancient commentary to *Nemean* 7, the Alexandrian scholar Aristarchus believed that Pindar was excusing himself in this ode for some uncomplimentary references he had made to Neoptolemos in a paian. In 1908, a papyrus containing substantial portions of Pindar's *Paian 6* was discovered. Its contents seemed to justify the theory that Pindar was taking pains in *Nemean 7* to clear himself before his Aiginetan audience of the charge that he had been disrespectful toward Neoptolemos, an Aiakid hero dear to the Aiginetans. The mysterious manner in which Pindar introduces Neoptolemos into the ode would seem to support such a theory. Pindar refers to a journey he himself had made to Delphi "in vindication," alluding, perhaps, to the performance of *Paian 6* at Delphi and to its basically laudatory intent. Whether or not this is the case, the differences between *Paian 6* and *Nemean 7* are instructive.

The relevant section of *Paian 6* reads as follows:

. . . (Neoptolemos), who sacked the city of Ilion. But he never saw his dear mother again, nor the horses of the Myrmidons in his father's fields, as he led the bronze-helmed host. He came to the Molossian land near Tomaros, escaping neither the winds nor the far-shooter with the broad quiver (Apollo): for the god had vowed that he would not reach his kindly home nor come to old age, because, leaping upon the altar near the hearth, he had slain the aged Priam; Apollo killed him, then, as he fought with the attendants over the honors due him in the god's own precinct by the broad navel of earth (i.e., at Delphi). (104–20)

There are significant points of difference between the account in the paian and that given in *Nemean* 7. In the paian, Apollo vows to bar Neoptolemos from returning home because he had killed the aged Trojan king, Priam, at the palace altar; and it is the god himself who kills Neoptolemos at Delphi. In *Nemean* 7, Neoptolemos goes to Delphi to offer Apollo the firstfruits of his Trojan war spoils—there is no mention of Apollo's role in keeping him from returning home; and he dies by the hand of a man—it is not Apollo who kills him. The people of Delphi grieve for his death, but the whole tragic event is transfigured by the future: Neoptolemos has died at Delphi in order that one of the descendants of Aiakos might have heroic honors there.

The mythical section of the ode comes to an end in the third turn. From here Pindar gradually modulates to praise of the victor's father, then of the victor himself. Between the two he inserts a self-justification, which occupies much of the first two stanzas of the fourth triad. The triad opens with a claim to acceptance at home and abroad. "An Achaian man" would find no fault with Pindar, nor would his own fellow citizens. Pindar may have chosen an Achaian man to vouch for him abroad because the descendants of Neoptolemos still enjoy the kingship in Molossia (stand 2), which can be imagined to lie "above the Ionian Sea." There Pindar also locates the home of his friend, the Achaian man. The mention of the Achaian man's approval would have special point if Pindar were vindicating himself in regard to Neoptolemos. He is unlikely to have discredited Neoptolemos without alienating that hero's Achaian descendants. But he has remained in their good graces and is, presumably, innocent.

The pentathlon event, in which Sogenes competed, provides Pindar with a metaphor for his own performance in this ode at the end of the fourth turn and the beginning of the following counterturn. Competitors in the pentathlon had to jump, throw the discus, hurl the javelin, run a race, and wrestle. Pindar imagines a situation in which losing the third event, the javelin throw, would cost a competitor his chance to enter the final event, the wrestling. It is significant that the imaginary javelin failure is not due to lack of strength but to lack of control: Pindar denies having "overstepped the line." This suggests that he has conducted himself properly in the previous part of the ode, where the main concern had been to glorify the heroes of the victor's city. What is left in the "competition" between the poet and his task is the celebration of the victor himself.

The last triad pays tribute to the favor of Herakles, enjoyed by Sogenes and his family. Apparently, they lived in a house situated between two precincts sacred to Herakles, their "neighbor." Pindar asks Herakles to continue blessing Sogenes and his descendants.

At the end of the ode, Pindar returns to Neoptolemos, of whom we have heard nothing since the beginning of the third triad. The return itself is emphatic, but even more emphatic is the language in which Pindar denies ever having treated Neoptolemos with disrespect.

The poem ends with a mysterious phrase, "Corinth of Zeus," usually interpreted as a reference to a nursery tale or a children's game. Pindar's audience are not children—he need not repeat himself to be understood.

The more obscure passages of the ode make sense when read as part of Pindar's self-justification to the Aiginetans. However, if Aristarchus had not expressed his opinion, and if no trace of *Paian 6* remained, the ode would still bear many resemblances to Pindar's other odes, and these resemblances would help us to understand it. Pindar's defense of his friend (*xenos*) Theariôn against "blame" in the third stand, for example, is strongly reminiscent of his rejection of Archilochos the "blameful" poet in *Pythian 2*. *Nemean* 7 might be considered a full-scale treatment of the poet's role as the victor's friend or *xenos* (see the Introduction, *Pindar's Genre*), with emphasis on its negative aspect: the poet not only praises, he also defends, his friend. A poet, however, emphasizes a theme for a reason. *Paian 6* casts light on the dark parts of *Nemean* 7. Whether it is the right light may well remain uncertain.

Turn 1

Eleithyia, enthroned beside the profound Moirai,
daughter of Hera in her great strength,
hear me, deliverer of children:
without you
we can have no vision
of day or dark night,
no share in the blessings
of Hebe, your sister, with the shining limbs.
Yet we do not all draw the breath of life
for equal destinies:
each is yoked
to his own fate,
each constrained
in his own way.
Still, with your help,
Sogenes, son of Thearîon, is supreme
in the pentathlon, and has become,
for his achievements,
a glorious theme of song. (1–8)

Counterturn 1

For he dwells in the music-loving city
of Aiakos' sons, warriors with clashing spears.
They are eager to embrace
a spirit tried in contention.
And if a man succeeds
in an exploit, he casts
a delightful theme
upon the streams of the Muses.
For great deeds of strength, if they lack songs,
are sunk in deep obscurity,
and we know
of only one
mirror
for noble achievements:
if Mnamosyna
in her shimmering veil consents
to let a man find
reward for toil
in the song of verses, givers of glory. (9–16)

Stand 1

And men of discernment, aware that the wind will rise
on the third day, are not hurt by the thought of gain.
Rich and poor alike fare onward to the tomb
of death.
I even suspect that Odysseus' fame
was greater than his worth, through the sweet words of Homer. (17–21)

Turn 2

For in his lies and in his winged devices
there is an awesome power:
wisdom is deceptive, seducing
with its myths,
and the masses
of mankind
have a blind heart,
for if they could have seen the truth,
powerful Aias, angered over the armor,
would not have plunged
the smooth sword
into his breast—
Aias, except for Achilleus,
mightiest in battle
of all
who went to bring back
blond Menelaos' wife from Troy,
riding
the escorts of Zephyros' breath (22–29)

Counterturn 2

to Ilion. But the wave of Death moves
over all and falls upon
the known and the unknown alike.
Glory is born
when a god
makes a man's fame grow
luxuriant after death.
It was, I tell you, in vindication
that I went to the great navel-stone
of broad-bosomed earth.
There, in Pytho's sacred ground,
Neoptolemos is laid to rest
because he had sacked
Priam's city—
the Danaans too
had struggled for it. But then, sailing home,
he missed the island
of Skyros
and came, wandering, to Ephyra. (30–37)

Stand 2

And he was king in Molossia for a brief time—
an honor his posterity now enjoy forever.
And then he left,
bringing firstfruits of Trojan spoils for the god
at Delphi
where, in a quarrel over sacrificial meats,
a man stabbed him with a knife. (38–42)

Turn 3

His Delphian hosts were deeply grieved,
but he had paid the debt of fate,
for one of the mighty Aiakidai
was destined to remain
in the ancient grove,
near the god's strong-walled temple,
for the rest of time,
and to dwell there, divinely appointed
to oversee processions honoring heroes,
rich in sacrifice.
Justice,
named in loveliness,
will find
three words are enough:
no lying witness
presides, Aigina, over the deeds
of yours and Zeus' children.
It is mine
to speak thus boldly, finding (43–50)

Counterturn 3

within myself a source of words with power
        to honor glittering prowess.
But in every matter
                                intermission is sweet:
    even honey
        and the flowers of Aphrodite
            bring satiety.
    And each of us differs from birth
in the endowments of life—one thing is yours,
                another is mine,
and for one man
    to attain
        every happiness
            is impossible.
                                    I cannot say to whom
Moira has offered this achievement
    in secure possession.
For you, Theariôn,
                                an hour of joy deserved (51-58)

Stand 3

is her gift,
                nor does she blight your mind
as you win to the boldness of noble acts.
                                                    I am your friend—
I will praise the man I love, warding away lurid blame
and bringing him true glory, like a stream of water.
This is the proper reward for the good. (59-63)

Turn 4

An Achaian man, dwelling above the Ionian Sea,
will not reproach me
when I meet him—
I trust in his friendship.
And among my fellow citizens
my glance is bright.
I do not overreach myself,
but keep all violence from my path.
May future time approach me kindly.
Men will understand
and say outright
whether I come
with a crooked phrase
upon my lips,
singing out of tune.
Sogenes, scion of the Euxenidai,
I swear I have not
overstepped the line,
not launched my word (64–71)

Counterturn 4

on its swift way, like a brazen javelin
whose thrower, with strong neck
dry of sweat, disqualifies himself
from the wrestling
before he enters the lists
in the blazing sun.
If there was toil,
greater the delight that follows after.
Let me be! If, carried somewhat
to excess, I cried aloud,
I am not ready
to refuse a victor
his due of song:
I find it easy
to plait him garlands.
Strike up the lyre! Look, the Muse
is twining together gold
and white ivory
and gathered coral, lily of the sea. (72–79)

Stand 4

Now, remembering Zeus in Nemea's honor, rouse
the chant of praise, but softly:
it is fitting
that we laud the King of the gods
with gentle voice upon this holy spot,
for here they say
he sowed the seed of Aiakos in Aigina's womb— (80–84)

Turn 5

Aiakos, destined to govern in my glorious city
and to be for you, Herakles,
brother and true friend.
If one man
has any knowledge of another,
he would say
a loving-minded neighbor
is a joy to value over all.
And if a god as well
endorse that precept,
Sogenes would pray
to go on dwelling
through your grace,
O slayer of giants,
in good fortune
and devotion to his father,
in the richly built
sacred avenue
where his ancestors have dwelt— (85–92)

Counterturn 5

for he has his house between your holy grounds,
like the yoke in a four-horse chariot,
to right and left of him
as he approaches.
O blessed one,
it is fitting
that you should sway
the heart of Hera's consort
and his bright-eyed daughter's will.
Often you are able
to give men strength
in intractable disasters.
So may you join
to his youth
and shining old age
a life of enduring vigor, weaving it through
happily to its end,
and may
his children's children enjoy forever (93–100)

Stand 5

the honor of this moment
and more in after time.
But my heart will never say that it has mauled
Neoptolemos with ruthless words.
To turn the same matter
three and four times over turns into futility, like idly
barking at children: *Corinth of Zeus!* (101–5)

NEMEAN 8

Deinis of Aigina, double foot race, 459 (?) B.C.

Nemean 8 celebrates a victory won in the double foot race at Nemea by Deinis of Aigina, who competed in the boys' division. His father, Megas, had won in the same event at Nemea before him, and Pindar mentions both victories together. It is clear from the end of the ode that the father is no longer alive. Father and son belonged to the clan of the Chariadai. Apart from these facts, we know virtually nothing about the circumstances of the ode's production.

It begins with a hymn to Youth (*Hora*), the "season of desire." The sexual emphasis at the start is appropriate for an ode written in honor of a victor who is just emerging from boyhood to manhood. In the course of the hymn, Pindar mentions two sorts of passion, one good, the other ruinous, and this leads him to a mythical example of the better kind: the union of Zeus and Aigina. From that union sprang the great hero Aiakos, founder of the line of mythical heroes who made Aigina resplendent in legend. Aiakos became king of the island, which Pindar calls by its older name, Oinona: "Vineland."

In the first stand, Pindar speaks of touching the knees of Aiakos in supplication. The language suggests a religious occasion, such as the dedication of the victor's crown, perhaps before a statue of Aiakos. Pindar prays here on behalf of Aigina: he wants her to enjoy prosperity from the gods. God-given happiness then reminds him of Kinyras, king of Kypros, whose wealth was proverbial. He is an example of human bliss secured by the favor of the gods. He is also appropriate here because he was a priest of Aphrodite, the goddess with whom the ode began.

The myth of the ode concerns one of the descendants of Aiakos, his tragic grandson Aias, whose suicide Pindar deals with also in *Nemean* 7 and again, a third time, in *Isthmian 4*. Here the story illustrates the destructiveness of envy. In the background is the dispute over who is to inherit the arms of Achilleus. According to Homer (*Odyssey* XI. 541–52), captive Trojans and the goddess Athena acted as judge and chose Odysseus over Aias; in Pindar, the Greeks themselves decide the issue, and it is decided in a secret ballot. Pindar darkly alludes to the rhetorical powers of Odysseus, as if he had won the people over to his side by cajolery. Aias, a man of few words, cannot compete in this way, and so he is defeated. His suicide is an example of the consequences of true merit going unrecognized.

The ode is light at the beginning and at the end, but dark in the center. Starting with the youth of Deinis and the feeling of love stirred by his beauty in those who see him, it moves to the love between Zeus and Aigina and to their offspring, Aiakos, whose reputation for justice once brought all Greece to his court for a fair decision. In the center of the poem, we have almost the exact opposite: all the Greeks rendering an unjust decision against Aiakos' grandson. Here, instead of love, there is hate; instead of birth, death; and instead of justice, injustice.

At the culmination of the myth, Pindar returns to the theme: envy and its chief expression, slander. The latter existed in ancient days, as it does now. Pindar avers that he is no slanderer, but a good judge of men, willing to speak his mind and able to make of his words a gift second in value only to immortality. If slander and the refusal to bestow true praise have been with us a long time, so too have their opposites, praise and its vehicle, the epinician ode. In fact, to take Pindar's expression precisely, the poetry of celebration has been with us a little longer, before Adrastos led the famed expedition of the Seven against Thebes. This would put it at least a generation earlier than the tragedy of Aias at Troy. Praise, then, has a more ancient pedigree than envy.

Turn 1

Herald of Aphrodite's awakening,
Youth, season of desire, enthroned
in the glances of maidens and boys—
there are those who feel
your force in gentleness
and those whom you move
another way.
In all I do
I would wish
to observe decorum,
and meet
with the better love, (1–5)

Counterturn 1

such love as hovered over the bed
of Zeus and Aigina, tending
the gifts of Aphrodite:
and there came to flower
a son, the King of Oinona,
supreme in might
and counsels.
Many a time
men prayed to behold him,
heroes of the lands
who hastened in peace,
eager to observe his decisions—

Stand 1

both those who ranged their hosts
in rocky Athens and the Pelopid
marshals of Sparta.
A suppliant of Aiakos
on behalf of his city and his people here,
I touch his sacred knees, bringing
a crown of Lydian fabric, intertwined
with whistling strains of the flute,
to adorn
Deinis and his father Megas, winners
in the double race at Nemea.
The happiness
sown by a god's hand endures the longer— (11–17)

Turn 2

Kinyras felt it once and flourished
with wealth in Kypros of the sea.
I stand on light feet now,
catching breath before I speak.
For there are songs in every style,
but to put a new one to the touchstone
for testing is all danger.
Words are a morsel
to the envious,
and their envy always
fastens on the noble,
but leaves the base alone. (18–22)

Counterturn 2

It bit into the son of Telamon
and doubled him onto his sword—
a man, surely, with no glib tongue
but proud of heart, now lies crushed
in darkness, under bitter strife.
For they gave the best prize
to the glistening lie:
the Danaans with secret votes
favored Odysseus, and Aias,
stripped of the golden arms,
rolled
thrashing in his own blood. (23–27)

Stand 2

Surely they were different wounds
that they tore in the warm flesh
of their foes and then pulled back for shelter
in the shadow of his spear—
around Achilleus' body
and on other days when the fighting
raged.
Yes, hateful slander existed
long ago, partner of flattering tales,
hatcher of schemes, doer of evil, reproach
that overwhelms the brilliant
and lifts into view
the spurious glory of the obscure. (28–34)

Turn 3

May I never have such a character, father Zeus!
May I tread the simple paths of life,
leaving behind in death
no infamy to taint my children.
Some men pray for gold,
others for limitless land,
but I would wish
to lay my limbs in earth
beloved by my fellow citizens,
because I praised the praiseworthy
and scattered blame
on those who deserved it. (35–39)

Counterturn 3

Like a tree fed by fresh dews,
virtue soars into the air,
raised among the good and the just
toward the shimmering ether.
From those we love
we know a thousand favors
valued most in times of trouble.
But in joy too
we feel the need of something
to rely on.
O Megas,
to bring your soul back to life again (40–44)

Stand 3

is not open to me:
empty hopes
fatten on emptiness.
But I hasten to raise
this stone of the Muses for Aigina
and the Chariadai, honoring your speed
and your son's, victorious twice.
And I rejoice in having cast
a boast to befit what I have done.
Once a man charmed the pain out of toil
with incantations,
and the song of praise
also existed long ago, even before
Adrastos and the Kadmeians came to blows. (45–51)

NEMEAN 9

Chromios of Aitna, chariot race at Sikyon, 474 (?) B.C.

The last three Nemean odes have nothing to do with the Nemean Games. See the Introduction, *The History of the Text* (The Second Century Selection).

Nemean 9 is the second poem Pindar wrote in honor of Chromios, son of Hagesidamos. The first, *Nemean 1*, was written for him when he dwelled at Syracuse. The second, *Nemean 9*, was written when Chromios, Hieron's brother-in-law and political ally, was acting governor of Aitna until Hieron's son Deinomenes should come of age and assume the kingship (see the preface to *Pythian 1*).

The poem is written in repeating stanzas instead of triads. The occasion seems to be a procession to Chromios' house, in celebration of a victory won in the chariot race at Sikyon, sacred to Apollo, whose mother and sister are included in the opening invocation. The games at Sikyon had been founded by Kleisthenes, but Pindar attributes their foundation to the hero Adrastos, son of Talaos, who set them up in thanks for his escape from Amphiaraos. Amphiaraos, the son of Oïkles, had usurped power in Adrastos' original home of Argos. Later Adrastos married his sister Eriphyla to Amphiaraos, and in this way made up the quarrel between them. Eriphyla was responsible afterward for the participation of her husband Amphiaraos in the abortive siege of Thebes, the subject of Pindar's myth in this ode. At the conclusion of the siege, Zeus saved Amphiaraos from disgrace, possibly because he was an unwilling participant in that doomed venture.

The choice of myth has at least two motivations. First, the connection between Adrastos and Sikyon, where Chromios' victory was gained, provides an easy bridge to the story of the siege, since Adrastos was one of the seven chieftains who participated in it. Second, the ode is full of references to actual military events. Chromios was a distinguished soldier. He had fought against the Carthaginians at Himera in 480 B.C. Though the Greeks had triumphed in that battle, the danger of renewed war with Carthage was ever-present. This is why Pindar breaks off the story of the war against Thebes in stanza 6, with a prayer to Zeus that the struggle between the Sicilian Greeks and the Phoinikian Carthaginians be put off indefinitely. Hieron and Chromios had fought against the Etruscans in the naval engagement at Kuma in 474, a battle alluded to by Pindar in stanza 7. Chromios had also fought at the battle of the Heloros River in 492. Pindar mentions this battle by name in stanza 8, because of its importance to Hieron: from it dated the foundation of the Deinomenid dynasty.

The struggle of war and athletic competition yields in the last two stanzas to the relaxation of the banquet. We see Chromios drinking wine from the silver cups that were his prize in the games at Sikyon. Thus Pindar puts in relief the gentler aspects of this warrior-athlete's character. It was not mere savagery that moved him to his warlike deeds, but the goddess Aidos, Shame or Modesty, who inspired him to turn the course of battle (stanza 8). Pindar adds that ordinarily she cannot survive among men who are rich. Chromios and his friends are an exception to that rule.

1 Come, Muses, leave Apollo's side—
let us go from Sikyon
to the newly built town of Aitna,
the rich house of Chromios,
whose doors are flung wide, though not wide enough
for all the guests streaming in!
But strike up the hymn, the joyous song!
For he mounts the chariot, reins in his steeds,
and calls for a loud invocation
to the mother and her twin children,
watching together over the heights of Delphi. (1–5)

2 Men have a certain saying:
hide not in the ground, in silence,
a noble deed accomplished—
wonder of song and pride of speech is fitting then!
So rouse the strumming lyre,
let the flutes resound
in praise of the best of horse races,
founded by Adrastos in Phoibos Apollo's honor
by the streams of Asopos.
Remembering that deed of his,
I will exalt him in my song. (6–10)

3 He was king at the time in Sikyon,
and with new festivals,
the trial of men's strength
and speed of wrought chariots,
he glorified the city, gave it a name among men,
all in thanks for his escape—
he had come there fleeing dread Amphiaraos
and the deadly strife at home in Argos.
For the sons of Talaos, crushed in that struggle,
were princes no more. The man of greater might
puts an end to the order of old. (11–15)

4 But the sons of Talaos, betrothing
Eriphyla the man-subduer
as a pledge of trust to Oïkles' son,
once more were mightiest of the fair-haired Danaans,
and in time they led a host of men
to seven-gated Thebes.
No propitious omens sent them on their way,
nor did Kronos' son,
hurling the lightning bolt,
bid them, in their madness, to set forth from home—
rather to refrain from going. (16–20)

5 But they were massed together,
hastening to sure disaster
with brazen arms and caparisoned steeds:
yielding up all hope of a sweet return,
they fattened the white bloom of smoke
with their corpses;
by the banks of Ismenos,
seven pyres fed on their youthful flesh.
But with all-powerful thunder
Zeus cleft the deep-breasted earth for Amphiaraos
and hid him from sight, chariot and all, (21–25)

6 before the spear of Periklymenos
could strike him in the back
and shame his warrior spirit.
Panic sent by the gods
makes even their own sons fear and flee.
Zeus, if I can, I put far off
the proud, impending life-and-death struggle
against Phoinikian spears!
and ask you to bestow
on the children of Aitna
a life of peace and order for long years to come (26–30)

7 and ever to assemble their people
in splendor of public celebrations.
Here, father Zeus, are knightly men,
with hearts above the lure of gain.
Incredible praise, I know:
for profit imperceptibly
overshadows Aidos, giver of glory.
But had you served with Chromios
among the spearmen, the cavalry, or the ships,
you would have judged—
in the peril of the shrill war cry— (31–35)

8 how that goddess moved him
in his soldier's heart
to beat back the havoc of Enyalios:
and few indeed are those
who keep, in the midst of bloodshed,
presence of mind and strength
to turn the storm
against their enemies' ranks.
They say that glory bloomed for Hektor
by Skamandros' streams.
By the steep banks of the Heloros, (36–40)

9 called by men *Areia's Passage,*
the same splendor shone
on the son of Hagesidamos
in his earliest prime.
I will proclaim the many deeds he wrought
at other times, on dusty land or nearby sea.
But after toils borne
in youth and justice,
a gentle life begins to dawn toward old age.
Let him know he has received
wondrous happiness from the gods. (41–45)

10 For if to his abundant riches
he has added glory,
he cannot—being mortal still—
set foot on any higher or more distant peak.
Meanwhile repose loves the drinking party,
victory newly planted
blooms with gentle singing,
and voices grow more joyous
around the wine bowl.
Let someone stir it,
sweet prophet of revelry, (46–50)

11 and pass from hand to hand
the mighty child of the vine,
in the silver goblets
Chromios' mares have won and sent to him,
together with Apollo's garlands
woven in holy rite, from sacred Sikyon.
Father Zeus, grant that I praise
this triumph with the Graces' favor,
and that I honor victory by my song
preeminently, casting my javelin
nearest the Muses' mark! (51–55)

NEMEAN 10

Theaios of Argos, wrestling, 444 (?) B.C.

The occasion of this ode is the victory of Theaios, son of Oulias, in the wrestling match at the Hekatombaia of Hera in Argos.

The ode opens with a catalogue of mythical splendors belonging to the victor's city. From there it moves, in the second triad, to the various successes gained by Theaios and a wish that he might add an Olympian victory to his record (a triumph in the Panathenaia at Athens, where the prize was olive oil in precious jars, is mentioned in the second stand as if it were a prelude to greater things—i.e., to an Olympian victory). The third triad begins with a list of successes won by Theaios' fellow Argives and ends with the statement that his athletic prowess is easily explained: he enjoys the favor of the twin brothers Kastor and Polydeukes, patrons and guardians of the Olympian festival. This favor is part of the family heritage of Theaios, whose maternal ancestor Pamphaes had once entertained the twins when they visited Argos. The last two triads are devoted to the myth of the ode, the story of the conflict between Kastor and Polydeukes on one side, and Idas and Lynkeus, sons of Aphareus, on the other.

Among the myths briefly alluded to in the opening catalogue is the story of Hypermestra, daughter of Danaos, the only one of his fifty daughters who disobeyed her father's command to kill their husbands on their wedding night. Hypermestra, Pindar tells us, kept her sword sheathed rather than murder her husband Lynkeus, who is not to be confused with the Lynkeus who fights together with his brother Idas against the twins at the close of the ode. The Lynkeus named in counterturn 1 married Hypermestra and became king of Argos. He was the son of Aigyptos. The Lynkeus who fights with the twins in counterturn 4 was the son of Aphareus. Pindar avoids confusion by naming Aphareus when he introduces the second Lynkeus into the ode.

Another myth receiving slightly more elaboration in the catalogue is told by Pindar in the first stand: when Amphitryon, husband of Alkmena, was away fighting the Teleboai, Zeus, disguised as Amphitryon, visited Alkmena and engendered Herakles. Later, Amphitryon came to her and sired Herakles' twin half-brother Iphikles. A similar event occurred in the family of Tyndareus and Leda, parents of the twins Kastor and Polydeukes. Zeus, in the form of a swan, made love to Leda and sired the immortal Polydeukes. Leda's mortal husband Tyndareus became the father of the mortal Kastor. We hear of this from the mouth of Zeus himself at the conclusion of the ode.

The theme of the myth is announced at the end of the third stand:

"Truly, the race of gods can be trusted." The words, echoed later by Polydeukes when his brother Kastor is dying, climax the description of the twins as tutelary heroes of athletic festivals, and the mention of Herakles here would call Olympia to mind (see the preface to *Olympian 3*). In the second triad, Pindar had placed unusual emphasis on Theaios' desire to win at Olympia. His ancestral connection with the twins, his previous athletic career, his inborn ability, and his reverence toward the gods would seem to make him worthy of their favor. Their reliability is then illustrated in the story of how Polydeukes, the immortal twin, consented to give up part of his immortality out of love for his brother.

In keeping with this lofty image of the twins, Pindar seems to have acted as editor in their behalf. According to one tradition, the twins, having been invited to the wedding of their cousins Lynkeus and Idas, seized both brides and fled with them. A struggle ensued and Kastor was mortally wounded. Pindar makes no mention of the relationship between the two sets of brothers, of the wedding, or of the rape, naming instead as the reason for the fight "a quarrel over cattle."

Turn 1

Sing, Graces, the city of Danaos
and his fifty daughters
throned in splendor,
Argos, Hera's home, a place
fit for the gods.
The radiance of a thousand exploits
shines about her, the gleam of her bold deeds.
Great are the acts
of Perseus, conqueror of Gorgon Medusa;
many the towns
founded in Egypt by Epaphos;
and Hypermestra did not swerve,
keeping shut in its sheath
the one sword in fifty
that cast its vote for life! (1-6)

Counterturn 1

And once bright-eyed Athena
made prince Diomedes an immortal god.
The earth at Thebes, cloven
by the thunderbolt of Zeus,
opened to receive
the son of Oïkles, Amphiaraos,
prophet and cloud of war.
And from of old
Argos has excelled
in her women's loveliness:
Zeus, in the arms
of Alkmena and Danaä,
brought that truth to light.
In the father of Adrastos and in Lynkeus, his gift
was intellect wedded with perfect justice. (7-12)

Stand 1

And Zeus exalted the spear of Amphitryon
who, matchless in prosperity, came
even into kinship with the god
when in bronze arms
he slew the Teleboai:
assuming his likeness,
the King of the immortals entered the palace
bearing the seed of Herakles,
whose bride Hebe—
loveliest of goddesses on Olympos—
walks beside Hera lady of marriage. (13-18)

Turn 2

Too great a task for lips of mine—
counting all the glories
that are the heritage of sacred Argos.
That way lies men's surfeit,
harsh to encounter.
But strike the melodious lyre
on the theme of wrestling.
The contest for bronze prizes
lures the people
to Hera's sacrifice
and the judgment of her games,
where Theaios,
the son of Oulias, has won
the victory twice and gained
forgetfulness of pains endured. (19–24)

Counterturn 2

He awed the Hellenic host at Pytho once.
Luck was with him when he went
for crowns at Isthmos and Nemea,
giving the Muses ground to till—
three times winner
at the sea's gates
and three times
on the sacred plain,
in Adrastos' games.
Father Zeus, he does not cry aloud
his mind's desire.
But you are the source
of every achievement: without the effrontery
of a heart unschooled in toil,
he prays for your favor. (25–30)

Stand 2

The gods know the meaning of my song,
so too the man who strives for the crown
in the highest of contests.
Pisa is supreme—
the games of Herakles are hers.
And yet,
by way of prelude, sweet voices twice sang of Theaios
in Athenian ritual chant, and Hera's
heroic people welcomed what he won—
the oil
in earthen vessels fired to black brilliance. (31–36)

Turn 3

And often, with the aid of the Graces
and the sons of Tyndareus,
glory has come, Theaios,
to the famed race
of your maternal ancestors.
If I were a kinsman
of Thrasyklos and Antias,
I would not veil
the brightness of my glance in Argos!
With what triumphs
has the city of Proitos,
rich in horses,
flourished in the valley of Corinth!
And among the Kleonaians
four times it burst in bloom. (37–42)

Counterturn 3

And Argives came away from Sikyon
with silver wine goblets
gathered to their arms,
and from Pellana they departed
with fine woolen cloaks
draped over their shoulders.
But there's no way
to number the bronze prizes—
greater leisure
than I have
would be needed for it—
endless prizes
Kleitor and Tegea, the upland towns of Achaia,
and Mount Lykaion set up beside the course of Zeus
for swift feet and strong hands to win. (43–48)

Stand 3

No wonder yours is a race of born athletes:
Kastor and his brother Polydeukes
came once to feast in friendship with Pamphaes,
and they—
lords in the broad land of Sparta—
share with Hermes and Herakles
in the arrangement of flourishing contests.
Deep
is their regard for men of justice.
Truly, the race of gods can be trusted. (49–54)

Turn 4

They live their lives by turns—
one day at the side
of father Zeus, another day
in the caverns of earth,
in Therapna's chambers underground,
each sharing
in the other's destiny.
Polydeukes,
rather than be a god
and dwell on Olympos forever,
chose this fate
when Kastor fell in battle.
For Idas, enraged
in a quarrel over cattle, wounded him
with the point of his brazen spear. (55–60)

Counterturn 4

Watching from Mount Taÿgetos,
Lynkeus had seen the twins
seated on a hollow oak trunk—
of all men on earth
he had the keenest eyes.
With swift feet then
the sons of Aphareus moved and were there.
Quickly
they planned a mighty deed
and suffered for it
at the hands of Zeus:
without delay
the son of Leda came in pursuit.
Near their father's tomb they took
their stand against him. (61–66)

Stand 4

There they seized into their hands the gravestone of Hades,
a polished boulder,
and hurled it against the breast
of Polydeukes.
But it neither crushed nor deterred him—
he swept in upon them with his swift spear
and thrust the bronze point between Lynkeus' ribs,
while Zeus let fall on Idas a smoking red bolt of thunder.
They burned at the same time, but apart.
How harsh it is
for men to clash in strife against their betters! (67–72)

Turn 5

Polydeukes ran to his brother's side
and found him still alive
but gasping in death's throes.
The warm tears fell amid his groans
as Polydeukes cried aloud:
"Father Kronion,
what relief from pain
will there be now?
On me too, lord,
together with him,
pass sentence of death.
A man deprived of those he loves
has seen his honor go,
though in times of suffering few
among mortal men can be trusted (73–78)

Counterturn 5

to share the burden." He spoke,
and Zeus appeared before him, face to face,
saying: "You are my son.
Your mother's husband
came to her after me
and left in her womb
the mortal seed
that is your brother there.
But hear me:
I grant you a choice
of two alternatives:
if you yourself, avoiding
death and loathsome old age,
would dwell on Olympos with me,
with Athenaia, and Ares of the dark spear— (79–84)

Stand 5

you may, such is your inheritance.
But if you strive
in your brother's behalf, intending
to share in all things equally with him,
then you may live
beneath the earth half the time,
the other half
together in the gold halls of Olympos."
So Zeus spoke, and Polydeukes felt
no hesitation in his mind, but opened the eyes
and restored the voice of Kastor clad in bronze. (85–90)

NEMEAN 11

Aristagoras of Tenedos, 446 (?) B.C.

Nemean 11 celebrates the installation of Aristagoras as president of the Council for the ensuing year.

It opens with a prayer to Hestia, goddess of the sacred hearth of the city, located in the council chamber where Aristagoras will preside. Although the poem is not a victory ode in the usual sense, Pindar proceeds very much in his usual epinician manner. He praises Aristagoras and the people of Tenedos for their lavish public hospitality, then turns to the wealth, beauty, and athletic prowess of his patron. All these personal attainments, magnificent as they are, remind Pindar of human mortality. The first triad concludes with the dark reminder that death waits for Aristagoras as it waits for all.

But death is no reason not to celebrate when the opportunity arises: the second triad opens with praise of Aristagoras for his local athletic victories. In the second counterturn, another dark note is sounded: Aristagoras has not won at Olympia or at Delphi, not through any lack of ability, but because his parents did not have enough confidence to support him in the attempt. The triad concludes with the reflection that hesitation can do no less harm to the more gifted man than rash pride can do to the less gifted.

The third triad opens with a brief account of Aristagoras' ancestry. He is descended from the Spartan Peisandros, who led Aiolian colonists from the mainland to Tenedos, and from the Theban Melanippos. This illustrious ancestry, boding well for the career of Aristagoras, is evident in his physical appearance, but the lack of a pan-Hellenic victory to his credit leads Pindar to reflect now on the mysterious alternation that governs the transmission of innate talent and energy from one generation to the next. As in *Nemean 6*, human families are here compared to the fields that yield abundant crops one year, but not in another. Yet the final lines of the ode, with a stern warning against ambition and impossible desires, imply that Aristagoras has enough to content him, or any man.

On the diction of the ode, with its thematic emphasis on negative volition, see the opening remarks on Translation in the Introduction.

Turn 1

Daughter of Rhea, mistress of the city's council, Hestia,
sister of Zeus on high
and Hera throned beside him:
kindly welcome Aristagoras to your chamber
and kindly receive
beside your gleaming scepter
his friends, who guard
the glory of Tenedos and often honor you (1–5)

Counterturn 1

first among gods in their worship,
in libation and savor of sacrifice.
In their halls, the lyre and the song resound
and Zeus lord of hospitality
beholds that virtue lavished
at their laden tables.
But grant that Aristagoras reach the end
of his year of office in glory, with heart unwounded. (6–10)

Stand 1

I call this man blest in his father Arkesilas,
blest in the wonder of his body
and the courage bred within it.
But if someone possessing wealth outshines others
by beauty also, and by strength in the contest,
he should remember
that he wears a mortal set of limbs
and last of all will put upon himself a cloak of earth. (11–16)

Turn 2

Yet it is right that the people of Tenedos
greet Aristagoras with ennobling words;
and right for us to glorify him
in the din of song, sweet to his ears.
Sixteen radiant victories,
won in the regions round about,
in wrestling and the proud pankration, have crowned
him and his famous fatherland. (17–21)

Counterturn 2

Only the too diffident hopes of his parents
barred their son from testing his mettle
in the games at Pytho and Olympia.
For I will swear, had he gone to Kastalia
and the thickly wooded Hill of Kronos,
he would have returned
more nobly than the wrestlers
pitted against him in the struggle, (22–26)

Stand 2

having celebrated the five-year festival
established by Herakles, and having bound
his hair in purple garlands.
But among mortals,
one man's puffed-up pride casts him
short of success;
another, too much
belittling his own power, feels a timid spirit
drag him by the hand and rob him of his proper glory. (27–32)

Turn 3

The blood of Peisandros from Sparta of old
was easy to discern in him—
Peisandros, who left Amyklai with Orestes
and brought to Tenedos a host
of Aiolians armed in bronze;
and Theban blood,
from Melanippos his maternal uncle,
commingles in him too. But ancient qualities (33–37)

Counterturn 3

put forth their strength in alternate
generations of men. The black earth
does not yield continual harvest,
and the trees will not break
in fragrant flowers
of equal richness
with every turn of the circling years. Even so
destiny governs the mortal race (38–42)

Stand 3

of man.
There comes from Zeus no certain sign
for men to read, yet we set sail for mighty
ambitions, coveting deed upon deed
because our limbs are bound by shameless hope,
and the streams of foreknowledge flow far off
from us.
We must hunt for the measure of gain.
Too sharp is the madness of unattainable desires. (43–48)

"Surely you know
of the blood-spattered might of Aias
impaled on his own sword in the late night,
casting reproach
on the sons of the Hellenes who went to Troy."

–*Isthmian 4*, 35–38

Black-figured belly amphora, showing the suicide of Aias. Courtesy, Musée des Beaux-Arts et d'Archéologie, Boulogne sur mer. Photo by Devos.

THE ISTHMIAN ODES

ISTHMIAN 1

Herodotos of Thebes, chariot race, 458 (?) B.C.

Pindar, engaged in writing a poem in honor of Apollo and Delos to be sung at Keos, has decided to suspend work on that song in order to compose the present ode, *Isthmian 1*. Since the ode celebrates a Theban victor, Pindar makes his decision into an expression of filial piety: he asks Delos to yield to Thebes, his mother city.

The ode falls into three divisions: praise of the heroes Kastor and Iolaos, praise of Asopodoros, the victor's father, a citizen of Orchomenos, and praise of the victor himself, Herodotos of Thebes.

The fact that Herodotos drove his own chariot to victory inspires Pindar to join his praises to a hymn in honor of the hero-charioteers Kastor and Iolaos. The hymn begins in the first stand and comes to an end in the second. The major part of it is a catalogue of athletic distinctions won by the Spartan hero Kastor and by the Theban hero Iolaos. There is a hymnal farewell to them in the second stand, where Pindar turns from them to the praise of Asopodoros, the victor's father.

In the third turn, Pindar refers to certain misfortunes that have come upon Asopodoros. The metaphor of shipwreck probably means that he had fallen upon hard times politically—that he may, perhaps, have suffered exile.

The third counterturn, an elaborate transition to the victor, is taken up with the idea that the proper response to achievement is praise. The stand goes on to develop the idea further by illustration from various walks of life. Herodotos belongs to the final class of men listed here.

An allusive catalogue of his victories occupies the fourth turn. Gratitude owed to Poseidon is a reiteration of Herodotos' success in the Isthmian Games sacred to Poseidon. "The sons of Amphitryon" called on next are Herakles and Iolaos, whose mention here signifies that they have favored Herodotos with a success in their games, held at Thebes. The mention of Minyas means a win at Orchomenos (see the preface to *Olympian 14*). Then follow victories at Eleusis and Euboia. All these places are referred to summarily for their "winding courses," a way of telling us that each of the triumphs was gained in a race.

The final stand is a prayer for further triumphs. It ends with reflection on the expenditures Herodotos will incur in pursuit of other victories. On the miser, implicitly contrasted with Herodotos here, see the Introduction, *"There is no Muse of translation."*

Turn 1

Mother, Theba of the golden shield,
yours is the moment now:
I will set you above
my want of leisure.
May rocky Delos, in whose praises
I have been absorbed,
not reproach me.
What is dearer to the good
than their own beloved parents?
Yield, O island of Apollo!
With the gods' help, I will achieve both songs together, (1–6)

Counterturn 1

dancing in honor
of Phoibos the unshorn
on wave-fringed Keos
with her island people,
and honoring in dances the ridge
of the Isthmos, guarded by the sea:
for it has given
six crowns from its contests
to the host of Kadmos,
the glory of victory
to my fatherland, where Alkmena bore (7–12)

Stand 1

her fearless son,
who once made the snarling dogs of Geryon whimper.
But I, composing in Herodotos' honor
a prize for victory in the four-horse chariot,
because he guided the reins himself,
with his own hands,
desire to join him
to a Kastor-song or a hymn of Iolaos.
For among heroes in Lakedaimon and in Thebes,
they were born to be the mightiest charioteers, (13–17)

Turn 2

and they won prizes
in the greatest number of contests
and beautified their homes
with tripods and cauldrons
and golden goblets,
winning the crowns of victory.
And still there is a shining
in the glory they gained
in the races run naked,
and in the races
run by men in arms with their shields clashing, (18–23)

Counterturn 2

and when they hurled
the javelin in their hands,
and when they cast
the stone discus.
For there was no pentathlon yet—
the prize was set up
for each achievement only.
Often binding their hair
in garlands from these events,
they shone forth
close by the streams of Dirka and by the Eurotas— (24–29)

Stand 2

the son of Iphikles, being of one folk
with the race of the Sown Men;
and the son of Tyndareus,
dwelling among Achaians in Therapna above the plain.
Farewell to you both.
Now, embracing Poseidon
in the folds of my song—and the sacred Isthmos,
and the shores of Onchestos—I will,
in honor of this man, proclaim
the lot of his father Asopodoros
supreme in glory, (30–34)

Turn 3

and likewise his ancestral city
Orchomenos
that received him
shaken with shipwreck,
in the chill of disaster
from the boundless sea.
But now again
his native luck
has spread above him
the fair skies of old.
And suffering brings the sufferer's mind foreknowledge. (35–40)

Counterturn 3

If a man has spent himself—
his wealth and his efforts—
on lofty achievements, he should receive,
when he has triumphed,
the proud vaunt of praise,
with no thought of envy.
For wise men,
in return
for labors of every kind,
willingly give noble recognition,
a song honoring the man and his people. (41–46)

Stand 3

For each has his deed's reward, each his enjoyment—
the shepherd and the plowman and the trapper of birds
and he whom the sea supports.
All men are intent
on warding brute famine from their bellies.
But he
who has won luxuriant renown in games or war,
once he has been well praised, receives
the greatest of gains:
regard in the speech
of his fellow citizens, and on the lips of strangers. (47–51)

Turn 4

And now we must bestow
return of glory
upon our neighbor and benefactor
Poseidon,
earth-shaking son of Kronos,
lord of chariots and of horses running,
and call upon
your sons, Amphitryon,
and upon the glen of Minyas,
upon Demeter's glorious grove
at Eleusis, and upon Euboia, for their winding courses; (52–57)

Counterturn 4

and I include, Protesilaos,
your precinct
of Achaian men
in Phylaka—
but the song,
with its brief measure, forbids
listing all the triumphs
Hermes god of contests has given
to Herodotos and his horses.
And often indeed
leaving a thing unmentioned brings us greater pleasure. (58–63)

Stand 4

May it be granted him, uplifted on the Pierian
Muses' bright wings,
to wreathe his hand hereafter
in garlands from Pytho too, and in the choice
blooms of Alpheos and Olympia, winning honor
for seven-gated Thebes.
But he who hoards
his wealth indoors, in secret, scorning others
less fortunate, is poor in glory—unaware that he pays
his soul in tribute to the god of death. (64–68)

ISTHMIAN 2

Xenokrates of Akragas, chariot race, 470 (?) B.C.

Isthmian 2 is the second poem Pindar wrote in honor of Xenokrates. Like the first, *Pythian 6*, it speaks not to Xenokrates, but to his son, Thrasyboulos. Almost at the very end, we are surprised to find that the ode—which has seemed all along to be addressed directly to Thrasyboulos—is actually a message entrusted by Pindar to a certain Nikasippos for delivery to Thrasyboulos in Akragas.

Pindar begins with an ironic comparison between the love poets of former times and the poets of the present day. The latter are, like Pindar, epinician poets who work for hire; the former wrote spontaneous love songs for boys. Ancient and modern critics alike agree that Pindar is here referring to the love poetry of Alcaeus, Ibycus, and Anacreon. The poetic scene, Pindar says, has changed considerably since their day. The Muse of choral song, Terpsichora, has approved the words uttered by Aristodemos the Argive, one of the Seven Wise Men: "Money, money is the man!" At this point Pindar abruptly compliments Thrasyboulos for being wise. He is the sort of listener who will not miss the point of Pindar's opening, which ironically overstresses one aspect of the Muse's public nature, namely, that she works for hire, and understresses another, that she bestows fame on deeds.

The central portion of the ode is a catalogue of victories. First on the list is the triumph that has occasioned the present poem. Next comes the Pythian victory of 490, already celebrated by Pindar in *Pythian 6*. Third is a victory in the chariot race at the Panathenaic festival in Athens. Xenokrates' charioteer on that occasion was Nikomachos, friend of the Elean heralds who proclaimed the opening of the Olympian festival to the states of Greece. The reference to Olympia reminds Pindar of the victory won there by Xenokrates' brother Theron, in whose honor Pindar had written the second and third Olympian odes. At this point, Pindar mentions Xenokrates and Theron together as "the children of Ainesidamos." The change from the individual to the family name enables Pindar to include Thrasyboulos, who is not a victor, in the standard epinician praise of wise generosity (see the Introduction, *Pindar's Genre*).

In the final triad, Pindar praises Thrasyboulos' family for their devotion to poetry and for hospitality. His father Xenokrates was a zealous host, as his name (*Xeno*-krates) would suggest. When Pindar says that he sailed to the Phasis in summer and to the Nile in winter, he means that Xenokrates did everything demanded by the highest ideal of hospitality. The Phasis was a river in Kolchis, on the eastern shore of the

Black Sea, which was open to Greek sailing only during the summer months. This use of extreme points on the geographical map to express the limits of moral achievement is common in Pindar. He does not mean Egypt and Kolchis literally, but metaphorically, and the same is true of winter and summer: Xenokrates was, at all times, everything a good host could be.

Pindar's use of the past tense throughout suggests that Xenokrates was dead when the ode was composed. His brother Theron, tyrant of Akragas, died in approximately 472. Theron's son Thrasydaios, who succeeded to the throne, quickly alienated the people of Akragas and fell from power (see the preface to *Olympian 12*). *Isthmian 2* concludes with ominous phrases on the theme of envy, but these need not allude to the disaster that eventually overtook the family. The power and eminence of its members would have made them the object of envy in any case.

Turn 1

In the olden days, Thrasyboulos, when poets
mounted the Muses' chariot
armed with the glorious lyre,
they shot their arrows
on the run,
honeyed serenades
to a darling boy—
whoever, in his beauty,
had the bloom
of Aphrodite's flower in his cheeks. (1–5)

Counterturn 1

For the Muse was not in love with money then—
she didn't work for hire,
nor would wanton songs
with silvered faces saunter
from melodious Terpsichora's shop
into the market place.
But now she'd have us
install the Argive's maxim,
words that very
nearly hit the truth: (6–10)

Stand 1

Money, money is the man! he said
when he lost his friends,
together with his wealth.
But you are wise—
not unfamiliar
is the triumph that I sing,
won by Xenokrates' horses
in the Isthmian games.
Poseidon
was behind it, Poseidon
sent him the wreath of Dorian parsley
to bind about his brow, (11–16)

Turn 2

glorifying a man good with the chariot,
the light of Akragas.
Mighty Apollo
smiled on him in Krisa,
the sons
of Erechtheus,
in glittering Athens,
clothed him with splendor,
and he found
no fault with the hand of his driver— (17–21)

Counterturn 2

Nikomachos, guiding the team at full rein:
the criers of the seasons—
Eleans who proclaim
the peace of Zeus Kronidas—
knew him, for they had proof
of his friendship
in the past.
The glad shout of their voices
welcomed him
to the arms of Victory (22–26)

Stand 2

in their own land,
called by them proudly
the grove of Zeus,
Olympia's god.
There the children
of Ainesidamos have mingled
with undying honor—
undying,
for yours is a house,
Thrasyboulos, not unfamiliar
with revels and the honey
boast of song. (27–32)

Turn 3

When we escort the Muses here,
to the halls of famous men,
we find no obstacle in the way;
the path is easy.
But I have hurled the discus far:
now may I throw the javelin
as far as Xenokrates
has spread his fame for kindness
beyond all rivals.
His neighbors found him noble, (33–37)

Counterturn 3

devoted to the Panhellenic code of horsemanship.
There was no holiday
when he did not entertain—
no shrill blast of wind
made him furl the sails
aboard his friendly table,
but he crossed to the Phasis
in summer, and in winter,
sailing,
he reached the steep banks of the Nile. (38–42)

Stand 3

Now while envious hope spreads
its shroud over the minds of men,
may he never stifle
his father's prowess
in the silence,
                    still less
this song: for we know
I did not compose it
to stay at home.
                    All this,
Nikasippos, dispense
when you come to my good friend. (43–48)

ISTHMIAN 3

Melissos of Thebes, chariot race, 473 B.C.

In the counterturn of *Isthmian 3*, Pindar mentions two victories won by Melissos: an Isthmian victory, contest unspecified, and a Nemean victory in the chariot race. The chariot then becomes the theme of celebration in the stand. For this reason, the chariot victory at Nemea seems to be the occasion of this ode and the Isthmian victory mentioned just before it is most likely the victory in the pankration celebrated earlier in *Isthmian 4*. If this is so, we have in *Isthmian 3* an example of a Nemean ode placed among the Isthmians.

Melissos was descended from Kleonymos, who married into the house of Labdakos, the Theban royal family. The vicissitudes endured by that family—by Laios, Oedipus, and the children of Oedipus—account for the sudden appearance of the theme of vicissitude at the end of the ode.

Turn

If a man, fortunate in the enjoyment
of glorious prizes or the might of wealth,
keeps his thoughts above restless ambition,
then he deserves
the praise of his fellow citizens.
O Zeus,
mortal man's prowess springs from you.
Greater the span of his happiness
when he reveres you,
while for perverse minds
it is not so—their joys
neither prosper nor abide lifelong. (1–6)

Counterturn

But, in return for his deeds of glory,
we must remember the noble man,
and as he celebrates
we must embrace him in soft folds of song.
Melissos has for his portion
not one but two successes
to sway his heart with rejoicing:
he received the crown
in the glens of Isthmos,
and in the hollow valley
of the grim-chested lion
he caused Theba to be proclaimed (7–12)

Stand

when he won with his horses.
He cast no doubt
on the manly character bred in his blood.
Surely
you have heard of Kleonymos' ancient renown
gained with the chariot—
his descendants,
kin to the sons of Labdakos on their mother's side,
have lavished their wealth on the toils of team racing.
But life, as the days wheel past, overthrows
all things in their turn.
Only
the children of the gods are unwounded. (13–18b)

ISTHMIAN 4

Melissos of Thebes, pankration, 474 (?) B.C.

Isthmian 3 and *Isthmian 4* both celebrate the same victor. They are also written in the same meter. This probably led to their combination in some of our manuscripts, where they appear as a single poem, with *Isthmian 3* forming the first triad of an ode consisting of five triads, and *Isthmian 4* the rest. The best manuscripts, however, keep the two apart. Their metrical identity is indeed unique, but with so little of Pindar's poetry to judge from, metrical identity in itself is not enough to prove the two poems were originally written as one. It may indicate that they were sung by the same chorus, perhaps even consecutively, with a brief pause between. The strongest argument for keeping them apart is their poetic independence. *Isthmian 3* is a complete poem and would form a rather odd prelude to *Isthmian 4*, which can also stand by itself.

Isthmian 4 makes no mention of the Nemean chariot victory celebrated in *Isthmian 3*. This is another indication that *Isthmian 4* was written first and *Isthmian 3* later, after the chariot victory was added to the roster.

The theme of vicissitude, sounded at the close of *Isthmian 3*, is of major significance in *Isthmian 4*. Four members of the victor's family have fallen in a single battle; now, thanks to Poseidon, patron of the Isthmian Games (counterturn 2), the victor's success redeems the tragedy. Later in the ode (stand 2–turn 3), Pindar reflects on another tragedy, the fate of Aias. Aias is introduced into the ode just after mention of the attempts made by the victor's clansmen, the descendants of Kleonymos, to win the chariot race in the great games. Pindar thus implies that, like Aias (see *Nemean 8*), they should have won the victories which, for some reason, they failed to win. In *Nemean* 7, Pindar suggests that Aias was neglected by Homer. In *Isthmian 4*, it is Homer's poetry that redeems Aias, as Pindar's redeems the Kleonymidai.

Melissos, like Herakles, was a Theban. In the third stand, Pindar compares Melissos the pankratiast with Herakles the wrestler against the giant Antaios. The ode concludes with a list of three victories won by Melissos in the Theban games honoring Herakles and his sons. Herakles' eight sons by his wife Megara were all killed by the hero himself in a fit of madness sent upon him by his immortal enemy Hera (for another instance of her persecution of him, see *Nemean 1*). Melissos won his first victory at these Theban games while competing in the boys' ranks. Hence Pindar mentions his trainer Orseas at the end.

Turn 1

By the will of the gods
I have a thousand roads in every direction
to follow your deeds of greatness in my song—
for you, Melissos, have given me the power
by winning at Isthmos;
and the Kleonymidai,,
ever flourishing in exploits,
live life through to its mortal end
favored by a god.
But all men are driven
along the way, hither
and thither, by the shifting breezes. (1-6)

Counterturn 1

They, honored at Thebes from the beginning,
are known as trusted envoys
to the surrounding states
and as men who show no arrogance.
Testimonials to their renown
circulate among us
while they are alive and after their death—
these they have earned
in all perfection.
By their supreme feats of courage
they set out from home
and reached the Pillars of Herakles: (7-12)

Stand 1

they have no need of further glory.
They proved themselves
to be rearers of fine horses
and found favor with Ares clad in bronze.
But in a single day the blizzard of war
bereaved their blest hearth of four men.
Now,
after the wintry darkness of the months,
like the ground dappled with red roses,
their line has bloomed again (13-18b)

Turn 2

as the gods have designed:
the Mover of Earth,
who dwells in Onchestos
and keeps the sea-bridge before the walls of Corinth,
has given their family
this wondrous song,
and raised from its bed the ancient glory
of their famous deeds,
for it had lain dormant.
And now, awakening, it is radiant
like the morning star,
brilliant beyond others in the sky. (19–24)

Counterturn 2

Having proclaimed their chariot triumphant
on the high ground of Athens
and in the games
of Adrastos in Sikyon,
their fame had brought them
even such leaves of song as these,
from men living then.
Nor did they keep their chariots
from entering the Great Games:
contending with the Panhellenes,
they rejoiced in expenditures on horses,
for oblivion awaits the untried. (25–30)

Stand 2

Yet there is also darkness on the outcome,
while men struggle, before
they reach their highest aim,
for luck is fickle,
and the trickery of lesser men has gripped
and overthrown the better man before.
Surely you know
of the blood-spattered might of Aias
impaled on his own sword in the late night,
casting reproach
on the sons of the Hellenes who went to Troy.
(31–36b)

Turn 3

But Homer has spread his honor among men—
at the wand-stroke of his wondrous words,
it rose and shone
in all its glory
for generations to delight in.
For what a man says well
goes forth with immortal persuasion—
over the earth that bears all fruits
and across the sea,
the light of glorious deeds
shines,
imperishable forever. (37–42)

Counterturn 3

May we find the Muses willing,
so we may kindle that torch of songs
for Melissos, scion of Telesiadas,
and crown as it deserves
his pankration victory.
For he has heart,
bold as a wild roaring lion in the struggle,
while in cunning he's a fox,
lying on its back,
ready for the eagle's swoop:
one must obliterate one's foe
no matter how. (43–48)

Stand 3

For his is not the bulk of an Orion—
no,
he's unimpressive to look at
but grim to fall in with.
A man, small in build
but adamant in spirit,
once went from Kadmeian Thebes to wheat-bearing Libya
to the house of Antaios,
to wrestle him
and put an end to his roofing Poseidon's temple
with the skulls of strangers—
it was he, (49–54b)

Turn 4

Alkmena's son, who reached Olympos
when he had explored the earth
from end to end,
and even the chasmed hollow of the gray ocean bed,
and had smoothed the way
for sailing ships.
Now he abides with aegis-bearing Zeus,
embracing perfect happiness,
and he has won glory
in the friendship of the immortals,
with Hebe for his bride,
lord of a golden house and son-in-law of Hera. (55–60)

Counterturn 4

For him we citizens of Thebes
spread the feast
outside the Elektran Gate
and lay fresh garlands on his altars,
heaping high the flame of sacrifice
to the eight who died—
wielders of bronze swords:
Megara, Kreon's daughter, bore them to him,
his sons, for whom, at dusk,
the rising blaze burns, unceasing
through the night,
grazing heaven with its fragrant smoke. (61–66)

Stand 4

And all through the following day
there is the culmination, the yearly games,
the work of might.
In these contests,
binding his head in shining myrtle,
Melissos has been victorious twice,
and once before
he won in the boys' division,
when he followed the resourceful advice of his pilot
guiding the tiller.
For I will glorify Orseas
together with him, shedding delight of song on both. (67–72b)

ISTHMIAN 5

Phylakidas of Aigina, pankration, 478 (?) B.C.

Pindar wrote two poems for Phylakidas, son of Lampon of Aigina. In *Isthmian 6*, he mentions only one Isthmian victory gained by Phylakidas; in *Isthmian 5*, he mentions two, and a third gained at Nemea. Hence, we infer that *Isthmian 5* is the later poem. Phylakidas' older brother Pytheas had also won at Nemea in the pankration, a victory celebrated by Pindar in *Nemean 5*. At the end of *Isthmian 5*, Pindar praises Pytheas for being an effective coach to Phylakidas. Kleonikos, the grandfather of the two brothers, is also praised in the course of the ode.

The ode opens with a hymn to Theia ("Divine One"), who appears in Hesiod's *Theogony* (371–74) as wife to Hyperion and mother of the Sun, the Moon, and the Dawn. It is as mother of the Sun that Pindar invokes her.

We can date *Isthmian 5* to sometime after September 480, when the Greeks defeated the fleet of the invading Persians at the battle of Salamis (see the Introduction, *Pindar's Life and Times*). Herodotus (VIII. 93, 122) tells us that the Aiginetans, Phylakidas' countrymen, had particularly distinguished themselves at Salamis, home of Aias. In this ode, Pindar represents their recent bravery as a continuation of the bravery shown by their legendary heroes, the Aiakidai. Chief among these is Achilleus, slayer of Kyknos, Hektor, Memnon, and Telephos, all of whom are named by Pindar in the second stand. These exploits are so well known that Pindar does not need to name Achilleus as the author of them. He also leaves Telamon's name to be supplied: that Aiakid hero had been with Herakles at the first siege of Troy, another Aiginetan exploit famous enough not to need detailed presentation.

As often happens in odes for Aiginetans, Pindar refers to the island also by its older name, Oinona ("Vineland").

Turn 1

Mother of the Sun, Theia,
goddess of countless names,
by your will men have made
gold a thing of might
beyond all others,
and it is through the glory
you shed upon them
that ships contending on the sea
and horses yoked to their chariots
shine in the whirl and flash of contests, (1–6)

Counterturn 1

likewise the man whose brow
many crowns have graced
achieves a longed-for glory
in athletics,
triumphant with his hands
or the speed of his feet.
It is a dispensation of the gods
that gives men their might.
And two things only
tend life's sweetest moment: when in the flower of wealth (7–12)

Stand 1

a man enjoys both triumph and good fame.
Seek not to become Zeus.
All is yours
if the allotment of these two gifts
has fallen to you.
Mortal thoughts
befit a mortal man.
And yet for you,
Phylakidas, the glory of two triumphs
abides at Isthmos, and at Nemea
you and Pytheas both
won in pankration.
But my heart
tastes not of song without singing of the Aiakidai.
I've come with the Graces for Lampon's sons (13–21)

Turn 2

to this harmonious city.
If she has chosen the pure path
of god-given deeds, let no one hesitate
to interweave a boast
in her song, sung
in payment for her struggles.
Yes, the brave in war
deserve the praise
of heroes, who are hymned to the music
of lyres and flutes sounding together (22–27)

Counterturn 2

to the end of time, because,
with Zeus' will, the reverence
in which they are held has given
wise poets a theme:
at the luminous sacrifices
of the Aitolians, the Oineïdai are mighty;
at Thebes, Iolaos, master of horses,
holds the honor;
Perseus in Argos; and by the stream
of Eurotas, the spear of Kastor and of Polydeukes; (28–33)

Stand 2

but here in Oinona the might
of Aiakos and his sons
holds sway.
Twice in battle
they sacked Troy city—
with Herakles first, and then the Atreidai.
On then, O Muse! Drive on!
Tell me who killed Kyknos,
and Hektor,
and Memnon,
wielder of the bronze sword, fearless
marshall of Ethiopians?
And whose spear was it
that wounded noble Telephos
upon the banks of Kaïkos? (34–42)

Turn 3

It was theirs, whose lips proclaim
Aigina their fatherland,
illustrious island
reared in ancient days,
a tower for high courage
to ascend: my voice is ready
with many a swift word
in her praise.
And in our day, in war, the city of Aias
would swear that it was saved by her ships— (43–48)

Counterturn 3

Salamis, in the deadly
storm of Zeus, hailing
with the blood of countless men.
But drown this vaunt in silence!
Zeus dispenses good and ill,
Zeus, the lord of all.
And yet, the honor of this occasion
puts us in a mood
to sing the glad victory chant.
Let a man contend in deeds (49–54)

Stand 3

when he has thoroughly tested
the race of Kleonikos.
The great labors
of their men have not been blotted out,
nor has the expense that fed their hope
come to nothing.
Among pankratiasts,
I praise Pytheas for having steered
his brother's blows aright—
he's clever with his hands
and a match in wits.
Take up his crown,
his fillet of fine wool,
and send him this winged new song! (55–63)

ISTHMIAN 6

Phylakidas of Aigina, boys' pankration, 480 B.C.

Pindar mentions three victories in *Isthmian 6*. First is the victory of Phylakidas in the pankration at the Isthmian Games, the occasion of this ode. Second is the Nemean victory, also in pankration, won by Phylakidas' older brother Pytheas and celebrated by Pindar in *Nemean 5*. Finally, there is an earlier Nemean victory of Euthymenes, maternal uncle to the two brothers. At the end of the ode, we hear of Themistios, also mentioned by Pindar in *Nemean 5*. He was the maternal grand-uncle of the two brothers. All belong to the clan of Psalychiadai. But the member of the family receiving the most attention in the present poem is the father Lampon, son of Kleonikos. Pindar praises him in the first counterturn and again at the end of the ode. He was not a victor himself, but his encouragement of his two victorious sons is strongly commended by Pindar, who adds that Lampon is a good example of the conduct urged in a famous line of Hesiod, now proverbial: "devotion furthers your work." In Hesiod (*Works and Days*, 412), the phrase refers to economic labors; in Pindar, to the aristocratic business of achieving fame through athletics.

The ode opens with an elaborate simile comparing this, Pindar's second song for Lampon's family (*Nemean 5* being the first), to the second libation at a symposium. At the conclusion of the first turn, he goes on to pray for yet a third victory, to be followed by a third draft of song. He does not explicitly name an Olympian triumph as the object of his prayer, but a reference to Olympian Zeus here reveals that that is what he has in mind.

The myth of the ode is told in two phases, the later part first. It deals with the expedition of Herakles against Troy, quickly told by Pindar in the second turn. The second counterturn goes back further in time, to the appearance of Herakles at the halls of Telamon, son of Aiakos. Herakles had come seeking Telamon's company on the expedition to Troy just described. In this part of the myth, Pindar employs a pun impossible to translate. Herakles prays to Zeus to grant Telamon a heroic son; Zeus in answer sends down an eagle; Herakles then interprets this as an omen favoring the prayer he has just made and advises Telamon to name the child who will be born to him "Aias" after the eagle (*aietos*) that had just appeared.

Turn 1

As at the height of the men's symposium
we mix the second bowl, so now
here is the second song
poured by the Muses
for Lampon's family of fine athletes:
the first was for the crowns they received
from you, O Zeus, at Nemea;
and now another
has come from the Lord of the Isthmos
and the fifty daughters of Nereus,
for the triumph
of Lampon's youngest son,
Phylakidas:
and may it be ours
to fill a third bowl, pouring it out
to Zeus Olympian the Savior,
libations of sweet songs streaming over Aigina. (1–9)

Counterturn 1

For if a man has known enjoyment
in spending and in struggle
and has gained distinction
from the gods,
and if a god has fostered
his delight in glory,
already he has cast his anchor
at the furthest shore
of happiness,
honored of heaven:
the son of Kleonikos prays
to welcome death and gray old age
with such feelings in his heart,
and I call by name
on Klotho throned above
and on her sister Moirai,
to heed the prayer for glory of the man I love. (10–18)

Stand 1

But it is my clearest obligation
when I set foot upon this island
to shower praises on you,
O sons of Aiakos,
in your golden chariots!
Unnumbered are the roads
your deeds of greatness travel,
cut a hundred feet wide from end to end
and leading south beyond the springs of Nile
and north to the midst of the Hyperboreans.
Nor is there a town so barbarous,
so perverse of tongue, it has not heard
of the renown of Peleus, hero, blest son-in-law of gods, (19–25)

Turn 2

or does not know the fame of Aias,
son of Telamon, or of his father
whom Alkmena's son
brought with the Tirynthians
to bronze-loving war, an eager ally
aboard the ships for Troy,
that toil of heroes,
to avenge the treacheries of Laomedon.
And he took the citadel
and with Telamon at his side
he slew the tribes
of the Meropes
and the ox-herder,
Alkyoneus, huge as a mountain,
whom he found at Phlegra,
and the loud bow's string
twanged unceasing in the hands (26–34)

Counterturn 2 of Herakles. But when he came to summon
Telamon upon that journey,
he found him at a feast.
And Telamon invited him,
the son of Amphitryon,
mighty with his spear, standing
in his lion's pelt,
to lead the way
with nektar-sweet libations
and offered him
the wine-bowl
glittering with gold.
And Herakles, raising
invincible hands toward the sky,
uttered this prayer:
"If ever, O father Zeus,
with willing heart you heard my entreaties, (35–43)

Stand 2 now I beseech you, now, in supplication:
bring to birth from Eriboia a mighty son,
destined to be my guest-friend,
for Telamon here, a son
unbreakable in body, even as the hide
that winds about me now, the skin of the lion
I killed at Nemea, foremost
of all my exploits;
and may he have
a lion's courage."
When he had spoken thus,
the god sent down a great eagle, prince of birds,
and a sweet joy thrilled within him, (44–50)

Turn 3

and he said, like a man of prophecy:
"The child you desire, O Telamon,
will come to you,
and you must name him
for the eagle that appeared—
mighty Aias, the awe of his people
in the toils of Enyalios."
So having spoken
he took his seat again.
But for me
to go through all the glories
of the Aiakidai, is a great task:
I have come as master of revels
for Phylakidas, O Muse,
and for Pytheas and Euthymenes.
What I have to say, then, will be said
in the Argive manner, without elaboration. (51–59)

Counterturn 3

For they have won three triumphs in pankration—
one from Isthmos,
two from wooded Nemea,
Lampon's radiant sons
and their maternal uncle:
what an allotment of songs
they have brought to light!
They nurture the clan
of the Psalychiadai
with the glittering
waters of poetry,
and they exalt the house
of Themistios, inhabiting
this city, beloved of the gods.
But Lampon, lavish
in *devotion to work*, truly keeps alive and honors
Hesiod's advice, and recommends it to his sons, (60–68)

Stand 3

bringing glory to his city in the eyes of all.
He is loved for his kindnesses to strangers, following
measure in his thoughts, achieving
measure in his deeds.
His speech never wanders
from his mind's control.
You could say of him
that he is, among athletes, a Naxian whetstone
among other stones, a sharpener of bronze.
I will offer him to drink of the sacred water
of Dirka, which the slim-waisted daughters
of Mnamosyna in her gold robes have made to spring
by the strong gates of Kadmos. (69–75)

ISTHMIAN 7

Strepsiadas of Thebes, pankration, 454 B.C.

The entire first triad of *Isthmian 7* is an extended rhetorical question: Pindar asks the goddess Theba, for whom Thebes was named, what event from her mythical past most delights her. At the end of the catalogue of possible answers, the past yields to the present: Pindar comes to a recent Theban accomplishment, the victory of Strepsiadas in the pankration at at the Isthmian Games.

Strepsiadas enters the ode in the second turn. The counterturn modulates from him to his maternal uncle, also named Strepsiadas. This elder Strepsiadas, son of Diodotos, had died heroically in battle. Pindar praises his bravery and mourns his loss down to the third turn, where he comes to the present occasion again: Poseidon, god of the Isthmian Games, has, in a sense, redeemed the loss of the elder Strepsiadas by glorifying the younger one with victory (compare *Isthmian 4*, stand 1–turn 2). In the rest of the ode, Pindar celebrates this occasion for joy and prays that the gods will not resent his happiness.

Turn 1

In which of the ancient glories
of this country
do you most delight your heart,
O blessed Theba?
Was it when you raised into the light
Dionysos,
comrade of Demeter
for whom bronze cymbals clash?
Or when you welcomed
in the dead of night
the mightiest of gods,
a snow of gold— (1-5)

Counterturn 1

when, having stood in the doorway,
he came to the wife
of Amphitryon
and begot Herakles?
Or is it the deep mind of Teiresias?
Or Iolaos,
skilled with horses?
Or the Sown Men, relentless
with their spears?
Or when from the dread
din of battle you sent
Adrastos away, deprived (6-10)

Stand 1

of all his allies, fleeing to Argos,
nurse of horses?
Or when you established
on a secure footing
the Dorian colony of the Lakedaimonians,
and the sons of Aigeus, your descendants,
took Amyklai?
But the grace of old
drops to sleep, and mortal men forget (11-17)

Turn 2

whatever has not intermingled
in the glorious streams of verses,
and come to flower
through a poet's skill.
Then sing the sweet-voiced song
for Strepsiadas too—
victorious in pankration at Isthmos,
he is awesome in strength
and handsome to see,
nor does the distinction
he has achieved
put his looks to shame. (18–22)

Counterturn 2

The dark-haired Muses make him glow.
To his maternal uncle and namesake
he has given
a flowering garland
to possess in common—
Strepsiadas,
for whom brazen Ares mixed
the draft of death: but honor
rewards the brave.
Let him, who in the storm's onset
turns the hail of blood
from his dear country, (23–27)

Stand 2

hurling havoc amid the enemy host,
know well that in his life
and in his death, he magnifies
his city's glory more than any.
And you, son of Diodotos,
in emulation of warlike Meleagros,
of Hektor and Amphiaraos,
in the flower of your strength
breathed out the breath of life, (28–34)

Turn 3

fighting in the forefront
where the best men
stayed the strife of battle
at the edge of hope.
Unspeakable is the sorrow I have borne.
But now Poseidon
has calmed the storm,
and I will sing,
fitting my head with garlands.
May no envy
of the gods
fall upon me (35–39)

Counterturn 3

that in pursuit of delight
as it comes each day,
I go in peace
toward old age
and the mortal limit of life:
for we all perish,
though our luck varies.
If a man gazes in the distance,
he is too short
to reach the bronze-paved
home of the gods:
winged Pegasos shook from his back (40–44)

Stand 3

Bellerophon, his rider, striving
to enter the dwellings of the sky
and join Zeus' company.
Most bitter is the end
of a sweetness not our right.
For myself, O Loxias, I wish another
flourishing garland, from your games at Pytho! (45–51)

ISTHMIAN 8

Kleandros of Aigina, boys' pankration, 478 B.C.

Isthmian 8 is written in a single stanza repeated seven times. In the opening phrases, Pindar calls on a band of young men to sing the song on their way to the house of Kleandros, son of Telesarchos. The ode, then, was probably meant to be sung in procession rather than by a dancing chorus.

In the first two stanzas, Pindar refers to a recent deliverance of Greece from the dread of catastrophe. It is generally agreed that he means by this the defeat of the army of Xerxes at the battle of Plataia in 479. Pindar makes the anxiety of the war itself, and probably also recent sorrow for the fallen, into a foil for the joy of the present occasion. On the role played by Pindar's city Thebes in the Persian Wars, see the Introduction, *Pindar's Life and Times.*

The victor is from Aigina, the myth is Aiginetan. Pindar begins it toward the end of the second stanza by drawing attention to his own connection with the victor's homeland. Aigina and Theba were sisters, the youngest daughters of Asopos. Thus Pindar the Theban and Kleandros the Aiginetan are, in a sense, cousins. Pindar speaks of Theba in the third person at the end of stanza 2; he speaks to Aigina directly at the start of stanza 3, where he also mentions "Oinopia," another form of the name by which the victor's island home was called before Zeus brought Aigina there.

The myth treats of three generations of heroes, beginning with Aiakos, son of Zeus and Aigina; moving on to the wedding of Peleus and Thetis and the quarrel on Olympos that preceded it; and concluding with the funeral of Achilleus, at which the Muses themselves sang the dirge. This final episode leads into the last stanza, where Pindar briefly eulogizes Nikokles, cousin of the victor. As the Muses had sung for the dead Achilleus, so Pindar, with the Muses' inspiration, sings for the dead Nikokles. He then passes on to Kleandros' victories in the games of Alkathoös at Megara and in the games at Epidauros. The ode ends with the claim that Kleandros deserves the praises he has received from Pindar and others.

1 For Kleandros and his youth, let someone go
to the bright doors of Telesarchos, his father,
rousing the revel song in glorious recompense for his struggles,
to pay him for his triumph at Isthmos
and for showing his might in the Nemean games.
And therefore I too, though grieved at heart,
have been requested to summon the golden Muse.
And having been delivered from great sorrows,
let us not go ungarlanded—
do not nurse your own troubles.
No, turning away from intractable evils,
let us perform a song especially sweet after our toil.
For some god has turned aside
the stone of Tantalos
that loomed over our heads, (1-10)

2 an unbearable strain for Hellas. But now
it is gone, and my strong anxiety is at an end.
It is always better to heed the present.
The future is deceptive—
it hovers before us, full of distortions.
Yet mortals can recover even from this, if they are free.
A man must be hopeful.
A man raised in seven-gated Thebes
must make first offering
of the Graces' finest song to Aigina,
for she and Theba were born twin daughters of Asopos,
youngest of his children.
And they found favor with Zeus the King,
who made one to dwell by the bright spring of Dirka,
mistress of a chariot-loving city; (11-20)

3 but you he brought to the island of Oinopia,
and the bed of love.
You bore him a son, dearest of mortal men
to the deep-thundering father:
divine Aiakos, who settled disputes even among gods,
whose godlike sons and warrior grandsons
were supreme in courage,
confronting the brazen throng of battle rich in groans.
And they were wise and prudent of heart.
Even the assembly of the gods took note of this,
when Zeus and gleaming Poseidon clashed
over the wedding of Thetis, each desiring
to make her his beautiful bride, for passion possessed them.
But the immortal minds of the gods
did not fulfill that marriage, (21–30)

4 once they had heard the oracles—
wise Themis in their midst proclaimed it fated
that the goddess of the sea
bear a son mightier than his father,
a lord who would speed from his hand
another weapon, more powerful than thunder
or Poseidon's relentless trident,
if she joined in love with Zeus or Zeus' brother:
"But let it not be so! Let her marry a mortal instead
and see her son killed in battle,
a son equal to Ares in might of hand
or to the lightning bolt in speed of foot.
It is my counsel to give her as a wedding prize
to Aiakos' son Peleus, reputed to be
the most righteous man the plain of Iolkos has reared. (31–40)

5 Let the announcement go at once
to Chiron in his immortal cave—
and let not the daughter of Nereus
put into our hands again the leaves of strife.
May she loosen the bridle of her virginity
in the hero's arms on the evening of full moon."
So the goddess urged the children of Kronos
who bent immortal brows, assenting.
And the fruit of her words did not perish,
for they say even Lord Zeus joined
in honoring the wedding of Thetis. And there
the songs of skilled poets revealed to those who knew it not
the young valor of Achilleus,
who stained the vine-clad Mysian plain
with the black blood of Telephos, (41–50)

6 and bridged a return for the sons of Atreus,
and freed Helen,
cleaving the sinews of Troy with his spear—
all those who strove to keep him
from marshaling the deadly work of war upon the plain:
the proud strength of Memnon, and Hektor,
and others of the best men for whom Achilleus, Aiakid champion,
showed the way to Persephone's house
and so brought glory to Aigina and his lineage.
Nor did songs abandon him even in death,
but the maidens of Helikon stood at his pyre
and beside his tomb, pouring upon it the dirge of glory:
thus the immortals themselves chose to make
even a man who had perished
a theme for the hymns of goddesses. (51–60)

7 And there is reason for it still—
the Muses in their chariot hasten to proclaim
the memory of Nikokles, the boxer: glorify him,
who gained the Dorian garland in the grove at Isthmos;
he too once vanquished
those who lived in the surrounding country,
confounding them with inescapable blows.
And his cousin, Kleandros, does not disgrace him.
Let one of the youths plait him
a garland of myrtle for his pankration victory,
and because the gathering of Alkathoös
and the young men at Epidauros
welcomed him in triumph before.
We may praise him justly, for he has not consigned
his youth to oblivion, bereft of noble deeds. (61–70)

APPENDIXES

I. The Dating of Pindar's Odes

The dates of Pindar's *Olympian* and *Pythian Odes* are known to us from notices in the ancient commentaries based on victor-lists available in antiquity and, for the Olympians at least, still available today: *Oxyrrhynchus Papyrus* ccxxii contains a list of victors at Olympia from 480 to 468 and from 456 to 448 B.C. For the complete list of Olympian victors, see Luigi Moretti, *Olympionikai, I Vincitori Negli Antichi Agoni Olimpici* (Rome: *Atti della Accedemia nazionale dei Lincei. Classe di scienze morali, storiche e filologiche. Memorie*, Ser. 8, v. 8, fasc. 2, 1957).

The situation is otherwise for the *Nemean* and *Isthmian Odes*: the ancient commentators did not make use of lists of Nemean and Isthmian victors; consequently, establishing dates for these odes depends on identifying historical allusions or tracing the chronological development of Pindar's style, both of which are extremely hazardous. The dates given with or without a question mark after them in my prefaces to the individual Nemean and Isthmian odes are almost always as they appear in the Greek text that I have used for my rendering, the Teubner edition of Bruno Snell and Herwig Maehler.

Poetic inscriptions commemorating athletic victors are collected in Joachim Ebert, *Griechische Epigramme auf Sieger an Gymnischen und Hippischen Agonen* (Berlin: *Abhandlungen der Sächsischen Akademie der Wissenschaften zu Leipzig, Phil. hist. Klasse* 63.2, 1972).

II. Geographical Distribution of Pindar's Odes

Odes for Sicilian victors (total of 15):

Olympian 1:	Hieron of Syracuse	*Pythian 2*:	Hieron
Olympian 2:	Theron of Akragas	*Pythian 3*:	Hieron of Syracuse
Olympian 3:	Theron of Akragas	*Pythian 6*:	Xenokrates of Akragas
Olympian 4:	Psaumis of Kamarina	*Pythian 12*:	Midas of Akragas
Olympian 5:	Psaumis of Kamarina	*Nemean 1*:	Chromios of Aitna
Olympian 6:	Hagesias of Syracuse	*Nemean 9*:	Chromios of Aitna
Olympian 12:	Ergoteles of Himera	*Isthmian 2*:	Xenokrates of Akragas
Pythian 1:	Hieron of Aitna		

Odes for Aiginetan victors (total of 11):

Olympian 8:	Alkimedon	*Nemean 7*:	Sogenes
Pythian 8:	Aristomenes	*Nemean 8*:	Deinis
Nemean 3:	Aristokleidas	*Isthmian 5*:	Phylakidas
Nemean 4:	Timasarchos	*Isthmian 6*:	Phylakidas
Nemean 5:	Pytheas	*Isthmian 8*:	Kleandros
Nemean 6:	Alkimidas		

Odes for victors from mainland cities other than Thebes (total of 7):

Olympian 9:	Epharmostos of Opous
Olympian 13:	Xenophon of Corinth
Olympian 14:	Asopichos of Orchomenos
Pythian 7:	Megakles of Athens
Pythian 10:	Hippokleas of Pelinna (Thessaly)
Nemean 2:	Timodemos of Acharnai (Athens)
Nemean 10:	Theaios of Argos

Odes for Theban victors (total of 5):

Pythian 11:	Thrasydaios
Isthmian 1:	Herodotos
Isthmian 3:	Melissos
Isthmian 4:	Melissos
Isthmian 7:	Strepsiadas

Odes for victors from Kyrana (Cyrene, North Africa; total of 3):

Pythian 4:	Arkesilas
Pythian 5:	Arkesilas
Pythian 9:	Telesikrates

Odes for Italian victors (total of 2):

Olympian 10:	Hagesidamos of Western Lokroi
Olympian 11:	Hagesidamos of Western Lokroi

Odes for victors from islands other than Aigina (total of 2):

Olympian 7:	Diagoras of Rhodes
Nemean 11:	Aristagoras of Tenedos

III. Myths in the Odes of Pindar

Olympian 1: Pelops: the spurious tale of his ivory shoulder; Poseidon's passion for him; the wooing of Hippodameia; the race to the death with Oinomaos; Pelops the prototype of the Olympian charioteer.

Olympian 2: The daughters of Kadmos: Semela and Ino; other descendants of Kadmos: Laios, Oedipus, Polyneikes, Thersandros (ancestors of Theron, the victor);

The soul's fate after death: punishment of the wicked; reward of heroes—the island of the blest.

Olympian 3: How the olive tree was brought to Olympia: Herakles' first journey to the land of the Hyperboreans in quest of the Keryneian doe; the founding of the Olympian games; the second journey, to bring back the olive.

Olympian 4: Erginos the Argonaut ridiculed by the Lemnian women.

Olympian 5: None.

Olympian 6: Poseidon and Pitana: the birth of Evadna; her adoption by Aipytos; Apollo makes love to Evadna;

the birth and exposure of Iamos, ancestor of the victor's clan; he is fed by serpents in the woods; he receives the gift of prophecy from his father Apollo.

Olympian 7: The myth of Rhodes (moving backward in time): Tlapolemos, founder of the Dorian cities on Rhodes, kills his illegitimate grand-uncle Likymnios in Tiryns and flees to Rhodes; Athena's birth there; the birth of the island itself.

Olympian 8: The walls of Troy: Apollo and Poseidon summon Aiakos to help build the city's walls; three serpents leap at the tower; the omen interpreted by Apollo, who prophesies the fall of Troy.

Olympian 9: The myth of Herakles' combat with the gods (rejected);

The flood: the repopulation of the earth; the ancestry of the Opountian nobility traced back to Zeus;

Patroklos and Achilleus.

Olympian 10: The founding of the Olympian games: Herakles defeats Augeas and the sons of Molione and founds the games to commemorate the victory; the first Olympian festival, with a list of the first victors.

Olympian 11: None.

Olympian 12: None.

Olympian 13: Catalogue of Corinthian heroes: Sisyphos, Medea, Glaukos, Bellerophon;
Bellerophon and Pegasos: the invention of the bridle; martial exploits; the fall of Bellerophon.

Olympian 14: None.

Pythian 1: Zeus and Typhon: Typhon's imprisonment beneath Mt. Aitna; the eruption of the volcano;
Hieron compared to Philoktetes.

Pythian 2: The myth of Ixion: his attempt to seduce Hera an expression of ingratitude; his punishment suits his crime;
Kentauros, offspring of Ixion's union with the cloud-Hera; Kentauros mates with the mares of Mt. Pelion and sires the race of Centaurs.

Pythian 3: Apollo and Koronis: Koronis, while pregnant with Apollo's son Asklepios, makes love to a stranger; her punishment; the god rescues his son from the dead mother's body on the funeral pyre; Asklepios is reared as a physician;
Asklepios brings a man back from the dead; his punishment by Zeus.
Kadmos and Peleus as examples of the highest human happiness: Kadmos marries Harmonia, Peleus marries Thetis; both suffer, Kadmos through his daughters, Peleus through his son Achilleus, who dies at Troy.

Pythian 4: The colonization of Kyrana from Thera: Medea and the Argonauts on Thera;
The voyage of the Argo, with emphasis on the confrontation between Jason and Pelias that precedes it.

Pythian 5: Battos, first king of Kyrana, arrives on the site of the city from his home in Thera.

Pythian 6: The death of Nestor's son Antilochos at Troy, an example of filial devotion.

Pythian 7: None.

Pythian 8: "The Sons of the Seven" (The *Epigonoi*) march against Thebes; prophecy of Amphiaraos regarding his son Alkman.

Pythian 9: Apollo and Kyrana: the god brings the girl from her original home to the site of the city in North Africa that will bear her name; birth of Aristaios, her son by Apollo.

Pythian 10: The blissful existence of the Hyperboreans; Perseus arrives in their midst.

Pythian 11: Klytaimestra murders her husband, Agamemnon, and his concubine Kassandra; she is killed in turn by her own son, Orestes.

Pythian 12: Athena invents the flute, inspired to do so by the sound of wailing made by the two Gorgons when Perseus killed their sister Medusa;
Perseus and his mother Danaä.

Nemean 1: The birth of Herakles and Iphikles; Hera sends serpents to devour the infants; Herakles strangles them; Teiresias prophesies that, after performing various exploits, Herakles will join the gods.

Nemean 2: None.

Nemean 3:	Herakles explores the limits of the world (set aside in favor of an Aiakid subject). Peleus and Thetis; Telamon and Iolaos. The young Achilleus: his journey to Troy, his exploits there, the killing of Memnon.
Nemean 4:	Herakles and Telamon (Troy taken, Alkyoneus defeated). Catalogue of Aiakid heroes: Teukros, Aias, Achilleus, Neoptolemos, Peleus. Peleus, Hippolyta, and Akastos; Peleus marries Thetis.
Nemean 5:	Peleus, Telamon, and Phokos (set aside as unsuitable for telling). Hippolyta's sexual advances rejected by Peleus; her husband Akastos lays an ambush for Peleus; Zeus gives Thetis in marriage to Peleus in return for his virtuous conduct.
Nemean 6:	Achilleus and Memnon.
Nemean 7:	The suicide of Aias; the death of Neoptolemos at Delphi.
Nemean 8:	Odysseus awarded the arms of Achilleus; Aias, the more deserving man, commits suicide.
Nemean 9:	Adrastos founds the Games at Sikyon; the expedition of The Seven against Thebes.
Nemean 10:	Catalogue of Argive heroes and heroines: Perseus, Epaphos, Hypermestra, Diomedes, Amphiaraos, Alkmena, Danaä, Talaos, Lynkeus, Amphitryon. Polydeukes, in order to save his brother Kastor, mortally wounded, consents to spend half the time with him in the underworld.
Nemean 11:	None.
Isthmian 1:	Athletic prowess of Kastor, Polydeukes, and Iolaos.
Isthmian 2:	None.
Isthmian 3:	None.
Isthmian 4:	The disgrace and suicide of Aias redeemed by Homer's poetry. Herakles and Antaios. Herakles deified after his exploits.
Isthmian 5:	Catalogue of Aiakid heroes and their exploits. Aiginetan bravery at the battle of Salamis.
Isthmian 6:	Herakles and Telamon sack Troy; their other exploits; prophecy of the birth of Aias.
Isthmian 7:	Catalogue of Theban gods and heroes: Dionysos, Herakles, Teiresias, Iolaos, The Sown Men, Adrastos and The Seven defeated, the taking of Amyklai. The victor's uncle, killed in battle, compared with Meleagros, Hektor, and Amphiaraos. Bellerophon as warning example of the limits attainable by mortal man.
Isthmian 8:	Zeus and Poseidon clash over Thetis; she is given to Peleus instead; birth, exploits, and death of her son Achilleus.

IV. Variant Readings

This is a translation of Bruno Snell's text of Pindar's victory odes: *Pindari Carmina cum Fragmentis. Pars I. Epinicia*, post B. Snell edidit H. Maehler (Leipzig: B. G. Teubner, 1971).

At times I have preferred a punctuation different from Snell's, but I make no mention of this below, since Pindar himself made no use of punctuation.

I mention only the places where the text I rendered differs from Snell's, and I give the author of the emendation in each case, adding, when appropriate, the name of the scholar whose arguments I found persuasive.

Readers interested in other conjectures will find them conveniently assembled in Douglas E. Gerber's *Emendations in Pindar 1518–1972* (Amsterdam: A. M. Hakkert, 1976).

Olympian 10. 25: *πόνων*, conjectured by W. Christ in *Pindari carmina prolegomenis et commentariis instructa* (Leipzig, 1896) and defended by L. R. Farnell in his *Commentary*, p. 81.

Pythian 2. 90: *τινος* wrongly changed by Snell to *τινες*. See Hugh Lloyd-Jones, "Modern Interpretation of Pindar," *Journal of Hellenic Studies* 93 (1973): 125, note 100.

Pythian 6. 47: retain *ἔδειξεν*, omit *ἅπασαν*: Farnell, *Commentary*, pp. 187–88.

Pythian 9. 91: *εὐκλέϊξας* instead of *εὐκλεΐξαι*: G. Hermann, *Emendationes Pindaricae*, in *Opuscula* VII (Leipzig, 1839) p. 163. See R. W. B. Burton, *Pindar's Pythian Odes* (Oxford: Oxford University Press, 1962), pp. 50–54.

Nemean 1. 66: *φᾶσέ νιν δώσειν μόρῳ*: August Boeckh, *Pindari Epiniciorum Interpretatio Latina cum Commentario Perpetuo* (Leipzig, 1821), p. 360.

Nemean 4. 16: *υἱὸν* instead of *ὕμνον*: T. Bergk, *Poetae Lyrici Graeci* (Leipzig, 1878). See Adolf Köhnken, *Die Funktion des Mythos bei Pindar* (Berlin: Walter de Gruyter, 1971), p. 215, note 104.

Nemean 4. 58: *χρησαμένου* instead of *χρησάμενος*: Köhnken, *Die Funktion des Mythos*, pp. 201–3.

Isthmian 3. 7: *ὑμνᾶσαι*, the reading of the manuscripts, explained as deriving from * *ὑπ-μνᾶσθαι* by Bernhard Forssman, *Untersuchungen zur Sprache Pindars* (Wiesbaden: Otto Harrassowitz, 1966), p. 76.

Isthmian 7. 28: *λοιγὸν ἄντα φέρων*: F. Thiersch, *Acta Philologorum Monacensium* 2 (1815–16): 287–88.

Isthmian 8. 11: *παροιχόμενον* instead of *παροιχομένων*: L. R. Farnell, *Commentary*, p. 378.

V. Athletic Contests

For a full description of the religious and athletic program at the Olympian Games, see M. I. Finley and H. W. Pleket, *The Olympic Games. The First Thousand Years* (New York: The Viking Press, 1976).

On Greek athletics in general, see the works of Gardiner and Harris cited in the Bibliography.

The Pythian Games consisted originally of musical competitions only. The earliest event was the hymn in honor of Apollo, sung to the lyre. In 582 B.C., when the Pythian Games were reorganized as a pan-Hellenic festival, athletic contests on the model of the Olympian Games were introduced, and contests in singing to a flute accompaniment and in flute solo were added. There were no musical contests at Olympia.

Following is a list of the athletic events. There was no two-lap or long race for boys at Olympia. The mule car race was discontinued at Olympia in 444 or 440 B.C. The order of events at Olympia is disputed. Some think the chariot race came first, on the second day of the festival (the first day being taken up with religious ceremonies); others think the chariots raced on the last day.

1. Single-lap foot race, c. 200 meters.
2. Double-lap foot race, c. 400 meters.
3. Long foot race, c. 4800 meters.
4. Pentathlon (5 events): contestants competed in the short race, broad jump, discus and javelin throw, and wrestling match.
5. Wrestling.
6. Boxing.
7. Pankration (all-strength): a combination of boxing and wrestling.
8. Boys' foot race.
9. Boys' wrestling.
10. Boys' boxing.
11. Race in armor.
12. Chariot race: two-wheel chariots drawn by four-horse teams for twelve laps in the Hippodrome at Olympia, approximately nine kilometers.
13. Horse race: approximately 1600 meters.
14. Mule car race.

GLOSSARY

Following is a list, with brief annotations, of the proper names occurring in Pindar's victory odes. The list is complete, except for citations. Readers interested in particular subjects will find fuller references to their occurrence in the odes under the proper entry in the Index.

Where references are given, "O" stands for "Olympian," "P" for "Pythian," "N" for "Nemean," and "I" for "Isthmian." The numeral immediately following gives the number of the ode in question, and the number in parenthesis designates the relevant line.

Abas: King of Argos; son of Lynkeus and Hypermestra. See **Argos**.

Achaia: Southeastern Thessaly and the north coast of the Peloponnesos, between Elis and Sikyon.

Achaian: In Homer, the Greeks who went to Troy, specifically the followers of Achilleus and Agamemnon.

Acharnai: The largest of the Attic demes, in the northwestern corner of the Attic plain.

Acheron: A river of Thesprotia, in southern Epirus, reputed to be the entrance to the underworld. Also a river in the underworld. P11 (21), N4 (85).

Achilleus: Son of Peleus and Thetis, hero of Homer's *Iliad*, greatest of the Greek warriors who fought at Troy. See **Aigina**.

Admatos: Son of Pheres; cousin of Jason.

Adrastos: Son of Talaos; brother of Eriphyla; king of Argos; driven from Argos by Amphiaraos: N9 (13–15); his daughter Argeia married Polyneikes and became by him the mother of Thersandros, Theron's ancestor; sole survivor of the first expedition against Thebes (see **Thebes**); leader of the Epigonoi; founder of games at Sikyon; in N10 (28) Pindar alludes to the tradition that the Seven against Thebes founded the Nemean Games. See **Argos**.

Agamemnon: Son of Atreus; brother of Menelaos; husband of Klytaimestra; leader of the Greek expedition against Troy. See **Klytaimestra**.

Aglaia: "Brilliance," one of the three Graces.

Agreus: "The Hunter," epithet of Aristaios.

Aiakidai: Sons or descendants of Aiakos.

Aiakos: Son of Zeus and Aigina, founder of the Aiakid line. See **Aigina**. Famed for his justice, Aiakos became a judge in the underworld.

Aias: (1) Son of Oïleus; also known as "Aias the Lesser," to distinguish him from Aias the son of Telamon (below); a Lokrian hero: O9 (112); known for his blasphemous boasting and punished for it by the gods. (2) Son of Telamon; a hero of Salamis, second only to Achilleus among the heroes who went to Troy: N7 (27–30); committed suicide after the arms of Achilleus were awarded to Odysseus: N8 (23–34). See **Aigina**.

Aidos: Shame or Modesty; personified by Pindar in N9 (36).

Aietas: Son of Helios and father of Medea; king of Kolchis.

Aigai: A town in Achaia, sacred to Poseidon.

Aigeus: One of the five surviving Spartoi or Sown Men who sprang from the dragon's teeth sown by Kadmos; they were reputed to have become the ancestors of the Theban aristocracy; the sons or descendants of Aigeus (not to be confused with the father of Theseus) were a clan with branches at Thebes, Sparta, and Thera. Whether Pindar himself was one of them is in dispute. They helped the

Dorians take Amyklai and establish Sparta as the new chief power in the Peloponnesos: P5 (75), I7 (15).

Aigimios: Father of Pamphylos and Dymas; friend of Herakles' son Hyllos; ancestor of the Dorian race, divided into three branches called Pamphyloi, Dymanes, Hylleis. See P1 (61–66).

Aigina: An island in the Saronic Gulf, off the coast of Attica; also the nymph Aigina, daughter of Asopos and Metopa; sister of Theba; mother of Aiakos by Zeus. See also Oinona, Oinopia. The descendants of Zeus and Aigina are one of the most illustrious families in Greek mythology:

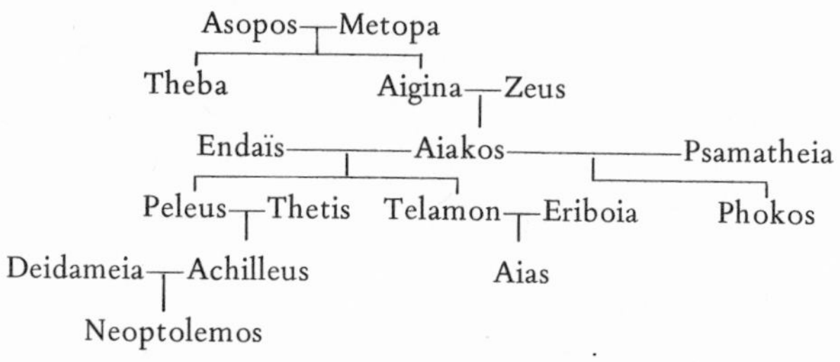

Peleus and Telamon killed their illegitimate half-brother Phokos and had to flee from Aigina. Peleus went to Iolkos, Telamon to Salamis. Telamon joined with Herakles in the first sack of Troy, Aias and Achilleus with Agamemnon in the second (see **Troy**). Achilleus died before the city was taken; his son Neoptolemos was summoned by the Greeks to replace him.

Aigisthos: Son of Thyestes; cousin of Agamemnon; lover of Agamemnon's wife Klytaimestra; killed by Orestes: P11 (36).

Aigyptos: Egypt; son of Belos and brother of Danaos. See **Argos**.

Aineas: Leader of the chorus in O6; not to be confused with the hero of Vergil's *Aeneid.*

Ainesidamos: Father of Theron and Xenokrates; grandfather of Thrasyboulos.

Aiolian: A Greek tribe, descended from Aiolos. The Aiolians originally inhabited Thessaly. Under pressure from the Dorian invasions of c. 1100 B.C., they migrated eastward across the Aegean Sea to the islands of Lesbos and Tenedos and the northern coast of Asia Minor: N11 (34–35). Aiolian is the dialect of the lyric poets Sappho and Alcaeus, who lived on Lesbos.

Aiolos: Son of Hellen; father of Salmoneus, Sisyphos, Athamas, and Kretheus; grandfather of Aison; great-grandfather of Jason and of Bellerophon the grandson of Sisyphos; founder of the Aiolian race; ancestor of the Aiolidai.

Aipytos: Son of Elatos and, according to Pindar, adoptive father of Evadna, the mother of Iamos by Apollo: O6 (32–34); Pindar makes him king of Phaisana; brother of Ischys.

Aison: Father of Jason; for the genealogy, see **Aiolos**.

Aitna: A volcano in Sicily; also the city founded by Hieron near the volcano: P1 (29–33). Pindar calls Zeus god of Aitna in P1 (30), O6 (96), N1 (6).

Aitolian: The Elean umpire at the Olympian Games in O3 (12), Elis having been settled by Aitolians; the Aitolians were a people in northwestern Greece. See **Oineïdai.**

Akastos: Son of Pelias; husband of Hippolyta; treacherous host to Peleus in Iolkos: N4 (57), N5 (30).

Akragas: A city in southwestern Sicily founded by Geloans in 580 B.C.; also the river Akragas, flowing through the city: P12 (2).

Akron: Father of Psaumis.

Aktor: Father of Menoitios by Aigina; grandfather of Patroklos.

Alatas: Great-great-grandson of Herakles; a leader of the Dorian invasion of the Peloponnesos; established Dorian power at Corinth; Pindar addresses the Corinthians as descendants of Alatas: O13 (14).

Alatheia: Truth, personified by Pindar as daughter of Zeus: O10 (4).

Aleuas: Son of Herakles and king of Thessaly: ancestor of Thorax; the Aleuadai or Sons of Aleuas were the leading aristocratic family of the Thessalian town of Larissa.

Alexibias: Father of Karrhotos the charioteer in P5.

Alexidamos: Ancestor of Telesikrates; winner of the race for the hand of Antaios' daughter: P9 (103–25).

Alkathoös: Son of Pelops and Hippodameia, in whose honor games (the Alkathoia) were held at Megara: I8 (67). See **Nisos.**

Alkidai: Descendants of Alkaios the father of Amphitryon, who was foster father of Herakles. See **Argos.**

Alkimedon: The victor in O8.

Alkimidas: The victor in N6.

Alkmaion: Founder of a noble Athenian family prominent in politics; ancestor of Megakles.

Alkman: Son of Amphiaraos and Eriphyla; avenged the death of his father by killing his mother; went with the Epigonoi against Thebes. See **Eriphyla** and **Thebes.**

Alkmena: Daughter of Elektryon; wife of Amphitryon; mother of Herakles by Zeus. See **Argos** and **Teleboai.**

Alkyoneus: A giant slain by Herakles with the aid of Telamon. See **Giants.**

Alpheos: The largest river of the Peloponnesos, flowing from southern Arkadia past Olympia and into the Ionian Sea; often used by Pindar as another way of referring to Olympia or the Olympian Games. See **Arethusa.**

Altis: The precinct of Zeus at Olympia, built by Herakles: O10 (45).

Amazons: Mythical female warriors who lived at the edge of the known world; attacked by Telamon and Iolaos in N3 (38) and by Bellerophon in O13 (87–89).

Ammon: A cult title of Zeus in Libya.

Amphiaraos: Son of Oïkles; father of Alkman by Eriphyla; Argive hero; a prophet, he participated against his will and better judgment in the siege of the Seven against Thebes. See **Eriphyla** and **Thebes.**

Amphitrita: Daughter of Nereus and Doris; wife of Poseidon.

Amphitryon: Son of Alkaios; husband of Alkmena and father of Iphikles, whose twin brother Herakles was the son of Zeus by Alkmena; Pindar often calls Herakles "son of Amphitryon." See **Argos.**

Amyklai: An ancient town on the river Eurotas south of Sparta.

Amyntor: Father of Astydameia, the mother of Tlapolemos by Herakles.

Amythan: Brother of Aison and father of Melampos; for the genealogy, see **Aiolos.**

Ancient: Nereus.

Angelia: Announcement, personified by Pindar as daughter of Hermes in O8 (82).

Antaios: (1) A giant, son of Poseidon and king of Libya, killed by Herakles (see preface to N1). (2) King of Irasa in Libya; father of Barkê (see preface to P9).

Antanor: A Trojan, counselor to Priam, said to have been spared by the Greeks because he had advised the Trojans to restore Helen to her husband; his sons were said to have settled at Kyrana: P5 (83).

Antias: A victor, maternal relative of Theaios.

Antilochos: Son of Nestor, killed by Memnon at Troy: P6 (29–42).

Aphareus: Father of Idas and Lynkeus (2).

Aphrodite: "The Foam-born" goddess, goddess of love, said to have been born from the sea-foam and to have come ashore on the island of Kypros, where she was worshipped.

Apollo: Son of Zeus and Leto; patron deity of the Pythian Games; celebrated by Pindar as a god of medicine and music and prophecy in P5 (63–69); god of poetry, often associated with the Muses; father of Iamos, Asklepios, Aristaios; brother of Artemis. See **Loxias, Paian, Phoibos.**

Archestratos: Father of Hagesidamos.

Archilochos: A famous poet, native of Paros, who lived sometime in the seventh century B.C.; known particularly for his bitter attacks on his enemies; twice named by Pindar: O9 (1), P2 (55).

Areia: A place on the Heloros River in southeastern Sicily.

Ares: Son of Zeus and Hera: god of war; often identical with battle and carnage.

Arethusa: A daughter of Okeanos and nymph of Arkadia pursued by the river Alpheos; she became the famous spring at Ortygia.

Argo: The legendary ship in which Jason and his comrades went to fetch the Golden Fleece.

Argos: A city located about three miles from the sea on the southern part of the Argive plain. Extraordinarily rich in mythical tradition, beginning with the union of Zeus and Io, daughter of the Argive river Inachos:

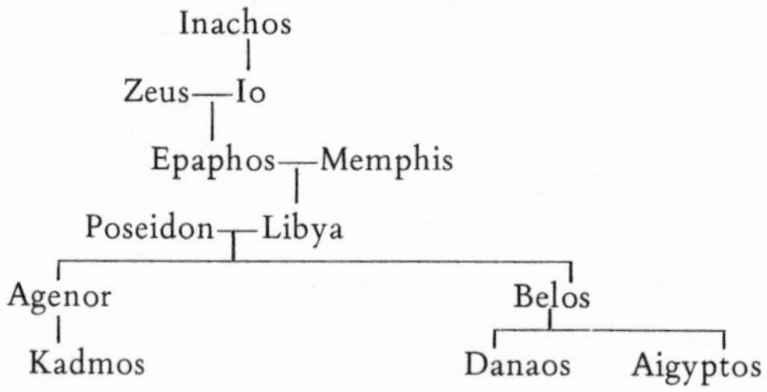

Driven by the jealousy of Hera, Io left Argos and went to Egypt. Her great-great-grandsons Danaos and Aigyptos quarreled, and Danaos with his fifty daughters fled from Egypt to Argos, pursued by the fifty sons of Aigyptos, who wanted to marry their fifty cousins. On the wedding night, acting under the instructions of Danaos, forty-nine of the daughters killed their husbands. The exception was Hypermestra; her husband was Lynkeus (1); from them Perseus descended, and, ultimately, Herakles:

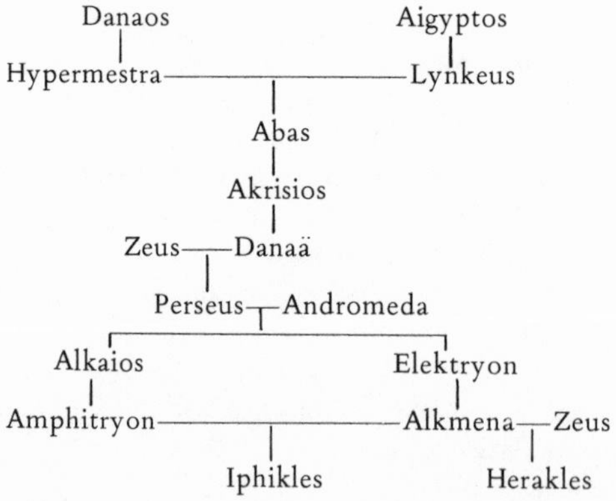

Aristagoras: A citizen of Tenedos whose installation as president of the council is celebrated by Pindar in N11.

Aristaios: Son of Apollo and Kyrana; named by Pindar in P9 (65).

Aristokleidas: The victor in N3.

Aristomenes: The victor in P8.

Aristophanes: Father of Aristokleidas; not to be confused with the Athenian comic poet of the same name.

Aristoteles: The original name of Battos, founder and first king of Kyrana: P5 (87).

Arkadia: A mountainous region in the central Peloponnesos, east of Elis and west of Argolis.

Arkesilas: (1) The victor in P4 and P5. (2) Father of Aristagoras.

Arsinoa: The nurse of Orestes: P11 (17).

Artemis: Daughter of Zeus and Leto; sister of Apollo; goddess of hunting and of the wild.

Asia: Asia Minor.

Asklepios: Son of Apollo and Koronis; raised as a physician by Chiron: P3 (45–46); killed by Zeus for having raised a man from the dead: P3 (54–58); afterward a god of medicine.

Asopichos: The victor in O14.

Asopodoros: Father of Herodotos.

Asopos: A river in Boiotia; also the river god, husband of Metopa and father of Aigina and Theba. See **Aigina.**

Astydameia: Mother of Tlapolemos by Herakles: O7 (24).

Atabyrion: The highest mountain on the island of Rhodes; there was a temple of Zeus there: O7 (87).

Athena: Daughter of Zeus; her birth is described by Pindar in O7 (35–38); goddess of Athens; patroness of arts and crafts: O7 (50–53); also called Athenaia by Pindar, "bright-eyed," "goddess of horses," and, most often, "Pallas."

Athens: Chief city of Attica, near the Saronic Gulf.

Atlas: Son of Iapetos and Klymene, a Titan condemned to support the weight of the sky on his shoulders: P4 (289).

Atreidai: See **Atreus.**

Atreus: Son of Pelops; brother of Thyestes; father of Agamemnon and Menelaos who are often referred to as the "sons of Atreus" (**Atreidai**).

Augeas: King of Epeians; slain by Herakles for his refusal to pay for the cleansing of his stables: O10 (42).

Bassidai: A clan of Aigina to which Alkimidas belonged.

Battidai: Descendants of Battos; the royal line of Kyrana.

Battos: A nickname given to Aristoteles; the name apparently means "Stammerer": P5 (55–62).

Bellerophon: Corinthian hero; son of Glaukos (for the genealogy, see **Aiolos**); tamer of Pegasos; attempted to enter Olympos. See **Pegasos.**

Blepsiadai: A clan of Aigina to which Alkimedon belonged.

Boibias: A lake in Thessaly; Koronis lived nearby.

Boiotia: A district in central Greece, bordering on Attica; Thebes, Pindar's home, was located there.

Boreas: Son of Eos (Dawn) and Astraios; the North Wind; father of Zetas and Kalaïs.

Centaur: A mythical being, half human, half horse. In Pindar, usually Chiron, the teacher of Achilleus, Asklepios, and Jason.

Chariadai: A clan of Aigina to which Deinis belonged.

Chariklo: Wife of Chiron.

Chimaira: Offspring of Typhon and Echidna; a triple-form monster slain by Bellerophon: O13 (90).

Chiron: The wise and benevolent Centaur, son of Kronos (hence "Kronidas" in P4 [115]) and Philyra; his mother is said to have taken the form of a mare in order to escape the embraces of Kronos—hence the half human, half horse form of their offspring; not to be confused with the monstrous Kentauros; Chiron, though immortal, was wounded by a poisoned arrow from the bow of Herakles; the wound would not heal, and Chiron chose to give up his immortality; hence Pindar refers to him as "dead and gone" in P3 (3).

Chromios: The victor in N1 and N9.

Corinth: A Dorian city on the Isthmos connecting the Peloponnesos with the rest of Greece; said to have been built by Sisyphos.

Daidalos: Son of Eupalamos; a descendant of Erechtheus; legendary Athenian craftsman and artist of wondrous skill.

Damagetos: Father of Diagoras.

Damaios: Tamer (of horses), an epithet of Poseidon at Corinth.

Damophilos: An exiled Kyranaian nobleman of democratic sympathies, who apparently asked Pindar to write P4 in order to ingratiate himself with the king, Arkesilas.

Danaä: Daughter of Akrisios who imprisoned her in a tower to prevent her from becoming pregnant. Zeus visited her in the form of a golden rain, and she became the mother of Perseus: P12 (17). See **Argos.**

Danaans: A name given to the people of Argos from Danaos their king; later applied to all the Greeks who went against Troy; used by Pindar in P4 (48) to refer to the peoples displaced by the Dorian invasions; in P8 (52) the name refers to the army of the Epigonoi.

Danaos: Son of Belos; descendant of Zeus and Io; father of fifty daughters, the Danaïdai, who fled the sons of their uncle Aigyptos from Egypt to Argos. See **Argos.**

Dardans: Descendants of Dardanos, legendary king of Troy; used to refer to the Trojans.

Dawn: The goddess **Eos,** daughter of Hyperion and Theia; mother of Memnon, the Ethiopian prince: O2 (83).

Deinis: The victor in N8.

Deinomenes: (1) Father of Hieron. (2) Hieron's son, installed as king of Aitna: P1 (58–65).

Deinomenidai: Descendants of Deinomenes.

Delos: An island, one of the Cyclades; reputed to have been the birthplace of Apollo and Artemis and for that reason sacred to Apollo.

Delphi: Site of the Delphic Oracle of Apollo and of the Pythian Games sacred to Apollo; located some 2,000 feet above the Gulf of Corinth on the lower southern slopes of Mount Parnassos; according to mythology, the center or navel (omphalos) of the earth: P4 (74), P6 (3)

Demeter: Sister of Zeus; wife of Hades; mother of Persephone; goddess of the earth and the fruits of the earth.

Deukalion: Son of Prometheus and husband of Pyrrha; he and his wife, only survivors in the Greek version of the flood myth (see O9 [41–53]), repeopled the world by casting stones over their shoulders.

Diagoras: The victor in O7.

Dika: Justice, one of the Horai: O13 (4); personified by Pindar in O7 (13) and P8 (1, 71).

Diodotos: Father of Strepsiadas (2).

Diomedes: Son of Tydeus; valiant Greek warrior at Troy; deified by Athena in N10 (7).

Dionysos: Son of Zeus and Semela; god of wine and ecstasy.

Dirka: A famous fountain in Thebes; often used by Pindar to designate the city.

Dodona: A sanctuary of Zeus in Epirus; famed as the center of an oracle.

Dorians: Last of the Greek peoples to have entered Greece from the north in c. 1100–1000 B.C.; settled especially in Elis, Lakonia, Argos, Corinth, Sikyon, Epidauros, Megara, and Aigina; also the islands of Krete, Melos, and Thera; and portions of Asia Minor.

Doryklos: Named by Pindar among the first Olympian victors in O10.

Earth: See **Gaia.**

Earth-Shaker: An epithet of Poseidon.

Echemos: Named by Pindar among the first Olympian victors in O10.

Echion: Son of Hermes and Antianeira; brother of Erytos; member of the crew that sailed with Jason aboard the Argo.

Echo: Personified by Pindar in O14 (21).

Eirena: Peace, one of the Horai.

Elatos: Father of Aipytos and Ischys.

Elean: See **Elis.**

Eleithyia: Goddess of childbirth; daughter of Hera in N7 (1).

Elektran Gate: At Thebes, looking toward Plataia.

Eleusis: A town in Attica famous as the seat of the Eleusinian Mysteries in honor of Demeter and Persephone; site of games in honor of Demeter.

Elis: A plain of northwestern Peloponnesos, where Olympia was located; the Eleans presided over the Olympian Games; the Elean Heralds proclaimed the beginning of the Olympian festival to the states of Greece: I2 (24).

Emmenes: Grandfather of Theron; ancestor of the Emmenidai.

Emmenidai: The descendants of Emmenes; a clan of Akragas that claimed descent from Kadmos through Polyneikes; Theron and Xenokrates were Emmenidai.

Endaïs: Daughter of Chiron; wife of Aiakos; mother of Peleus and Telamon: N5 (12). See **Aigina.**

Enyalios: A war god, sometimes the companion of, sometimes identical with, Ares.

Epaphos: Son of Zeus and Io; born in Egypt; father of Libya: P4 (14). See **Argos.**

Epeians: The ancient inhabitants of Elis, where Olympia was located.

Epharmostos: The victor in O9.

Ephyra: (1) Capital city of Molossia in Epirus: N7 (37). (2) Ancient name of the Thessalian town Krannon: P10 (55).

Epialtas: A giant; son of Iphimedeia and Poseidon, according to Pindar; brother of Otos: P4 (89); the two brothers planned to scale the heavens by piling Mount Ossa on Olympos, Mount Pelion on Ossa, but were killed by Apollo before they could do so.

Epidauros: A small state in Argolis, famed chiefly for its sanctuary of Asklepios, in whose honor games were held there.

Epigonoi: Those Born After, the sons of the Seven against Thebes who avenged the deaths of their fathers by successfully attacking the city. See **Thebes.**

Epimetheus: Son of Iapetos and Klymene; brother of Prometheus; husband of Pandora; his name means "Afterthought."

Eratos: Founder of the Rhodian clan of the Eratidai or "sons of Eratos," the clan to which Diagoras belonged.

Erechtheus: Son of Earth, reared by Athena; legendary first king of Athens; the "sons of Erechtheus" in I2 (19) are the Athenians.

Erginos: The son of Klymenos; sailed with Jason aboard the Argo.

Ergoteles: The victor in O12.

Eriboia: Wife of Telamon; mother of Aias: I6 (45). See **Aigina.**

Erinys: The avenging spirit who punishes crimes against kindred.

Eriphyla: Daughter of Talaos and sister of Adrastos, who married her to Amphiaraos in order to make up their quarrel: N9 (13–19); Eriphyla, bribed by Polyneikes, who offered her the necklace of Harmonia, compelled her husband Amphiaraos to join the ill-fated expedition of the Seven against Thebes; her son Alkman avenged his father's death by killing his mother. See **Thebes**.

Eritimos: Son of Terpsias and nephew of Ptoiodoros; relatives of Xenophon.

Erytos: Son of Hermes and Antianeira; participated with his brother Echion in the voyage of the Argo.

Ethiopia: In Africa, south of Egypt; home of Memnon.

Euboia: An island extending from the Gulf of Pagasai to Andros.

Eunomia: Law, one of the Horai.

Euphamos: Son of Poseidon; an Argonaut connected with the foundation of Kyrana: P4 (22, 44, 175, 256).

Euphanes: Grandfather of Timasarchos: N4 (89); dead at the time of the ode's composition; apparently a poet and musician.

Euphrosyna: Festivity, one of the three Graces.

Euripos: Strait between Euboia and the mainland; the Greek fleet, assembled for the expedition against Troy, was stranded here; here Agamemnon sacrificed his daughter Iphigeneia: P11 (22).

Europa: Daughter of Tityos, according to Pindar; mother of Euphamos by Poseidon: P4 (44–46); according to others, daughter of Agenor the king of Tyre. In N4 (70) "Europa" means "Europe."

Eurotas: The river near which Sparta was located.

Euryala: Wide-Leaper, one of the three Gorgons: P12 (20). See **Gorgons**.

Eurypylos: A son of Poseidon; one of the Tritons or Greek mermen; see P4 (33).

Eurystheus: Son of Sthenelos; king of Tiryns; he made Herakles perform his twelve labors; killed by Iolaos in revenge for that: P9 (79–81).

Eurytos: Son of Molione by Poseidon; nephew of Augeas; brother of Kteatos. See **Molione**.

Euthymenes: Maternal uncle of Pytheas and Phylakidas.

Euxenidai: A clan of Aigina to which Sogenes belonged.

Euxine Sea: Ancient Greek name for the Black Sea: N4 (49). The name means "Hospitable." See **Inhospitable Sea**.

Evadna: Daughter of Poseidon and Pitana; mother of Iamos: O6 (29–57).

Gadeira: Cadiz, where the Pillars of Herakles were located; on the coast of Spain, northwest of Gibraltar.

Gaia: The Earth; offspring of Chaos; mother of gods and men: see N6 (1–4).

Ganymede: Son of Tros; Zeus fell in love with him and carried him off to Olympos, where he became his cupbearer: O1 (43–45), O10 (105).

Geryon: Son of Chrysaor and Kallirrhoe; a giant said to live at Gadeira; Herakles' tenth labor was to steal the cattle of Geryon and bring them back.

Giants: Children of Gaia from the blood of Uranos, according to Hesiod; enemies of the gods; the giants mentioned by Pindar are Alkyoneus, Epialtas, Otos, and Porphyrion.

Glaukos: A descendant of Bellerophon who fought on the Trojan side against the Greeks: O13 (55–62).

Gorgons: Medusa and her two sisters, Stheno ("Mighty") and Euryala; daughters of Phorkos and Keto; monstrous beings of Greek mythology, with serpent hair and eyes that turned people to stone.

Graces: Aglaia, Euphrosyna, Thalia: daughters of Zeus and Eurynome, worshipped at Orchomenos (O14); often associated with the Muses.

Greece: See **Hellas**.

Greeks: See **Hellenes**.

Hades: Son of Kronos; brother of Zeus and Poseidon; husband of Persephone; and god of death.

Hagesias: The victor in O6.

Hagesidamos: (1) The victor in O10 and O11. (2) Father of Chromios.

Hagesimachos: Great-great-grandfather of Alkimidas.

Haimones: A people of Thessaly: N4 (56).

Halirothios: Son of Poseidon and father of Samos.

Harmonia: Daughter of Ares and Aphrodite; wife of Kadmos: P3 (91); mother of Semela and Ino. See **Thebes.**

Hebe: Daughter of Zeus and Hera; her name means "Youth." She is the wife of the deified Herakles: N1 (72).

Hektor: Son of Priam and Hekaba; greatest of the warriors defending Troy; slain by Achilleus: O2 (81), I5 (39), I8 (55).

Helen: Daughter of Zeus and Leda; wife of Menelaos; her abandonment of her husband for the Trojan prince Paris led to the Trojan War.

Helenos: Son of Priam; called by Pindar the cousin of Memnon at N3 (63). See **Memnon.**

Helikon: The largest mountain in Boiotia, where was located a sanctuary of the Muses: Pindar several times calls the Muses Helikonian.

Helios: Son of Hyperion; father of Aietas; god of the sun; worshipped at Rhodes: O7.

Hellanios: A cult title of Zeus as god of the Hellenes.

Hellas: Originally the region around Dodona in Thessaly; later applied as a name to all Greece.

Hellenes: The people of Hellas; the Greeks; used without distinction by Homer to designate the Greek people; descendants of Hellen, son or brother of Deukalion.

Heloros: A river in Sicily. Hippokrates of Gela defeated the Syracusans at the battle of the Heloros in 492 B.C.

Hephaistos: Son of Hera; the lame god of the forge; his name is often synonymous with fire itself.

Hera: Daughter of Kronos and Rhea; sister and wife of Zeus.

Herakles: Son of Zeus and Alkmena (see **Argos**); often called "son of Amphitryon" from the name of his foster father, the husband of Alkmena: N10 (13–17); Hera, jealous of Alkmena, tried to destroy Herakles in his infancy: N1 (35–50). Greatest of all Greek heroes, famed for his Twelve Labors (see **Eurystheus**); renowned as an explorer: N3 (20–26), I4 (55–58); as slayer of the Nemean lion: I6 (37, 47–49) and of Alkyoneus: N4 (27), I6 (33); sacked Troy to avenge the treachery of Laomedon (see **Laomedon**); comrade-in-arms of Telamon (see **Telamon**); founder of the Olympian Games: O10 (24–59). The Pillars of Herakles at Gadeira symbolized the end of the known world: O3 (43–45), N3 (20–21). See **Gadeira.** Immortalized and accepted among the gods as bridegroom of Hebe: N1 (69–72).

Hermes: Son of Zeus and Maia (a daughter of Atlas); born on Mount Kyllana in Arkadia above Stymphalos; the messenger of the gods; also the psychopomp who conducts the souls of the dead into the underworld.

Herodotos: The victor in I1.

Hesiod: Boiotian poet who lived several centuries before Pindar; author of the *Theogony* and the *Works and Days*; named in I6 (67).

Hestia: Daughter of Kronos and Rhea; goddess of the hearth, both public and private.

Hesychia: Peace, personified by Pindar in O4 (16) and P8 (1).

Hieron: Son of Deinomenes; tyrant of Syracuse; patron of the arts; Pindar's most powerful patron; celebrated in O1 and in the first three Pythian odes; succeeded to the tyranny of Syracuse in 478 and died in approximately 467 B.C.

Himera: A city on the north coast of Sicily, founded in approximately 649; site of the battle of Himera in 480: P1 (79–80), when Theron of Akragas and Gelon of Syracuse defeated the Carthaginians; see the prefaces to O2 and O12.

Hipparis: A river in southern Sicily.

Hippodameia: Daughter of Oinomaos; wife of Pelops: O1 (75–89), O9 (9–10). See **Oinomaos.**

Hippokleas: The victor in P10.

Hippolyta: Daughter of Kretheus; wife of Akastos; she attempted to seduce Peleus, who rejected her advances: N5 (25–36).

Homer: Author of the *Iliad* and the *Odyssey*. His "Sons," the *Homeridai*, were a guild of epic rhapsodes. See the preface to N2.

Honesty: *Atrekeia*, personified by Pindar in O10 (13).

Horai: The Seasons, daughters of Zeus and Themis. They are Dika, Eirena, and Eunomia.

Hybris: Pride, personified by Pindar in O13 (10).

Hyllos: Eldest son of Herakles by Deianeira; founder of the Dorian tribe of Hylleis. See **Aigimios.**

Hyperboreans: Mythical people who lived in the far north. According to Delphic legend, Apollo spent the winter months in their company. Pindar depicts them as a blissful people, free of sickness and death, in P10 (37–44).

Hyperian: A fountain near Pherai in Thessaly.

Hyperion: A Titan, husband and brother of Theia; father of the sun, the moon, and the dawn.

Hypermestra: Daughter of Danaos; wife of Lynkeus (1). See **Argos.**

Hypseus: King of the Lapithai and father of Kyrana: P9 (12–18).

Hypsipyleia: Queen of the Lemnian women; she received the Argonauts in Lemnos and had two sons by Jason.

Ialysos: Grandson of Helios and Rhodes; also a Rhodian city.

Iamos: Son of Apollo and Evadna; legendary ancestor of the clan of Iamidai, who administered the oracle of Zeus' altar at Olympia: O6.

Iapetos: A Titan; son of Uranos and Gaia; father of Prometheus.

Ida: A mountain in Krete; Zeus was said to have been born there in a sacred cave, invoked by Pindar in O5 (18).

Idas: Son of Aphareus; brother of Lynkeus (2). Idas wounded Kastor and was slain by Zeus: N10 (71).

Ilas: Trainer of Hagesidamos (1).

Ilion: Another name for Troy.

Inhospitable Sea: The Black Sea, afterward called the Hospitable Sea (i.e., the Euxine Sea). It was Inhospitable until Jason and the Argonauts opened it up to navigation: P4 (203).

Ino: Daughter of Kadmos and Harmonia: P3 (96–98); driven mad by Hera because she had nursed the infant Dionysos, son of Zeus and Semela; in her madness she killed her son Learchos and leaped into the sea with her other son Melikertes; she and Melikertes then became sea deities: O2 (28–30). See **Leukothea.**

Iolaos: Son of Iphikles the twin brother of Herakles (see N1); companion to his uncle Herakles; avenged the sorrows caused to Herakles by Eurystheus: P9 (79–81); an example of loyalty and family devotion; also a patron of athletic competitions.

Iolkos: A city in Magnesia, in Thessaly; famous as the home of Jason and the starting point for the voyage of the Argo; subdued by Peleus singlehandedly in revenge for the treachery of Akastos and Hippolyta: N3 (34), N4 (54–61).

Ionian Sea: The Adriatic; sometimes the term included also the sea coast of Sicily.

Iphigeneia: Daughter of Agamemnon and Klytaimestra; sacrificed by her father in order to calm the winds, that the Greek fleet might embark for Troy: P11 (22).

Iphikles: Son of Amphitryon and Alkmena; twin half-brother of Herakles; father of Iolaos. See **Argos.**

Iphimedeia: Wife of Aloeus; mother, by Poseidon, of Otos and Epialtas, giants destroyed by Apollo. See **Epialtas.**

Iphion: Father of Alkimedon.

Irasa: A city in Libya, ruled by Antaios (2): P9 (106).

Ischys: Son of Elatos and lover of Koronis: P3 (25–32).

Ismenos: A river flowing past Thebes; near it was the Ismenion, a temple and oracle of Apollo Ismenios: P11 (6).

Isthmos: The neck of land separating the Corinthian Gulf from the Saronic Gulf; Corinth, on the Isthmos, was the seat of the Isthmian Games held every two years in honor of Poseidon.

Ixion: A Thessalian hero; father of Kentauros the ancestor of the Centaurs (see **Kentauros**). In the underworld, he is fastened to an ever-spinning wheel in punishment for ingratitude; also the first man to shed kindred blood: P2 (21–48).

Jason: Son of Aison; leader of the Argonauts; hero of the myth in P4.

Kadmeians: Descendants of Kadmos, i.e., the **Thebans.**

Kadmos: The son of Agenor, king of Tyre; cousin of Danaos and Aigyptos (see **Argos**); when Zeus took his sister Europa over the sea, Kadmos was told by his father to bring Europa home or not return. Kadmos founded the city of Thebes in Boiotia; he sowed the dragon's teeth whence sprang the Spartoi or Sown Men. See **Thebes.**

Kaïkos: A river in Mysia, in Asia Minor.

Kalaïs: Son of Boreas; brother of Zetas.

Kallianax: Ancestor of Diagoras.

Kallias: A boxer; one of the Bassidai of Aigina: N6 (36).

Kallikles: Deceased uncle of Timasarchos.

Kallimachos: Deceased relative of Alkimedon.

Kalliopa: Calliope, Lovely Voice, the Muse of epic poetry: O10 (14). See **Muses.**

Kallista: The Most Beautiful (Island), the early name of Thera: P4 (258).

Kamarina: A city in southern Sicily. Also, the nymph of the city.

Kamiros: Grandson of Helios and Rhodes; also, a Rhodian city.

Kaphisos: A river springing from Mount Parnassos, watering Phokis and northern Boiotia, and emptying into Lake Kopaïs; haunted by the Graces: O14 (1). Father of the nymph Kopaïs, alluded to in P12 (27).

Karneiadas: Father of Telesikrates.

Karneios: Epithet of Apollo as god of the Karneia, a festival in Thera and Kyrana: P5 (80).

Karrhotos: Son of Alexibias and driver of the winning chariot for Arkesilas of Kyrana, celebrated by Pindar in P5.

Kassandra: Daughter of Priam and Hekaba; priestess of Apollo; a prophetess; Agamemnon's concubine after the sack of Troy.

Kastalia: A spring on Mount Parnassos sacred to Apollo and the Muses; Pindar often refers to Delphi, Pytho, and the Pythian Games by mentioning Kastalia.

Kastor: Son of Tyndareus and Leda; brother of Polydeukes; patron of equestrian activities. See **Tyndaridai.**

Kastor-song: Apparently, a song celebrating a chariot victory: P2 (69).

Kentauros: Monstrous son born of the union between Ixion and the cloud Hera. See the preface to P2, for an explanation of the significance of his name. Kentauros was the ancestor of the violent and brutal race of Centaurs, creatures half horse, half man. Chiron, the good Centaur, was not related to him.

Keos: An island just east of Cape Sounion.

Kilikia: A district of southern Asia Minor; birthplace of Typhon: P1 (17), P8 (16); Typhon's connection with Kilikia indicates the Near Eastern origin of the myth of the struggle between gods and giants.

Kinyras: Legendary king of Kypros and ancestor of the Kinyrades, priests of Aphrodite. Kinyras was a prophet and musician also, a favorite of Apollo. His name became a proverb for wealth and beauty: P2 (15), N8 (18).

Kirrha: A town in the coastal plain below Delphi, often used by Pindar to denote Pytho, Delphi, the Pythian Games. See **Krisa**.

Kithairon: Mount Kithairon, separating Attica and Boiotia. On its northern slopes, the battle of Plataia was fought: P1 (77).

Kleandros: The victor in I8.

Kleitomachos: Uncle of Aristomenes.

Kleitor: A city in Arkadia, where games were held in honor of Persephone: N10 (47).

Kleo: Clio, Glorifier, one of the nine Muses: N3 (83). See **Muses**.

Kleodamos: Deceased father of Asopichos.

Kleonai: A city near Nemea. The Kleonaians administered the Nemean Games.

Kleonikos: Grandfather of Pytheas and Phylakidas.

Kleonymos: Ancestor of the Kleonymidai, the clan to which Melissos belonged.

Klotho: One of the Three Fates or Moirai. See **Moira**.

Klymenos: Father of Erginos.

Klytaimestra: Daughter of Tyndareus and Leda; sister of Helen; wife of Agamemnon and mother of Orestes, Iphigeneia, Elektra. She became the lover of Aigisthos and murdered her husband Agamemnon on his return from Troy. Her son Orestes killed her to avenge his father: P11 (17–37).

Knossos: The principal city of Krete.

Kolchis: A region at the eastern end of the Black Sea, south of the Caucasus Mountains; famed as the home of Medea.

Koronis: Daughter of Phlegyas; mother of Asklepios by Apollo, who destroyed her for making love to Ischys while still pregnant with Asklepios: P3 (8–37).

Koros: Ambition, personified by Pindar at O13 (10).

Kreoisa: A naiad, mother of Hypseus: P9 (16).

Kreon: King of Thebes; father of Megara.

Kreontidas: Ancestor of Alkimidas.

Krete: A large island, southeast of the Peloponnesos in the Mediterranean Sea.

Kretheus: Son of Aiolos; brother of Salmoneus; father of Hippolyta; grandfather of Jason. See **Aiolos**.

Krisa: A town near Kirrha. In Pindar's time, the contests of the Pythian Games were held at Krisa. Krisa and Kirrha are often used interchangeably for the site of the Pythian Games.

Kroisos: Son of Alyattes; last king of Lydia before its conquest by Cyrus the Great; Kroisos was famed for his generous gifts to the Oracle of Apollo at Delphi and his enormous wealth.

Kronidas: Son of Kronos.

Kronos: Son of Uranos and Gaia; a Titan; consort of Rhea; father of Zeus, Poseidon, Hades, Hera, Chiron. Zeus is often called "the son of Kronos" or "Kronidas," also "Kronian" Zeus, or Kronion. There was a hill called the Hill of

Kronos at Olympia, often mentioned by Pindar as a periphrasis for Olympia or the Olympian Games.

Kteatos: Son of Molione by Poseidon; brother of Eurytos; nephew of Augeas. See **Molione**.

Kuma: Cumae, the earliest Greek colony in Italy, not far from Naples; settled by Chalkidians in 750 B.C.

Kyknos: (1) A son of Ares who waylaid pilgrims bringing offerings to Apollo's shrine at Delphi. Herakles killed him with Athena's help: O10 (15). (2) A son of Poseidon; slain by Achilleus at Troy: O2 (82), I5 (39). He was invulnerable, so Achilleus choked him to death. After his death, Poseidon changed him into a swan (*kyknos* means "swan").

Kyllana: A mountain in Arkadia; birthplace of Hermes.

Kypros: Cyprus, an island in the Levant, some fifty miles south of Kilikia; sacred to Aphrodite.

Kyrana: (1) Cyrene, a city in North Africa. (2) The nymph Kyrana, daughter of Hypseus; loved by Apollo who brought her from her home on Mount Pelion to her new city in Libya: P9 (5-75).

Labdakos: Son of Polydoros; father of Laios; grandfather of Oedipus. See **Thebes**.

Lachesis: One of the Three Fates or Moirai. See **Moira**.

Laios: The father of Oedipus; named at O2 (38). See **Thebes**.

Lakedaimon: The ancient name of Sparta, chief city of the Peloponnesos.

Lakereia: A town near Lake Boibias in Thessaly.

Lakonian: Spartan.

Lampon: Father of Pytheas and Phylakidas.

Lampromachos: A citizen of Opous, apparently the friend of Epharmostos.

Laomedon: Son of Ilos and father of Priam; legendary king of Troy; when Herakles saved Laomedon's daughter Hesione, Laomedon refused to pay Herakles the horses he had agreed to pay for this feat, and Herakles, together with Telamon, sacked Troy and killed Laomedon in revenge: I6 (29).

Lapithai: A people of Thessaly; ruled by Pirithoös; they fought against the Centaurs.

Leda: Daughter of Thestios the king of Aitolia; wife of Tyndareus; mother by him of Klytaimestra and of Kastor; Zeus made love to her in the form of a swan and became the father of Klytaimestra's twin sister Helen, and of Kastor's twin brother Polydeukes. Leda's two children by Zeus were immortal, the two by Tyndareus mortal.

Lemnos: An island in the northeast Aegean; visited by Jason and the Argonauts: O4 (19-27), P4 (252). Philoktetes was marooned there.

Lerna: A coastal district of Argolis, where Herakles killed the Lernaian Hydra.

Leto: Daughter of Koios and mother of Apollo and Artemis by Zeus; often named by Pindar in reference to her children.

Leukothea: The White Goddess, an epithet and cult title of Ino: P11 (2).

Libya: (1) The Daughter of Epaphos. See **Argos**. (2) The land of Libya, i.e., North Africa, where Kyrana was located.

Likymnios: Son of Elektryon and his concubine Midea; killed by his grandnephew Tlapolemos: O7 (27–30).

Lindos: Grandson of Helios and Rhodes; also a Rhodian city.

Lokris: (1) Eastern Lokris, a strip of land along the Euboian Gulf, bordered by Phokis in the west and Boiotia in the south. (2) Western Lokris, an area bordered by the Corinthian Gulf in the south and Aitolia in the north. Opous was located in Eastern Lokris. Western Lokris, in the mainland of Greece, is not to be confused with Western Lokroi (Epizephyrian Lokroi), a Greek colony located in the southeastern end of the Italian peninsula.

Lokros: Eponymous Lokrian hero, king of the city of Opous in Eastern Lokris; adoptive father of Opous, after whom the town was named: O9 (59–66).

Lord of Ships: Poseidon.

Loxias: An epithet of Apollo in P3 (28), P11(5), I7 (49). The name is derived from the adjective *loxos*, "slantwise," "crooked," and was thought to belong to Apollo because of the ambiguity of his oracles at Delphi.

Lydia: A land in the west of Asia Minor, home of Kroisos; the adjective "Lydian" is often applied to music and musical instruments.

Lykaian: Of Lykaion, a mountain in Arkadia where there was an altar of Zeus, and where games were held in his honor. Hence Pindar calls Zeus "Lykaian" in O9 (96) and O13 (108).

Lykia: A mountainous country in southwestern Asia Minor, home of Sarpedon. The Lykians were allies of Priam in the Trojan War. Apollo had a shrine at Patara in Lykia; hence Pindar calls him "Lykian" in P1 (39).

Lynkeus: (1) Son of Aigyptos; husband of Hypermestra. See **Argos.** (2) Son of Aphareus and brother of Idas; killed by Polydeukes: N10 (70).

Magnetes: The people of Magnesia in southeastern Thessaly, where Mount Pelion is located.

Mainalos: A mountain in Arkadia, where Zeus made love to the mother of Opous: O9 (57–61).

Mantinea: A city in Arkadia.

Marathon: An Attic deme. Games were held there in honor of Herakles. It was the site of the battle of Marathon 490 B.C.

Medea: Daughter of Aietas and granddaughter of Helios the Sun God; queen of Kolchis, who left her father and her country with Jason aboard the Argo and came with him to Greece: O13 (53–54), P4 (218–19).

Medusa: The mortal sister of the immortal Gorgons Stheno and Euryala; her name means Queen; slain by Perseus: P10 (46), P12 (16). See **Gorgons** and **Pegasos.**

Megakles: The victor in P7.

Megara: (1) The daughter of Kreon, king of Thebes; wife of Herakles and mother by him of eight sons, all killed by Herakles himself in a fit of madness. Pindar refers to them as "the eight who died" in I4 (63). (2) A Dorian town on the Isthmos of Corinth where games were held in honor of Alkathoös and Apollo. See **Nisos.**

Megas: Father of Deinis.

Meidylidai: The clan to which Aristomenes belonged.

Melampos: A seer; the cousin of Jason: P4 (126).

Melanippos: A Theban champion, descended from the Sown Men; he mortally wounded, and was mortally wounded by, Tydeus at the siege of the Seven against Thebes. Maternal ancestor of Aristagoras.

Meleagros: Son of Oineus; famed as a valiant warrior in the defense of his city: I7 (32).

Melesias: An Athenian trainer of athletes.

Melia: An Okeanid, mother, by Apollo, of Ismenos and Teneros.

Melissos: The victor in I3 and I4.

Memnon: Son of the Dawn, an Ethiopian prince who came to the aid of Priam and the Trojans. He killed Nestor's son Antilochos in battle: P6 (29–42) and was himself killed by Achilleus: O2 (83), N3 (63), N6 (50), I5(41), I8 (54). Memnon's father Tithonos was the brother of Priam. Hence Priam was Memnon's uncle and Memnon was the cousin of Helenos, one of Priam's sons: N3 (63).

Menandros: An Athenian trainer of athletes, praised by Pindar in N5 (48).

Menelaos: Son of Atreus; brother of Agamemnon; husband of Helen.

Menoitios: Father of Patroklos: O9 (70).

Meropes: An ancient people that once inhabited the island of Cos and were destroyed by Herakles and Telamon: N4 (26), I6 (31).

Messana: A region in the southwest of the Peloponnesos.

Messanian: Nestor's city, Pylos, was located in Messana. Hence Pindar calls him "the old Messanian" in P6 (35).

Metopa: A nymph of Stymphalos; mother of Theba and Aigina: O6 (84). See **Aigina.**

Midas: The victor in P12.

Midea: (1) The concubine of Elektryon and mother of Likymnios: O7 (29). (2) A town in Argolis, belonging to Elektryon: O10 (66).

Minyans: An ancient people of Boiotia, living around Orchomenos.

Minyas: Son of Poseidon; legendary founder of Orchomenos; ancestor of the original crew of the Argo.

Mnamosyna: Memory, a Titan, mother of the nine Muses.

Moira: The Greek word for "portion" or "allotment." Personified, and often appearing in the plural Moirai, it has the meaning of "fate" or "destiny." The three Moirai or Fates, daughters of Zeus and Themis, were Klotho (O1 [26], I6 [17]), Lachesis (07 [64], and Atropos. Klotho ("Spinner"), the youngest of the three, carried the spindle and spun the thread of life. Lachesis ("Allotment") measured the length. Atropos ("Implacable") cut the thread. Only the first two are mentioned by name in Pindar.

Molione: Mother of Eurytos and Kteatos by Poseidon. The sons of Molione ambushed the army of Herakles, who killed them in revenge: O10 (26–34).

Molossia: A region in Epirus; later known as Thespriotis. The royal house of the Molossoi claimed descent from Neoptolemos.

Mopsos: A prophet who sailed with Jason aboard the Argo: P4 (191).

Mother Goddess: Rhea.

Muses: The nine daughters of Zeus and Mnamosyna; goddesses of poetry. See **Helikon** and **Pieria.**

Mykenai: Mycenae, an ancient city in the northwestern part of the Argive plain; the leading center of Mycenaean culture until it was destroyed c. 1200 B.C.

Myrmidons: The earliest inhabitants of Aigina, who emigrated with Peleus to Thessaly (see **Aigina**). The Myrmidons were said to have sprung from ants in answer to Aiakos' prayer to Zeus for a people to inhabit Aigina. *Myrmêx* is Greek for ant.

Mysia: A region of Asia Minor; south of Phrygia and north of Lydia. See **Teuthras** and **Telephos.**

Naiad: The naiads were water nymphs, divine female beings living in lakes, rivers, springs, and fountains.

Naxian: Of Naxos.

Naxos: The largest of the Cyclades; an island famous for its wine and for the worship of Dionysos. According to tradition, Apollo killed Otos and Epialtas on Naxos: P4 (88).

Nemea: A valley in the territory of Kleonai; here Herakles slew the Nemean lion: I6 (47–49), and here the Nemean Games, sacred to Zeus, were held every two years, in the second and fourth year of each Olympiad.

Nemesis: The Apportioner, Fate, personified by Pindar at P10 (44).

Neoptolemos: Son of Achilleus and Deidameia. He slew the aged Trojan king, Priam. According to Homer (opening of Book 4 of the *Odyssey*), Neoptolemos returned from Troy safely and married Hermione, daughter of Helen and

Menelaos. According to Pindar in N7, Neoptolemos died at Delphi on the return home. See **Aigina**.

Nereid: A daughter of Nereus and Doris; a nymph of the sea; Thetis, the mother of Achilleus, was a Nereid.

Nereus: Son of Pontos (Sea); consort of the Okeanid Doris; father of the Nereids, fifty daughters whose names are listed by Hesiod in *Theogony* 240–64. Nereus is "the old man of the sea" or "sea's Ancient," a god of great wisdom and foreknowledge: P9 (94).

Nestor: Son of Neleus; king of Pylos; father of Antilochos; an elder chieftain among the Greeks who fought at Troy.

Nikasippos: Victory with Horses; Pindar entrusted I2 to him for delivery to Thrasyboulos in Akragas: I2 (47).

Nikeus: One of the first Olympian victors listed by Pindar in O10.

Nikokles: Cousin of Kleandros.

Nikomachos: The charioteer of Xenokrates in I2 (22).

Nile: The river Nile in Egypt.

Nisos: Mythical king of Megara, whose daughter Skylla betrayed him to Minos. Pindar refers to games at Megara by mentioning the "hill of Nisos": P9 (91). See **Alkathoös**.

Nomads: A tribe of Libya, living near Irasa: P9 (123).

Nomios: An epithet of Aristaios as "Herder" or "Pasturer" of flocks.

Nymphs: Female spirits of mountains, springs, woods; also goddesses of cities: Theba, Aigina, Metopa, Kyrana, Akragas.

Oanos: A river flowing past Kamarina.

Odysseus: Son of Laertes; hero of Homer's *Odyssey*; not one of Pindar's favorites: N7 (20–30), N8 (23–34). See **Aias** (2).

Oedipus: Son of Laios and Jokasta; the tragic king of Thebes who solved the riddle of the sphinx, killed his father, married his mother, and blinded himself. His curse upon his sons led to their mutual slaughter during the first siege of Thebes. Alluded to by Pindar in O2 (38) and named in P4 (263). See **Thebes**.

Oïkles: Father of the seer Amphiaraos.

Oineïdai: Descendants of Oineus the king of Kalydon; husband of Althaia, and father of Meleagros and Deianeira the wife of Herakles. Oineus was a great-great-grandson of Aitolos, who gave his name to Aitolia: I5 (31).

Oinomaos: King of Pisa and father of Hippodameia. Suitors for the hand of Hippodameia were compelled to flee her father in a chariot race. If Oinomaos caught up with them, he would spear them in the back. See O1 (75–89).

Oinona: The ancient name for the island of Aigina before the nymph Aigina was brought there by Zeus. It means "Vineland."

Oinopia: A variant of the ancient name for Aigina: I8 (21).

Oionos: One of the first Olympian victors listed in O10.

Okeanos: Ocean, a Titan; son of Uranos and Gaia; husband of Tethys and father of the Okeanidai.

Oligaithos: Founder of the clan to which Xenophon belonged.

Olympia: The site of the Olympian Games, sacred to Zeus, in Elis, near the river Alpheos; personified by Pindar in O8 (1).

Olympos: The highest mountain of the Greek peninsula, between Macedonia and Thessaly. It rises to an elevation of 9,573 feet and was reputed to be the home of the Olympian gods.

Onchestos: A town in Boiotia on Lake Kopaïs, sacred to Poseidon.

Opous: (1) According to Pindar, an Epeian of Elis; his (unnamed) daughter, pregnant by Zeus, was taken from her home in Elis and given as bride to the childless

Lokros. (2) Son of the daughter of Opous (1), and named after him. (3) The town in the district of Eastern Lokris. See the preface to O9.

Orchomenos: An ancient city in Boiotia; reputed to have been established by Minyas. The Graces were worshipped there: O14.

Orestes: Son of Agamemnon and Klytaimestra; avenged the death of his father by killing his mother and her lover Aigisthos: P11 (17–37).

Orion: A gigantic hunter who pursued Pleione and her daughters, the Pleiades, until pursuer and pursued were transformed into the constellations of Orion and the Pleiades. According to another tradition, he was slain by Artemis.

Orpheus: The son of Apollo by Kalliopa; a poet of magical power; husband of Eurydice.

Orseas: The trainer of Melissos.

Orthosia: A cult title of Artemis at Sparta.

Ortygia: An island near Syracuse; site of the fountain Arethusa: N1 (2).

Otos: A giant, brother of Epialtas. See **Epialtas**.

Oulias: Father of Theaios.

Paian: The Healer, an epithet of Apollo: P4 (270). Also, a song in honor of Apollo.

Pallas: An epithet of Athena, apparently signifying "Maiden."

Pamphaes: Maternal ancestor of Theaios.

Pamphylos: Son of Aigimios; founder of the Dorian tribe of Pamphyloi. See **Aigimios**.

Pan: Son of Hermes; an Arkadian god: P3 (78).

Pangaion: A mountain in Thrace, between the lower Strymon and the sea coast.

Panhellenes: All the Greeks.

Parian: Of Paros, an island famous for its fine marble: N4 (81).

Paris: Son of Priam and Hekaba; also known as Alexandros. His abduction of Helen caused the Trojan War.

Parnassos: A mountain of the Pindos range, rising to a height of 8,200 feet. The plain of Krisa and the high valley of Delphi are located on its southern slope; often mentioned by Pindar in reference to Pytho, Delphi, the Pythian Games.

Parrhasians: An Arkadian people.

Parthenia: Maiden: a cult title of Hera in Arkadia: O6 (88).

Patroklos: Son of Menoitios; beloved friend of Achilleus: O9 (70–79), O10 (19); his death in the *Iliad* precipitates the climax of the epic.

Pegasos: Fabulous winged horse that sprang from the blood of the slain Medusa; tamed by Bellerophon: O13 (63–90), who tried to ride him into the halls of Olympos: I7 (41–47).

Peirana: A fountain on the acropolis in Corinth.

Peisandros: Ancestor of Aristagoras; left Sparta, together with Orestes, and colonized Lesbos and Tenedos: N11 (33–35).

Peleus: Son of Aiakos and Endaïs; father of Achilleus; famed for his righteousness: I8 (40); married to Thetis on Mount Pelion: P3 (87–95), N5 (22–25). See **Thetis** and **Aigina**.

Pelias: Son of Poseidon and Tyro; half brother of Aison the father of Jason; king of Iolkos and father of Akastos.

Pelinna: A small town in Thessaly, near the river Peneios; home of Hippokleas.

Pelion: A mountain in Magnesia, in Thessaly, 5,700 feet high; reputed to have been the home of Chiron.

Pellana: A town in Achaia where games were held, the prize for victory being a woolen cloak.

Pelops: The son of Tantalos who came from Lydia to Pisa to compete with Oinomaos for the hand of his daughter, Hippodameia. According to one tradition, he founded the Olympian Games; he was buried at Olympia: O1 (90–93); the Peloponnesos was named after him (Island of Pelops); his father Tantalos was a son of Zeus; hence Pindar refers to Pelops as "Kronian Pelops," a descendant of Kronos through Zeus. Pelops and Hippodameia became the parents of Atreus, father of Agamemnon and Menelaos. In O1, Pindar rejects the story that Tantalos fed Peleus to the gods.

Peneios: A Thessalian river.

Pergamos: The citadel of Troy.

Periklymenos: Son of Neleus; one of the defenders of Thebes: N9 (26). Also an Argonaut: P4 (175).

Persephone: Daughter of Demeter; raped by Hades and carried by him into the underworld, where she became Queen of the Dead.

Perseus: Son of Zeus and Danaä; slayer of Medusa: P10 (46), P12 (16); ancestor of the Persians. See **Argos**.

Phaisana: A town ruled by Aipytos, adoptive father of Evadna; it was situated beside the river Alpheos in the borderland between Arkadia and Pisatis.

Phalaris: Tyrant of Akragas c. 570–54 B.C.; notorious for his cruelty: P1 (96).

Phasis: A river in Kolchis.

Pherenikos: Victory Bringer, Hieron's race horse, victorious in the Pythian Games of 482 and 478 B.C. and in the Olympian Games of 476.

Pheres: Uncle and supporter of Jason in his bid to regain the throne of Iolkos from Pelias: P4 (125).

Philanor: Father of Ergoteles.

Philoktetes: Son of Poias; bitten by a snake on Lemnos and left there by the Greeks, who summoned him later because Troy could not be taken without his bow (see **Poias**). Pindar compares the ailing Hieron to Philoktetes in P1 (50).

Philyra: An Okeanid; mother of Chiron by Kronos.

Phintis: Driver of the mule car for Hagesias.

Phlegra: Ancient name of Pallene in Thrace; site of the battle between gods and giants: I6 (33).

Phlegyas: Son of Ares; king of the Lapithai; father of Koronis.

Phleious: A city near Nemea.

Phoibos: An epithet of Apollo meaning "Bright" or "Pure."

Phoinikian: Phoenician, i.e., Carthaginian.

Phokos: Son of Aiakos and Psamatheia; murdered by his half-brothers Peleus and Telamon. See **Aigina**.

Phorkos: Son of Nereus and Gaia; father of the Gorgons and the Graiai: P12 (13).

Phrastor: One of the first Olympian victors listed in O10.

Phrikias: Father of Hippokleas.

Phrixos: Son of Athamas and Nephele; brother of Helle; rode the back of the golden ram to safety in Kolchis: P4 (160, 242).

Phrygia: A country in the central plateau and western flank of Asia Minor, just south of the Propontis. The Phrygians fought on the Trojan side against the Greeks.

Phthia: A region of Thessaly; home of Achilleus.

Phylaka: A city in Phthiotis, with a shrine to Protesilaos.

Phylakidas: The victor in I5 and I6.

Pieria: A district on the northern slopes of Mount Olympos in Thessaly, sacred to the Muses who are often called "Pierian," "Pierides," "maidens of Pieria," etc.

Pindos: A mountain range in northern Greece, separating Thessaly and Epirus. Pindar's name seems to have been derived from it.

Pisa: The district in which Olympia was located; often used by Pindar to mean Olympia or the Olympian Games.

Pitana: (1) Daughter of the river Eurotas and mother of Evadna. (2) A township of Sparta: O6 (28).

Pleiades: Daughters of Atlas and Pleione, pursued, along with their mother, by the giant Orion. Called by Pindar "the mountain Pleiades" in N2 (11) because they lived on Mount Kyllana.

Poias: Father of Philoktetes; the dying Herakles entrusted his bow to Poias, who passed it on to his son.

Polydektas: The king of Seriphos, where Danaä and her infant son Perseus came ashore after being cast adrift in a box by her father Akrisios; Polydektas tried to force himself on Danaä: P12 (15).

Polydeukes: Son of Zeus and Leda; brother of Kastor. See **Tyndaridai.**

Polyïdos: The One Who Sees Much; son of Koiranos; a seer of Corinth: O13 (75).

Polymnastos: The father of Battos.

Polyneikes: Son of Oedipus and Jokasta; father of Thersandros the ancestor of Theron: O2 (46). See **Thebes.**

Polytimidas: Friend or relative of Alkimidas.

Porphyrion: King of the Giants; slain, according to Pindar in P8 (15–18), by Apollo; according to others, by Zeus. See **Giants.**

Poseidon: Son of Kronos and Rhea; brother of Zeus; god of the sea; often called "Earth-Shaker"; patron of the Isthmian Games.

Praxidamas: Grandfather of Alkimidas.

Priam: Son of Laomedon; king of Troy; father of Hektor, Paris, Kassandra, Helenos, and many others.

Proitos: Son of Abas; brother of Akrisios, with whom he quarreled over the throne of Argos; Proitos then became king of Tiryns.

Prophasis: Excuse, personified by Pindar as the daughter of Epimetheus in P5 (28).

Protesilaos: Commander of the contingent from Phylaka at Troy; first of the Greek invaders to set foot on Trojan soil and to die there.

Protogeneia: Daughter of Deukalion and Pyrrha; ancestress of the Opountian Lokrians: O9 (41).

Psalychiadai: Aiginetan clan to which Phylakidas belonged.

Psamatheia: Sand Goddess, mother of Phokos by Aiakos. See **Aigina.**

Psaumis: The victor in O4 and O5.

Ptoiodoros: Grandfather of Xenophon.

Pylades: Son of Strophios; friend of Orestes, who fled to Strophios after the murder of his father Agamemnon: P11 (15); Pylades stood at Orestes' side when the latter slew Klytaimestra.

Pylos: A place in Messana; traditionally the home of Nestor.

Pyrrha: Daughter of Prometheus; wife of Deukalion: O9 (43). See **Deukalion.**

Pytheas: The victor in N5.

Pytho: Alternative name for the shrine and oracle of Apollo at Delphi; so called because Apollo's first exploit there was the slaying of the giant serpent Python that presided over the site before the god's arrival; site of the Pythian Games, sacred to Apollo; another name for Delphi; Apollo's close association with the place resulted in his epithet "Pythian."

Pythonikos: Father of Thrasydaios.

Rhadamanthys: Son of Zeus and Europa; transported to Elysium before his death; there he was a ruler and judge. Pindar depicts him as a judge of souls in the underworld. In P2 (73–75) he exemplifies intellectual discernment.

Rhea: A Titan; wife of Kronos and mother of Zeus.

Rhodes: (1) An island off the coast of Karia; settled by Dorian Greeks; a center for the worship of Helios: O7. (2) The nymph Rhodes, bride of Helios: O7 (14).

Salamis: An island in the Saronic Gulf just north of Aigina; home of Aias the son of Telamon: N2 (13), N4 (48), I5 (48–50); the Persian fleet of Xerxes was defeated at the battle of Salamis in September, 480 B.C.; Pindar names the battle in P1 (76) and I5 (49).

Salmoneus: Son of Aiolos and father of Tyro; hence grandfather of Pelias, the usurper of the throne of Iolkos; Salmoneus pretended to be Zeus and was punished by Zeus with death.

Samos: One of the first Olympian victors listed in O10.

Sarpedon: Son of Zeus; a Lykian ally of the Trojans.

Semela: Daughter of Kadmos and Harmonia; mother of Dionysos by Zeus; a victim of Hera's jealousy, she perished, but was resurrected and transported to Olympos through the influence of her son Dionysos: O2 (26).

Seriphos: An island, one of the Cyclades, where Danaä landed with her infant son Perseus.

Shaker of Earth: Poseidon.

Sicily: Large island to the south of the tip of Italy; colonized extensively by Greeks from 735 B.C.; many of the victors celebrated by Pindar were Sicilians: see Appendix II.

Sikyon: A city to the west of Corinth, site of games whose foundation Pindar attributes to Adrastos in N9 (11–12).

Sipylos: A Lydian city, where Tantalos feasted the gods: O1 (38).

Sisyphos: Son of Aiolos; traditional founder of Corinth; famed for his cunning: O13 (52).

Skamandros: A river at Troy, rising in Mount Ida and flowing into the Hellespont; site of Hektor's exploits: N9 (39).

Skyros: An island in the northwest Aegean, due east of Euboia; birthplace of Neoptolemos: N7 (37).

Sogenes: The victor in N7.

Sokleidas: Great-grandfather of Alkimidas.

Solymoi: A people living between Lykia and Pamphylia in Asia Minor; defeated by Bellerophon: O13 (90).

Sostratos: Father of Hagesias.

Sown Men: The Spartoi, who sprang from the dragon's teeth sown by Kadmos. See Aigeus.

Sparta: Chief city of the Peloponnesos, on the banks of the river Eurotas; also called Lakedaimon; the great Dorian rival of Athens.

Strepsiadas: (1) The victor in I7. (2) His maternal uncle.

Strophios: The father of Pylades.

Stymphalos: A town in Arkadia; home of Metopa; seat of the maternal ancestors of Hagesias.

Syracuse: A Greek city on the eastern coast of Sicily, founded by colonists from Corinth.

Tainaros: A Lakonian city near Cape Tainaron; Tainaron was the central peninsula of South Peloponnesos; Herakles was thought to have dragged Cerberus from the underworld through a cave there.

Talaos: Father of Adrastos.

Tantalos: Son of Zeus and father of Pelops; punished in the underworld by having a boulder suspended over his head, forever threatening to fall on him: O1 (55–64), I8 (10–11).

Tartaros: The underworld.

Taÿgeta: Daughter of Atlas; she gave her name to Mount Taÿgetos. According to some sources, she was changed to a hind by Artemis, angered because Zeus had loved her. According to Pindar, it was she who dedicated the golden-horned hind to Artemis: O3 (29).

Taÿgetos: A mountain range in Western Lakonia, rising to a height of 7,800 feet and overlooking the plain of Sparta.

Tegea: A town on the southwestern plain of Arkadia.

Teiresias: Son of Eueres and Chariklo; one of the descendants of the Spartoi or Sown Men; a legendary blind Theban seer who retained even in death his prophetic ability.

Telamon: Son of Aiakos and Endaïs; brother of Peleus; father of Aias and Teukros; comrade-in-arms of Herakles, in whose company he sacked Troy and destroyed the Meropes and the giant Alkyoneus: I6 (26–30), N4 (25–30); in N3 (36–39) Iolaos replaces Herakles as Telamon's ally against Troy and the Amazons.

Teleboai: Inhabitants of the Taphian Islands opposite the district of Akarnania in eastern Aitolia, south of Epirus; they harassed Elektryon, father of Alkmena, who required her new husband Amphitryon to take vengeance on them; while Amphitryon was off fighting the Teleboai, Zeus visited Alkmena in the guise of Amphitryon and became the father of Herakles by her: N10 (11–18).

Telephos: Son of Herakles; king of Mysia; wounded in battle by Achilleus when the Greeks, on their way to Troy, mistakenly landed at Mysia and were met as an invading force: O9 (73), I5 (41), I8 (50).

Telesarchos: Father of Kleandros.

Telesiadas: Father of Melissos.

Telesikrates: The victor in P9.

Tempe: A narrow valley in northern Thessaly, between Mounts Olympos and Ossa, with the river Peneios flowing through it. According to tradition, it was created by Poseidon, god of earthquakes. *Poseidon Petraios*, or Poseidon of the Rock, is Pindar's way of alluding to this tradition in P4 (138).

Tenedos: An island off the coast of Asia Minor, settled by Aiolians.

Terpsias: A relative of Xenophon.

Terpsichora: Delighting in the Dance, the Muse of choral song, hence of epinician poetry, Pindar's genre. See **Muses**.

Teukros: Illegitimate son of Telamon; half-brother of Aias (2); a warrior at Troy famed for his archery.

Teuthras: A king of Mysia, referred to as "Teuthras' plain" in O9 (71). See **Telephos**.

Thalia: Bloom, one of the three Graces.

Theaios: The victor in N10.

Theandridai: The clan to which Timasarchos belonged.

Thearion: The guild-hall of the *Theoroi* or sacred envoys sent from Aigina to Delphi: N3 (70).

Theariôn: Father of Sogenes.

Theba: Daughter of Asopos and Metopa; sister of Aigina; eponymous nymph of Thebes.

Thebes: The main city of Boiotia; home of Pindar; founded, according to legend, by Kadmos, sower of the dragon's teeth (see **Sown Men**), husband of Harmonia, and ancestor of the royal House of Labdakos, to which Oedipus belonged:

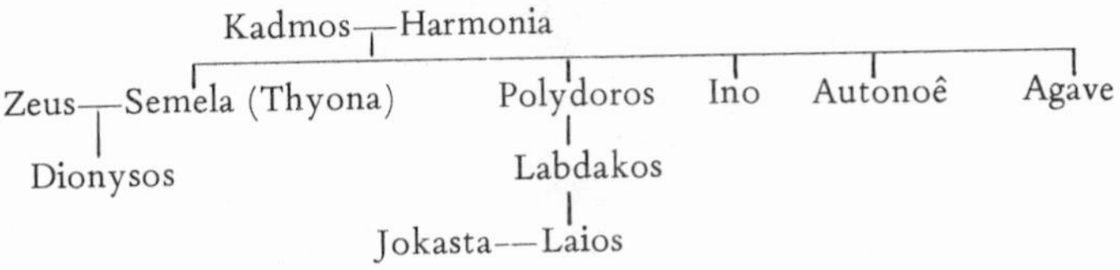

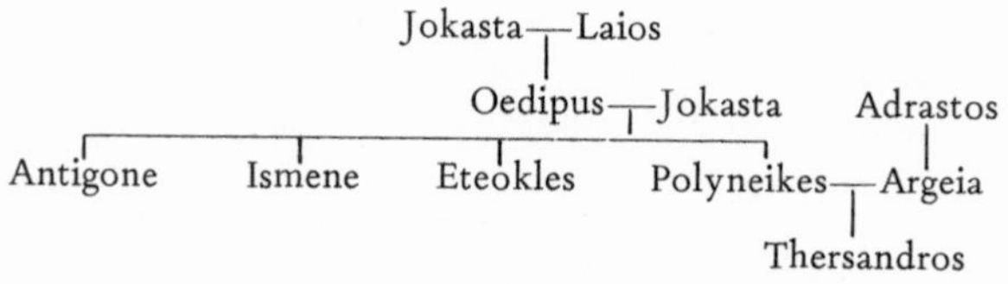

The sons of Oedipus, cursed by their father, disputed the succession after his death. Polyneikes, driven from the city, formed an alliance with Adrastos, marrying his daughter Argeia and gathering an army with which he hoped to drive his brother Eteokles from the throne of Thebes. This army, called the Seven against Thebes for its seven leaders, met with disaster: Polyneikes and Eteokles fell by each other's hands: O2 (41–42), and five of Polyneikes' six allies perished in the siege: Tydeus, Kapaneus, Hippomedon, Parthenopaios, and Amphiaraos. The seventh, Adrastos, lived to participate in the second siege: O6 (12–17), successfully undertaken by the sons of the first leaders, the Epigonoi: P8 (41–45), among whom were Thersandros the son of Polyneikes, Diomedes the son of Tydeus, and Alkman the son of Amphiaraos. See **Argos.**

Theia: Divine One, a Titan, sister and wife of Hyperion and mother by him of the Sun, the Moon, and the Dawn; hailed at the opening of I5 as the source of all that is glorious in life.

Themis: A Titan, daughter of Earth; Zeus' second consort by whom he has several children; her name means "Right" or "Justice."

Themistios: Maternal grand-uncle of Pytheas and Phylakidas.

Theognetos: Uncle of Aristomenes.

Thera: An island, one of the Sporades, famous for its wine. Kyrana was colonized by immigrants from Thera.

Therapna: A town on the Eurotas, southeast of Sparta; Helen and her brothers Kastor and Polydeukes were worshipped there: P11 (63), N10 (56), I1 (31).

Theron: Son of Ainesidamos and tyrant of Akragas; traced his descent to the royal line of Thebes through Thersandros, son of Polyneikes: O2 (46); one of Pindar's richest and most powerful patrons; victorious in the battle of Himera (see **Himera**); the victor in O2 and O3.

Thersandros: One of the Epigonoi; the son of Polyneikes and Argeia; see **Thebes.**

Thessalos: Father of Xenophon.

Thessaly: A district of northern Greece, rich in wheat, horses, and cattle; site of Iolkos, where Peleus went from Aigina.

Thetis: Daughter of Nereus and Doris; sister of Amphitrita; fated to bear a son mightier than his father, she was given by the gods in marriage to Peleus and became the mother of Achilleus: I8 (27–48). See **Aigina.**

Thorax: A Thessalian prince, lord of Larissa; a descendant of Aleuas; he cooperated with the Persians during the invasion of Greece by Xerxes in 480 B.C.

Thrasyboulos: Son of Xenokrates; though not a victor, he is addressed by Pindar in P6 and I2.

Thrasydaios: The victor in P11.

Thrasyklos: A maternal relative of Theaios.

Thyona: An alternative name for Semela: P3 (99).

Timasarchos: The victor in N4.

Time: *Chronos*, personified by Pindar in O2 (17) and O10 (55).

Timodemidai: The clan of Timodemos.

Timodemos: The victor in N2.

Timokritos: Father of Timasarchos.

Timonoös: Father of Timodemos.

Timosthenes: Brother of Alkimedon.

Tiryns: An ancient city on a rocky hill on the Argive plain; home of Herakles: O10 (31) and of his son Tlapolemos: O7 (29, 78).

Titans: The generation of gods preceding that of the Olympians; children of Uranos and Gaia: Okeanos, Hyperion, Iapetos, Mnamosyna, Theia, Rhea, Kronos, Themis.

Tityos: Son of Zeus and Elara; a giant who tried to rape Leto and was killed by Artemis.

Tlapolemos: Son of Herakles and Astydameia; having killed his maternal granduncle Likymnios, he was advised by Apollo's oracle to leave Tiryns and colonize Rhodes: O7 (27–38).

Tritonis: A lake in Libya.

Troy: The city in Asia Minor, twice taken by the Greeks, first by Herakles (see **Laomedon**) and then by the sons of Atreus (see **Helen**); the second siege forms the background for Homer's *Iliad* and *Odyssey*.

Tycha: Goddess of Fortune: O12 (2).

Tyndareus: The husband of Leda; father of Kastor and Klytaimestra.

Tyndaridai: The sons of Tyndareus, Kastor and Polydeukes, tutelary heroes at Olympia, patrons of athletic festivals. See **Leda**.

Typhon: Monstrous son of Earth and Tartaros; a chaos demon who tried to usurp the rule of Zeus; according to Pindar, he lies pinned beneath Mount Aitna: P1 (13–28).

Tyre: A Phoinikian city, famed for its purple dye.

Tyro: Daughter of Salmoneus; mother, by Poseidon, of Pelias.

Tyrsanoi: Etruscans, the earliest historical occupants of the region between the Tiber and the Arno in Italy (modern Tuscany); their naval expansion was checked by Hieron at the battle of Kuma in 474 B.C. See P1 (71–75).

Uranos: The sky, consort of Gaia, the earth; together they were parents of the Titan generation of gods. See **Titans**.

Victory: *Nika*, the goddess of victory.

Western Lokroi: Epizephyrian Lokroi, a Lokrian colony in the extreme southeastern end of Italy.

Xanthos: The name given by the gods to the river Skamandros.

Xenarkes: Father of Aristomenes.

Xenokrates: The victor in P6 and I2.

Xenophon: The victor in O13.

Youth: *Hora*, personified by Pindar at the opening of N8.

Zephyros: God of the west wind; son of Eos (Dawn) and Astraios.

Zetas: Son of Boreas, the north wind; brother of Kalaïs: P4 (182).

Zeus: Son of Kronos (hence "Kronidas") and Rhea; chief of the Olympian gods; father of Apollo and Artemis, Athena, Hermes, the Muses, and many other gods and heroes; the patron god of the Olympian and Nemean Games.

BIBLIOGRAPHY

Barrett, W. S. "Pindar's Twelfth *Olympian* and the Fall of the Deinomenidai." *Journal of Hellenic Studies* 103 (1973): 23–35.

Benjamin, Walter. *Illuminations*, edited and with an introduction by Hannah Arendt. New York: Schocken Books, 1969.

Benn, M. B. *Hölderlin and Pindar*. 's Gravenhage: Mouton, 1969.

Bergk, Theodorus. *Poetae Lyrici Graeci.* Leipzig, 1878.

Boeckh, August. *Pindari Epiniciorum Interpretatio Latina cum Commentario Perpetuo*. Leipzig, 1821.

Bowra, C. M. *Pindar*. Oxford: Oxford University Press, 1964.

Brower, Reuben A. *Mirror on Mirror: Translation, Imitation, Parody*. Cambridge, Mass.: Harvard University Press, 1974.

Bundy, Elroy L. *Studia Pindarica* I and II. Berkeley: *University of California Publications in Classical Philology* 18 (1962).

Burton, R. W. B. *Pindar's Pythian Odes.* Oxford: Oxford University Press, 1962.

Bury, J. B. *The Nemean Odes of Pindar.* London, 1890.

—. *The Isthmian Odes of Pindar*. London, 1892.

Dale, A. M. *Collected Papers*. Cambridge: Cambridge University Press, 1969.

Drachmann, A. B. *Scholia Vetera in Pindari Carmina* I–III. Leipzig. 1903–27.

Duchemin, Jacqueline. *Pindare. Poète et Prophète.* Paris: Société d'Édition Les Belles Lettres, 1955.

—. *Pindare. Pythiques.* Paris: Presses Universitaires de France, 1967.

Farnell, Lewis Richard. *The Works of Pindar, II: Critical Commentary.* London: Macmillan and Co., 1932.

Fennell, C. A. M. *Pindar: The Olympian and Pythian Odes.* Cambridge, 1893.

—. *Pindar: The Nemean and Isthmian Odes.* Cambridge, 1899.

Finley, Jr., John H. *Pindar and Aeschylus*. Cambridge, Mass.: Harvard University Press, 1955.

Forssman, Bernhard. *Untersuchungen zur Sprache Pindars*. Wiesbaden: Otto Harrassowitz, 1966.

Fränkel, Hermann. *Early Greek Poetry and Philosophy*, translated by Moses Hadas and James Willis. New York: Harcourt, Brace, Jovanovich, 1975.

Fussell, Paul. *English Augustan Poetry.* Edited and Introduced by Paul Fussell. New York: Anchor Books, 1972.

Gardiner, E. Norman. *Athletics of the Ancient World.* Oxford: Oxford University Press, 1930.

Gerber, Douglas E. *A Bibliography of Pindar, 1513–1966*, Philological Monographs of the American Philological Association No. 28 (Case Western Reserve University, 1969).

—. *Emendations in Pindar, 1513–1972.* Amsterdam: A. M. Hakkert, 1976.

Gildersleeve, Basil L. *Pindar. The Olympian and Pythian Odes.* New York, 1890.

Hamilton, Richard. *Epinikion. General Form in the Odes of Pindar*. The Hague and Paris: Mouton, 1974.

Harris, H. A. *Greek Athletes and Athletics*. London: Hutchinson and Co., Ltd., 1964.

Highet, Gilbert. *The Classical Tradition.* New York: Oxford University Press, 1949.

Huxley, George. *Pindar's Vision of the Past.* Belfast, 1975.

Irigoin, Jean. *Histoire du Texte de Pindare.* Paris: C. Klincksieck, 1952.

Köhnken, Adolf. *Die Funktion des Mythos bei Pindar.* Berlin: Walter de Gruyter, 1971.
Lefkowitz, Mary R. "ΤΩ ΚΑΙ ΕΓΩ: The First Person in Pindar." *Harvard Studies in Classical Philology* 67 (1963): 177–253.
—. "Pindar's Lives." *Classica et Iberica.* Worcester, Mass.: College of the Holy Cross, 1975, pp. 71–93.
—. "The Influential Fictions in the Scholia to Pindar's *Pythian 8.*" *Classical Philology* 70 (1975): 173–85.
—. *The Victory Ode.* Park Ridge, N.J.: Noyes Press, 1976.
—. "Pindar's *Pythian 8.*" *Classical Journal* 72 (1977): 209–21.
—. "The Poet as Hero." *Classical Quarterly* 28 (1978) 459–69.
—. "Pindar's *Nemean 11.*" *Journal of Hellenic Studies* 99 (1979): 49–56.
Lloyd-Jones, Hugh. "Modern Interpretation of Pindar: The Second Pythian and Seventh Nemean Odes." *Journal of Hellenic Studies* 103 (1973): 109–37.
Maas, Paul. *Greek Metre*, translated by Hugh Lloyd-Jones. Oxford: Oxford University Press, 1962.
Maddison, Carol. *Apollo and The Nine. A History of the Ode.* London: Routledge and Kegan Paul, 1960.
Meillet, Antoine. *Aperçue d'une Histoire de la Langue Grecque.* Paris: C. Klincksieck, 1975.
Nisetich, Frank J. "*Olympian 1.* 8–11: An Epinician Metaphor." *Harvard Studies in Classical Philology* 79 (1975): 55–68.
—. "Convention and Occasion in *Isthmian 2.*" *California Studies in Classical Antiquity* 10 (1977): 133–56.
—. "The Leaves of Triumph and Mortality: Transformation of a Traditional Image in Pindar's *Olympian 12.*" *Transactions of the American Philological Association* 107 (1977): 235–64.
Norwood, Gilbert. *Pindar.* Berkeley: University of California Press, 1945.
Pfeiffer, Rudolf. *History of Classical Scholarship from the Beginnings to the End of the Hellenistic Age.* Oxford: Oxford University Press, 1968.
Pickard-Cambridge, Sir Arthur. *Dithyramb, Tragedy, Comedy.* Oxford: Oxford University Press, 1969.
Pound, Ezra. *The Literary Essays of Ezra Pound*, edited by T. S. Eliot. New York: New Directions, 1968.
Puech, Aimé. *Pindare.* Paris, 1922–23.
Schadewaldt, Wolfgang. *Der Aufbau des Pindarischen Epinikion.* Halle, 1928.
Schroeder, Otto. *Pindari carmina.* Leipzig, 1900.
Slater, W. J. *Lexicon to Pindar.* Berlin: Walter de Gruyter, 1969.
Steiner, George. *After Babel. Aspects of Language and Translation.* Oxford: Oxford University Press, 1975.
Thummer, Erich. *Pindar. Die Isthmischen Gedichte* I und II. Heidelberg: Carl Winter, 1968.
Verdenius, W. J. *Pindar's Seventh Olympian Ode. A Commentary.* Amsterdam: North Holland Publishing Company, 1972.
Wilamowitz-Moellendorff, Ulrich von. *Herakles.* Berlin, 1895.
—. *Pindaros.* Berlin, 1922.
Young, David C. *Three Odes of Pindar. A Literary Study of Pythian 11, Pythian 3, and Olympian 7.* Leiden: E. J. Brill, 1968.
—. "Pindaric Criticism." *Wege der Forschung* 134 (Darmstadt, 1970).
—. *Pindar Isthmian 7, Myth and Exempla.* Leiden: E. J. Brill, 1971.

INDEX

(Italic numbers refer to the maps)

The Johns Hopkins University Press

This book was composed in IBM Aldine Roman text and Phototypositor Columna and Palatine display types by Horne Associates, from a design by Susan Bishop. It was printed by Universal Lithographers, Inc., and bound by The Maple Press Company.